TODAY'S
WOMAN
in WORLD
RELIGIONS

McGill Studies in the History of Religions,
A Series Devoted to International Scholarship
Katherine K. Young, Editor

TODAY'S WOMAN
in WORLD
RELIGIONS

edited by
ARVIND SHARMA

introduction by
KATHERINE K. YOUNG

State University of New York Press

Published by
State University of New York Press, Albany

For information, address State University of New York Press, State
University Plaza, Albany, N.Y., 12246

Production by E. Moore
Marketing by Theresa A. Swierzowski

Library of Congress Cataloging-in-Publication Data

Today's woman in world religions / edited by Arvind Sharma.
        p.   cm. — (McGill studies in the history of religions)
    Includes bibliographical references and index.
        Contents: Aboriginal women's religion / Diane Bell—Women in
Hinduism / Katherine K. Young—Women in Buddhism / Nancy Schuster
Barnes—Women, the state, and religion today in the People's
Republic of China / Miriam Levering—Women and Chinese religion in
contemporary Taiwan / Barbara Reed—Today's Jewish women / Denise
L. Carmody—Christianity and women in the modern world / Rosemary
R. Reuther—Women in Islam / Jane I. Smith—Studying women and
religion / Rita M. Gross.
        ISBN 0–7914–1687–9 (alk. paper). — ISBN 0–7914–1688–7 (pbk. :
alk. paper)
        1. Women and religion.   I. Sharma, Arvind.   II. Series.
BL 458.T63   1993
291.1'78344—dc20   92–40319
                                                                           CIP

10 9 8 7 6 5 4 3 2 1

When I came to the West I was taught that in Hinduism women cannot take *sannyāsa*.

The first person in my life I ever saw wearing the saffron robes was my grandmother.

This book is dedicated to her memory.

"Their words [the words of women] will have the same authority as the scriptures."

—Mahatma Gandhi (1869–1948)

CONTENTS

Arvind Sharma

PREFACE

It is impossible to decipher not only the outcome but even the origins of one's actions. Over a decade ago I undertook to put together a book on world religions in which women scholars would write about the position of women in the religions of the world. It was to be a book by women about women for women—and for men. As I proceeded to compile such an unprecedented book, this act of academic temerity may have caused me to falter but for the surprising and spontaneous support the project received from all the scholars I approached regarding it.

The success of that book, *Women in World Religions* (SUNY Press, 1987), also highlighted its limitations: it did not, even if only because it could not, cover as many religions as one would have liked. And while it offered a historical survey of the position of women in the religions it did cover, it did not tackle the contemporary issues pertaining to women in the various traditions. The treatment of the past, howsoever rich, can never be an adequate substitute for the treatment of the present, howsoever turbulent.

I must thank Bill Eastman for responding with enthusiasm to my suggestion that these shortcomings be rectified by the publication of two companion volumes. *Religion and Women* would extend horizontally the discussion of the position of women beyond the seven traditions of Hinduism, Buddhism, Confucianism, Taoism, Judaism, Christianity, and Islam to include Native American, African, Shinto, Jaina, Zoroastrian, Sikh, and Baha'i religious traditions as well; and *Today's Woman in World Religions* would extend the discussion of the seven traditions, initiated in *Women in World Religions*, vertically into contemporary times and thus bring it up to date. What began as one book thus ended as three—as a trilogy, a development that should not take most of the readers familiar with the Christian tradition by complete surprise! The publication of this book completes the trilogy.

It is a matter of great personal satisfaction and gratitude for me that virtually the entire team that produced *Women in World Religions* has participated in the publication of the present volume. Theresa Kelleher had to bow out but Miriam Levering and Diane Bell came aboard. I must also acknowledge here the support I received in putting this book together from Julia D. Howell and Louise Edwards of Griffith University, Faye Sutherland of the University of New South Wales, and Tamara Jacka of the University of Adelaide—all from distant Australia! My indebtedness extends further and lies closer to home as well, for I must also thank Ella Laffey and Laurel Bossen of my own university, Norma Diamond of the University of Michigan, Ann Anagnost of the University of Washington, Emily Honig and Helen Siu of Yale University, Ellen Judd of the University of Manitoba, Margery Wolf of the University of Iowa, Terry Woo of the University of Toronto, and Lee Raynui of Memorial University, Newfoundland, for pointing me in the right direction when I might have gone astray. My sense of thankfulness to them induces the wry self-reflection that those whose friends and colleagues have talent need not fret too much over their own!

It has been said that no project is really finished; it is merely abandoned. And so as I now abandon this project, I hope not prematurely, I am happy to leave the matter in the hands of the reader.

Katherine K. Young

INTRODUCTION

This book is about how the women's movement is affecting traditional religions and civilizations throughout the world. Where it will lead is not yet certain, but one thing is clear. We can no longer understand our world, much less direct its course, without coming to terms with this phenomenon. Understanding the global impact of the women's movement on religion, however, is a daunting task. It has been difficult to recover the history of women in various religions of the world and search for a comparative perspective, and it is even more difficult to understand the flow of history *in medias res*. Identity, economics, politics, economics, ideology, and scholarship collide. In some countries, the women's movement is being shaped by the first wave of industrialization accompanied by the breakdown of extended families, rural communities, and traditional gender roles. In others it is shaped by the identity crisis that usually follows colonialism. Because the women's movement began in the West, it has been associated with cultural imperialism and secularism—anathema to new nations searching for identity in their own religious traditions. In the West itself, the advent of postindustrialism is causing profound upheavals in the workplace and basic social institutions leading some to question the meaning of progress.

The contributors to this volume have written extensively on the history or anthropology of women in Hinduism, Buddhism, Taoism, Confucianism, Judaism, Christianity, Islam, and Australian aboriginal religion. And yet some have found that even less research has been done on women and religion today than was done at earlier times. In fact, the primary materials have often never been gathered.

Diane Bell, an anthropologist, says that "if we begin with the ethnography—that is, what women are doing—and build from there to map women's strategies, we are writing a special kind of situated ethnography, one where the participant observation is with women, and one that relies on what can be learned from women of women's business." Bell studies Australian aborigine women's religion. Through her description of the women's domain, she is able to explain anomalies and points of confusion in the interpretations of her male colleagues. Drawing on her extensive field work on Australian aboriginal women and her job as an applied anthropologist— this involved mediation between the women and the Australian government over land—Bell explores upheavals in the religious lives of aboriginal women.

Katherine K. Young reports on interviews with both leaders of the women's movement in India and those worried about current threats to Hinduism. She thus exposes a growing tension in Indian society over the position of women. Nancy J. Barnes utilizes her Buddhist networks to piece together information of the nun's order in some Buddhist countries and on what is being done about reviving it in others. She also tells us about the accomplishments of exemplary Buddhist women today: spiritual leaders, religious teachers, reformers, and academics.

After assessing whether the position of women has improved in communist China, Miriam Levering looks specifically at women today in Chinese Christianity, Taoism, and Buddhism to see how have they been effected by the Chinese revolution. Barbara Reed analyzes published materials and interviews to understand the current relation between women and religion in Taiwan. Jane Smith examines a variety of sources to analyze the dialectic of religion and politics in four Islamic countries—Egypt, Saudi Arabia, Iran, and Pakistan.

To do justice to the global story of women and Christianity, Rosemary Radford Ruether reports on a questionnaire she devised and sent to female church leaders in west European, Latin American, North American, Asian, and African countries. Besides basic information on Christianity, she asked about women's church activities, the extent of professional ministry done by nonordained women, whether women are ordained, how many are ordained, how many female students and professors are in theological schools, the teaching of women's studies in those institutions, the networks of women in theology, and the major issues that feminist theologians address. Denise Lardner Carmody examines various Jewish experiments to bring women into sacred learning and religious leadership in both Israel and the United States.

Drawing on her knowledge of three religious traditions (Judaism, Australian aboriginal religion, and Buddhism), Rita M. Gross offers her methodological insights on women and religion. She explores the delicate issue of directing feminist criticism against other religious traditions. Because historians of religions are trained to understand other religious traditions with empathy—which involves bracketing out their own presuppositions in order to approach the religion on its own terms—it has been considered inappropriate to criticize them. Gross argues that it is "more appropriate to criticize one's own cultural-religious situation and the scholarly methods derived from it than the 'other'; when dealing with 'others' we should do the scholarly task of description and leave the judgment to the reader."

Research on women often goes beyond description; a feminist analysis subjects the topic of women and religion to critique. This has been the approach of several of the scholars in this book. Bell draws attention to the political nature of the study of women and religion in her discussion of the Australian aborigines. She argues that religion and politics (local, national, and academic) are so intertwined that to write of the former means becoming involved with the latter. Although Bell exposes the political dimension of religion and scholarly writing about religion, she does so without becoming ideological. Her interpretations are not politicized in the sense of weapons forged for an ideological battle; rather they serve to illumine the interactions of Australian aboriginal women and men as well as their interaction with male government officials and scholars of both sexes. Through her research, Bell recovers women's religious views and practices. Her findings allow her to appreciate the deep egalitarianism of former aboriginal religion and the complementarity of gender roles; these are fast being eroded by cultural assimilation into the frontier society of the Australian outback where men dominate. Because egalitarianism is at the core of the aboriginal worldview, Bell experiences no conflict between the restoration of traditional aboriginal values and her own goals as a woman. In this sense, her task is easier than that of other scholars represented here who find hierarchy and marginalization of women at the core of traditional religions.

THE WOMEN'S MOVEMENT: RELIGION, MODERNITY,
AND IMPERIALISM REVISITED

Articulating a widespread view of feminists, Carmody claims
that there are two matters that shape the women's movement: one
is patriarchy and the other is the unique needs and contributions of
women as a class. By "patriarchy" she means the predominance of
men in formulating beliefs and institutions, and the fact that men,
when defining the concept of humanity, have made women mere
"helpers." Patriarchy, in other words, represents the experiences and
desires of men (androcentrism) and legitimates a hierarchy of men
over women (sexism). This is viewed as unjust (the underlying assumptions being that women have different experiences and needs,
and that subordination is exploitation). She believes, for instance,
that "the majority of Jewish women nowadays are aware that patriarchy is neither inevitable nor just." Gross draws attention to much
the same thing when she refers to the idea of women naming their
own reality and demonstrating that patriarchy is not a biological
given. Critiques of patriarchy and hierarchy are closely related to
the critique of domestic segregation of women and the call for
women to move into the public sphere through jobs, education, and
leadership positions. The women's movement is preeminently one
for equal rights, equal status, and freedom to decide life patterns and
careers. As Gross says: "The old gender hierarchy proclaimed that
men have rights that women do not, and that gender dualism gave
men the public domain and taught women to value the private."

Critiques of androcentrism, hierarchy, and segregation lead to a
critique of the family, since it is structured and legitimated by patriarchal values. They also lead to a call for the solidarity of all
women worldwide, the presupposition being that androcentrism,
hierarchy, and segregation are extremely widespread if not universal. Feminist theology for third-world women, according to Ruether,
is the "eruption within the eruption of an oppressed and dominated
people."

Levering notes that in communist China the male-dominated
party tried hard to prevent such an eruption. With its interest in
class struggle, it classified women according to the status of their
fathers and husbands, oblivious to the fact that even women of the
landlord class had never owned property. Although they organized a
women's federation to mobilize women, male party leaders did not
allow it to represent women's interests. Accordingly, control of the
party remained in men's hands. Western feminists argue that in the

final analysis critiques must be extended to all forms of hierarchy and segregation, be they defined by race, class, or sex. They have traced the origins of today's patriarchal societies to major beliefs of the world religions. For example, Ruether says of Christianity that "patriarchy or male headship over women in both the family and in the larger society was understood as the divinely mandated 'order of creation.'" Feminists argue that these same religions legitimate current patriarchal institutions—political, economic, and social—and are themselves a microcosm of patriarchy. Feminist critique, accordingly, is often critique of the world religions.

In the modern period, women's critique of patriarchy began in the West, primarily in Britain and the United States. Mary Wollstonecraft's *A Vindication of the Rights of Women*, published in England in 1792, called for women to have the same opportunities in education, work, and politics. In England these demands were taken up by the Chartist movement of the 1840s, by prominent liberal intellectuals such as John Stuart Mill and his wife Harriet in the 1850s, and by a number of movements, in the late nineteenth and early twentieth century, to give women the vote. In 1928 British women gained the right to vote. Young points out that early British feminism was transported throughout the British colonies by administrators and missionaries. Ironically, they instituted some reforms for women in the colonies long before such measures had taken root in Britain itself. Colonialism was rationalized in terms of freeing native women from their oppressive husbands, religions, and cultures. In short, part of the "white man's burden" was a need to improve the lot of women. The British Raj, in fact, rationalized its domination of the Indian subcontinent on the basis of the need to put an end to the severe problems of Hindu women—their lack of education, inequality in divorce, plight as widows and suttees.

Other cultures took similar criticisms to heart. "Beginning at the end of the last century," observes Smith when writing on Islam in Egypt, "early feminism was part of Egyptian response to Western colonialism and the drive toward national independence." Of Buddhism and imperialism, Barnes observes that Asian Buddhists have had a painful confrontation with the ideas, institutions, technologies, and colonial powers of the West for the past century. Colonial governments and Christian missions profoundly undermined local political, social, economic, and religious traditions creating a dislocation that had not been experienced since the days of Islam. While wars of national independence and Marxist revolutions have ended direct Western rule, they have not ended the debilitating influence of modernity introduced by the West. For some Asian countries, such as Cambodia and Tibet where Buddhist monks have been massacred and institutions destroyed by Marxist revolutionaries, the damage, says Barnes, has been extreme. For other countries, the colonial experience has acted as a catalyst for Buddhists to creatively respond to the West and Christianity through reinterpretation of their own traditions. In short, the experience of imperialism distinguishes the women's movement in other parts of the world from that of the West.

The relation between the women's movement and religion in the United States is explored by Ruether. She observes that the women's movement—beginning in the 1840s with women's participation in the abolitionist movement, which created awareness of their legal bondage—gave rise both to feminism in the church and in civil society. Women's demands for legal standing, voting, education, and jobs initially had little support from the churches, sources of conservatism and legitimators of the patriarchal order. But opportunities for theological education and the ministry developed gradually in some of them. The first turning point, argues Ruether, occurred in 1921 when women obtained the rights of full citizenship. Although women gave up good jobs when men returned from World War I, as they did during the great depression and after World War II, they could not forget how new experiences and their own income had increased their self-worth and power both within the family and in public.

The second turning point, says Ruether, occurred after many churches sided with the civil rights movement in the 1960s. Once again, as in the 1840s, women compared their own restricted roles to those of African-Americans. Opportunities for women in theological education and the ministry expanded rapidly, though not always at the same rate.

The third turning point is now occurring with the export of American feminism to churches in other parts of the world. Ruether observes that feminist theology, much of it from North America, is read by women in western Europe, Asia, and Africa. Books have been translated into German, Korean, Spanish, and other languages. This creates a common forum for discussion of topics such as biblical hermeneutics, interpretation of Christian symbols, anthropology, ecclesiology, christology, mariology (for Roman Catholics), sexuality, reproductive rights, violence to women, peace, economic justice, and ecological harmony.

Ruether's analysis of the dissemination of Western feminist thinking is confirmed by the other authors of this volume. Carmody observes that "American Jewish women probably are the vanguard of Jewish feminism." Although Barnes looks to Asia first as the homeland of Buddhism in her survey of the women's movement, she notes how often the momentum for change has come from the West. Leadership for restoration of the nun's order has come from "educated Asian women (and some men) who are well acquainted with Western culture and familiar with modern Western ideas on the equality of women. Joining them are many Western women who have received the lower ordination into the Theravada or one of the Tibetan Buddhist sects and aspire to full ordination." Because religions such as Christianity and Buddhism have international organizations, ideas are transmitted very quickly, at least among the educated elite. Transmission also occurs when women from various parts of the world are educated in North America and return home with feminist plans for the transformation of traditional religions. Levering mentions that there have been women students sent from China to Western theological seminaries who have returned with knowledge of Christian feminist theology. Their views have a "wonderful resonance within contemporary Western feminist theological discourse. Whether they have any of the same kind or degree of resonance within the discourse of the now very indigenous Chinese Protestant churches remains to be seen." Reed gives us a good example of the influence of Western feminist thinking in her profile of the Taiwanese feminist, Lu Hsiu-lien, who was educated at Harvard.

The relation of the women's movement to religion is best understood against the backdrop of the changes introduced by modernity and imperialism. Women's critique of hierarchy, after all, can be traced to liberal, egalitarian, and reformist ideals that informed political life in the modern West from the time of the Enlightenment. The women's movement initially spread around the world with Western imperialism. Democracy, socialism, and especially Marxism subsequently inspired movements for national liberation, women's liberation, and lay activism in various countries. Changes brought by the industrial revolution also played a part. The machine, for instance, equalized male and female bodies in the labor force; men's size, strength, and mobility were no longer relevant for many industrial jobs (and even less so with the subsequent advent of the computer age). The development of the condom (and subsequent forms of birth control) also contributed to the equalization of male and female bodies, for women no longer had to fear pregnancy and could be a stable member of the work force. Protection against pregnancy also gave them the same carefree access to sexual pleasure that men had always enjoyed.

Modernity emphasized materialism and well-being in this world (rather than the divine realm). The prosperity of the industrialized West highlighted the poverty of other places. Christian missionaries took up the idea of the social gospel and criticized other religions for neglecting the social welfare of the people. This inspired both Christian missionaries and the other religions themselves to correct the situation. Women in particular took up the challenge. Ruether observes, for instance, that women in Christianity do the majority of lay, voluntary service; Christian women in India run schools, hospitals, and so forth. Barnes notes a this-worldly emphasis in Buddhist revivalism: it is responsible for schools, orphanages, disaster relief, and projects to aid the poor, the sick, and the elderly. "The reformers have been sophisticated, educated individuals," says Barnes, "and they are willing to modify tradition for the sake of goals relevant to modern life and reformist agendas." Young draws attention to the current popularity in India of *lokasaṅgraha,* or working for the welfare of the world. According to Smith, Egyptian urban women at the end of the late nineteenth century focused on social welfare efforts for their lower-class sisters. More recently, a this-worldly emphasis in religions reflects the growing secularism of the modern era and supports international efforts for third-world development.

Finally, with modernity came new forms of rapid communication and transportation. This played a role in transmission of ideas, which contributed to the sense of a women's movement first in the West and then elsewhere. In short, the women's movement has not occurred in a vacuum. It has been part of larger historical forces related to equality (made possible by political, economic, and technological development), hierarchy (increased by imperialism), a this-worldly orientation (connected to materialism, Christian notions of social gospel, secularism, and development projects), and globalism (inspired by new forms of communication and transportation).

CHANGES IN PRIVATE AND PUBLIC REALMS

This section will look at general changes in women's lives in private and public realms traditionally legitimated by religions; specific changes in religious spheres and patterns of religious leadership; and limits to reform (especially limits imposed by issues of identity).

One way that religion is affected by the women's movement is by the breakdown of domestic segregation and by the entrance of women into religious spheres outside the home. The corollary of the breakdown of segregation is change in traditional family structures and the religious laws, customs, and ideals regulating them with reference to questions of lineage, suitable marriage partners, desired number of children, usage of contraception, segregation, divorce, and remarriage. The first wave of attack on traditional family structures came from imperialists and missionaries: India, Muslim countries, and China were particularly affected. Young, for instance, notes that during the nineteenth century the Hindu family was severely criticized by the British Raj and Christian missionaries. Elite brahmanical values had endorsed arranged marriage, furthered the subordination of women to men in the hierarchy of the extended family of the husband's village, segregated women in the household, denied education to female children, made dowry the price of marriage for a woman, placed a premium on the birth of sons, encouraged a woman to love her husband as a god, prevented women from divorcing men or remarrying, and allowed only an ascetic mode of widowhood or suttee (the very rare practice of immolation on the funeral pyre of her husband should he die first).

Levering also notes similar problems faced by women in the traditional Chinese family system: arranged marriage, dowry and bride price, no divorce, the selling of women who were not needed or could not be supported by a family, and segregation inside the family. Both Hindu and Chinese elite family systems insisted on women being dependent on their fathers, husbands, and sons, a denial of independence.

The second wave of critique came from reformers within the religions who took up the challenge to transform family structures in order to measure up to the expectations of foreign rulers. Young describes how in India during the nineteenth century Indian men campaigned against child marriage, suttee, polygamy, female infanticide, lack of education and property rights for women, seclusion, and the ban on divorce and remarriage. About the same time, according to Smith, an early Egyptian response to Western colonialism was feminism. By the 1920s, segregation and veils were disappearing and Egyptian women were entering the work force in increasing numbers. In China after the May Fourth Movement of 1919, urban intelligentsia—communists, nationalists, and feminists—saw the traditional family system as an embarrassment to a modern nation and sought to reform it. Similarly, from the 1920s, women's lives were liberalized in Turkey. In the nationalist movement of Jinnah, which led to the formation of Pakistan, the education and participation of women was promoted, as it was under Bhutto. And in Iran the lives of urban women were changed under the Shah.

The third wave came from people within various societies who had come to accept the tenets of Western Marxism, socialism, or secular feminism, and worked to change not only family structures but also to eliminate religion itself. There has been a new generation of such Western-style feminists, for instance, in Egypt since the 1970s. In India, feminists, Marxists, and socialists are active in various causes related to women. Young describes a play called "A Daughter is Born," which has been performed by Marxists and others in the various villages of the province of Maharashtra to encourage reform. In China, says Levering, the communist party promised to end women's oppression because of the traditional Confucian ideology and its effect on the social and economic system by encouraging them to participate more actively in economic production, politics, and family life.

Out of these various waves, which often overlapped in time, has come new legislation in some countries. Young reviews the vast legal changes in India over the past century and the call today for a new uniform legal code so that all Indian women will be governed by the same law. Levering points to the marriage law of 1950, which gave Chinese women freedom to choose their marriage partners and to seek divorce. Smith notes changes in Muslim law (Turkey, for instance, introduced a secular civil code in the 1920s while the Shah in Iran and Bhutto in Pakistan liberalized Muslim laws).

In some countries, there is only now a call for change. Reed speaks of the Taiwanese woman Lu Hsui-lien who has written a book criticizing Chinese family structure and its features of patrilineality, ancestor worship, filial piety, preference for sons, taking the husband's name, denial of education to girls, dowry, bride price, and segregation of women in the private sphere. As a lawyer and political activist, she has fought these practices and has been imprisoned. Lu Hsui-lien suggests that women should abandon their husband's name, that their earning power should be the substitute for dowry and bride price, and that spatial segregation and job discrimination should end. Arguing for a truly equal society, she thinks that "feminist power is needed to eliminate the prejudices of patriarchal Chinese tradition and to build a new society based on rationality." But the government of Taiwan sees its identity in traditional Confucian culture; it promotes Confucianism in the schools and celebrates Confucius's birthday annually. Confucian "Chinese Culture" is advocated by those men who want unification of Taiwan and mainland China.

Lin Mei-jung, an anthropologist, finds that an attack on traditional values affecting women has been interpreted by the men in power as an attack on the very definition of what it means to be Taiwanese. She recently wrote a book arguing against Confucian values because they represent a double superimposition—that of the elite on the masses and that of the dead Confucian values of mainland China before the revolution on the living, pluralistic values of a Taiwan that has developed its own distinct culture.

It is striking that there is no report on Buddhism when the topic is women's work and changes in family life aside from one cryptic statement by Barnes: "women appear to be no more highly regarded or better off than in many non-buddhist societies. This is a disturbing incongruity." But Buddhism, even in its earliest period, rarely addressed questions of family life.

Although new laws certainly help to bring about change, they may not be very effective. Sometimes a new government will even eliminate liberal laws. In Turkey fundamentalists today, against the government's will, are encouraging a return to Islamic dress and domestic segregation. In Pakistan Zia al-Haq reversed Bhutto's policies. In Iran the Ayatollah's Islamic revolution undid the Shah's reforms. But when legal changes are accompanied by industrialization and secularization, enormous change takes place. In India, for instance, new laws had little effect curbing practices such as dowry, but with industrialization, urban upper-caste women are entering the work force and traditional citadels such as arranged marriage and dowry are weakening. According to one report, urban young women, emboldened by interaction with men in the workplace and exposure to sexually expressive films, television programs, and videos are dating and a few even desiring sexual thrills to eliminate boredom. Levering reports that in China, too, young persons are more likely to choose their own marriage partners.

Even when there are no new laws in place to foster change, the very fact that women have begun to work outside the home has helped to breakdown domestic segregation and hierarchy. Smith, for instance, describes how providing education and jobs for women—which is proceeding at different rates throughout the Muslin world—has challenged the spatial segregation of women in the home. Women are no longer confined to certain rooms, and they are taking a more active role in decisions that affect the family. In China during the Cultural Revolution from 1966 to 1976, political and economic roles were expanded for women, and women suddenly had greater freedom and mobility.

When domestic segregation breaks down and women begin to move into public realms, they start to demand participation in religious spheres outside the home. They seek access to exclusively male religious spheres or create counterparts for women. Women are also breaking down hierarchy by seeking entrance to the exclusively male spheres of religious power. When entrance is difficult, they seek positions of power in lay or female organizations.

Barnes describes in detail the restoration of the Buddhist nun's order that had fallen into oblivion or was seriously weakened in many Buddhist countries. She examines the problem of a valid ordination procedure and the politics surrounding it. Whereas one would expect this to be a battle of women against men, the lineup is no by means so clear. Some women's spiritual communities, such as the *dasasilmattawa* in Sri Lanka, enjoy their current independence. If they were to formalize their community into an order (*sangha*), they would have to be governed by traditional monastic rules; this would put them under the nominal domination of monks. Also the *dasasilmattawa* prefer to seek their spirituality through radical withdrawal rather than catering to the lay community and its modern penchant for reforming society through social work. Along with the *dasasilmattawa,* many Buddhist monks have not supported the ordination process for women. Barnes observes that it is mainly educated Asian women and men familiar with the West—and Western Buddhist women—who want the order restored.

Levering points out that after 1978 a few major monasteries were reopened in China. Seminaries are now functioning to train both male and female novices, and rural women are attracted to the convents. Many men and women are becoming monastics. For women in particular this provides opportunity to become part of the international network of Buddhism with its promise of travel to Hong Kong, Singapore, Malaysia, Indonesia, Taiwan, and the United States. Chinese Buddhist nuns are also trying to help Theravada nuns reestablish their lineage by accepting them into Chinese seminaries. There seems to be one innovation: some sources say that Chinese nuns and monks can now marry. As for the Taoist female adepts, they are also restoring their traditions at Taoist monasteries.

Ruether traces the history of women's demand for ordination in Christianity and the closely related demand for theological education. She notes the very uneven rate of change. The Salvation Army, Holiness churches, the Church of God, the United Church of Christ, and Disciples of Christ were pacesetters, while many liberal Protestants churches such as the Presbyterians were much slower. A number of conservative Protestant churches and Roman Catholicism have not yet changed their policies. Theological education for women became more common in the 1970s. By 1987, reports Ruether, half the students in liberal seminaries were women. She surveys the history of ordination in Canada, Europe, and elsewhere. Access to ordination is only one problem; women also have lower rank, salary, and administrative positions than men. As for bishops, Methodists and Episcopalians had one apiece. Despite all these changes, notes Ruether, female ministers are still at the bottom of the profession in status and seniority with few chances to influence things except in three areas—inclusive language, clergy-lay relations, and new liturgies. While women have access to theological education in Europe, there are few female professors. In the third world, graduate education, women on faculties, and feminist courses are still rare.

Levering reports that in 1990 the first class of educated Roman Catholic nuns after the revolution in China graduated from St. Joseph's convent: nursing, English, cooking, and sewing were to be their professions. Since the Chinese church has not had an official connection to the Vatican since 1957, says Levering, there would seem to be opportunity to ordain nuns, but so far church leaders have not taken this initiative and seem more concerned with the maintenance of traditions. As for Protestants, there are few women ministers in the cities, though in some of the main seminaries half of those in the program now are women, a third of those who go abroad are women, and there are also a number of women on theological faculties. In the rural areas, however, women are very active as leaders for prayer groups, which may be attended by as many as a thousand people, though they may turn to men to perform the sacraments.

In Rabbinic Judaism, claims Carmody, "learning has been the badge of merit and women have generally been excluded from learning . . . ; [there was] virtually no entry to the precincts where the religious elite dealt with the questions shaping what it meant to be a Jew." One liturgical experiment related to Jewish feminism is that of a group called the Upstairs Minyan. This congregation at the Hillel Foundation of the University of Chicago is affiliated with Conservative Judaism. After its founding in 1965, women gradually participated in different parts of the service until they were leading regular Saturday morning services, wearing the prayer shawls and skull caps typically worn by men for Sabbath worship, changing prayers to include women, and training women in Hebrew and musical tradition. Jewish women have also sought entrance to seminaries. In the early 1970s Sally Priesand graduated from the Reformed Seminary of Hebrew Union College and became the first woman rabbi. Other women of the Reformed tradition followed suit. Women also began to attend the Jewish Theological Seminary and became Conservative rabbis. And women in the Reconstructionist tradition did the same. Besides becoming rabbis, women have become cantors.

Some women are taking on positions of religious leadership in Islam. Smith notes that there are a few Muslim women in Egypt who teach the Qur'ān and the Islamic tradition (albeit just to other women, given the context of segregation of the sexes), though this role has usually been reserved for men. In Indonesia, the Aisyihah movement—named after the Prophet's wife A'isha who was learned in religious matters—educates women about Islam; a few women are also functioning as imams (prayer leaders).

Young reports that in the modern period there are now ashrams in India for women or female sections of ashrams. A few women are foregoing marriage to become ascetics; this has been virtually unheard of in traditional Hinduism. A number of famous Hindu gurus have chosen a woman as their successor, and a few women have independently become gurus. In several Hindu sects, women have also taken up study of the Vedas and performance of Vedic rituals, once a male, Brahmin preserve. This, in turn, may qualify them for future roles as priests, though this is still rare.

Those religions that have a laity have been more willing to accept female lay leadership than to open positions of formal priestly or monastic leadership to women. Reed, for instance, reports that Buddhism, Taoism, and especially Chinese popular religion are proving attractive to women today in Taiwan as they look for ways to avoid the constraints of Confucianism. Women have access to religious experience and leadership through oracles, divination, and healing. In these religions, women with grown children are volunteers in temples, though the official roles are still played by men.

Barnes draws our attention to the growth in Buddhist lay movements, some of which have become sects in their own right. Modeled on Christian organization and proselytism, they are established to institute reforms and serve the community. With the development of Buddhist lay movements, leadership opportunities for women have increased; women have become "spiritual leaders, teachers, scholars, organizers, and shapers of a new Buddhism for the modern world" in countries formerly dominated by monks. The lay movement has also brought more women into the practice of meditation in Sri Lanka, Thailand, and Burma; many of the teachers have been women. According to Levering, there is a great amount of lay activity in China: women chant sūtras or go on pilgrimage together, and some attend sessions where the leader goes into trance, communicates with Guanyin, and practices healing.

Ruether comments on new volunteer lay roles in Roman Catholicism and lay professional ministries that are completely female. In addition to her documentation, it may be useful to examine the Canadian experience reflected in a document prepared by the Anglican and Roman Catholic churches of that country.[1] It observes that both churches have been promoting lay ministries and lay apostolates. For Roman Catholics, the Vatican II decree *Lumen Gentium* (1964) argued that there are two priesthoods—the common one of the faithful and the hierarchical one of the clergy; both in their distinctive ways participate in the *one* priesthood of Christ. In Canada, women serve on pastoral teams and sisters have been appointed to vacant parishes. Both laywomen and nuns have been authorized to preside over the liturgy of the Word and to administer communion from reserved elements. For Anglicans the resolutions of the Lambeth Conference state that all Christians, not just those who are ordained, are to minister to God. All major issues in the church, moreover, are to be decided only with full participation of lay and ordained people.[2] Ruether observes that Protestant women in India have inherited large networks of social, health, and educational institutions built by female missionaries and run them as lay professionals. One of these institutions completely run by women is the YWCA. In fact, in many Asian and African countries, women leaders, both in the church and in society, have had their initial training in the YWCA. Similarly, Levering reports that because there is a shortage of clergy in China, nuns and lay leaders preach, lead prayers, and offer pastoral care, though they do not offer the sacraments.

In the above instances, we find a number of changes that can be called reforms. New laws bring about changes in family life. Reforms are also introduced from within the religions. These are sometimes along sectarian lines. Some sects decide to restore ancient practices that had been abandoned in the course of time. Certain Buddhist groups, for instance, are restoring the order for nuns that was established at the time of Buddha but had been abandoned in some countries. Some Protestant Christian denominations are accepting women as ministers and teachers, which had precedent in the early church or an early phase of the sect (especially those founded by women). And some branches of Islam are allowing women to function as imams and teachers to groups of women, which had been the case during the life of the Prophet himself. Even when no precedent can be found, established branches or sects of a religion have also taken the initiative to introduce changes. Reformed, Reconstructionist, and Conservative branches of Judaism have opened their seminaries to women, have made women rabbis, and have introduced changes into their liturgies to incorporate women's experience. Some Hindu sects have introduced radically new changes by passing the mantle of guru to a woman or by training women in the sacred knowledge and rituals of the Vedas, which qualifies them for Brahmanical priestly roles. Such reforms (whether based on earlier practices or current changes), however, have taken place within general institutional structures that have been broadened to include the participation of women. On a few occasions changes have stimulated the formation of new sects.

———————————

While reforms—both those restoring former practices or introducing new changes within existing institutional structures—have occurred, they are by no means universal. There may be a difference between precept and practice. Through reforms, women may now be eligible for leadership positions, but the actual number of women placed may be few. Reforms are also not universal, since some sects or branches of a religion appear not to have changed. Orthodox and Hasidic Jews, fundamentalist Christians, Roman Catholics, and Muslims in Saudi Arabia are cases in point. Many orthodox Jewish women, for example, reject reforms and feminism, and look to orthodoxy as a way to discover and develop their identity. Hasidic women also scrupulously preserve tradition. They see in the feminist critique of male and female roles in the family a cultural imperialism of Western Jews (who assimilated into gentile traditions) over east European Jews or an affirmation of secular values over religious ones. Most women of these more orthodox Jewish traditions, then, want to maintain traditional family forms, symbolism, theology, and ritual (P. Nathanson; personal communication).

In Christianity, some traditionalists have refused to change, claiming that the issue is one of religious identity established by scripture and tradition. In Canada the position of Roman Catholic women and the need for changes were explored in a study kit called *Women in the Church*, more popularly known as the green kit, published in 1985.[3] The green kit inspired conservatives to promote their own position in what became known as the "blue kit." The bishops, however, did not endorse its distribution to parishes. As a result of such conflicts, the role of women in Roman Catholic churches varies by region and diocese. Nevertheless, women are represented nationally on bishops' study committes and internationally on their synods. While some female leaders continue to support the church, others have left over the issue of ordination.[4] In short, although some churches have officially remained traditional, they are experiencing internal tensions over the role of women.

The recent "Anglican-Roman Catholic Dialogue Agreed Statement" for Canada—after surveying the position of women in these two Canadian churches with reference to history, geography, national identity, social activism, women's Christian movements, and the experience of women in Canadian society—concludes that the experience of the frontier improved the position of women over that in the European mother countries, while the experience of industrialization moved women into the economic mainstream. Today, with a growing number of working and professional women and with federal and provincial human rights legislation in place, there is an insistence that discrimination on the basis of sex become a thing of the past. Some Canadian Christian women, says the statement, are increasingly aware that "in the church more than in any other sphere their sex is a discount, if not a discredit . . . ; some have left the church altogether; some others have changed denominations; still others, while remaining loyal to their communion, have joined groups seeking change; and many are quietly resentful. On the other hand, more traditional Canadian Christians argue that there is no necessary analogy between what the secular world considers the proper status of women and what divine revelation establishes as the proper status of women.[5]

In China there is also difference of opinion. Urban people may seek reforms but, according to Levering, people in the rural areas are not so keen on reform. They wished to restore traditional family structures by having enough money to be able to afford a wife, or to be able to keep the one they have and not be threatened by divorce.

Issues of reform are closely related to issues of identity. Reaffirmation of traditional identity has already led some to criticize Western women who are held responsible for the sexual revolution. Many Muslim women praise modest Islamic dress, for example, as a way to avoid the immorality of Western woman. Smith reports that "most would say that Islamic dress is their consciously and freely adopted symbol of identification with a religious system to which they wish to express a deep commitment and allegiance." Hindus have long praised the chastity of Hindu women and compared it to what is perceived as the promiscuity of Western women. With the recent crisis of Hindu identity, this idea is currently popular in certain circles. Even Lu Hsiu-lien, who has criticized the traditional Chinese family, does not want to eliminate the notion of chastity. She wishes to reinterpret it as a means of maintaining self-respect, a self-motivated behavior for character training, a love of self rather than fear of social disapproval, and a moral principle for both sexes. Western feminism is also held responsible for the deterioration of the family. The escalating divorce rate, single-parent families, and neglect of elderly parents are all held up as problems caused by Western feminism. Many women of other countries do not wish to go in this direction; this is why they wish to make changes on their own terms. Even some third-world activists of a more secular hue are quick to criticize any superimposition of Western feminism on their identity.

Young reports how Madhu Kishwar, an Indian activist on women's issues, rejects the label "feminist" because it is culture bound (a product of European and American thought), reflects a unidirectional flow of power from West to East, and is a tool of cultural imperialism. She observes that although Western feminists attacked them and pressured them to follow Western thinking, they avoided imitation. Nowhere was this more obvious than on the issue of men's partication in the women's movement. Leaders of the Indian women's movement rejected confrontation with men on a priori grounds (contrary to Western separatist feminists) just as they rejected unconditional acceptance of men's participation (contrary to socialist feminists). Rather, they acknowledged a diversity of responses on various issues. Because of this nonideological response, says Kishwar, they received over the years much support from men.

Some Western feminists consider rejection of Western feminist ideas as uncritical (a naivety regarding the nature of patriarchy, an emotional reaction against anything Western, or even a fundamental misunderstanding of what is causing the profound social changes in the West). Other Western feminists argue that they are sensitive to the importance of "context" in their studies: variations from one country to another, from the first world to the third, from rural to urban areas, from upper to lower classes, from socialist to capitalist countries. Even though the women's movement as a whole monitors problems caused by sexual behavior and family organization in general, local groups emphasize particular issues: genital incision and excision are a cause célèbre in Africa, for instance, while dowry-deaths are in India. But some women in the third world argue that there is a potential problem with the concept of contextualization. When Western women presume that women's movements in various countries are merely variations on a Western theme, they ignore some real differences, especially the concerns of these third-world women who see in the invitation to throw off oppression a threat to their own national, religious, and familial identity.

FUTURE DIRECTIONS

What is in the future for women and religion? One author in this volume is optimistic. Barnes sees a vibrant future for a reformed Buddhism on its "triumphant . . . march westward in collusion with feminism." She also judges the Buddhist record on religious symbolism to be good. Attributing dualistic, conflictual, and hierarchical thinking to Western religions such as Judaism, Christianity, and Islam, Barnes finds in the Buddhist concept of nondualism a new model for feminist thinkers who "have valued connectedness rather than separation and opposition. . . . It is now time for Buddhists and feminist thinkers to blend their insights and intellectual skills, and borrow from each other's strengths. From its joining of forces it should be possible to establish powerful alternatives to a dualistic outlook on our complex, tormented modern world."

Another author in this volume is pessimistic. Bell suggests that the subtle interplay of independence and interdependence in Australian aboriginal religion may be lost, since aborigines have lost control of their lands and their hunter-gatherer mode of subsistence. They must now deal with laws, courts, and white male frontier society in the northern part of the continent where paternalism and sexism are pervasive. Aborigine women are losing some of their former power with the breakdown of aboriginal society and religion. To counter this, they are becoming involved with the "institutions of self-determination related to the state, statutory authorities, and development lobbies." In the future, thinks Bell, this may take them more and more away from their traditional ritual activities, communal values, and negotiations with men.

Most authors in this volume still maintain some hope for change, though they are cautious. Many suggest that tension, if not confrontation, will mark the future of religions as they struggle to come to terms with the women's movement. Questions of identity will influence the future as they have the past. For some third-world women, the problem will continue to be how to maintain some authentic selfhood that is different from the West. More religions may react negatively to the growth of secularism by trying to preserve some continuity of religious identity. Even in the West, parallel religious communities, calls for a radical transformation of symbolism, theology, and ritual, and a separatist orientation that rejects men (all of which amounts to the call for a new religion) are causing issues of identity to arise.

Religious identity, according to Smith, will continue to be very important for Muslim women. The fact that Islam claims to be a universal religion means that, at least in the background, there will be an expectation of common traditional roles for women. Many Iranian women will continue to veil themselves to show solidarity with Muslim men against Western imperialism, Marxism, and secularism. While they are searching for an Islamic approach—and often look to models provided by women in the early days of Islam, such as that of the prophet's daughter Fatima—they are also against feudalism and extremist fundamentalism. Smith thinks that Islam will be marked by more strife. She observes that the value of education and jobs for women have generally increased in the Muslim world, though there are great differences between urban and rural areas, and reforms in personal status laws lag behind the political rhetoric. Underlying these debates is the tension between needing women for modern national development and observing traditional religious restrictions. Underlying this tension is an even deeper one: the struggle between secularist ideology and Islamic revivalism. Smith is confident that Muslim women will find a way to resolve or live with the tension in such a way that it does justice both to being Muslims and being women.

But despite their desire to affirm the family along with new power for women (expressed as greater participation in making decisions and insistence on monogamy), some women are experiencing problems. In Saudi Arabia, reports Smith, it is increasingly difficult for educated women to get married, because young men feel threatened by an educated wife, because the bride price for one is too high, or because they prefer a wife who is younger. With the growth of nuclear families, child care for working mothers will become even more of an issue. Smith thinks that there will be more confusion on the part of both women and men. They want education and jobs, and they "fear that too rapid movement may lead to instability in the family and in society." Hence, "the tensions are real and inevitably growing for Saudi women."

Young sees ongoing tension in India as well. The Hindu revival now occurring may escalate as Hindus perceive their identity increasingly threatened by the Indian secular state and by Marxists, socialists, and feminists who dominate Indian intellectual circles and ally themselves with the minority religions such as Islam and Christianity. This will lead to greater polarization between secularists and Hindu fundamentalists, and may affect the position of women. If the secularists triumph, they may do so by introducing a uniform civil code (the Hindu minimum demand for continued acceptance of India as a secular state); this may enhance the legal position of women in India, especially those of the minority communities. But if a Hindu state is created, the position of women may be determined by whether liberals or conservatives define policy. If the former, there may be few changes aside from the introduction of a uniform civil code and a Hindu sacred canopy. But if the latter, there may be reintroduction of traditional Hindu laws and segregation to bolster the family and preserve Hindu identity. The future position of Hindu women may be determined not only by politics, but also by economics. Young sees two trends. If women continue to move into industrial jobs, they may gain more economic leverage and status in society, though their domestic security may be eroded by upheavals in family life through divorce. But if there is high unemployment, pressure may also grow for women to return home, making more jobs available for men. This may find expression in reassertion of traditional Hindu elite values such as segregation.

In the religious realm, there are two possible directions. The number of female ascetics and gurus may increase if women's status generally increases and men remain supportive of these changes. But if Hindu men begin to feel threatened economically or feel that Hindu identity is threatened, they may decide not to initiate women or turn their spiritual mantel over to them. Because Hinduism is so decentralized and each guru is able to act independently, it would be difficult to stem this tide. (Of course, by the same token of decentralization women could define themselves as gurus—at least on the basis of spiritual experience if not Vedic expertise—and could initiate their own disciples. This, however, could lead to separate religious spheres if men refuse to be disciples of a female guru.) Whatever the future, it is sure to be marked by tensions and even polarization with the women's issue at the center of political and economic agendas.

Levering speaks of how the Communist Party discouraged women from exercizing their new rights. Even the Women's Federation did not strive to help women see their own issues as in some way separate from the larger issues, and never encouraged them to mobilize against the male leaders of the party. In the countryside, the local cadres did not seriously try to protect women in abusive relations, did not encourage people to make their own decisions about marriage, did not make divorce easily accessible, and did not eliminate the practice of expensive weddings, and the practice of adopting a female child for a future bride. Even today, women still do not have equal access to education and good jobs with equal pay, nor do they have adequate child care facilities. After the Cultural Revolution, says Levering, the iron girl model (women are equal to men in capacity for work and revolutionary activities), promoted during both the Great Leap Forward and the Cultural Revolution, is discredited. Today women are told that they are better at embroidery, sewing, child-rearing, and languages but not science, higher education, mechanical, technical, and engineering work. The old gender roles are reappearing. With the new insistence on having only one child, Levering thinks that it will be very difficult for women to return to full-time domestic duties.

In the final analysis, says Levering, despite the slippage to old gender roles, there are "opportunities in Catholic, Protestant, Taoist, and Buddhist institutions for Chinese women to practice their religion as laywomen and as religious specialists. These opportunities are limited by the heavy work demands placed on women, and by government control, but they are nonetheless real. There are also opportunities for women to serve their religious communities. Women lay leaders served throughout the darkest days of the Cultural Revolution, and now continue to serve." There is token representation of them on the highest religious bodies. According to Reed, the future for women in Taiwan may also depend on politics, whether or not the government clings to the idea of restoring the

Confucian past or whether the new pluralism of Taiwan is officially recognized.

From this discussion, it seems that a dialectic between reform and tradition will characterize the immediate future of a number of world religions. The call for reform in Christianity is captured in the Canadian Anglican and Roman Catholic position paper. The authors argue that churches must understand both the positive and negative experiences of women (poverty, sexual abuse, or mistreatment because of one's sex); the ambivalent role of sexual stereotypes in the history of Christian thought (identification of maleness with spirit and reason, and femaleness with matter and emotion); Jesus' positive treatment of women; and the fact that his saving work transcends all sexual barriers. As for the maleness of God, they see it as metaphorical, insist that God's nature cannot be captured or exhausted in descriptions, and point out that, in any case, scripture sometimes describes God with female imagery and qualities.[6] Finally, they point to a Canadian context supportive of the ordination of women—from their legal equality to the shortage of ordained ministers to the example set by the other churches—yet tread very softly because of the Roman Catholic refusal to ordain women as priests.[7]

But there are also signs of a radical departure from the path of reform in Western Christianity. The future relation of women and religion may be quite different than in third-world countries because the demands are more radical, because society is more secular, and because reproduction, which is often regulated by religion, is no longer a central concern. Ruether argues that the future of Christianity depends on how open established churches will be to women's initiatives. And she implies that the churches must change on women's terms or women will start churches for themselves. Some Christian women have already established "women church." The entry of women to theological schools and the ministry is only "the first part of the story," observes Ruether; "the second stage is how the critical mass as students and clergy has begun to make an impact on the substance of the Christian faith . . . the way it is symbolized, organized, and understood." This will occur through the introduction of feminist courses, the hiring of full-time feminist professors, feminist research and publication, and the integration of feminism throughout the curriculum—Bible, history, ethics, theology, and pastoral care. Networks of feminist scholars, caucuses, and sections in established professional societies, and more feminist journals are also goals to be achieved. When basic method and content are rethought to "transform the tradition through the presence of women's experience," the women's movement will have fully arrived in the churches. A woman's professional society exclusively dedicated to feminism and religion along with autonomous, degree-granting institutions with a feminist perspective are yet to come. Ruether thinks that fundamental rethinking of patriarchal theology leads to a questioning of "male generic language for God." Without this, there is mere tokenism and no real change of consciousness. She finds substituting terms such as lord or sovereign too abstract, and so calls for feminine imagery to be created by mystics, poets, and exegetical committees. Ruether sees some problems, however, when this involves a return to pre-Christian religions, for this could open the door again to patriarchal religions. A return to female shamanism in Korea might initially seem attractive, but would a return to the past bring with it Confucianism? Would a return to pre-Christian African goddesses also reintroduce clitoridectomy? Moreover, what if a critique of patriarchal religion is understood as a critique of Judaism, thereby contributing to anti-Semitism?[8] Ruether thinks that "feminist reclaiming of pre-Christian and non-Christian religions of national cultures is easier when these religions have lost their male leadership and power." This, however, is rarely the case unless the religions are dead.

Religious symbolism is intimately related to theology and ritual. Changing the former means changing the latter. Of Judaism, Carmody observes that women's raised consciousness demands that they deal with ritual and theology, since only when ultimate reality "provides for the female as much as the male" will they finally achieve equality. But the internal dynamics of communities such as B'not Esh and the Upstairs Minyan, which have opened all aspects of Jewish life to women's participation, have forced them to realize that "any significant reform to make women the full equals of men was holistic—a recasting of the entirety of their Jewish awareness." The more radical feminists in Judaism are also calling for the imagery and language of a goddess to replace that of a god. They argue that this is necessary if religion is to reflect their own experience. Carmody draws our attention to the thinking of Jewish feminists such as Judith Plaskow and Rita Gross on this issue. Because Plaskow finds a biblical period when both gods and goddesses were worshiped, she finds a precedent for goddess worship today. But she wishes to maintain the idea of monotheism; hence the idea of the *one female* deity.

Gross prefers to rework Hindu and Buddhist concepts of the goddess into ones that can be recognized as Jewish. She takes the most radical approach of all. At times she calls for deconstruction of the existing religion by "radically relativizing and deabsolutizing" it through use of the comparisons provided by other religions. This is to be followed by its reconstruction and enrichment with "input from other, nontraditional resources." At other times, she calls for a radically new world construction based on a selection of sources from the world religions. Just as she calls for scholarship based on an androgynous model (by which she means the inclusion of the lives of both men and women for study), Gross argues for a remythologization of the transcendent to include both male and female. She is amazed that few feminists have followed this course and thinks that it goes "back to the proclivity of theologians to privilege culturally familiar religious concepts and resources in their world-construction." Finally, she argues that every scholar already engages in world-construction when giving an introductory course or writing an article, because of the selections and subjectivity involved in interpretation.

All of this suggests that for some Western feminists the issue is not just that of *adding* something to what is already there; it is *replacing* what is there with something quite different. Feminism supersedes other points of view. Carmody refers to the fact that significant reform involves recasting the entirety of Jewish awareness; Ruether speaks of changing the substance of Christianity, how it is symbolized, organized, and understood. When the call is to so change a religion that "significant reform" means "an entirely new awareness" and different "substance," the call is really for revolution and founding a new religion.

In some cases the move to new religions is a gradual process. This happened in Japan. As products both of the synthesis and fission of earlier Japanese religions (primarily Shinto and Buddhism) and of a response to the problems of modernity, postwar chaos, and loss of identity, new religious groups developed. Although they did not specifically address the problems of women, many of them were founded by women. According to Barnes, the founders, called "living Buddhas," provided continuity for female shamans, diviners, oracles, proselytizers, and healers of older popular religious traditions. They were family religions, says Barnes, and compatible with Japanese women's family role, but they also provided an outlet for these women to express their spirituality beyond the home. At first such religious groups viewed themselves as a branch of Buddhism or

Shinto. It was scholars of Japanese religion, in fact, who first labeled them the New Religions of Japan. Be that as it may, the New Religions gave Japan "alternative religions" and indirectly addressed the issue of women in public religious space and positions of leadership (though they did not challenge the prevailing social structure).

Ruether speaks of "women church," a kind of parallel community, which may have some loose ties with the large church. In Judaism, there are also some parallel communities that belong to the general movement of alternative congregations called *havurah*, and there are some ad hoc adaptations of mainstream congregations. At a certain point, the parallel community may find that it no longer has much in common with the original group. Carmody sees, for example, in the "all-female community of *B'not Esh*, a group assembling annually to work on Jewish feminism," a need to confront the problem of what to do in ritual. If members stay too close to the traditional liturgy, they are accused of following the "hierarchical, male-dominated, aspects of the liturgy." But when they radically depart from it, they confront the problems of their own pluralism: "such differences among them as their range of sexual orientations: straight, lesbian, bi-sexual, celibate, single, married with children, without children, and so forth."

When ritual, symbolism, and institutional structure are radically changed, the result will be new religions. Many Western feminists, of course, have already made a formal break with Christianity and Judaism, and have started new goddess cults. The concern with feminine symbolism today is not surprising. Historically, when religions existed in periods of political and economic stability, more dual sex and feminine symbolism are found. But also female leadership and feminine symbolism are found in marginal religious groups at a time of rapid change. Perhaps both these factors are working in the West today; there has been a long period of stability free from internal warfare and catastrophic economic depression. But there is also currently a period of rapid social change as secular worldviews replace religious ones.

From what Ruether and Gross say themselves and report here, it sounds as though other new religions led by women may be in the making even though some women currently are reluctant to take the step of completely breaking off from existing groups, preferring instead to rework them to their own agendas, albeit with a rhetoric of reform. This is legitimated as an important step in transforming society by changing its major institutions (though cynics claim that they only want to inherit the material assets of the community and not have to inspire others to leave and start anew). Of some Jewish feminists, Carmody reports: "On the one hand, they are insisting that they do not want to be Jewish at the price of denying their gender or experiencing it to be shortchanged. On the other hand, they are insisting that they are Jewish, not secular or religious in any other mode. The two words 'Jewish' and 'feminist' stand as mutually qualifying yet ineluctably joined. Sometimes you can speak of Jewish feminists. Other times you can speak of feminist Jews. On the whole, the terms demand equal emphasis. Criticize or slight the Jewishness and you will get a rebuke from the side of religious tradition. Criticize the feminism and you will get a rebuke from the side of sensitivity to gender rights. Criticize both, in the sense of asking both to bear on the identity of those asking what it means to be a Jewish woman today, and you will find yourself amid a wonderful ferment, full of diversity and pain, discovery and joy, and often wonderful creativity." Much the same can be said for some Christian feminists. It could be argued, however, that one cannot both rejoice in diversity and want to radically change a religion. This is a contradiction in terms. Sooner or later some reckoning will occur. Either the revolutionaries will dominate and mere reformers or traditionalists will be expelled, or vice versa. Of course, it is also possible that there will just be fragmentation and a collapse of religions already considerably weakened by the prevailing secular worldview.

But for some Western feminists, the call for change has gone too far. They are beginning to ask questions related to religious identity. If a goddess or goddesses were introduced into Judaism, for instance, would the new theology still be Jewish? If the Jewish tradition came to be defined, at least partly, by its rejection of goddess worship at some stage of its history, how can it now do the reverse? As for "reworking Hindu and Buddhist concepts of the goddess into ones that can be recognized as Jewish," is this not arguing that pork should be considered kosher? (Even reform Jews refrain from doing that; they merely say that the term "kosher" is irrelevant in the first place; P. Nathanson, personal communication.) In the final analysis, will most religious Jews admit that these ideas may or may not be useful, but still assert that they are not Jewish? For some, this is not only conflict but conflict that has been carried too far. It is striking that even Betty Friedan, called the mother of feminism in the United States, has declared that she is in favour of enriching Judaism with contributions from women, but not replacing God with a goddess. "I'm very quizzical about this Goddess stuff; I don't believe that there was a wonderful world where women were worshipped and that the Jews killed them off. Monotheism is what the Jews did. If God is seen as a male God, then that is a limitation. But you do not replace it by a female God. There is one God. And I, as a Jew, have no use for this Goddess-stuff. I have great use for how women theologians and rabbis are enriching the Jewish tradition by bringing rubrics that come from female experience, but the Goddess.... So, to say, 'You had your God, that was a male God. Now we're going to have our goddess'—that's ridiculous. That's not liberation." Many Christians find themselves asking similar questions. As some Western women begin to think about identity, they begin to appreciate the concerns about identity of religious men and women in non-Western countries. They also become more sensitive to the effect of secularism on religious life in general. And they even begin to understand problems of identity from a man's perspective.

For many men, the feminist agenda for religion is potentially disturbing. In the existing literature on women and religion today, there has been virtually no attempt to understand how the new experiments and proposals by women will affect men. In the West there has been only moral condemnation of men for the problems of patriarchy. Separate women's communities may be initiated by the desire for change. But they introduce a historically unprecedented separatism. There is a rejection not only of men's religion but of men as well. Many Western feminists argue that because of socialization or innate nature, men have created rampant militarism, environmental destruction, global poverty, and injustice. By contrast, women have "feminine" traits such as relatedness and caring that are keys to human survival, peace, and justice; women must bring their values center stage if there is to be a better world. Such a characterization divides the world into immoral men and moral women. In that patriarchal religion is the product of immoral men, it is evil and should be replaced, not reformed. In that men are immoral, they should be shunned.

Such separatism is distinctly different from the traditional separate spheres of the Australian aborigines. Comparing the two provides some intriguing insights. Bell observes how at the core of Australian aboriginal religion is a tradition common to both men and women; they both have direct access to the dream time. Women have real power (as gatherers they contribute to subsistence in a fundamental and valued way) and real knowledge (as experts in myth and ritual). Some rituals are secret and closed to men, some are jointly performed by men and women, and some are secret and closed to women. In aboriginal religion, women are thought to have a special connection to peace, health, and social welfare, which is modeled on the creative force of the dream time itself. Thus, women feel responsible for and are given special recognition for their contributions to these dimensions. But since men, too, have access to the dream time, the ultimate source, they are not excluded from expression of these activities. If women are given special recognition for their roles, men are also given recognition for other roles such as provider and protector. According to Bell, there is the playing out of independence and interdependence of the sexes in the spiritual domain.

There is often no appreciation of men's contribution to society and religion in the separatist forms of Western feminism. Prophecy, for instance, is said to be "innate to women;" the biblical male prophets are completely ignored. "Relatedness" and "community" are women's traits; the Islamic concept of brotherhood, the Christian notion of community, the Buddhist idea of the order (sangha) are ignored. Peacefulness and nonviolence are viewed as feminine; the Buddhist, Jaina, and Hindu notions of ahimsā are not mentioned. The total rejection of what is perceived as men's religion and men leads to a historically unprecedented separatism. The fact that many Christian congregations in mainstream churches are now mainly composed of women suggests that there is indeed a gender factor in the exodus from the churches. While women have threatened that they will leave, what has happened is that far more men are quietly departing.

Even if there is not a total rejection of men, there may be a demand that they change identity on terms defined by women. But Gross suggests that men should look anew at men's religion—not because it is normative or superior, but because it may shed more light on how culture contributes to the creation of masculinity, and the solving or disguising of problems specific to men. "Because in androcentric scholarship, the difference between the masculine and the human has been so thoroughly glossed over and ignored, we discover almost as much about men as about women in androgynous scholarship." (Presumably this is because a certain amount is already known about men's religion, which belongs to the public realm and has been recorded.) A new men's movement is already addressing issues of identity. Just as women feel women's identity cannot be dictated by men but must reflect the special capabilities and needs of women, so some men are now saying that men's identity cannot be dictated by feminists (which does not mean that aspects cannot be changed). The future may well see more debate and confrontation between men and women as men begin to reply to the separatist feminism of the 1980s.

SOME REFLECTIONS OF A COMPARATIVE NATURE

If the rise of kingdoms is a common type of historical process and is important for comparing the world religions in their formative phases, the rise of modernity is also important for comparing women in world religions today. More specifically, the age of exploration, which helped inspire imperialism, and the enlightenment—with its liberal, egalitarian, reformist, and scientific ideals that inspired, in turn, democracy, socialism, and the industrial revolution—informs the topic of women in world religions today.

Despite the historic attempts at reform in the foundational periods of many world religions, patrilineal and patriarchal structures prevailed. Today we are witnessing another major attempt at reform in the world religions. This time around, however, much of the initiative has been by women themselves instead of by male leaders more concerned about the universal appeal of their message (and the correction of social abuses brought about by experiments with hierarchy) than the problems faced by women per se. The women's movement has sought to remove (1) the dominance of men in formulating beliefs and institutions (androcentrism) and (2) the legitimation of hierarchy of men over women (sexism). Elite and middle-class women in many countries have ended centuries of seclusion or restriction of life plans to motherhood and the domestic sphere and have sought education and jobs in the public sphere. In the process, they have criticized scriptural and theological passages that serve to limit women's options. Where women once had public religious roles but such roles had disappeared in the course of time, they have reinstituted them or are currently trying to do so. Where such roles never existed, they have created them. In both cases, they have demanded training in religious schools. While they have been relatively successful in the educational department, they have been less successful in employment; when they do get religious jobs or roles, they are often at the low end of the hierarchy. Some branches of religions have also been unwilling to allow women to take on religious roles traditionally done by men, though they have generally tried to be more inclusive of women otherwise. When all is said and done, however, there appear to be limits to reform. Separatist feminists reject reform outright, arguing that it does not go far enough. Some men, and women having had a taste of reform, are also rejecting it, claiming that it has already gone too far.[9]

Ironically, though the women's movement started in the West, which was home to the Enlightenment and the industrial revolution, it was initially more difficult to change androcentrism and sexism there than in third-world countries. The attempt also led to greater polarization between men and women. This, I suggest, was related to a double standard related to imperialism: Western men criticized their colonial male subjects for their hierarchy over women. Men in India, China, and the Muslim world responded to this foreign attack on their morality and religious values, and took seriously democracy, socialism, or communism, all of which advocated equality, including sexual equality. Muslim leaders, such as Jinnah, Bhutto, and the Shah, and Hindu leaders such as Ranade, Vidyalankar, Tagore, Dayananda Saraswati, Keshab Chandra Sen, Jotirao Phule, E. V. Ranaswami, Gandhi, and Nehru were willing to institute reforms. In China, leaders even went so far as to eliminate the religion (Confucianism) because it was considered a barrier to progress. It may be argued that colonialism created heavy stress for men in colonized countries, for they were stripped of their power and treated as women. Real men, they were told by the colonizers, treat women equally not hierarchally. This inspired religious reforms of patriarchal society by men. Women identified both with the subjugation of their men and with the critique of male subjugation of women.

The solution to this potential polarization was for both men and women to champion reforms in the name of national independence. This led to the weakening of patriarchy. And so it seems that, in Victor Turner's terms, the liminality of sexual distinction was overcome by the communitas of common oppression and struggle.[9] Third-world men and women came together closer and moved further. The movement of women into new wage jobs created by industrialization and international development schemes also broke down patriarchy both in capitalist and socialist developing countries. Such changes often accompanied liberation struggles and the initial period of new nations. Moreover, there were new laws to improve the position of women.

But just as things seemed to be improving in many new nations for women, piecemeal changes and outright reversals related to the development of fundamentalism have begun to occur in places such as Egypt, Iran, Pakistan, and, more recently, India. (Even in China, in the past few years, there has been a more conservative note.) Chhachhi[10] suggests that these changes need to be understood with relation to the collusion of governments and conservative religious forces to address issues related to growing economic inequalities. These, in turn, lead to political unrest stimulated by democratic, socialist, and communist agendas for equality. Unrest reflects the fierce competition for jobs in new nations with burgeoning populations. Such economic competition may contribute to communalism as old animosities between religious groups flare up, and the competitor is perceived as belonging to another religious group. (Even in the colonial period, says Chhachhi, communalism flared up mainly over secular issues such as government jobs, educational opportunities, and political positions.) Economic competition may also contribute to sexual polarization when men perceive women as competing with them for the few jobs. These tensions are particularly severe for middle-class men who perceive their identity, status, and economic welfare to be threatened. They look to traditional religious symbols for reassurance and to male militaristic organizations for a renewed sense of masculine identity. Chhachhi notes the great increase in class, caste, communal and sexual violence in South Asia since the mid-1960s. As all these tensions give rise to oppositional movements, one tendency is for the state to support communalism and fundamentalism (which are often found together). The nation asserts religious and patriarchal power to control factious political groups and economic competition in order to preserve the fragile unity of the nation and the stability of the family, since the legitimacy of nation and family are increasingly under attack. The old tactic of eulogizing the independence movement no longer works for national identity and unity in these competitive times. The struggle becomes one of secular versus religious forces, or one religion against another; it is accompanied by a growing authoritarianism and sexual polarization.

The growth of communalism and fundamentalism, argues Chhachhi, threatens to erode the gains that women have made over the past century backed by religious forces drawing on traditions of reform. She observes the close tie between issues of religious identity and law related to the family. Because modern laws have tended to change family law regulating marriage, divorce, and inheritance to improve the position of women, a reassertion of religious identity can challenge the new laws. It is striking that this is happening at precisely the same time that more and more women are seeking wage employment to survive or to gain some measure of economic clout, and more and more men are wanting women back in their traditional roles in the home to eliminate job competition and the threat to their manhood. Communal identities, Chhachhi argues, are not primordial essences but created identities "that attempt to homogenise other differences within the community. In this process of identity creation, women figure in crucial ways—at a symbolic level they become symbols of culture and tradition—that is, identity markers while at the material level their particularized feminine identity forms the complementary pole to enhancing a particularized masculine identity. The crux of the fundamentalist rhetoric, a call to return to culture and tradition, is almost always a call first addressed to women. When western dress is rejected, no one demands that men stop wearing suits and ties."[11] (But sometimes, as with the Iranian revolution, women themselves reassert their identity—in contrast to Western secularism and in solidarity with men—by wearing traditional dress again.)

That the subjugation of men during the colonial period led to a hypermasculinity after national victory (which is seen in the militarism of fundamentalist groups), says Chhachhi, also means that this hypermasculinity may lead to a new subjugation of women in the family to exemplify male control. It may lead to rape of the women of other groups. And it may lead to men as a group enforcing the norms of society by punishing any woman who steps out of line. Chhachhi points out that the call for women to return to the home also happens at the same time as the growing strength of the women's movement, women's awareness of their legal rights, and women's agitation against violence and practices of subordination, especially in the family. All of these increase men's fear of loss of power and identity, and may lead to an escalation of violence. "But if we are not to fall into the biological trap of seeing inherent evilness in these acts of violence," says Chhachhi, "then it is necessary to look not only at the material basis but also the legitimizing belief systems which sanction such practices."[12]

Looking for the real cause of violence against women is an important reminder to those feminists who think that men are inherently evil. Violence, according to this analysis, is a variable within history, not a constant. According to the male aggression scale, a high degree of male aggression is defined by the presence of macho characteristics, exclusively male spheres, frequent quarreling, fighting, wife beating, rape, and raiding other groups for wives.[13] The growth of fundamentalism, the renewed insistence on male spheres, family violence, and rape seem to be increasingly common in many third-world countries despite legal and social reforms for women. The West, too, is experiencing new levels of family violence and rape. In the West as well, violence against women is recently becoming an increasing concern of women; this, too, may be a reflection of the stress caused by job competition and loss of male identity as progenitor, provider, and protector, not to mention the loss of power and sense of relative deprivation that many men are experiencing with the loss of jobs in postindustrial societies. If male stress is one of the reasons for these changes, then this issue has to be addressed in a way that also takes into consideration the problems of men.

In addition, a nation has to be willing not to condone violence by men and to use its power and resources to ease the transition to greater participation by women in the economic and political realms. The old male solution for decreasing violence against women by taking economic and political power away from them will never be accepted by women today, since it solves only the male problem and ignores the female one. In some past societies, another solution was to allow men nominal male dominance in some spheres but also to ensure economic and political power for women. This was more conflictual and necessitated careful management to prevent an escalation of violence; yet some of the needs of both men and women were addressed. Today, of course, to entertain even the idea of nominal male dominance is anathema to many women.

Chhachhi observes that some feminists in South Asia have sought a different cultural identity to fundamentalism in religious reform, while others have sought one in an oppositional culture. This observation is similar to the approaches being tried in the West: religious reform and new religions based on the thinking of separatist feminists. Religious reforms do little to address issues of male stress caused by economic, political, and identity factors, though they eliminate serious problems of stress for women related to domestic confinement and dependence. In the past, religious reform did not overlap with women's quest for economic, political, and reproductive power. While ethnic religions during the stressful time of the rise of states witnessed the rise of supreme male gods, reform and nature religions witnessed an increase in androgynous or female symbolism. But because the patrilineal family was maintained and elite men had political and economic power, women's public religious roles and androgynous or female symbolism was not threatening. It is possible that an oppositional culture today could aggravate male stress and violence, since it is premised on polarization. Nature religions (Buddhist and Hindu Tantra) in the past developed in historical periods of comparatively less stress or were proposed as a way to reform very stressful societies (Taoism as a solution to the warring states period) by advocating complementarity and harmony. Although ostensibly separatist, feminism is returning to nature religions for their message of complementarity and harmony; it is combining this return with a rhetoric of war against men (backed up by female economic, political, and reproductive power) and an interpretation of goddesses as figures of supreme power (queens). The result may not be a change from real to nominal male dominance as in the past or equality as envisioned today for the future, but a return to extreme male dominance—either sporatic expressions of male frustration and hostility, or more institutionalized expressions of aggression.

The relation between the religious and political realms may be an important variable in this discussion. Where the relation between the two spheres is integral, as in theocracies, the stress is likely to be highest because both the secular and sacred realms bear the brunt of chaos, experimentation, and oppression. Reversal of reforms is also most easy in state religions. Some Muslim countries, for instance, have recently become theocracies and have reintroduced traditional Muslim law. If a militant, conservative Hindu nation were to come into being, it is conceivable that the constitution could be rewritten and recent laws designed to improve the situation for women removed and replaced by traditional ones. Levering points out that in China gender ideology remains closely related to the state and its view of the family as it did in the past. Even the communist state supports a particular cosmological and moral order that influences views of gender and the family. In this sense, the relation between the state and religion remains integral.

When a religion has a predominantly ethnic base, moreover, any threat to the family is also a fundamental threat to the religion. Threats to the family in Judaism and Hinduism are cases in point. China, by eliminating Confucian thinking, also eliminated threats to identity based on threats to the Confucian order of the family. To the extent that Islam acts like an ethnic religion with its emphasis on the family, despite its origin as a reform religion, it too is extremely sensitive to attempts to undermine the patrilineal family. In that Christian and Buddhist scriptures rarely mentioned the family, these religions are presumably less threatened by changes to it.

Another difference is worth noting. As I argued in _Women in World Religions_ (SUNY Press, 1987), the rise of kingdoms historically was often accompanied by the rise of a supreme male deity. In those religions where this occurred against the backdrop of a pantheon of many deities, some of whom were feminine, the supreme male deity, in the course of time when there was less societal stress, would come to take on a consort or wife. In those societies with even less stress, a supreme goddess came to be accepted (albeit with some male rivals for supremacy). In the West today, many women perceive the issue of feminine symbolism to be a major problem. Because the religions are monotheistic, it is problematic to introduce alongside the male deity a female one. Because of tradition, it is also problematic to change the sex of the deity. In most non-Western religions such as Hinduism, Buddhism, and Taoism, the sex of the deities has not been a major concern, because they already have divine female figures and do not have to worry about the problem of monotheism in the same way. The fact that divine symbolism does not create such a theological and historical problem may be one reason why these religions focus more on the mundane issue of how to maintain an identity that is distinct from the West than the supramundane issue of the sex of the divine. Islam bridges these two problems; although it is a Western religion whose God has many masculine epithets (though it is argued that the deity transcends anthropomorphism), it has not focused on the issue of masculine epithets, because of the more pressing concern to maintain a Muslim identity in the face of economic, political, or cultural imperialism from the West.

To conclude, there have been many reforms related to women and religion to date. And there has been the birth of new sects and religions. There have also been some reversals of reforms, in part due to political and economic factors. There are no signs that tension generated by the women's movement will abate. Debates between branches of a religion, between old and new religions, between Western and third-world feminists, and between women and men will likely go on as questions of identity, politics, and economics collide. Although egalitarian changes occurred more quickly in the third world, so did the reversals as fundamentalist forces came to dominate more and more movements. By contrast, Western women had to fight against men to define their rights, and in some ways their movement is peaking only now. It may be argued that the potential for swing may be less in the West and greater in third-world countries because the former can build on the stabilizing factors of strong nationhood and industrialization, while these factors are often fragile in the latter. Despite such differences, women and men desirous of a more egalitarian society should not forget what has been the historic pattern of such reforms for women to date. While reforms characterized a formative period of many world religions, which was correlated with a maturing period of nation-building, a closure to this progressive spirit often characterized the change to nation maintenance. Perhaps the closure in some third-world countries that we are witnessing today is an expression of this larger trend. In this case, it is even more important to understand the dynamics involved. I, for one, suspect that the distinctive problems of both women and men must be addressed if we are to find a lasting solution to the issue of sexual inequality. But there must be institutional and legal safeguards against slippage to old ways. Understanding religion today is one thing; transforming religion for tomorrow is quite another. For both, *Today's Woman in World Religions* offers ample opportunity for reflection.

Diane Bell

ABORIGINAL WOMEN'S RELIGION: A SHIFTING LAW OF THE LAND

> My father was *kurdungurlu* for that place. It was his to
> look after. He looked after the two places, Waake and
> Wakulpu and then I lost him; he passed away. Now it is
> up to me looking after my own country, Jarra Jarra and
> also Waake and Wakulpu. As my father could not go on
> to that country so from when I was a young girl I kept
> on doing the *yawulyu* [women's ceremonies], looking
> after the country. . . . My sisters, Mona and Nancy, they
> are looking after that country too. . . . We do that *yaw-*
> *ulyu* for Wakulpu all the time . . . for fruit. So it will grow
> up well, so that we can make it green, so that we hold
> the Law forever. My father instructed me to hold it al-
> ways this way, so I go on holding *yawulyu* for that coun-
> try. Sometimes we dance, man and woman together. For
> Wakulpu. So we can "catch him up," "hold him up."
> Mollie Nungarrayi, 1981 (quoted in Bell 1983a, 119, 132)[1]

This testimony, given in the context of a Central Australian land
claim,[2] aptly summarises the nature of women's relationship to and
responsibility for country, and takes us to the very heart of Aboriginal religion: the focus on kin and sacred sites, the integration of
spiritual with economic life in ritual celebration, generational
transmission of knowledge, and a sex division of labor (see Bell
1983a; 1987c). It is the latter, the sex division of labor, and the existence of sex-specific bodies of secret-sacred knowledge, that render
research and analysis of Aboriginal women's religious beliefs and
practices so problematic (see Berndt 1965, 241–7; Bell 1983a, 229ff.;

Goodale 1971, 338; Hamilton 1987, 45–49; Maddock 1982, 139–40).
To gain access to the intimate ritual worlds of women, one needs to
be female (and, as I suggest below, not just any female). There have
been few women in the field and not all have been interested in
women, let alone religion.[3] Those who have written of women's
lives faced a dilemma in the presentation of their data.[4] How do the
worlds of women and men articulate? How are contradictory sex-
specific perceptions to be accommodated? Is it sufficient to accept
the ideology of male dominance as a timeless, enduring actuality?
What of regional differences? How do our own assumptions regarding gender relations shape our fieldwork experiences and subsequent analyses?

From the testimony of Mollie Nungarrayi another aspect of Aboriginal life, which impinges on any discussion of religion, is plain.
The contemporary contexts within which we may learn of women's
commitment to "hold onto" traditional knowledge are limited, and
often hostile to hearing what women have to say on serious matters.
Nungarrayi spoke in a legal context, an environment that does little
to put women at ease. Land claims are a telling example, albeit one
of many, where the constraints on recognition of women's contribution to Aboriginal society are manifest (see Bell 1984/5; 1988c).
The politics of knowledge and gender relations in Aboriginal society, and the points of articulation with institutions of the wider
Australian society, shape our approaches and appreciations of Aboriginal women's religious beliefs and practices (Bell 1983a, 240–46;
1989, 6–9; Bell and Nelson 1989, 408–11). Indeed, the politics of Aboriginal religion and the politics of the study of Aboriginal religion
have intertwined so intricately that to write of religion necessarily
entails engaging with local politics, academic politics and those of
the nation state (see Bell and Marks 1990, 98–104). As these do-
mains are ones in which women's voices are muted, to focus on
women is to call attention to the situatedness of the ethnographic
voices.

A FEMINIST ETHNOGRAPHY OF ABORIGINAL RELIGION

Here I address two basic questions: what are women doing in
the ritual domain, and what does this mean for our understanding of
Aboriginal religion? I begin from within the ritual worlds of women
and map their contribution to the religious domain. But we cannot
leave it there, for Aboriginal religion is the political forum within

which women and men negotiate authority, power, meaning, and relationships. Thus I explore ceremonial contexts within which women and men participate in the construction of representations of Aboriginal religion. My field methodology—participant observation—is necessarily situated, perspectival, relational, contextual, and my rendering of my field experience in the writing of ethnography is similarly framed. This, I suggest, is so of all ethnography, but where ethnographic reporting has produced images consonant with those cherished by the dominant society, and consonant with current scholarly theorizing about gender and women, the relation of the anthropologist to his or her field remains unscrutinized (Hondagneu-Sotelo 1988). In other words, the epistemology is undeclared; male experience is privileged; reality is presented as unmediated by the observer, and the voices of the less powerful are muted (Mascia-Lees et al. 1989). The difference for feminist anthropologists is that we can not feign disinterest, and, as I am arguing here, the sex division of labor in the religious domain presents an enigma which feminist critiques of "culture" and "gender-relations" illuminate (Moore 1988, 186ff.).

I have chosen an ethnographic presentation for several reasons. First, there is little written on Aboriginal women's ritual life.[5] Secondly, what does exist variously ignores women; is blind to the historical transformation of gender relations; nonreflectively endorses as holy writ male expressions of power and social reality, or categorically excludes woman's activities from the religious domain.[6] Thirdly, by beginning with a detailed account of one region, one where the separation of the sexes is particularly marked, it is possible to demonstrate that much of the generalizing about women's religious life has been premature and its sureness of vision has constrained research.[7] Finally, a woman-centred ethnography reveals that certain behaviors of women, which appear anomalous if religion is mapped with male as ego, are part of a consistent, coherent set of practices.

I begin with the assumption that what women are doing, and say they are doing, is worth recording; that differences between male and female interpretations of religion are not necessarily evidence that one has erred, but a challenge for the anthropologist to find ways of writing of a society with gendered views. My position is that an ethnography which is explicitly feminist in giving voice to women, not only illuminates women's worlds, but also leads us to a more dynamic reading of Aboriginal religion, and thereby to a critique of the ways in which we represent our fieldwork. In addressing these issues, I am in open dialogue with current feminist debates concerning reflexivity, politics, and epistemology (Caplan 1988; Clifford 1988; Hawkesworth 1989; Mascia-Lees et al. 1989). Following Caplan (1988, 10), I am arguing that we can be both "reflexive and political" and that to acknowledge our power as ethnographers is not to forgo our interest in the foundations of knowledge.[8] It is a profoundly political act to decenter man ethnographically as subject, or authority, and the terms in which feminist analyses have been reviewed in Australia are ample evidence of this.[9]

Although Aboriginal beliefs and practices are not consistent across the continent, at core is the concept of the dreamtime (*jukurrpa, altjirra, wongar, bugari*), a moral code that informs and unites all life. The dogma of dreaming states that all the world is known and can be classified within the taxonomy created by the ancestral heroes whose pioneering travels gave form, shape, and meaning to the land (Stanner 1979). Here a rocky outcrop indicates the place where the ancestral dog had her puppies, there a low ridge the sleeping body of the emu; the red streaks on the cliff face recall the blood shed in a territorial dispute; ghost gums stand as mute witness to where the lightning brothers flashed angrily at their father rain; the lush growth of bush berries is the legacy of prudent care by two old grandmothers; the clear, sweet water holes, the home of the rainbow serpent, which may only be approached by those schooled in the "business" (the term used for the work necessary to maintain the law of the dreamtime), remain pure.

The law binds people, flora, fauna, and natural phenomena into one enormous interfunctional world. It is the responsibility of the living, who trace direct relationships to these ancestors, to give form and substance to this heritage in their daily routines and their ceremonial practice: to keep the law, to visit sites, to use the country, and to enjoy its bounty. It is in the living out of the dreamtime heritage, particularly in the ceremonial domain, that we see how the past is negotiated in the present, how women and men position themselves vis-à-vis each other and vis-à-vis the law. Staging ceremonies which celebrate the dreamtime heritage is a sacred trust shared by men and women, both of whom have sacred boards, the title deeds to land; both of whom know songs and paint designs which, in cryptic graphics, encode knowledge of the dreamtime. The common core concerns the structural level of knowledge of ancestral activity (the major sites and their spiritual affiliations), the rights of living descendants, and the responsibilities of the ritual bosses of the business.

How each sex then fleshes out this common core of beliefs and knowledge, as "men's business" and "women's business," is dependent upon their perception of their role and of their contribution to society. These are elaborated in sacred sex-specific spaces (the ceremonial ground and the ritual storehouse) before being brought into shared spaces. Thus this portrait of Aboriginal religion stresses the sex division of labor, but as a mode of maintaining a complex system of beliefs and practices, and a means of revitalizing the common core of knowledge of the dreaming. By exploring the contexts in which meanings are negotiated and decisions made by men and women, we can see the importance of the existence of separate power bases. Separation does not necessarily entail fixed hierarchies, but rather generates shifting context-dependent moments. Aboriginal society presents a fascinating dilemma for the anthropologist who is willing to struggle with situated ethnographies and grapple with cultural models which accommodate societies where women and men have separate residential structures, ceremonial cycles, social strategies, and where there is no clearly defined public domain in which to "balance" one view against the other.

The politics of place and person, age and ambition, ceremony and sentiment, knowledge and kin, shape ritual practice. As each generation works with the resources at hand, it is important that we locate our studies historically and geographically. This ethnography draws on fieldwork (both lengthy periods of participant observation and shorter periods of applied research), undertaken in central and northern Australia since 1976, and is sensitive to the contexts within which Aboriginal women make known their religious belief and practices. In an oral culture, the law can only be given meaning through the expressions of the living which, in the Aboriginal case, are inscribed on the land itself. As long as one has contact with the land and control over the sites, the dreamtime as the ever-present, all encompassing law, can be asserted to be reality. Under these conditions the dreamtime is enduring and timeless: women and men negotiate common ground within a closed system. But land, as the central tablet, as the sacred text, is no longer under Aboriginal control across the continent. Ritual politics must now encompass a dramatically changed cast of players and forces.

A critically important change, which impacts dramatically on religion, is the shift from a hunter-gatherer mode of subsistence to a more sedentary one (Bell 1983a, 94–106). Aborigines must now deal with the state, its agencies, its policies, its laws and modes of distribution. Dispossessed of their land by the British in 1788, Aborigines' struggle for land rights has brought Aboriginal beliefs into the public arena. Under existing Northern Territory legislation, to gain title to their land, Aborigines must now prove traditional ownership in an Australian court, and this entails demonstrating their religious ties to land.

ABORIGINES IN AUSTRALIAN SOCIETY

At the time of the arrival of the British in Australia in 1788, there were hundreds of different languages spoken, by the million or so persons who were the undisputed owners of the continent.[10] The colonization of the land was uneven: Aboriginal groups in the southeast bore the brunt of the first wave of the invasion and for many peoples of northern Australia, intensive contact with whites dates only from this century. It is still possible to attend Aboriginal ceremonies that proceed in a way very close to those observed by men such as Spencer and Gillen (1899) at the turn of the century. However, the context has changed dramatically. Alternate land use by pastoralists, miners, urban and rural developers, has shattered the nexus between economic and spiritual practice. Once Aboriginal religion offered a comprehensive reading of the rhymes and rhythms of the world, and set the parameters of social, economic, and political life. Now, dependent on social security, subject to Australian laws, poorly housed and nourished, Aborigines suffer high rates of imprisonment, infant mortality, and interpersonal violence; endure low levels of educational certification and employment. The sense of self and community derived from religion today is thus markedly different from a century ago, and the shaping factors are not all amenable to religious interpretation and manipulation.

Aborigines constitute approximately 1.4 percent of the Australian population (i.e., about 200,000 people), but apart from indicating their electorally weak standing, this statistic reveals little of their situation, and nothing of the issues facing women. Indeed analyses that give salience to gender are resisted as not in the interests of the new elites, or in the interests of the wider society (Bell and Nelson 1989, 414–15; Bell and Marks 1990, 98–104). The highest proportion of Aborigines to non Aborigines is in the north, but even there residential sites range from urban, the fringes of the town, to cattle stations (ranches), missions, government reserves, homeland centers and Aboriginal land. What is consistent is that this is frontier society, a man's world, and the positions of power, the ability to name, and to confer meaning, in the emerging political order are not for women (Bell 1983a, 249–50). The official policy is self-management but this is a colonial artifact, which reverberates with paternalism and sexist practices (Bell and Ditton 1980, 5–15; Bell and Nelson 1989, 413–15; Bell 1990).

Across the tropical north of Australia (Queensland, Northern Territory, and Western Australia) and into the desert regions of central Australia, there are large tracts of land where Aborigines are the dominant population, and in some areas, where they have land rights, they are able to exclude outsiders. It is in these regions that ceremonial life is intense. Freed from the constant threat of intrusion, on their own land, and able to manage much of their own affairs, the impact of dispossession of land and disruption of family life is ameliorated. The shift from a hunter-gatherer life to a more sedentary one, the establishment of centers of population where groups who would not have sustained close relations are in daily interaction, has had a mixed impact on religious practice, and more particularly on women. New possibilities for sustained ceremonial life arise, but there are also new possibilities for tensions, jealous fights, and conflicts over distribution of the resources that flow from the politics of self-determination. There are important differences for those resident on cattle stations, settlements, missions, outstations, and towns (Bell and Ditton 1980, 29–90; Bell 1983a, 76–81).

One of the resources generated at the interface of the two cultures is the authorative documentary accounts of Aboriginal life. These reflect the preoccupations and purposes of the writers as surely as they reflect the lives of Aborigines. Men's roles and perceptions have been well documented: women's are rather less well known. However, this has not inhibited generalizations (Bell 1984; Gross 1987, 41–42). Many of those that deal with religion in a contemporary context, acknowledge that Aboriginal religion is a political domain, but tend to cast men as the politicians and women as the pawns (Bern 1979a; 1979b). Les Hiatt (1987, 186), in the face of evidence from feminist anthropologists, acknowledged that women had a voice, but cast men as setting the agenda and women as resisting. Clearly there is an unease in dealing with reports of vocal, powerful women, and as Ken Maddock (1982, 140) allows in revising his 1972 text, "the established position" that men hold the keys to cosmic order (Munn 1986, 213) is under siege. We are poorly served in our search for meaning if we begin with the assumption that women are the profane and the passive, that men command and women comply. If we are prepared to look beyond assertions that men control the religious domain, and beyond the promise of security contained in the dreamtime dogma of immutability, to the reality of the persons, passions, and politics that generate current religious practice and shape beliefs; to map the activities which maintain Aboriginal religion; and to trace how ritual decisions are negotiated, we move into a more dynamic, albeit problematic, exploration of Aboriginal religion.

The community in which my children and I lived between 1976 and 1978 was home to some seven hundred fifty Aboriginal persons of four different language groups (Alyawarra, Kaytej, Warlpiri, and Warumungu), and about seventy-five whites. The settlement of Warrabri (now Ali-Curang), established in 1954 under a heavily assimilationist policy, was an unhappy place where intergroup rivalries shaped daily life (Bell 1983a, 73–94). Around the periphery of the settlement service core, where whites ran and controlled the police station, store, post office, garage, hospital, school, and power plant, were the Aboriginal camps. People whose land was to the east lived in camps oriented to that country, likewise those on the west oriented their camps to their traditional lands. An "elected" all-male village council, who administered funds from the federal Department of Aboriginal Affairs, "ran" the settlement.[11] Much remained outside the ambit of council decision-making, but its presence and resources were factors in the balancing of power between groups, between men and women, between young and old. The settlement area is now Aboriginal land, and people settled there against their will several decades ago, have moved away to nearby towns, and onto adjacent traditional lands, which have been secured under the Land Rights Act. The shift from a hunting and gathering subsistence mode, to welfare dependency and local enterprises registers differently on women and men. Thus, in writing of Aboriginal women and religion in contemporary contexts, I must necessarily take account of the impact of two hundred years of colonization of desert lands, government policy, legal reform, of the embeddedness of Aboriginal society in the wider Australian society. Here we see that the law, the state, religion are not gender blind in Australian society, anymore than in Aboriginal society (Bell 1990).

WOMEN'S WORLDS

At Ali-Curang, some younger women were engaged as teaching aids, house girls, assistants, and nursing assistants, but for most, having left school early, married, and begun a family, their choices were limited. Even those who had completed high school found that they had few options, and to get employment usually meant moving to town. The older generation of women who had grown up on the local missions, ration depots, and cattle stations, but still enjoyed a relatively mobile life, mourned the loss of youth to the "new law" (gambling, alcohol, television). Nonetheless, conscientiously and rigorously, they instructed the young girls in the ways of the law. Much of their daily life was taken up with work in family camps and women's camps, in hunting and gathering, and in ritual.

Instruction in "women's business" occurs in all female groups and the most prominent setting is the *jilimi*, the all female camps, which are taboo to men. *Jilimi*, a Warlpiri term (also used by Kaytej), is often translated as "single women's camp," but this has pejorative overtones of the place being peripheral, transient, junior, and lacking power. In fact the *jilimi* is home to the ritually important senior women. It is a symbol of women's independence, a refuge, the locus of daily activity, and information exchange (Bell 1983, 16–17, 82–84; 110–36). At any given time up to 25 percent of the adult female population of the settlement could be found there. At the residential core of the *jilimi* was the older and respected ritual leaders, who are usually divorced, widowed, or separated, and their dependent female relatives, women visiting from elsewhere; women who for any reason are not living with a man; women who are ill, too young for marriage, or reluctant to enter a marriage. During the day the *jilimi* was the focal point of women's activities; during the evenings it provided a refuge.

Because of the sex-segregated nature of Aboriginal society, it is extremely inappropriate (and in terms of in-depth fieldwork unproductive) to attempt to work equally with men and women. Usually one is identified with members of one's own sex and is able to move freely within that sphere. Fortunately for my study, women considered my position agreeable for one who sought ritual instruction. Had I been working with teenage girls, the relations established would have been very different. As a divorced woman in receipt of a government pension (pensioners are important people in Aboriginal communities), I was in a similar position to the ritual "bosses" of the Warlpiri and Kaytej *jilimi* with whom I worked: I was economically and emotionally independent of men and therefore potentially safe with women's secrets. Further, the social status I enjoyed by virtue of my two outgoing and energetic children allowed me access to the world of adult women. Ritual knowledge resides with the older women who, once freed from the immediate responsibilities of child care, devote their time and energies to upholding and transmitting their spiritual heritage to successive generations.

By being around the knowledgeable women of the *jilimi*, one learned through direct experience: there is no concept of vicarious learning, no hypothetical puzzles by which one is instructed. When young girls do not hunt with their female kin, they do not learn survival skills and "women's law" in an integrated fashion. Competing calls on the time of young girls have reduced quality teaching opportunities. One of the most dramatic losses of knowledge is that of sign language, which is learned through exposure to groups of older women who are communicating in this way. When a close relative dies, part of the mourning ritual requires that women do not speak and the taboo lasts for up to two years (Bell 1983a, 115; Kendon 1988). But because young girls no longer spend so many hours in women's company, they do not learn the signs, and consequently the speech taboo period is shortened so that there can be communications with younger women. Thus learning time is curtailed, and the practice falls into disuse for want of skilled "speakers." The knowledge of sign language, like knowledge of the environment, was once an integral part of religious observances, but is being lost in a downward spiral: ceremonial observations associated with mourning, and subsistence activities informed by mythological narratives of place, are truncated.

Participation in the ceremonial life of women made it possible to explore aspects of ritual practice and belief at first hand. I was learning in the appropriate manner but I had quite a bit to cram. I was incorporated in the kinship system and, as a classificatory mother, sister, and mother-in-law to various young men, participated in their initiations; as an older woman with two children—a son who was seen to be nearing the age of initiation, and a daughter approaching marriageable age—I was admitted into the ritual world of women and participated in many women's ceremonies. Further, because I had a roadworthy vehicle, was literate, and willing to assist with telecommunications, I was considered well resourced, and by settlement standards, for a woman, I was. When I later worked as anthropologist for the Aboriginal Sacred Sites Protection Authority, as consultant to the Aboriginal Land Councils, Legal Aid Services, the Aboriginal Land Commissioner, and the Law Reform Commissions, and gave evidence in cases involving customary law, I was able to draw on the knowledge of ceremonial practice and women's strategies learned in one place, to enter women's ceremonial worlds in others. Regional differences were made plain to me and a constant source of amusement for women in fieldwork sites north of Ali-Curang was to ask me to dance in the "desert style."

On the occasions when I was engaged in applied anthropological research, my resources and my relationships to community members were of a different order from those of a long-term fieldworker. My position in terms of mediating between two cultures was more transparent; my motives in seeking knowledge recognizably part of the era of self-determination. The points of articulation between the gender politics of the wider society and Aboriginal society were nonetheless a critical factor (Bell 1984/5; 1987a and b; Bell and Ditton 1980; Bell and Nelson 1989). This was not so much a consideration for local peoples as it was for their representative organizations, the bureaucratic agencies with responsibility in the area of Aboriginal affairs, and institutions and individuals dispensing academic patronage and fieldwork funds.

My documentation and analysis of central Australian Aboriginal women's worlds draws mainly on Warlpiri, Kaytej, and Alyawarra ceremonies, but I also attended Warumungu, Pintupi, Gurinji, Pitjantjatjarra, and Aranda ceremonies when, in the company of women I knew at Ali-Curang, we visited other communities. In their religious rituals women emphasized their role as nurturers of people, land, and relationships. Their responsibility to maintain harmoniously this complex of relationships between the living and the land is manifest in the intertwining of the ritual foci of health and emotional management. Through their *yawulyu* (land-based ceremonies) they nurture land; through their health and curing rituals they resolve conflict and restore social harmony; and through *yilpinji* (love rituals) they manage emotions. In *yilpinji,* as in their health-oriented *yawulyu,* women seek to resolve and to explore the conflicts and tensions which beset their communities. In centers of population concentration where Aborigines now live, jealous fights, accusations of infidelity, and illicit affairs occur on a scale impossible a century ago when people lived in small mobile bands. Thus today, women's role in the domain of emotional management, like their role in the maintenance of health and harmony, is truly awesome (Bell 1983a, 145–62).

In central Australia, ceremonies may be classified as those staged by women, which are secret and closed to men; those in which men and women participate; and those staged by men, which are closed and secret to women. Most analyses begin from within the latter. If, however, we begin from within woman's ceremonial world and explore her ritual domain, we find that women see their lives as underwritten by their independence and autonomy of action. These self-evaluations are not easily dismissed for they are legitimated by women's direct access to the dreamtime. Men and women politic to achieve personal ends, to establish favorable alliances between families and countries, and with fieldworkers whose analyses become part of other political campaigns—be the forum the law courts, the academy, or the bureaucracy.

YAWULYU

The *jilimi*, which is the focus of women's daily activities, is also where women begin to make plans for *yawulyu* activity. At the core of each *jilimi* are key individuals for a particular country and the *jilimi* is known by that name. In *yawulyu*, it is relations to land which are being stressed also. In central Australia, women and men alike trace their decent from the dreamtime through two distinct lines and here I am using the Warlpiri terms. From one's father and father's father a person has the rights and responsibilities of *kirda*; through one's mother and mother's father those of *kurdungurlu*. From one's mother's mother one also enjoys a special relationship to what is called one's *jaja* (granny) country. Other interests in land are stated in terms of conception dreamings, residence, marriage, place of death, burial, and sentiment. Through these overlapping and interlocking modes of expressing how one is "of the land," central Australian women and men locate themselves within the ancestral design (Bell 1983a, 264–66).

Place names, dreaming affiliations, and the relationship of particular individuals to land may be discussed within the *jilimi*, but when women wish to engage in *yawulyu*, or serious discussion concerning *yawulyu* places, women retire to their ceremonial ground. Situated within walking distance of the *jilimi*, but conceptually "in the bush," and thus beyond the settlement, are the ritual storehouse, bough-shelter, and "ring place," ceremonial ground (Berndt 1950, 43). This area is inaccessible by road, and not visible from the residential camps. Men travel circuitous routes to avoid even sighting the general area, and women, if disturbed by children during ritual activity at the "ring place," will carry through disciplinary threats, which at other times, because of the high levels of personal autonomy enjoyed by children, are not enforced.

The women's ritual area has two main divisions. One is a large clearing where women may sit to paint, display their boards, dance, and occasionally sleep. The second area, facing east, the site of more serious work, backs onto the "ring place" and has a storehouse where the ritual paraphernalia (sacred boards, stones, painting sticks, bleached feathers, ochres, hair string, and headbands) are stored, often on a ledge in one of the recesses of the structure. The area opens out into a bough shade, a private, secure place, from where the women keep all activity in the *jilimi* under surveillance and signal through only those visitors they wish to see. Gone is the ribald joking of the *jilimi*; instead women speak of the importance of caring for their treasures and the need to "hold" them always.

In the past women's "ring places" were where offenders were brought to trial and disputes resolved by ritual means. Men refer to their ceremonial ground as the "ring place" and it also has a function in dispute resolution. Important meetings concerning women are held in their "ring place." On occasions when I was putting together a background briefing on disputes which had found their way into Australian courts, I knew the matter entailed serious infringement of the law, if I was invited to the "ring place" for discussion. Although many of the functions have now been usurped by school, hospital, church, and police, the "ring place" is still considered to be a therapeutic place to sleep during trying times. For one thing, it is away from the daily hubbub of the camps and the demands of children and husbands, but it is also where women may state their authority and ability to manage their own lives, and to influence community affairs.

The atmosphere at the "ring place," while handling the sacred objects, is one of hushed reverence for the traditions being evoked. Introduced items, such as store-bought cleaners, wool, dripping (cattle fat), and cash, which have been incorporated through use, are treated as if they were the stone derived bleaches, hair string, emu fat, and exchange items. The availability of certain items has facilitated ceremonial activity. For example, once "hair string" could only be obtained through exchanges at initiation; now women may buy wool, red ochre it, and use it in ceremonies. On becoming part of the store, it is indistinguishable from ritual hair string. Now that women may buy small handle tomahawks in the store, they can cut wood for ritual poles with ease. Store-bought fat means ritual activity is no longer constrained by the availability of goanna or emu fat from hunting. Cash is incorporated into ritual exchanges and, to an extent, it is brought under the law. But inflation is rampant, because, unlike traditional exchange items, money is not produced by the participants.

In the past the contents of the storehouse moved with the ritual bosses (larger items remained at sacred sites), but today, where people are living in population intensive settlements, women want brick museums to protect their sacred paraphernalia from fire, theft, and accidental intrusion. Men have had success in gaining funding from government agencies and enjoyed support from local councils in obtaining such structures. However, when a women's submission comes before a male council, members of which have cause to fear the growing strength of women's ceremonies, or a government bureaucrat ignorant of women's business, funding is problematic (Bell and Ditton 1980, 6). Further, it is improper for women to be asking men for assistance in "women's business."

At one level the lack of outside support has meant that women have had less prying into their affairs than have men, but at another it means they are not taken seriously in the resource allocation that flows from the implementation of government policies of self-determination and management. Access to vehicles is a good example. Men, as drivers and owners of vehicles, have been able to consolidate and extend their social and ceremonial networks. Women, with fewer vehicles and little driving experience, have trouble visiting neighboring women and "mustering" women for ceremonies.[12] Thus while population intensive settlements and readily available materials facilitate the staging of *yawulyu*, other factors limit the impact and efficacy of the activity. Whereas once separation of women's and men's activities assured that women were consulted, because their resources were necessary for male activities, now it is the means of their marginalization. The political domain, in which resources are distributed, has become the male domain and women have been relegated to the domestic. The latter is an imposed category with no real traditional correlate save that which is generated by assuming that when women go out to gather food, they are engaged in "women's business" for women's benefit, not the production of the means of survival of the whole group (Bell 1983a, 54–56). Or, that when women talk in their own camps, it is the "gossip" of "highly vocal" "toothless old hags" (Hart and Pilling 1960, 14, 20; Meggitt 1962, 236) not the reflections of ritual sages (Bell 1983a, 16–17).

I had been in the community more than nine months before I moved with any ease in the "ring place." I needed to know a great deal of kinship relations, actual and classificatory, and these can be difficult to distinguish, but are a critical indicator of ritual politics. I needed to know the history of group movements, to have access to sites, and to know the range of country associated with individuals and groups. My clearest instruction included the structural level of interrelations of sites, persons, and dreamings—the grand design of mythological activity in the area. This was accompanied by visiting the sites, *yawulyu*, sand maps, and careful monitoring of my behavior to ensure that I spoke only of those matters of which it was proper to speak. I was being tested to see if I understood the politics of knowledge. It was not what I knew, but rather what I verbalized, to whom and in what context, that was critical. I was guided carefully, for to blunder would have been to endanger myself and others, and protected by always being in the company of other women, particularly my "sisters," with whom I shared major kin avoidances (Bell 1983a, 25).

Alongside the macro level of learning of what I have termed the "common core," was finer grain analyses of song texts, designs, and gestures. These were only forthcoming after I had participated; were sometimes quite elliptical; and usually built on the broader appreciations of the macro level. Once I began to take greater responsibility within the "ring place," and had been taken to visit the women's sites, I was expected to "know" more and was instructed accordingly. It was like having the outline colored in. The revelation of the details of ancestral activity through interaction with country is also one way in which women validate their rights and authority over the land and its bounty, both spiritual and economic (Bell 1983a, 110–28).

Yawulyu performances tend to cluster around the preparation for special events, during times of social unrest and illness. At other times women simply gather to work on ritual items, to plan, to share information. Although I have been present at some eighty *yawulyu*, generalizations are difficult for one group, let alone region or the continent. Nonetheless, it is possible to identify key aspects of the structure of women's ceremonies in desert regions, which are also manifest in the practice of women further to the north. All the *yawulyu* I have attended included a period of preparation which was sacred and secret, a "calling in" transition, a relatively open performance, and a solemn "finish up."All had an overt function—Nangala was ill; Nakamarra needed to visit a site; there was a land claim, a school excursion, a sacred site registration. Someone had to ask for *yawulyu* and being able to pin performances to external bodies alleviated tensions generated by jealous fights if one person "put herself up" as in charge. There is a difference between assuming that role, and being "mistress of ceremonies." When powerful interests are at stake, it is wise to be the one responsible for resolving conflict, but folly to claim responsibility for initiating the action. A similar mode of deflection of responsibility is manifest in the way in which women will say they "learned" of a particular ceremony: it came from elsewhere (especially powerful *yilpinji*); it was "found" in a "dream"; or it was in the mythology. Underpinning the stated ceremonial agenda, there were always deep simmering, long standing "troubles," ones which were rarely voiced, and are only known in the unfolding of individual and group histories, which spanned generations implicating the unborn and deceased.

The preparation for *yawulyu* usually begins early in the afternoon. Women gather at the "ring place" where they sit close, and speak softly as they take their sacred objects from the store. The objects are fondled, named, and then passed to the appropriate person for preparation. The women begin by greasing their own bodies with fat, and then the senior *kurdungurlu* begin the body painting of the *kirda*. More junior persons may then try their hand under the guidance of older women. Painting is a group activity, which allows novices to acquire the necessary knowledge and expertise. Onto the fat, on the upper torso, legs, and back red ochre is applied, and with broad brush strokes of the index finger, the painter maps out the basic contours of the design in black, yellow, or red (Berndt 1950; 1965; Munn 1986, 36ff.) Then with small painting sticks, the white enclosures are applied to produce dramatic symbolic representations of land, myth, and relationships. Bleached white headbands are painted with symbols from the same repertoire as those on the body and boards. The ritual pole is dressed, in the same manner as the human participants—white cockatoo feathers in the headband, designs running along the body of the board, and hairstring skirt. The particular designs being used depend on the site(s) and dreaming activity on which the *yawulyu* is focused.

While the women are preparing the ritual items and painting, they sing gently and harmoniously of the dreamtime experience, which validates their use of the objects. During this activity, the range of songs, harmonies, and symbolic meanings is far more extensive and complex than during the open and public singing which may follow in the "ring place." It is a private time when children and outsiders are not welcome; and the songs known as "dear ones"— that is, old and cherished—are sung; it is also when verbal instruction occurs, when ritual roles are sorted out, and when new information may be incorporated. For example, in the narratives of the places Waake and Walapanpa, the ancestor rain, an extremely important dreaming in the desert, is manifest as younger and older brother. This relationship should be reflected in the seniority of the lineages of the current generations with responsibility for the sites. But there is room for adjustment. The seniority of lineages is not reckoned by chronological age, but rather by sibling relations at the parent level, or more often grandparent generation level, and these relatives may be actual or classificatory. Thus the living ritual celebrants have room to maneuver and the status of seniority is conferred on the most able, most active, best positioned, ritual politicians. Once done, it is ratified by the law and thus not open to speculation by mortals.

When the body painting is completed, the boards greased, the feathers glistening, and the headbands brilliant white, the women move to the dancing place, sit facing west, and begin to sing the songs which call in those who may watch, which welcome strangers, and which begin the process of "bringing" the dreamings to the ceremonial ground. The fire in the center of the ground, a symbol of ritual continuity, is rekindled in the embers of previous fires. Following the "calling in" songs, the *kurdungurlu* introduce the country with several songs, which allude to, rather than explicate, ancestral activity. Then the senior *kirda*, holding the painted boards on high for all to see, dance forward in single file, until they arrive at the fire. This "wakens" the *kirda* and activates the power of the *jukurrpa* at that ceremonial site.

The seated *kirda* and *kurdungurlu* sing of the site at which the dreaming rests or visits, while senior *kurdungurlu* "plant" the boards. The power of the dreaming is thus brought to the "ring place," and is active for the duration of the ceremony. The past moves concurrent with the present. The planted boards are called by name and addressed affectionately by the kin terms. In this way both the ritual relationship and the deep emotional personal tie to country are given expression. The *kurdungurlu* dance flanking the *kirda* and thus reenact the way in which the ancestors made known these ritual roles. One narrative tells how little black birds danced alongside black berry in his tiring journey to Wakulpu. The meandering track of their travels is symbolized in the designs for this *yawulyu*, and is imprinted on the land by the dancing feet of the *kirda* and *kurdungurlu*.

The sacred board or ritual pole becomes the focus of the dancing, as the *kirda* and *kurdungurlu* weave patterns in the sand, which spell out the interactions of the dreamings. The broad design can be grasped by an outsider, but the rich texturing of the information in the songs is only available if one has been given previous ritual instruction. The *yawulyu* performance is short, alludes to the preparation, but in no way spells out the nature of the negotiations. The dance is the time to confirm the ritual roles to the assembled public, to tell a story for the pleasure of all present: it is truly a celebration of the dreamtime. A favorite *yawulyu* segment concerns the adventures of two "grandmothers" who were out collecting berries. As they filled their wooden dishes with fruit, young girls who were out playing in the country crept up from behind the older women and stole berries. When they discovered the loss, the grandmothers were surprised and turned this way and that looking for an explanation. The dance sequence is repeated several times for the further amusement of those present, and as a way of giving younger girls a dancing part in *yawulyu*.

In the final segment of *yawulyu*, the mood shifts back to one of hushed reverence. The dancing finished, the women sing the dreamings back into the ground and expect visitors to leave. Senior women smooth over all traces of where the boards have been, throw dirt to nullify any remaining power, and rub the painted boards onto their bodies to reabsorb the power. This transference of power is extremely dangerous, and when the *yawulyu* has resolution of conflict as a goal, constitutes the most sacred moment. Once stripped of their designs, the boards are returned to the storehouse. Some women return to the *jilimi* to sleep, others remain at the ground. The body paint is allowed to wear off, and often the fading designs are the only sign that women have been engaged in ritual.

Within the *yawulyu* context, ritual segments may directly address the needs of group members. For example, when the *yawulyu* is for health reasons, the fun performance is omitted, and only the gathering of women at the "ring place" occurs. The power evoked is that of women's relationships to land and their power to restore the harmony necessary for good health of individuals and communities. Through these ceremonies women may seek to achieve resolution of conflict or more specific symptomatic relief. There has, I think, been a subtle shift in the structuring of these health and well-being ceremonies, which are now organized according to the complementary lines of descent of relations to land and *yawulyu*, but once emphasized matrilineality more strongly (Bell 1983a, 152–54). This line, through the mother, is important in nurturance especially in matters of birthing and feeding. And, as I have argued elsewhere, the shift in the nature of conflict post contact, and especially on settlements, registers ceremonially (Bell 1983a, 248–49).

If the particular *yawulyu* focuses upon emotions (and these are closely linked to health), *yilpinji* songs will be included and the "secrecy" and "sex-exclusivity" indexes will be higher: only those directly involved can participate. The songs concern attraction, resistance, pacification, arousal, infidelity, abiding affection, and rejection, indeed the whole gamut of emotions manifest in male/female relations. A woman may request *yilpinji* if she is having trouble in a relationship, wishes to attract a new lover, or ensure the absent spouse will be faithful. The decision to stage *yilpinji* is not taken lightly, for women believe that their actions are not only efficacious, but release potent forces which, if handled improperly, may cause illness, conflict, and impotence. Emotions, it is acknowledged, are serious matters in which to delve and their management is part of women's business.

In the literature *yilpinji* is often glossed "love magic" (Bell 1983a, 176–79). For central Australia, if the songs are taken out of context, this may be sustainable, but if they are analyzed within *yawulyu*, then it is the broader management of emotions rather than an explicit concern with sex and sexuality which is being managed. Of course sex and sexuality are often at the base of fights and disturbances, and it is not surprising that they are richly represented in women's ritual symbolism. I have explored elsewhere the agenda (scholarly and indigenous) which supported the designation "love magic" and its pejorative overtones (Bell 1983a, 176–79). For the purposes of this discussion, suffice it to say that *yilpinji* deals with "troubles," a gloss which includes, but is not limited to, matters of sex. However, by giving a shorthand explanation of the activity as "love magic," older women deflect attention from other ritual agenda, and restrict younger women's access to certain ritual knowledge until they have the wisdom to use it "properly."

If we shift from the reading of woman as sexual object, and from the physical realm of reproduction to the symbolic constructions of woman in women's ceremonies, different interpretations of Aboriginal religion are available, and a different portrait of gender relations is generated. When women hold aloft their sacred boards on which are painted ideational maps of their country, when they dance hands cupped upward, they state their intention and responsibility to "grow up" country and kin. To Aboriginal women, as the living descendants of the dreamtime, the physical acts of giving birth and lactation are important, but are considered to be one individual moment in a much larger design. Their wide-ranging and broadly-based concept of nurturance is modeled on the dreamtime experience, itself one all-creative force. When women rub their bodies with fat in preparation for the application of body designs which, like the boards, symbolically encode information about sites, dreamings, and estates; when they retrace in song and dance the travels of the mythological heroes, they become as the ancestors themselves. Through ritual reenactment women establish direct contact with the past, make manifest its meaning, and thereby shape their worlds. The past is encapsulated in the present: the present permeates the past. In women's rituals the major themes of land, love, and health fuse in the nurturance motif, which encapsulates the growing up of people and land, and the maintenance of the complex of land/people relationships.

There are occasions when *yawulyu* performances are oriented to incorporating, or instructing men, and do so by actively engaging men in the performance. The most extensive ceremonial presence of men at a woman-controlled, woman-initiated, series of ceremonies that I have observed occurred on a cattle station and involved three distinct groups of women. Two were extremely knowledgeable and had an extensive ritual repertoire. The third, the local group, were desirous of extending their ceremonial authority, and by linking it to that of the other groups, accessing their expertise. This was accomplished over a series of visits and required that the men "witness" the authorative statements of the women in a performance which occurred at the final meeting of the groups. In a "surprise" which delighted the women, the men brought a short, compact, and dramatic ceremonial segment concerning the major dreaming being celebrated, to the women's ground. Another example of men's participation in women's ceremonies concerns *jarrarda*, the name given to women's *yawulyu/yilpinji*, farther north.

YUNGKURRU

Moving from women's *yawulyu* to ceremonies which entail co-operation of women and men, in *yungkurru* we find an excellent forum in which to explore commonalities and differences in male and female practice. In *yungkurru* women bring their ceremonial expertise to a ground shared with men. During these joint ceremonies, the sexual politics of ritual are evident. Each sex vies with the other in its brilliant display of knowledge. At the same time, each is constrained by the need to represent the dreamtime experience with meticulous fidelity and not to provoke jealous fights. Ceremonies at which men and women are present have the dual function of permitting monitoring of the activities of the other, and providing a forum of display to the other. Attendance means that the division of labor is made explicit and the physical layout of ceremonial activity is shared. Each is able to elaborate their interpretations of the common core of knowledge and to ensure neither errs is the necessary and continuous process of reinvention. It is at such times that the unity of the law, which underwrites the separation of the sexes, is open to observation, and it is possible for an anthropologist to learn what each knows of the practice of the other. In this context, common ground concerned the structural aspects of ancestral activity in land; the name of the *kirda* and *kurdungurlu* for the area; the sites and the major dreamings: sex-specific explanations concerned the content of the activity and the interpretation of the songs. Negotiations concerned who will be told what, when, by whom, and for what purpose: the politics of knowledge and gender were intertwined.

According to the participants, *yungkurru* ceremonies occurred infrequently, perhaps averaging one every three to four years. *Yungkurru* were to "make young men." They have as their focus one particular site and its interrelations with a number of intersecting dreamings. There needs to be an occasion worthy of the staging of a *yungkurru*, and settlement politics, rather than exclusively traditional concerns, generate rich contexts. It is, for instance, a way of introducing new people into the dreamtime design, and then declaring it to have always been thus. It is a way of redistributing knowledge, of sorting out ambiguous ritual relations by establishing, through practice, that this is "the woman" or "the man" of a particular place.

The *yungkurru* I was able to follow from beginning to end in 1977 was easily recognizable as the *ingkurra* of Spencer and Gillen (1899, 271ff.) and *inkura* of Strehlow (1947, 100ff.). Unlike their documentation, the one I saw was not associated with a particular initiation, but it was focused on a particular sacred site, and it was a means by which changes and new information were injected into the repertoire of practice and knowledge. Throughout, the participants were able to maintain the continuity of tradition by reference to an ancestral event that legitimated their activity. It was politically charged as needs, ambitions, and alliances were being negotiated, but superbly crafted as "the law" in the final performance.

The external reference point, which protected the instigators from being the subject of jealous fights, was the centennial celebrations at Hermannsburg, a Lutheran mission, southeast of Alice Springs. One of the then rising political stars of the settlement was from that mission and was seeking integration in the Ali-curang community. It was in the interests of the Kaytej to accommodate this man, for if he were to become president of the settlement, their interests would be well represented at the community level. The keen rivalry for his affections was obvious when the presiding council created difficulties over access to the community bus, needed for the trip to Hermannsburg.

The more deeply entrenched political agenda of the ceremony concerned the need to recruit men to an area of country to the west of the settlement. Nungarrayi, the woman whose father had been *kurdungurlu* for that country, and whose father's mother's father—that is, *kirda* for that country—had appeared to her in a "dream."[13] In the "dream" Jampijinpa had instructed Nungarrayi in the use of *jungkurru* songs; told her to take the business to the ring place; to build a brush shelter for the men; to hold the boards high so all could see; and then to make everyone sit and wait in the way the little birds had for bush berry in the dreamtime.

Women routinely use a "dream" to introduce, or more properly to reintroduce, information into the ritual realm. When a person dies part of the "sorry business" (mourning rituals) requires that all personal things are set aside, and this includes use of ritual objects, songs, designs, mythology, intimately associated with the individual. After a period of three or more years, a woman, usually in the *kurdungurlu* line, but certainly of the ritual cohort of the deceased, will have a "dream" in which the parent or grandparent of the deceased appears and instructs the "dreamer" to go forth, and perform the ceremonies, and use the items which henceforth will be associated with her. In this way the living may shape current ceremonial activity while maintaining that nothing changes. On the occasions when I have been able to observe the first reuse of a song, a number of women who had been present at previous performances gathered, and while the new "owner" intoned the words, these experts discreetly guided the action. Henceforth it was the law.

In the "dream" of Nungarrayi for the *yungkurru*, the interdependence of the roles of *kirda* and *kurdungurlu* were marked, the interrelations of the dreamings complex. Unity was achieved by Nungarrayi in her display of the sacred pole as Nangala, the daughter of the Jampijinpa of the dream, as the object which would be at the center of the dancing. Nungarrayi was able to show the men in the *kirda* line what had been revealed to her, thereby incorporating them within that frame, and extending their existing dreaming tracks into that country. This was anxiously sought by an older man who was her father's classifactory "mother's father" and it was an agenda she endorsed. One other consequence of the ceremonies, only apparent some tens years later, is that Nungarrayi was able to strengthen her daughter's relation to the dreamings and to make sure she would be able to marry into that country. Nungarrayi's daughter's children would then be in the *kirda* line for the country. Also she was able to establish a rationale for her relation to land as *kurdungurlu* through a line of descent which was unusual (through father's mother). She was of the right patrimoiety and this facilitated her playing that role, but to be a first-order *kurdungurlu*, she needed a more direct link. This strategizing by important women to position favored kin within their ritual worlds is not unusual. However, it is not pursued in an aggressive fashion—it just unfolds.

The *yungkurru* ceremony lasted for over a week, drew heavily on the resources of all involved, entailed the making of new boards, and the generation of new designs. All the designs were within the given symbolic repertoire, but by rearranging the colors (red, black, and white representing different manifestation of the dreamings), the elements (circles, semicircles, dots, and lines representing the presence of the dreamings at three sacred sites), Nungarrayi generated greater diversity for the ceremonial painting of bodies, boards, and headbands. Nungarrayi directed which boards the women would make and which would appear at Hermannsburg. Again this was a subset of the total production. In all the ceremonies I have attended, there have always been possibilities for further learning, and future exchanges. Retention of objects and holding back of knowledge maintains power in the hands of the persons hosting the ceremony. Indeed ceremonies are often "cut short" on the basis that the "next time we will be able to do that part," but just for now there is "not enough time."

Each afternoon the men and women gathered on a newly cleared ground to prepare materials and participants. The women worked as if these were *yawulyu* preparations, but the performance was on a shared ground, and involved women and men singing, and joint displays. The women invested a great deal of time and energy in the *yungkurru* and were quick to remind the men, if they were not taking up their share of the work, that it was they who wanted to be "level" with the women. In the *yungkurru*, the differences in public and private behavior, in terms of what each sex admits to knowing, was pronounced. One old man asked Nungarrayi for information and she responded: "Don't ask me, I'm a woman." Half an hour before she had been teaching the women just those details. What she was prepared to show were the designs she had elaborated. The men had expressed jealousy of the extent of her knowledge, and had she fallen ill this would have been given as a reason. She had already shed a certain amount of knowledge and bestowed associated paraphernalia on a neighboring group of women to allay such fears (Bell 1983a, 157–79).

In transforming a section of wood to a ritual object, the women chose an area from which it should be cut—one where the dreamings intersected—and thus the object could be a center piece for the travels of any of these dreamings, and could serve as a focal point for the ceremonial retracing and extension of the ancestral travels. The women rubbed the board with red ochre, sang it into the area, dressed it as a person, and henceforth it was known as Nangala. Each of the key participants could trace a relationship along a dreaming track to Wakulpu. These radiated outward and constituted extensions of the country already known and claimed. But, it was through the "dream," as related by Nungarrayi, that the dreamtime design was made explicit.

In the performance the women were quick to distinguish those *yawulyu* songs of Nangala for Wakulpu, which concerned mythology, from those *jungkurru* songs of Jampijinpa for Wakulpu, which concerned display. In terms of the maintenance of the dreamtime heritage, the *yungkurru* was an occasion on which women and men engaged in cooperative work. The final performance, which was viewed by many outsiders, black and white, was short, showed a fraction of what had been "rehearsed," and by itself gave no indication of the many ambitions, passions, and politics of the ceremony.

INITIATION

Initiation is a time when the whole society pauses, when all resources are directed at "making young men." However, while old men "make" boys into young men through the ritualized death and rebirth of circumcision, and thereby celebrate their role as spiritual procreator, old women organize the feeding of the boys, sit in all-night vigils with the boys, stage *yawulyu*, which celebrate the continuity of land and people associated with the boys, and nominate the mothers-in-law for the boys. Women make manifest their rights—which flow directly from the *jukurrpa*—by providing links between groups through marriage; by their ritual incorporation of outsiders; by their extension of knowledge through ritual action; and at initiation by nominating the mother of the girl the boy will eventually marry. Thus, women engage in key decision-making, which affects both ritual procedure and the aftermath of initiation. When we focus on the world of men and treat women's rituals as a subset, we blur the playing out of independence and interdependence of the sexes in the spiritual domain.

One conceptual difficulty in accounts of initiation is that woman's participation has been analyzed in terms of her kin ties to the initiate and not in terms of her relationship to the *jukurrpa* (Bell 1983a, 238). Once the ritual correlates of the kin roles are recognized, it is then possible to see the ways in which women's participation overlaps, extends, and complements that of the men. One of the consequences of seeing women as ritual status holders at initiation is that their role in marriage arrangements becomes an integral part of initiation for, like the act of circumcision, they are hedged in with ritual politics and serve to create new webs of relationships within the society.

A second problem in coming to an appreciation of initiation from a womancentric view has been that one must participate in the role of mother, mother-in-law, sister, grandmother, cross-cousin, in order to follow the action. It is inappropriate to ask what is happening if one has not been present, and one may only seek guidance from those involved; it is dangerous to speak of the business of others. Questions regarding initiation are not hypothetical, but involve real choices being made about actual persons, and this is not something about which one speculates. When I asked about a mother's role at initiation, I would be answered with questions: Which mother? Where is she from? Where did this happen? Thus, only after I had sat the all-night vigils with the mothers, been red-ochred and danced all night, answering the men's calls with a shrill trill for my "brother," did the design in the patchwork of women's participation emerge. Once it was assumed "I knew" the structure, my questions were often answered with reference to my own children, and my adoptive family would make claims as "aunts," "uncles," and in one memorable moment as "father-in-law."

During the periods spent in the field between 1976 and 1980 I attended the initiations of some twenty boys (often two or three boys of the same subsection classification would be initiated at the one ceremony).[14] Having boys to initiate is an indication of the strength of the law and some groups are said to be "rich" in young men. The ceremonies I attended were for Warlpiri, Warumungu, Alyawarra, and Kaytej peoples. While there are significant differences in the sequencing of the events, it is possible to identify a structure that holds for all. The differences speak to variations in marriage arrangements, land tenure, and kinship systems. While these are intriguing, especially for tracking the nature of the velocity (speed and direction) of change, they are outside the scope of this article (Bell 1980; 1988b). Here I highlight the moments which women emphasized as critical. One concerned decision-making: men decide who will be the circumcisor; women who will be the mother-in-law, and it was the latter decision which interested women. The decisions are made independently, yet ideally the woman and man chosen should be wife and husband. The action moves back and forth, and there are many negotiations, but the ideology says each decision is a surprise to the other. This is yet another example of the politics of knowledge in an oral culture.

The timing of initiation is one key decision which illustrates a particular patterning of ritual decision-making. Within family camps, husbands and wives discuss the forthcoming initiation season. A mother's decision that her son is ready is based on her assessment of his physical and emotional maturity, the availability of potential mothers-in-law with whom she may wish to establish an alliance, the availability of food to feed the influx of visitors, and the necessary resources for extended periods of ritual activity. There are considerable pressures on women to have adult sons and benefits accrue, but if a woman wishes to delay for a year, that is acceptable. Women should appear reluctant to lose their sons, should cry and worry about their safety, but in reality the boys have been living in single-sex peer groups for some time, and have been the bane of everyone's existence, mothers included. However, once the decision is made, it is no longer open to scrutiny. Only when boys are "grabbed" by neighboring groups in a hostile act are the merits of timing debated after the fact (Bell 1983a, 215–16).

The capture of the boys by the red-ochred men, who swoop through the camps to the sound of blood-curdling whoops, "grab" the boys, and take them to the men's ceremonial ground, where they are held "captive," is also supposed to be a surprise. But, because a number of observances are necessary, it cannot be too much of a surprise. For instance, one must not be on the "wrong side" of the party of captors. After a while I learned to read the signs of an imminent capture: the women would be sitting around quietly in their camps, there would be no hunting, no visiting, and the store would be virtually empty. These behaviors cannot be maintained for long: food cannot be stored for any time, people need to move around to chat and to keep news alive.

After the capture, which is often in the early morning, women dance at the initiation ground for a short period, "to soften the ground." This will ease the pain of the boys and prepare the area for the subsequent week of dancing. The women then return to their own camps (ones specially constructed for the duration of the ceremony), where they begin preparation of the ritual paraphernalia for their dancing that evening. On this occasion the mother is clearly directing the action, and it is the designs of her country (the ones for which the boys are *kurdungurlu*) that feature, and her daughter (his sister, who shares the boys' ritual affiliations) receives special attention.

At dusk the women return to the men's ceremonial ground, build a fire, one for the family of each initiate, and sit waiting for nightfall. The men send small concave boards to the women, which they hold until the end of the ceremony. A large cleared area, on an east-west axis, is prepared by the men for each year's initiations. To the east, the men sit singing behind the shallow semicircular windbreak. The women sit to the west. A deep groove made by the *kurdungurlu* joins the men's windbreak to a small fire and break at the western end. The long leafy poles, which will be stripped on the penultimate night of the week-long dancing, are visible on now overgrown initiation grounds of previous years.

On this first night the women dance all night in a formation that locates mothers, father's sisters (female fathers), and classificatory mothers-in-law at the center, with sisters flanking the huddle of dancers. Thereafter there are three or four "half-nights" of dancing by the women. Somewhere in the middle of this sequence, there is a day of rest to allow the "visitors" to arrive, preparations for the finale, and routine business to be done. Prior to each of the "half-night" dancing, the sisters and fathers' sisters—that is, co-*kirda* with the boys— stage *yawulyu*. Women who are visiting are incorporated at the level of patrimoiety and thus assigned affiliations with those present. By participating they extend their knowledge of country into the sites and stories of the local families. It is during these nights that the mother refines her decision regarding the mother-in-law, and this is evident in the order in which women are painted.

After the women's dancing at the men's ground, but before they return to their camps, is a feeding ritual in which women make plain they bore the child, nurtured him, and will now marry him. In Warlpiri initiations, the women carry the boy on their shoulders to a special area where, sitting on his mother's lap, he is fed by his sisters. The surrounding symbolism of this short sequence evokes birth: there are the smoky leaves and exhortations to grow strong. Rather than initiation being a time when women are negated as life-givers, the women cooperate in the symbolic rebirth. The Alyawarra practice, which makes explicit women's nurturance role, occurs during the capture of the boys: the women present the men with bags of flour to sustain the participants in their work. This compares with Warlpiri practice where the women provide food daily.

Nomination of the mother-in-law is a decision made by the mother of the boy in consultation with the mother of the girl, who will be the future mother of the boy's promised wife. The two mothers (of the boy and of his future mother-in-law) are likely to be of a similar age. Ideally the girl should be under twenty, not married, or if married have no children, and the mother-in-law should like the potential daughter-in-law. It is for young women one of the first opportunities to participate in ceremonial activities, and the person chosen must be willing to learn. She must also be present on the night when the fire-stick is passed. Thus young girls may exercise a degree of control over the choice. These personal and pragmatic constraints nestle within a constellation of factors dealing with ritual and country. The choices made are part of a wider pattern of reciprocation given form in marriage alliances and land affiliations which implicate three generations. "Keeping the families straight" is part of the women's responsibility (Bell 1980; 1983a, 269–72). Men ponder aloud who may be nominated, but it is not until the passing of the fire-stick that the choice is made public.

The Alyawarra procedure whereby the nomination is made known is a good example of the joint responsibilities and interaction of roles at initiation. At dusk the women go to the men's ground where they sleep until after midnight. On the call of *wadja* they move through to the dancing ground where mothers and mothers-in-law dance in a tight formation, flanked by sisters and mothers' mothers, the sisters call out to the brothers who answer. The patterns made by the dancing feet echo the groove cut by the men. At about 1 A.M. the women move to an area a little separate from the main ground and sit beside a fire lit by the men. Shields painted by the men with the country of the mother are laid on the blanket around which the women are sitting. A brother brings a fire-stick and gives it to the mother who passes it to the mother-in-law she has chosen. The sisters hold a torch to illuminate the mother-in-law's face. Mothers and mothers-in-law dance briefly together and then the brother places the white ritual fluff on the mother-in-law's head. The sisters then position themselves between the men and the mother-in-law, and dance until dawn twirling a bunch of head scarfs (traditionally possum tails).

At dawn the boys are escorted to the blanket where they sit in front of the mothers-in-law who rub their ochred bodies against the boys, in the way women rub sacred objects in their *yawulyu*. The boys are returned to the men's space where the women rush, fall upon the boys, and then, mothers supporting the mothers-in-law, depart to their own secluded area. Movement is restricted, speech and food taboos apply. The mothers-in-law are in a liminal state until the final "finish up," when weeks later payments and counterpayments are made to those who participated and all taboos are lifted.

While this structure is well known to all and could be generated from a reading of the classic desert ethnographies, the events taking place in the women's ritual area are not visible to male participants or observers. What is generally reported is the conclusion of the intensive ceremonial activity at the men's "ring place" with two nights of men's dancing. On the first night the men bring out the long poles and dance, and the following night the boys are circumcised. A male observer would see the women appear and disappear, but could not track them into their ceremonial camps. Here working from women's domain out, we see initiation is a time when women make certain statements about their importance in the presence of men, and do so in a way consonant with their construct of woman in *yawulyu*.

In my analysis of initiation, I have juxtaposed the men's circumcision of the boy with the women's nomination of the mother-in-law. Both are acknowledged as key events; both serve to crystalize male and female roles; both are political acts based on the ritual rights, responsibilities, and ambitions of the participants. Therefore, while at initiation the values of the society are writ large, it is a *complex* of values that is being celebrated. Initiation entails both separate ritual actions and cooperative endeavors: young men cannot be made without the assistance of women. There are male/female negotiations, and decisions that are the prerogative of each. Women continue to assert their nurturing role, not just as mothers, but within the context of relations to land in the *yawulyu*; to people in the choice of co-workers; and to their dreamtime heritage in the transmission of power by direct and indirect contact with the boys.

My ethnography of initiation is a far cry from depictions of initiation as an exercise in male power, as the time of negation of women, whose heads cowered, in fear of death, run to and fro the male initiation ground. Nothing I observed at the male ceremonial ground was substantially at odds with the observations of Meggitt (1962), Strehlow (1947), and Spencer and Gillen (1899). What was radically different was the way in which I was being guided to see and understand it. When the women "ran away," they went to their ceremonial ground where they worked on their ritual relations, which impacted on the male world of making young men. Further, behaviors which had mystified men like Spencer and Gillen (1899, 366–68, 374, 380), are rendered intelligible. The presence of women at men's ceremonies could not be accommodated within their analysis of ceremonies as male affairs and the "anomalous" behavior was left as noted in passing, but did not stimulate further questions.[15]

The ceremonies I have so far discussed were documented during a period of in-depth fieldwork in central Australia and reflect the politics of large settlements. One of the consequences of contact is that extended ceremonies are held in the times when other demands on Aborigines' time are limited: thus initiation tends to coincide with the long summer break from schools, and the stand-down for the wet season (summer months) in the cattle industry. This period is only six weeks to two months, and therefore the period of exclusion of the boys from heterosexual society has been shortened. Similarly the extended bush tours of the novice have been curtailed to accommodate time constraints. This is no longer on foot, and the route taken is constrained by the demands of vehicles for fuel, passable roads, and the competing needs of the participants to make no contact with "civilization," but to collect welfare checks to pay for the travel.

The period of initiation has gone from being a time of education to an abrupt transition from boyhood to manhood. The deprivations, which once taught men to respect women as a precious resource, no longer apply. Punitive aspects of initiation are now emphasized by initiating boys young. This is aimed at "settling down" wild boys, and the ceremonies do not include full instruction. This is intended as punishment, but also means boys, with significant "knowledge deficits," become men. Respect for the knowledge of elders has diminished, as it is evident that they no longer are in control. As marriages have become between persons closer in age, and fewer are the result of promises made at initiation, the standing of woman as spouse has changed. Once marriage is about choices based on attraction, not about productive relations and family alliances, women lose the network of powerful older women and initiation promises, which implicate kin networks, and must operate as individuals. They become dependents in households with a nominal male head, no longer independent producers in a hunter-gatherer economy (Bell 1980; 1988b).

LEGISLATIVE CONTEXTS AND SELF-DETERMINATION

In this section I am shifting from material generated by in-depth fieldwork in central Australia to comparative material generated by applied research farther north. The existence of special purpose legislation for Aborigines[16] has created novel fora in which to learn of women's religious life, but the existence of a weighty body of literature detailing the overriding importance of men in the religious domain has been a significant impediment to women's full participation in the new order (Bell 1984/5). Finding appropriate ways of bringing information regarding women's spiritual rights and responsibilities into the courts, and sensitizing the bureaucracy to the need to consult with women, has been fraught. One strategy pursued by women has been to allow ignorance of their rituals to go unchallenged, because they have feared loss of control if they are drawn into fora where the rules governing transmission of knowledge do not accommodate "women's business." This strategy has consequences where documents, such as registers of owners, or beneficiaries of a particular action, are drawn up and assume a life of their own (Bell 1983b).

From 1978 to 1987, I worked on some seven land claims and prepared exhibits which dealt especially with the rights and responsibilities of women in land (Bell 1981; 1982; 1984/5; 1987a). Women preferred to give evidence in ceremonial form, for that is the clearest way of answering the question: Who is the "owner" of this land? The problem for me, as consultant-anthropologist, then became how to render this information in a form which would be considered evidence by the court, and to do so in a way which would not jeopardize women's secrets in a public place. Segments of performances could be adapted for mixed company, but the private, secret part of the preparations could not, and that was where much of the critical information was accessible. We found ways of scaling down the court, of making it less intimidating for women, but still there remained the problem that women were giving less than a full account, because the court was predominantly male, and ultimately their evidence had to be seen by a male judge (Bell 1984/5). In the process of registering a sacred site, the material was to be reviewed by a male authority (Bell 1983b). This legislation has recently been amended and women now sit as members of the authority.

In 1981, as anthropologist to the newly formed Aboriginal Sacred Sites Protection Authority in Darwin, I was able to record and participate in a week-long *jarrarda*, a secret women's ceremony, held at a cattle station (ranch) in the Roper River area and attended by women from far-flung communities (Bell 1982; see also Berndt 1950, 30–37, 44; 1965, 254). In song and dance, in gesture and design, the assembled women celebrated the travels of the Munga-Munga ancestral women who pioneered the country from Tennant Creek to Arnhem Land. These female ancestors scattered across the Barkly Tablelands; they traveled from Macarthur River and from the junction of the Wilton and Roper rivers to a site on Hodgson River and thence to Nutwood Downs, where their tracks divide, one following the "road" to Alice Springs, the other to a site on Brunette Downs. The Munga-Munga assumed different forms, met with, crossed over, absorbed, and transformed the essence of other ancestors; their influence infused country with the spiritual essence of women.

In subsequent discussions of the ceremony with the participants, they retraced in sand maps the patterns made by the dancing feet on the ceremonial ground, and explained that Munga-Munga mapped the country for women; they were everywhere; they changed form, language, and style as they forged links between groups in the dreamtime. Within the context of this overarching responsibility for the dreaming, women also stated their responsibility for particular tracts of land and emphasized certain themes and, as with central Australian women: emotional management and health were the principal ones. At one level women gave form to a generalized notion of their responsibility for land, its dreamings and sites, in expressions such as "we must hold up that country," "not lose him." At another level the ceremony allowed certain divisions of labor for responsibility for country to be played out.

Although the terms are different, the multiplicity of ways of tracing a relationship to land remained a salient feature of the ceremonial activity.[17] Those who traced their relationship from their father and father's father as *minirringki* and from their mother and mother's father as *jungkayi*, and from their mother's mother as *dalyin*, had a particular role and the overlap with the division of labor of *kirda*, and *kurdungurlu* in central Australian *yawulyu* was considerable. Men were rigidly excluded from the ceremony at the women's "ring place," but at the conclusion of the activity on the women's ground, the women entered the main camp where the men had been sitting quietly. A gift exchange between men and women then took place. In this way the interdependence of men's and women's worlds was celebrated.

The northern literature, where it makes mention of women's rituals, speaks of crisis of life ceremonies (Berndt 1965, 238–43). Catherine Berndt (1950) writes of *tjarada, jawalju,* and *ilbindji,* but the emphasis in the literature on religion concerns the regional cults of Kunapipi and Yabaduruwa at which women have a shadowy presence. Bern (1979 a and b), Elkin (1961), and Berndt (1951) provide fine-grain ethnographic descriptions and analyses of male-controlled activities at which women are necessary, but their role is supportive: they cook; they are drawn to the verge of knowing men's secrets, but their own participation is limited (Bern 1979a, 418–19). The most confident generalizations regarding woman's profanity, and women's exclusion from all things sacred, have come from anthropologists working in these regions (Warner 1937; Maddock 1972; Bern 1979ab). Writing of Arnhem Land, Lloyd Warner (1937, 6) had summarized that women made little sacred progress through life but remained largely profane. Despite Kaberry's (1939, 221) counter that "men are the uninitiated at women's ceremonies," Warner has become the "Australian case."[18]

Through working with women in these contexts, having participated in women's ceremonies in the Roper River, Victoria River Downs, and Daly Rivers areas, and held meetings with women in eastern Arnhem land, I would suggest that the central Australian material provides as good a basis for generalization as the more popular northern fieldwork. By beginning with the desert material, we gain a different perspective on separation of the sexes. The work of Hamilton (1979, 1987) in the western desert would also offer interesting contrasts, where to infiltrate women's autonomous ritual world in the western desert men need to undermine the mother/daughter tie, because endogamous generation moieties organize ritual life.[19] The ceremonial life in central Australia consists of separate and shared ground, but as we move further north to the Roper River, Victoria River Downs, and Daly Rivers region and onto Arnhem Land, the markers of separation of the sexes are less dramatic. There are still women's grounds, and there is still "women's business," but there is not the same high level of independence structuring women's economic and ritual life. Men produce a greater percent of the reliable diet, polygyny rates are higher, and age difference at first marriage greater.

More work is necessary on the Munga-Munga and *jarrarda* before we can discuss women's ceremonies in this area as dealing with "personal reactions to physiological stress" (Maddock 1972, 155). In the revised edition of *The Australian Aborigines* Maddock (1982, 139) took into account that in central Australia there were women's ceremonies other than those focusing on crises of life, and that the evidence of land claims supported my ethnography. However, he noted that the scale of women's ceremonies does not rival that of men, and it seems unlikely the underreporting is a case of male bias. Wisely, he added, scale is not necessarily an indicator of importance or merit. Clearly we need to ask new questions of the material.

One question, worth reflection raised by the *jarrarda* I witnessed is: Could it be that the Munga-Munga is a women's regional cult, now truncated to a *jarrarda?* Certainly the ceremony encompassed a number of groups, covered vast tracts of land, and could travel from site to site. It had not been performed for many years and it is worth noting why this was so and why it was staged in 1981 (Bell 1982). This is an area where the logistic constraints on women's ceremonial life are marked. Women, isolated from each other on a number of cattle stations, needed access to transport to bring together the necessary personnel. Munga-Munga is dangerous business and released wild and uncontrollable forces, not ones that give men any great joy and for the duration of the ceremony they were under certain restriction of movement. To stage a *jarrarda* for Munga-Munga, women needed a compelling rationale. The activities of the Sacred Sites Authority provided a rationale and access to vehicles driven by women for the journey to the ceremonial ground required woman-specific activities and negotiations. The ceremonial activity had another prompt from the impending land claim hearing to the north of the cattle station, and that was one supported by the local land council.

In terms of the 1981 ceremony there was an interesting overlap in politics: women ritual "bosses," resident on the cattle station, were anxious to confirm their claim to the area, and this could be achieved through ceremonial activity on a site as a Munga-Munga place. If this site were protected by legislation, then it would be respected by station managers and visitors alike. It would give women a negotiating position in the politics of self-determination in that they would be registered, and therefore would be more likely to be consulted. And as John Bern's (1979a) exploration of politics in the Roper River region helpfully indicated, power plays drive ceremonial action. However, he excluded women as players because in his analysis religion is the business of men (1979a, 47) Here I am suggesting we factor women into the resource wrangles that characterize much of the institutional politics of the region.

As anthropologist to the Sacred Sites Authority, I was anxious to begin the task of alerting developers to the existence of women's sites and the need to consult with women. There had already been a lengthy dispute over a site in Alice Springs where, too late, women who controlled aspects of the site were acknowledged (Bell 1983b, 284). On that occasion, all reports had been done by men talking to men, and it was only when the site was about to be flooded that the importance of the women became apparent. Had the site not been threatened, the women's side would have remained unknown, secrecy had been the preferred strategy. Part of my work in 1981 entailed explaining the existence of the new sacred sites legislation and giving people the option of registering sites if they thought it offered protection. For the most part, if they could protect sites by keeping them out of the public eye, that was the path chosen. However, the situation was delicate, for once sites became the subject of disputes, there was always the suspicion, on the part of developers and the state, that they had been "invented" to thwart their work. Stopping development for a woman's site was even more problematic as the image of woman as excluded from the religious domain and as persons punished for violating sacred sites (Strehlow, 1971, 340) is pervasive.

The things left "undone" in 1981 *jarrarda* were addressed again in 1983 and 1984, but on these occasions the bureaucratic support was more intrusive (Merlan 1989) and the ritual agenda different: the site had already been confirmed as a Munga-Munga place. In 1981 we had asked the women initiating the ceremony, who should be invited and what should be said in telegrams, a favored way of communicating between communities. We traveled with one of the bosses, and at each community we asked again who should go, and attended meetings in family groups. Men were interested in what the women were doing, but made no attempt to attend. The preliminaries took longer than the ceremony and involved many decisions which then set the parameters for the ceremony. Had we been a mixed group, the ceremony would have been different; had the sacred sites authority not had a specific agenda regarding women, it would have been different. What distinguished this occasion was that there were resources available to women. Had the ceremony involved only men, it would have been part of a known history of ceremonies in the area. The recourse to external bodies to resolve ritual politics has led to an increasing level of engagement with bureaucratic politics and submissions for funding. The ceremonies staged will reflect these factors, but will also be driven by territorial disputes and a contesting of leadership. It is not particularly helpful to promote one ritual agenda as more authentic, untouched, or apolitical than another. However, I would suggest that the long history of women being denied (overtly or covertly) the means to gather for ceremonies has benefited male politicking through ceremonies.

My next example is from the Daly River where I had the opportunity to work with women on a land claim and to participate in series of closed and secret women's ceremonies (Bell 1981). The ceremonial cycle had engaged the services of all the women in the community, and was glossed as a girl's "puberty rite". Five girls were put through the ceremonies, but, as I already learned in central Australia there was likely to be a broader political agenda, and indeed there was, and it was relevant to a local land claim. The site on which the ceremony focused was a woman's site and without documenting its importance one area of the claim would have failed. I could only discuss structure, not content of the rite, with a fellow male anthropologist who had worked in the area, and I very much wanted to know what he had been told of such ceremonies (Bell 1987c, 238). The particular ceremony was similar to *yawulyu:* there was the private, women-only segment of preparation, painting, handling of sacred objects (including hair string): the performance and confirmation of the ritual status in a wonderfully staged segment, the stress on kin—the mother was in charge and the sister-in-law was classified as "wife." What I had not expected in a "crisis of life" ceremony was the invocation from the ritual "boss": "Help me in my ceremony. Make me happy for this land."

In terms of separation of the sexes, the men knew the ceremonies were in progress and one of the girls was the daughter of a principal claimant in the impending land claim. He was anxious to have another adult woman in his group. In the focused segments of the puberty rituals, the women worked in their own space. On the day when all women were welcome, they gathered in large numbers in a public space. The men had all vacated the mission for the day, and in a parade, bold and dramatic, the women brought their business through the main camp. The cries they let out were to warn anyone nearby not to look, and were reminiscent of those of the red-ochred men at the capture of the boys in initiation. The final segment of the ceremony involved the men and gift exchanges. The community now had more adult women and the men thanked the women for their work.

My evidence concerning these activities for the land claim hearing was carefully negotiated with the women. It fell into two parts: there was a submission, which dealt with the structure of the ceremony without referring to actual content, and a second containing photographs and descriptions of the meanings. This was to be available only to the judge and to female counsel. Establishing this "precedent" was another interesting illustration of the problems of gendered knowledge for a culture without the parallel legal structures: there was no women's "ring place" to which we could retire for a ruling. In the interests of fairness, the judge allowed the women's submission to be restricted to women. In so doing, he granted the women the same privileges that men's restricted submissions have always enjoyed (Bell 1984/5, 357–59). However, men's submission have not had to declare their masculinist-bias, because they present little disruption to a court.

Although the women's movement has had some impact on the practice of law, for the most part patriarchal values permeate Anglo-Australian law. Courts of law are not accommodating of women, and legal means of establishing rights present special problems for Aboriginal women (Bell 1984/5; Bell and Ditton 1980/4). Similarly, within the academy, although feminist scholarship constitutes a fundamental challenge to the pursuit of knowledge as value-free, women are marginalized, co-opted, treated as tokens, or their work dismissed as of concern for women only (Moore 1988; Mascia-Lees et al. 1989).

Other contemporary contexts in which we may learn of women's ceremonial life are ones where an external authority is the initiator: tourist performances; opportunities generated by film crews; historic occasions marked by a "traditional" celebration; the opening of a gallery; or an exhibition in an urban center. The contexts for ceremonial life continues to change. Berndt (1950) noted this some forty years ago, but her focus was on dimensions of cultural contact. In the 1990s Aboriginal women are moving into regional networks and the politics driving these new interactions are those of the institutions of self-determination. The politics concern, among others, the state, statutory authorities, and development lobbies (Bell and Marks 1990). It is my impression that with the politicization of Aboriginal affairs, the drawing of Aborigines into the bureaucracy, and the indigenization of service industries, a "brain drain" is occurring. Women ritual leaders now travel to Norway to address conferences on indigenous art, not to the next *jilimi* to negotiate *yawulyu*. The resources at hand are different, and so are the needs. Religious practice has always had the capacity to adapt, absorb, and accommodate change. Ceremonial life continues but its association with land as spiritual and economic giver of life is attenuated.

It is no longer possible to write of Aboriginal religion as if it existed in a closed world, isolated from the politics of the nation state, nor gender relations as if independent of the wider Australian society. Making explicit the broader factors which impact on the Aboriginal groups whose religious practice is the subject of enquiry, is a complex task and more elusive than merely speaking of "bias." I am endorsing the analysis which holds that the religious domain is where power, status, authority, resources are negotiated and distributed, but I arguing that women engage in these politics not just as pawns but as players; that if we begin with the ethnography (what women are doing), and build from there to map women's strategies, we are writing a special kind of situated ethnography, one where the participant observation is with women, and one which relies on what can be leaned from women of women's business. This is an exercise in power, and when it has the effect of bringing women's lives into sharper focus, it raises questions of knowing, knowers, and the known (Hawkesworth 1989).

The feminist ethnography presented in this article demonstrates that much of the earlier generalizing was premature: we know too little of actual practice, it varies regionally, and impact of contact has been dramatic. What does emerge is that there are common features to women's ceremonies across regions from the desert to the tropical north; that the structuring principles are age, kin, and ritual status; that ceremonies celebrate relations to land and sacred sites; that the religious domain constitutes an arena for political negotiations; that ceremonies manifest a division of labor which entails exclusions and interrelations with the men, exchanges of knowledge, power, and goods; that the focus of ceremonies shifts according to needs. There are regional variations, as there are in men's ceremonial life, in terms of the land that is being celebrated, the sustenance it provides, and the contexts in which it is made known. What varies is the basis of women's separation, the content of the ceremonies, and the contexts in which we learn of religious beliefs and practices.

Katherine K. Young

WOMEN IN HINDUISM

Indologists are fond of pointing out that the longevity of this religion—represented in its textual record of over three and a half millennia—must be attributed, at least in part, to the remarkable stability of the Hindu family. It has fulfilled many human needs; its system of formal relations has attended to the physical, psychological, social, and religious aspects of the individual throughout the life cycle. Inspiring the support of various family members and enforcing obligations through different mechanisms of control, the family has not only provided a caring environment for the individual, it has also provided the main mechanism for transmitting religion itself. Important for both tasks has been the Hindu woman. Through her traditional behavior and duties (strīdharma)—especially her chastity and loyalty to her husband, her role as mother, her telling of exemplary epic stories, her fasts for the welfare of all, and her deep piety—she has given the family its social and cosmic mooring.

Strīdharma and the institution of the Hindu family were especially important in helping Hinduism survive under Muslim and then British domination. At the end of colonial rule, however, Hindu culture was stagnant and the family (not to mention women) fatigued by the long ordeal. Moribund by the nineteenth century, the institution of the Hindu family was subject to devastating attacks by the British Raj and Christian missionaries. One response to these critiques was reform. Now, over a century later, reforms have been many, but the obstacles still seem insurmountable. In part, this is because of changing problems related to (1) the creation of a new nation (which has to unify people of many ethnic, linguistic, religious, educational, and economic differences); (2) population explosion; and (3) industrialization. While cynicism seems to be growing in some circles, there is still in many circles an indefatigable urge to work for the creation of a modern, more just society. This spirit is captured by the term *lokasaṅgraha* (working for the welfare of the world), a theme of the *Bhagavad Gītā* and the Hindu Renaissance of the nineteenth century.[1]

Over the past century, Hindu women have fought to eliminate female segregation and to have literacy, education, and good jobs. They have also fought for equality between men and women in family life. In this enterprise, they are part of a global movement for the liberation of women. As in other countries, desired changes and their implementation in women's lives are related to politics, economics, and religion. To examine the relation of women and Hinduism today, I will begin with an overview of social and legal reforms. Reforms are closely tied to family (or personal) laws since woman's issues fall under this legal category. I will then present profiles of three contemporary women activists and their views on religion. Finally, I will explore how the substantive and symbolic dimensions of women's issues figure in Indian economics and politics, especially recent Hindu calls for a "reformed" secularism or a Hindu state.

The relation between women and religion in India today is closely linked to political and economic changes over the past century. According to Sudesh Vaid,[2] in the 1850s to 1870s the organized struggle by women in Britain began in earnest with attempts to reform the Married Woman's Property Act, the publication of the first feminist journal called the *English Woman's Journal*, the foundation of the Society for Promoting the Employment of Women, the establishment of Victoria Press which was run by and for women, the struggle for women's admission to Oxford and Cambridge, and the entry of women into jobs and new occupations (one-third of the labor force was women in 1861). There was frequent discussion of the breakdown of the family. These changes led to a clash of two views. One doctrine was that men and women are equal by nature and women's current inferiority is due to social factors (John Stuart Mill, basing his case on utilitarianism, and the socialists, basing theirs on the French revolution's principle of equality and an opposition to capitalism). The other doctrine was that men and women are inherently different, women being inferior (Darwin), or its variant that women are superior in the moral and spiritual realm and must be protected in separate domestic spheres from the destructive forces of the outside world (Ruskin).

Theories of gender had an influence on imperialism in British India. Liddle and Joshi argue:

> The impact of foreign domination is an important factor in women's subordination, historically and in the present. Recognition of this link gives people in the West a framework for understanding women's struggles in ex-colonial and neo-colonial countries, for it helps to explain why Third World feminists have a different analysis of women's oppression than those that have arisen in the West. This analysis, focusing on both male domination and Western domination, needs to be incorporated into Western feminist analysis. The singular concern with men as a group, to the exclusion of other features of sex inequality, is clearly ethnocentric and inadequate.[3]

The British used one particular form that gender divisions took in India. When they tried to align British and Indian law, they made upper-caste Brahmin law the basis. More specifically, Warren Hastings in 1772 requested ten Bengali pandits to compile a digest of Hindu civil law. This subjected lower-caste women to strictures such as no divorce or remarriage that had not governed their lives before, since laws had varied according to caste (viśeṣa-dharma).

Although introducing even greater conservatism, British administrators and Christian missionaries blamed the conservatism on Hindus. This inspired Hindus themselves to take up the issue of reform. The nineteenth-century Hindu reform movement[4] was led by M. G. Ranade, Mrtyunjaya Vidyalankar, Raja Rammohan Roy, Ishwarchandra Vidyasagar, Dabendranath Tagore, Dayananda Saraswati, Keshab Chandra Sen, and Behramji Malbari among others. They examined the problems faced by women and campaigned against such practices as child marriage, suttee, polygamy, the ban on widow remarriage, female infanticide, the lack of education and property rights, seclusion, and violence against women. Largely a movement led by Brahmin men, its primary goal was to challenge the imperialistic British Raj—which understood its "white man's burden," in part, as a responsibility to improve the lot of Hindu women. (The British argued, for instance, that child marriage retarded the development of body and mind, and "created a nation that was an 'easy victim under every blessed tyrant that chose to trample upon them.' "[5]) A secondary goal was to counter missionary propaganda against Hinduism—it was considered stagnant and medieval, especially in its repression of women—by presenting Hinduism as a religion that could be compatible with progress, modern values, and improvement in the status of women. The reform and revival of Hinduism by Brahmanical leaders gave rise, in turn, to the anti-Brahmin movement. Non-Brahmin leaders such as Jotirao Phule, Subramaniya Bharati, and E. V. Ramaswami linked the oppression of women to that of outcastes and blamed both on Brahmins and Brahmanical Hinduism. Some Brahmin women, too, joined the attack against the latter. Perhaps the most famous was Pandita Ramabai (1858–1922). She had been trained as a Sanskrit and Vedic scholar by her father, but this highly unorthodox act led to such persecution of the family that Ramabai "steeled her heart against the Hindu religion and society, neither of which she could ever forgive."[6] After championing the cause of women (especially widows), traveling abroad, and writing a book, *Sthri Dharma Neeti* (Women's Religious Law), she converted to Christianity.

The British eventually passed a number of liberalizing laws against suttee, remarriage, and child marriage, thereby undoing some of the damage done by universalizing Brahmanical law. During the Indian independence movement, women played an active role, began to organize themselves, and championed the cause of women's independence along with the cause of national liberation. In the 1920s, for instance, they tried to consolidate the social reforms initiated in the prior century, lobbied the political parties and the government to meet their demands, and fought for the enfranchisement of Indian women. The Women's Indian Association published the periodical *Strīdharma* to deal with women's issues, comment on bills before the government, educate women, and inform them of what was happening in various parts of the subcontinent. Despite British legitimation of the Raj on the perceived need to improve the lot of Hindu women, British men themselves were reluctant to take action. They feared that it would inflame the religious sensitivities of various communities already inflamed by the Revolt of 1857 attributed to progressive changes—especially for women—which they had introduced. "This pragmatism on the part of government was condemned by the leaders of the women's movement. *Strīdharma* noted that a British civil servant had the maxim,

'Keep your hands off religion and women' impressed on him by his superiors and that this accounted in part for the difficulties the women's movement experienced in having any social legislation passed" (Strīdharma 1936, 173–76).[7]

The British were particularly reluctant to extend the vote to women. In 1917 the Women's Indian Association, which was connected to the British suffragette movement, was formed. Women first demanded the right to vote from Montagu, secretary of state for India, in 1917. Although he derided the idea and refused to even mention it in his report, it was discussed later in the Southborough Franchise Report (1919) and rejected for the following reasons. The culture was too conservative, the practice of purdah would make it hard to implement, and the lack of women's education meant that power would be used irresponsibly. Perhaps the real reasons, however, were (1) that British women themselves were not granted the vote until 1928 and (2) that it was useful to maintain the Indian status quo since the traditional subordination of women could be used as a reason why India was not yet capable of self-government and needed the British Raj.[8] When all major Indian political groups supported women's right to vote, the British government avoided action by allowing the new Indian assemblies to make the decision.

As a result, during the 1920s, women were winning the right to vote in Madras, Bombay, Uttar Pradesh, Bengal, and princely states such as Travancore, Mysore, Jhalawar, and Cochin. At the Round Table Conference in London in 1931, they argued for universal adult franchise and the right to be a candidate at any election. They were supported in these efforts by women members of the Parliament in England who lobbied for the extension of franchise and political representation to Indian women. Many were impressed by the support Indian men gave to women. Margaret Cousins, an Irish feminist who led women's movements both in India and in Britain, observed: "Perhaps only women like myself who had suffered from the cruelties, the injustices of the men politicians, the man-controlled Press, the man in the street, in England and Ireland while we waged our militant campaign for eight years there after all peaceful and constitutional means had been tried for fifty previous years, could fully appreciate the wisdom, nobility and the passing of fundamental tests in self-government of these Indian legislators."[9] In India, the All India Women's Conference was founded in 1927 to address women's issues, specifically the right to vote, reform of personal (family) law, and guarantees of sexual equality in any future constitution, should independence be achieved.

Mahatma Gandhi was instrumental in bringing Indian women into the struggle for national liberation. Many of his views on women seem contemporary:

Their "words will have the same authority as the *Shastras*" and command the same respect as those of their prototypes of yore.... The fact that women had been for so long "caged and confined in their houses and little courtyards" had a ruinous effect on their personality, narrowing their vision and stunting their interests to petty things.... This kind of denial of freedom to women leading to their infantilisation had to be put an end to notwithstanding the religious scriptures that legitimise such denial since they are "repugnant to the moral sense." In fact, according to Gandhi, Hinduism's essential postulate was the absolute freedom of every individual, man or woman, to do whatever he or she liked for the sake of self-realisation, for which alone every human being was born.... Though men owed it to themselves to help in the cause of women, "ultimately women will have to determine with authority what she needs." But if women were to assert themselves in family life "wives should not be dolls and objects of indulgence, but should be treated as honoured comrads in common service." Women must protest against being treated as sex objects: ... Gandhi insists on the inviolability of the personal dignity and autonomy of women. She had the right to say "No" even to her husband. "I want woman to learn the primary right of resistance. She thinks now that she has not got it." "And why is there all this morbid anxiety about female purity? Have women any say in the matter of male purity?" ... He believed that a wife had the right to live separately, if a husband was unjust: "if divorce was the only alternative" he would not "hesitate to accept it."[10]

Beside supporting various reforms for women, Gandhi encouraged them to join the agitation against the British. Indian women were fighting "nonviolently" for independence shoulder to shoulder with Indian men; of the eighty-thousand people who were arrested during the salt satyāgraha (1930), for instance, seventeen-thousand were women.[11] They also picketed, distributed nationalistic tracts, demonstrated, and spun cloth (the symbolic rejection of British manufacturing). Women's participation in the movement embarrassed the British as the 1932 Annual Reports of the Police Administration make clear:

A large presence of women in the campaigns upset British stereotypes of Indian women and exposed police brutality. More
significantly, it laid bare British hypocrisy over Indian men's
maltreatment of women, since British police and army officers
and government officials were quite prepared to intimidate,
beat and shoot women demonstrators. These actions undermined the legitimacy of Britain's rejection of Independence,
since the very women whom the British had claimed they
were there to liberate from the abuses of Indian men, were
taking up the fight against their foreign protectors.[12]

Just as Indian women provided numerical strength to the independence movement, so men were morally bound to meet women's
demands for their own liberation. If they seemed reluctant, they
were sharply reprimanded. Even Gandhi, who contributed in many
ways to the liberation of women (and benefited from women's support), was denounced when he suggested that women should raise
their status through renunciation. A writer in *Roshini* replied: "Indian women have a long tradition of renunciation and it has not got
us anywhere; we want our rights to improve our status."[13] Gandhi,
however, continued to see women primarily in their roles as mother
and wife, rather than working outside the home for wages. He upheld, moreover, women's contribution through their spiritual and
moral courage (symbolized by Sītā, Draupadī, and Damyantī) rather
than through their individual strength (symbolized by the Rani
of Jhansi).[14]

Many women rejected these limitations, made radical demands,
and attacked traditional values. They supported the national movement but in return demanded concessions, strategically playing
political parties against the government until they obtained their
way. "The realization that the national movement needed their
support provided a leverage which they were quick to use; to link
feminist aims to nationalistic aims legitimized their claims. Opposing a foreign government, wresting concessions from it, added
lustre to the campaign whether it was a specifically male or female
cause."[15] The fact that mothers, wives, sisters, and daughters of
male national leaders were involved in both the national and the
women's movement helped to link the two (and consequently men
and women) at the vortex of planning and activity.

Throughout this period, there was cooperation among women of
diverse religious communities in India, for many issues such as lack
of education and seclusion of elite women were shared, at least in
some regions and by some strata of society. While Hindu women

pressed for reforms, Muslim women tried to recover their traditional rights under Muslim law; these were considered progressive by the regional Indian standards of the day. Thus, Muslim women lobbied for their traditional rights regarding inheritance, dower, divorce, and remarriage. The Shariat Act in 1937 and the Dissolution of Muslim Marriages Act 1939 restored such rights to the law books. Through their organizations such as the All India Women's Conference (AIWC), the Women's Indian Association, and the National Council of Women, Indian women were so well organized that by the time of independence they were ready to help design the constitution. Under the leadership of Kitty Shiva Rao, they studied the changes that needed to be made in Hindu law for women and they drafted an Indian women's charter of rights and duties for the new constitution. The latter included:

> equality before law; no disability due to religion, caste, creed or sex, in public employment, power or dishonour, and in exercise of trade or calling; adult franchise; no difference in education; free health services; equal moral standards for men and women; equal pay for women workers and all amenities (creches for children and maternity benefits; housewives' right to part of husband's income to use as her own; husband should not have the right to dispose of his whole income without the consent of the wife; wife should be the beneficiary for the husband's social insurance; women should inherit equally with men; no polygamy; women's consent to marriage essential; no marriage for girls below 17 years and boys below 21 years; divorce rights; wife should be the equal guardian of the children; court should decide on custody; both husband and wife must decide on adoption; wife has the right to limit the family.[16]

With the growing intensity of Muslim separatist politics, though, the solidarity of Indian women was challenged. During and after partition, many Muslim women leaders, as part of the liberal Muslim middle class, migrated to Pakistan; the ones who remained were faced with conflicting identities as a Muslim minority in a largely Hindu population, on the one hand, and, as Muslim women, a minority among Indian women, on the other. The Muslim community sought to preserve identity through Muslim personal or family law, though the constitution declared that the country should work toward a uniform civil code. Before independence,

Muslim women seemed to have more liberal laws compared to those of other religious communities; after independence they seemed to be restricted to more conservative laws because of reforms in Hindu law. Before noting these changes, it should be pointed out that Muslim women found it difficult to insist on reform of Muslim personal law, which governed many aspects of their lives, and to seek the support of women from other communities and the government. Because Muslim personal law had become a symbol of Muslim identity, any change was considered threatening to the Muslim community. More specifically, when men felt stressed in the public economic and political realm, they found security and comfort in control over some aspect of their lives, in this instance over their families in general and women in particular.

Since independence (1947), India has developed a system of liberal legislation that can be used to improve the lives of women. According to the constitution, there is to be no discrimination on the basis of sex with reference to social, political, and economic acts. The government can also make special provision for women to improve their status. In addition, there are directives giving both men and women the right to an adequate livelihood and equal pay for equal work. Nehru, the first prime minister, thought that women should be economically independent and that the joint family system should be eliminated. Hindu personal or family law was fundamentally altered with the Hindu Marriage Act 1955 and the Hindu Succession Act 1956. These acts improved the position of women by making polygamy unlawful, raising the age of marriage to eighteen for girls and twenty-one for boys, and allowing women to petition for restitution of conjugal rights, judicial separation, and divorce. Laws also provided for maternity benefits and inquiry into cases of death under suspicious circumstances (related to the dowry problem), sexual harassment, assault, wrongful confinement (related to the practice of seclusion), cruelty on married women (related to difficulties associated with the extended family system), rape, and so forth. Some experts have concluded that although legislation can still be improved, the most urgent need now is to teach women about their rights under the law.

Much of this progressive legislation remains to be implemented. The document *Towards Equality: Report of the Committee on the Status of Women in India* (1974), the last major statistical study to be done looking at changes in the status of women since the early part of the century, reveals discouraging trends. The female population has declined, resulting in a steadily declining female to male sex ratio; women's life expectancy is lower than men's and the gap is widening over time; and female literacy rate is considerably lower (a half or third that of men in many states) though the gap between the two has closed slightly.[17] It has also been argued that the women's movement has declined. Provisional figures of the 1991 census show that the sex ratio continues to be adverse to women; the number of females has fallen to 929 per 1,000 males against 934 in 1981. Women's rights and progress, so it is said, have been marginalized because (1) social legislation was more a public symbol that arose out of a political context than the product of a women's movement that had to debate and fight social, political, and economic issues among women from different socio-economic groups; (2) once political independence had been achieved, men's support of women's issues waned; (3) women have not been central to economic developments after independence, and (4) when the movement for national integration gave way to an emphasis on ethnic identities, there was pressure to subject women again to traditional laws.[18]

But there are also many signs of a vigorous women's movement today. The ideal of *lokasaṅgraha* (acting for the welfare of the world) brings together women and men of many different political persuasions and economic classes to work for a better society. It involves big acts and small. An example of the latter is the case of a Brahmin high school teacher in Bombay who has changed a traditional Hindu ritual. Instead of offering gifts to her husband's family on the annual death ceremony of his parents, she buys school clothes for a scheduled caste student. Because the economic and political problems are enormous in modern India, such acts can disappear in the statistics. And yet, as I moved about the middle class in Bombay and read the newspapers and the popular magazines, I was struck by the devotion sometimes verging on religious commitment—to *lokasaṅgraha.*

Closely related to *lokasaṅgraha* is the concept of *satyāgraha* (literally grasping/insisting on the truth or as Gandhi himself put it: soul force). This term was originally coined by Gandhians to capture the idea of nonviolent, political activism for national independence. Since independence, though, it has come to mean activism for social change. Women have participated, for instance, in workers' strikes, peasant rebellions, and the struggles of tribals. They have also tried to raise the consciousness of both women and men regarding women's issues at the village level. This has led to changing power relations between men and women, especially when many women, including upper-class women, identify with the oppressed group and upper-class men are viewed as the oppressors.

These two concepts—*lokasaṅgraha* and *satyāgraha*—underlie the activism of three women: Jyoti Mhapesekara, Madhu Kishwar, and Uma Bharati. In a sense, *lokasaṅgraha* and *satyāgraha* are "swing" concepts that can bridge secular and religious realms. In this section, I will examine how the first two women represent a secular approach and the last a religious one. And yet there is a certain overlap between the secular and the religious.

JYOTI MHAPASEKARA

For the past fourteen years, Jyoti Mhapasekara of Bombay has taken the message of women's liberation into the rural districts of the state of Maharashtra. Along with a group of activists, she travels to villages, addresses students and puts up posters about women's issues, holds discussions, enacts folk dramas with a contemporary message set to music, and sells books on women at a nominal cost. Out of this experience has grown the movement called Strī Mukti (the liberation of women) and a play written by Mhapasekara entitled "A Daughter is Born." This play—in versified, rhythmic Marathi accompanied by *dholaka* drums—follows the format of the *tamasha* folk dramas. The traditional theme of these is how Lord Krishna obstructs the cowherdesses on their way to market. Its modern counterpart is about how women are overcoming traditional obstructions. Mhapasekara is quick to point out, however, that women do not want to obstruct, compete, or quarrel with men; on the contrary, they wish to become their equals. This play gives us an insight into one form of social activism to improve the status of women.

The traditional drama begins with salutations to Lord Gaṇapati. Its modern counterpart salutes nineteenth-century reformers such as Isvaracandra Vidyasagara who was against the practice of child marriages, Raja Rammohan Roy who raised his voice against suttee, and Jyotiba Phule who championed the cause of education for women in Maharashtra. The viewer is reminded that women had been confined to the four walls of the home; Manu, the most famous of the classical Hindu authors on *dharma* (law), had said that women were to be dependent on their fathers in youth, husbands in marriage, and sons in old age. Salutations are next made to Agarkar, a social reformer, Karve, the founder of the first women's university in Maharashtra, Pandita Ramabai who founded homes for widows, and Mahatma Gandhi and Nehru who called upon women to come out of their houses and join the struggle for independence. The salutations end with the call "Let us unite; we shall destroy the ancient traditions and make women free."

Several vignettes of witty dialogue between two women, Kamala and Mina, are periodically broken by the chants of choruses. In the first, Kamala says that as soon as a girl is born, she is beset by problems and suffers. One chorus chants "enough of women's life" and another sings "we prefer to be born as men." Mina disagrees and says that she is proud that she was born as a woman; though there are problems, they can be solved. Kamala then says that Indian culture is so high that a woman can be prime minister. Mina replies "True, but people say that she is the only man in the cabinet." She then asks, "Is it the monopoly of men to be valorous? Women also achieve some great things. If a woman achieves something, she is just labelled as a man. Women should have equal opportunity and not be called a man." A chorus chants "we want equal opportunity." Kamala then asks, "How can we have equal opportunity because nature has made women and men different?" Mina retorts, "Yes, but what about cultural differences?" If a son is born, the sweets distributed are called *pede*. If a daughter is born, they are called *barphi*. Therefore discrimination starts at birth.

Another vignette explores the issue of preference for sons and discrimination against daughters. Here the blame is leveled at both women and men, for mothers-in-law put great pressure on their daughters-in-law to give birth to sons. The audience is told that performing vows or worshiping the goddess Ambābāī at Kolhapur (a Maharashtrian pilgrimage spot) cannot determine the sex of a child; instead sex is determined by chromosomes. A mother then tells her daughter: "If I allow you to go to college I will have to find a son-in-law who is more educated. He will ask for more dowry. You just have to go and manage a husband's home. Since you have come of age and are in a dangerous stage of life . . . we must get you married. Just as we have to handle glass carefully, so we must protect your chastity."

When the daughter says that the spark in her will vanish if she just sits at home, the mother replies that she will become accustomed to this and will rear her child and manage her kitchen. She is a woman and must take the vow or regimen (*vāsa*) of being a woman. With rhythmic and alliterative words, the skit expounds on the duties of womanhood that restrict her to the home and make her a good householder (*sugṛhiṇī*): "wash, scrub utensils, cook and serve, clean, sew, sweep, make *rangolis* (auspicious designs), water the [sacred] tulasi plant, circumambulate the [holy] banyan tree, follow some vows, and walk with head down, not looking around when in public."

Later Manu's verse on the protection of women is again mentioned and the question is raised: "What kind of protection is there? Do men really protect women?" Six news broadcasts are mentioned to refute this idea of protection: a husband kills his wife after four months of marriage; an angry laborer murders his wife because there is not enough salt in the soup; a Dalit woman is raped while returning home (the suspect being the landlord's son); a woman in custody is raped by the police; sixteen Adivasi women in a tribal area are raped by an officer; a woman clerk is molested by an income tax officer in Bombay.

The next vignette parodies arranged marriage and the selection process; the audience is reminded how a ten-minute conversation results in the selection of a life-time partner. The last skit raises the issue of the stress of the working woman because there is no day care and men do not help with domestic tasks. The play concludes with a dramatic speech by a woman who says that "a daughter is as good as gold." Why should there be dowry? She will "smash down" dowry and will go ahead. All her friends will come together and fight the "dirty" traditions that are constraining their freedom. They will break the shackles. When asked why she is so confident, she says that when women are aware of injustice, they can revolt. She tells the audience:

> Don't look at a woman as a slave or a goddess or a thing of enjoyment but as a human being. There should be a common civil law, moreover, because the Constitution has given women equal rights. But some are excluded. Muslims and Catholics are not protected. . . . If all demands are accepted, women can be self-reliant and have self-confidence. But organization and unity is needed. This is the way of liberation (*mukti*). Tradition is shackles on our legs. Caste and religion destroy intellect. Men alone create differences. We shall destroy differences. We shall make the dream of the equality of men and women come true. We shall step ahead for socialist rule. Those who are labourers, let them be united and struggle for emancipation. Let us free all the downtrodden people and make the dream of a new society the reality.

Mhapasekara's play has become extremely popular not only in the rural areas but also in the cities; there have been numerous performances throughout the villages of Maharashtra and the slums of Bombay. Sometimes as many as fifteen-thousand people have gathered at one time to see it. In 1985–1986, at the height of its popularity, there were several performances a day. Seventy different organizations have been performing it (sometimes only after seeing a video) and some have done as many as forty performances. It has been shown on television several times. Even today there are five to six performances per month by Mhapasekara's own group. In fact, now that the play has been translated into seven languages including Hindi, Sanskrit, English, and Russian, Mhapasekara has lost track of its impact. When I interviewed her, she said that she was surprised the play had become so popular but was pleased that its reception by the public helped her organization Stri Mukti Sanghatana grow (eight hundred people have joined after seeing the play). This has made possible other projects for the "liberation of women." They investigate, for instance, complaints made by a woman about treatment by her husband or his extended family. When I asked why men would be willing to discuss these problems, she suggested that it was perhaps due to the fame of her organization. That day as I left her office, I saw a group seated on the ground; a wife and husband were presenting their versions of a conflict to a social worker, lawyer, and others in order to solve problems before the police were involved. Besides participating in these "vigilance committees," the members of Stri Mukti Sanghatana (which includes both men and women) have held demonstrations in Bombay on issues related to women.

Although her play concludes that "religion destroys the intellect," Mhapasekhara does not think that religion alone is responsible for the conditions of women in Indian society. Rather, religion, poverty, lack of political representation, and social custom have all contributed to the secondary status of women. According to Mhapasekara, her play has been criticized as both too bourgeois and too leftist. It has also been disliked by some religious groups and liked by others. She has been told (but has not verified) that some women of the conservative Hindu organization, the Vishva Hindu Parishad, went to Rajasthan to protest the suttee of Roop Kanwar in 1987 by performing her play. She also has been told that it was translated into Urdu and performed in Pakistan, but does not know for sure. Mhapasekara observes that even if the play has offended Hindus, it has been so immensely popular that religious Hindu groups do not make a direct attack on it.

Her organization has taken a stand against the recent growth of what she calls "religious fundamentalism." In an article in its publication *Lalakari* (March–April 1988), the organization's position on religion is described in more detail. The article argues that Buddhism, Bhakti Hinduism, Christianity, and Islam all have some good points because they promote compassion, forgiveness, and peace through declarations such as "let everyone be happy" or "everyone is equal before God" or "the kingdom of heaven does not belong to the rich." Because class stratification was prevalent when these religions began, they improved life. They supported the poor and those who suffered. Even so, religious leaders such as Buddha and Christ could not understand the economic basis of the sufferings of the people, did not take a stand against slavery, and did not encourage people to revolt against poverty, inequality, exploitation, and injustice. Rather, they told people to accept their lot, have faith in God, and not be attached to the world. We are told, moreover, that all religions are dominated by men and the elite class; women are subordinated and restricted in their activities. Practices such as [Muslim] divorce by pronouncing three times "I divorce you," viewing rape as adultery, promoting suttee, or prohibiting divorce and abortion are outdated and selfish. They should be abandoned. Although people still visit temples and bow before God, they now revolt against exploiters and use modern medicines; yet it will take another millennium before people are convinced that there is no God. Even in socialist countries such as Russia and Poland, the article points out, people still attend church and assemble to see the pope.

In the meantime, says the article, we must guard against divisions created by religion, caste, and sectarianism. We must also encourage everyone to be tolerant (*sahiṣṇu*); accordingly, International Women's Day was celebrated as antisectarianism or antifanaticism day (*dharmāndhatāvirodhī divas:* literally, the day that is opposed to the blindness of religion). When people say "my religion alone is great," they create hatred and fanaticism. Generally people are not fanatic; it is the politicians who provoke the masses into being antisocial. Consequently, the women's liberation movement must fight against fanaticism. Freedom of the press is necessary so that people can write seriously about other religions. The secular state must be maintained so that everyone has equal treatment irrespec-

tive of religion. Besides legal reforms, attitudes regarding maintenance of Muslim widows, Hindu dowry, and so forth, must be
changed. Behind this version of women's liberation (strī-mukti) is
Marxist ideology. Because the ultimate goal is to eliminate religion
and all social evils, Mhapasekara's movement is willing to capital-
ize on concepts such as lokasaṅgraha and satyāgraha, and to pay
some compliments to religion knowing that many people still identify themselves with Hinduism, Buddhism, Christianity, Islam,
Sikhism, Jainism, and Zoroastrianism. At the same time, it calls
for reforms of religious practices that affect the lives of women, rejection of religious fanaticism, and maintenance of India as a secular state. In the final analysis, it encourages followers to overcome
religion itself.

MADHU KISHWAR

Madhu Kishwar is another woman activist whose profile helps
us to explore the relation of women and religion in India today. Kishwar is best known for her association with *Manushi: A Journal
About Women and Society*. When interviewed for the cover story
"Woman Power: Ten Amazing Women of Our Times" of *The Illustrated Weekly of India*, she said: "I feel the need to devote the coming years of my life to the struggle to develop the institutions which
foster genuine self-governance by giving ordinary people greater
control over their own lives."[19] *Manushi* over the years has reported
on various struggles by and for women as the following titles of articles indicate: "Letter from Jail: Tribal Women's Fight for Famine
Relief;" "Confronting Male Power: An All Women Panel Contests
Panchayat Election;" "The Invisible Labour Force: Women Paper
Bag Makers in Delhi" "Women Mobilise in Raipur;" "A Report
from Meat Packing Factories;" and "Herstory: Women's Nonviolent Power in the Chipko Movement." Some of the articles are
updates on elections, women in Parliament, Indian broadcasting, or
some other aspect of national life. Some of them scrutinize recent
bills or laws regarding their impact on women. Some document particular problems faced by women such as polygamy, health hazards,
and illiteracy. Some explore the everyday reality of women's lives
as daughters, students, wives, mothers, and workers. Along with
its attempt to keep abreast of women's movements and women's
problems in different parts of the country at grassroot, state, and
national levels, *Manushi* features book reviews, short stories, and

poetry by women. It also analyzes how recent films and television shows portray women. Occasionally, it reflects on women in Indian history and religion.

Although *Manushi* has been called a feminist magazine, Kishwar rejects this label in an article called "Why I do not Call Myself a Feminist."[20] She begins by observing that when they launched the magazine in 1978, she did not openly challenge being called a feminist herself, though she wanted the magazine to become known more generally as a magazine for "the protection of the human rights of all the disadvantaged or discriminated groups in our society, while having a special emphasis on women's rights."[21] Today she distances herself from every "ism" be it Marxism, Gandhianism, humanism, or feminism, because they are either inadequate through reification or harmful. Of feminism she writes:

> Feminism was an outgrowth of eighteenth century humanist thought in Europe and the USA, reinforced by thinkers from many other schools of thought, such as utilitarianism and Marxism. This second type of ism may not be more time specific but is as culture specific. . . . While I stand committed to prowomen politics, I resist the label of feminism because of its over close association with the western women's movement.
>
> . . . given our situation today, where the general flow of ideas and of labels is one way—from west to east, in the overall context of a highly imbalanced power relation, feminism, as appropriated and defined by the west, has too often become a tool of cultural imperialism. The definitions, the terminology, the assumptions, even the issues, the forms of struggle and institutions are exported from west to east, and too often we are expected to be the echo of what are assumed to be more advanced women's movements in the west. . . .
>
> During all these years, despite these pressures and attacks on us, we studiously avoided duplicating the postures and responses of factions within the western feminist movement on the issue of men's participation in the women's movement. It seemed as foolish to take an *a priori* position of confrontation against men, as some separatist feminists insisted on doing, as it would be to insist, as a cardinal principle, on an unconditional alliance with men, as those who called themselves socialist feminists required of everyone. It made no sense to expect an undifferentiated response from all

men—or from all women for that matter. . . . Partly as a consequence, *Manushi* has over the years received an unusual
amount of support from numerous men owing allegiance to a
variety of ideological orientations.[22]

Kishwar challenges other assumptions of the Western feminist
movement. One is the need for homes for battered women, which
she thinks makes no sense in India; they rarely help women carve
out independent lives because of the different socio-economic context. She notes that the women's cause in India has been well represented in the mainstream mass media and does not deserve the
image of being a "persecuted movement" as Western feminists think
is true in the West. And she bemoans the fact that those Indian
women willing to call themselves feminists have been handsomely
rewarded by being absorbed into international feminist circles with
invitations to conferences all expenses paid. This has helped their
careers at home, but this has also meant that they are under pressure to accept certain Western positions without taking into account
the distinct features of the Indian context and possible solutions
that may be more appropriate. In this context she mentions:

> I was invited to attend a conference on reproductive technolo-
> gies to be held in Germany. However, since the invitation let-
> ter mentioned that those who attended the conference would
> be expected to campaign against the use of certain new forms
> of contraception and reproductive technologies being devel-
> oped in the west, I wrote back saying that while I was willing
> to discuss these issues, I was not prepared to commit myself
> in advance because, on the basis of available information, I
> had not yet been convinced about the need to oppose all these
> reproductive technologies. I was summarily told that in that
> case they would cancel the invitation they had extended.[23]

She thinks that the term "feminist" does not say "enough of
substance about those who use the term to describe themselves."[24]
She notes, for instance, that many feminists in India have called for
capital punishment for wife murderers or those who abet suttee. But
since she is categorically against capital punishment in any instance, she would have to campaign with others on this issue. Another demonstration of her independent thinking is her choice and
treatment of topic for the tenth anniversary issue of *Manushi*
(1989):[25] the Hindu women devotional saints of the medieval pe-

riod. She rightly observes that those Hindu women who dramatically defied the norms of marriage and motherhood were generally not branded as heretics or lunatics, but accepted as saints and gurus in the mainstream tradition. This, she remarks, was a very positive aspect of cultural tradition. While appreciating the fact that social space was made available to exceptional women, she notes that it did not change the roles for ordinary women (just as today having outstanding women in unusual roles does not translate into more basic human rights for ordinary women). Kishwar rejects the position of some Indian women that the medieval women saints are symbols for reactionaries, because they are associated with religion. She points out that most protest movements in the world for most of history have been expressed in a religious idiom, though they have both social and religious dimensions. Although the poetry of these saints has no social message for other women nor advocates equality between men and women, this does not mean it is inadequate, for equality between the sexes is a modern idea:

> To look for its expression in contemporary terms by these women would be to do both the past and the present an injustice. We need to understand the past on its own terms rather than saddle it with our own current preoccupations. In order to move our society in the direction of greater justice and freedom we need to develop a creative relationship with the more humane and potentially liberating aspects of our cultural traditions. *A people without a sense of their own past are a people without a sense of self.* To understand the past is not to glorify it or to perpetuate every tradition. We are not suggesting that today's protest movements express themselves in the idiom used by these movements. As Gandhi said: *"it is good to swim in the waters of tradition, but to sink in them is suicide".* . . . This issue of *Manushi* is intended as another small effort to educate ourselves.[26]

Even this phenomenological appreciation of Hinduism in the past aroused the ire of some Indian women. Kishwar observes that she was attacked for this position by a group of feminists at a women's college in Delhi University. They could see no good at all in female *bhakta* saints such as Mahadeviyakka or Mirabai because they had substituted slavery to a husband for slavery to a god. Her reply was that we must understand the age in its own terms: "The past ought not to be studied either to seek justifications for, nor faulted for not having lived up to our present day political inclinations, but viewed on its own terms, while acknowledging it as our inherited legacy."[27] Kishwar is a staunch supporter of India as a secular state, works arduously for women in the larger framework of human rights, and is ever-ready to lend support to minority women. In this article, Kishwar does not judge the Hindu past in categorically negative terms. In fact, one could assume that she keeps the door open for communication with Hindus who seek continuity with the past as they change for the future. In her article "In Defence of Our Dharma," she acknowledges:

> The liberal, secular intelligentsia is rooted more in the western liberal tradition and is often unable to comprehend, leave alone appreciate, the sentiments and cherished beliefs of India's diverse peoples. Their attitude is often similar to that of the erstwhile colonial rulers who contemptuously dismissed the social, religious and cultural beliefs of the Indian people as superstitious mumbo-jumbo. Today, a large body of Hindu opinion seems tired of the thoughtless and disrespectful critique of India's indigenous traditions and culture which has led to brutal neglect of indigenous learning and knowledge systems.[28]

And yet Kishwar claims that the movement for a Hindu state is not inspired by real Hinduism; people have not read the *Tulsī Rāmāyaṇa*, they have only seen a popular version on television. They are not taught about the great epic; they are only manipulated to be anti-Muslim and fascistic. Religion, argues Kishwar, must be saved from the politicians who are interested more in nationalism than Hinduism:

> We need to redeem Ram as a religious figure, religious in the sense of representing a revered moral, ethical code and as an embodiment of rare spiritual ideals which have inspired generations and generations of people to upright lives in this land. The appropriation of Ram by sectarian politicians to perpetuate communal massacres pours contempt on Ram, who in popular imagination stands as a symbol of love, compassion (patit pavan kripanidhan) self sacrifice and steadfastness to duty (kartavyanishtha). . . . We were taught that he triumphed over Ravan with moral force rather than through his superior

skills as a warrior. . . . He represented righteousness. . . . The BJP projects Ram as a national warrior hero, as opposed to a Hindu god.[29]

Any exercise of power on the part of the Hindu majority infuriates Kishwar. Concerned about the fascistic tendencies of the Bharatiya Janata Party (BJP) and the movement for a Hindu state, she sees in the current strife no religious dimension what so ever. Her politics are with Gandhi's vision of India. She claims a Hindu identity and a personal moral voice. Because her own family had to flee at the time of partition along with other Hindus into what was to become India and lost everything yet maintained respect for Muslims (and a vision of an India where both Muslims and Hindus can dwell in peace), she defends with passion the view of tolerant Hinduism. To support this view, her readings of Hinduism are also selective. She ignores the fact that the concept of avatāra in general and Rāma in particular have been used at different points in Indian history to rally Hindus against what were perceived as hostile religious forces.

UMA BHARATI

A different style of activism on women's issues is represented by Ms. Uma Bharati. She has been a BJP member of Parliament from Khajuraho. When she was interviewed in December, 1989, for *Times of India News*,[30] she described her life in the style of a sacred biography. She recalled, for instance, her early, extraordinary religious experiences:

I began having unusual experiences. At the age of six, I found myself giving discourses on the scriptures to the villagers. As far back as I can remember I have had this feeling of two existences within me—dual voices—one of a philosopher-scholar, the other of a child. It was almost an organic phenomenon; I can't explain it. It was as natural as breathing, to orate on religious matters or on the need for a spiritual revolution.[31]

The interviewer then asked how she was discovered as a religious prodigy. Bharati answered:

Well, one day some professors from a Tikamgarh degree college came to the village as part of a *baraat* (marriage party). When they heard me, they were so amazed, they did not even wait for the *bidaai* (nuptials). They bundled me into a car and I was admitted to a school in the town. Then followed years of participation at religious *sammelans*. I travelled abroad, toured in private planes, was feted and banqueted, nearly drowned in flowers from admirers. When the initial glamour of the adulation wore off, I began to feel caged in the worship. I wanted to appear ordinary, not the image of a *devi* or *avatar*, or live up to a created image.[32]

Bharati remarks that she was once engaged but broke off the relationship because of her "religious commitments." She thought of becoming a *brahmacāriṇī* until her mentor told her that being a *brahmacāriṇī* meant total renunciation—that is, complete withdrawal from the world. Because she wanted to serve the people and work for the welfare of the world (*lokasaṅgraha*), she decided against total renunciation (hence her sporadic wearing of the ochre robe). Working for the "welfare of the world" has meant working with outcastes and women in her native village and in Khajuraho. Of women, she said:

Women are inherently superior as a created species. Men are not such noble beings that women should fight for equality. Instead they should fight to be treated with respect. . . .

If Indian women combine the *madhurya* (sweetness), their femininity, with self-pride and political awareness, they can teach the whole world the path of liberation. . . .

You cannot sacrifice either aspect—sword in the hand and child on the back. Our women have to combine the heroism of Draupadi, Gargi, Savitri, Jabala, and Kunti. It is self-respect that will free us, not legislation. I don't eat in houses where, as per the tradition, women eat after men and observe *purdah* . . . for crimes like rape, I feel there should be [the] death sentence.[33]

When the interviewer asked her whether she has ever experienced sexual discrimination in political life, she replied, "No, because I am well known in my area. And in the BJP we give the woman a very exalted status." Then, with a twinkle in her eye, she told the reporter, "my religious image has helped women overcome their prejudices." Folding her ochre robes, she added "I have faith in my-self. . . . And may God give me some of the reformist energy of my idols—Rani Laxmi Bai and Swami Vivekananda."[34]

Uma Bharati sees no contradiction between working for the cause of women and being a member of the BJP Party, usually por-trayed in the press as the Hindu fundamentalist or militant party, and stereotyped as a regressive force on women's issues. Bharati is a Hindu liberal, at least on women's issues. But like many other Hin-dus she is disturbed at the loss of Hindu values and perceives sec-ularism under leaders such as Rajiv Gandhi negatively. When defending Indian voters, she remarks: "maybe they didn't like Ra-jiv's foreign wife . . . or his elite coterie of friends . . . or his mania for computerisation and breakneck modernisation in certain sectors when so many lakhs [100,000] were denied basic amenities."[35]

Her remedy for conflict brought on by communalism and re-ligious extremism is to make room for moderate religion in the public square:

> The fact is the Indians can only understand religion. We are an instinctively religious people. The police, law, science— these are external controls; even our communists are "astiks" (theists) in their heart of hearts. The best methods of control-ling communalism is to get moderate religious leaders on public forums to address the masses, spiced with examples from the scriptures. Those who are inflamed by religion can only be calmed down by religion, not by a slick or rational explanation.[36]

Bharati told the interviewer that all parties exploit religious senti-ment: "But the BJP believe in Hindutva ("Hinduness") and are proud of it and just because of this we are branded communal."[37] More recently, Bharati has become much more militant and vocif-erous against the Muslims. Prior to the projected showdown (re-garding the rebuilding of a Hindu temple to Lord Rāma at the site of a mosque) at Ayodhya on October 30, 1990, she made speeches in Hindi that were later made into cassettes and sold. The message was virulent:

> On October 30, by beginning the construction of the temple, our holy men will be laying the foundations of making Hin-dustan a Hindu [state]. Bharat Mata Ki Jai . . . Glory to Ma-hadev [the Great Deity]. Destroy the tyrant in the same way

that Ravana was vanquished. Do not display any love (nij preet). This is the order of Ram. Announce it boldly to the world that anyone who opposes Ram cannot be an Indian. Muslims, remember Rahim who longed for the dust of Lord Ram's feet. . . . Songs of Hindu Muslim brotherhood were sung by Mahatma Gandhi. We got ready to hear the Azaan along with the temple bells, but they can't do this, nor does their heritage permit them to do so. . . . The two cultures are polar opposites. But still we preached brotherhood. . . . We could not teach them with words, now let us teach them with kicks. . . . Let there be bloodshed once and for all. . . . Leftists and communists ask me if we desire to turn this land into a Hindu rashtra. I say it was declared one at the time of Partition in 1947—Hindustan, a nation of Hindus and Pakistan, a nation of the Muslims. Those Muslims who stayed behind could do so because of the tolerance and large-heartedness of the Hindus. . . . Declare without hesitation that this is a Hindu rashtra, a nation of Hindus.[38]

Uma Bharati finally took saṁnyāsa (formal renunciation) in 1992. It was prompted, some say, to clear her reputation after she was accused by the opposition parties of having an affair. Be that as it may, she shaved her head, was renamed Uma Shri Bharati, and began to wear only ochre robes. As the opposition was quick to point out, she did not give up her status as a member of parliament. She also continued to support the cause of rebuilding the Rām Janmabhoomi temple.

———————

All three women—Mhapasekara, Kishwar, and Bharati—have dedicated their lives to the transformation of Indian society. Accordingly, they express the modern ideal of working for the welfare of the world (lokasaṅgraha). In particular, they are all dedicated to improving the lives of women. While they themselves belong to the urban middle class or elite, their activism is directed at women, rural and urban, of all economic strata. If they converge in their dedication to improving the lot of women, they diverge in their views on religion. Mhapasekara herself refused to single out religion as the sole culprit in the troubles women face (placing blame also on economic and political factors). She showed no hostility toward religion in my interview with her; her organization's publication of *Lalakari* revealed, however, its Marxist bias with its occasional diatribe against religion. Although the final lines of her play also insinuate the group's Marxist orientation—"Caste and religion destroy intellect. . . . We shall step ahead for socialist rule"—few liberal Hindus (at least the ones I met) seem to have detected its antireligious stance, identifying instead only with the need to make women equal to men and to change religion in a progressive way to make this happen.

Kishwar, by contrast, repudiated all "isms." An example of her willingness to look at the merits of each case was her study of the medieval Hindu bhakti women saints who were to be understood on their own terms and not anachronistically by our modern evaluation. But Kishwar is quite capable (as we shall see in the next section) of categorically attacking modern Hindus who suggest that the Indian secular state supports religious minorities at the expense of the religious majority, as if Hinduism is to be entertained only when it is safely relegated to the past.

In contrast to both Mhapasekara and Kishwar who write on Hinduism from a secular, politicized stance (albeit ranging from antagonistic to historically sympathetic), Uma Bharati combines both politics (as a member of Parliament) and religion (as an ascetic albeit of a neo-Hindu type with her "renunciation for activism within the world"). Whereas both Mhapasekara and Kishwar denounce Hindu fundamentalism, indirectly or directly, Bharati is proud to be an elected representative of a party labeled fundamentalist or militant. She sees such labels as but the rhetoric of people who are against any kind of Hinduism. While at one time women such as Mhapasekara, Kishwar, and Bharati (and many others like them) shared a commitment and willingness to work together for improving the lives of women, from 1991 this alliance has been breaking down.

————————

The great epic *Mahābhārata* has recently been relived by over one hundred fifteen million people in India through the ninety-one episodes of a television megaserial. Its power to grip the nation has been attributed to the fact that its content is still relevant. Writing in *India Today*,[39] Sharmila Chandra notes:

Without doubt, the issues it has been dwelling upon are the ones that plague the present. Take for example Draupadi's *cheerharan* or disrobing scene. It has been used to raise a myr-

iad questions on female equality. Having lost all else in a
game of dice, Yudhishthir stakes his wife. He loses her too,
and his Kaurava cousins attempt to disrobe her. The questions
Draupadi raises in the royal court grab the viewer by the gut.
She asks her husband: "Who did you lose first, yourself or
me? Does a husband have the right to lose his wife in a gambling game?" She also asks the king and the other elders
present in the court as to how they could silently watch one
of their subjects being humiliated. . . .

Rupa Ganguly, 23, the Calcutta-based actress who bagged
the prize role of Draupadi, spells out why Draupadi is a
woman of our times. Says she: "Unlike Sita of *Ramayan*,
Draupadi does not believe in suffering silently. Like a modern
Indian woman, she reacts vociferously, demands apologies and
plans revenge. She is loyal to her husbands but can and does
rebel against them." Explains Rupa: "Her anger is well
received by the audience because it is not only natural, but
also righteous."[40]

While the *Mahābhārata* was unfolding on television, another
drama was, and still is, unfolding across the country. It is linked to
the epic *Rāmāyaṇa*, for it is a call by Hindus to rebuild the temple
at Ram Janmabhoomi, considered the birthplace of Lord Rāma at
Ayodhya. Hindus claim that the temple had been destroyed by Muslims who had erected in its place a mosque, the Babri Masjid. This
call, however, is much more than an ultimatum to rebuild a temple.
It is a cause célèbre for Hinduism in general and for Hindu power in
particular. Hindu militants, claiming to defend Hindu traditions,
have invoked the *Rāmāyaṇa* because of its focus on the "liberation"
of Ayodhya. What does this mean for women? Will the epic's heroine Sītā once again be viewed as the ideal woman? Will Sītā, often
self-effacing and eager to demonstrate her *pativrata*[41]—her chastity
and loyalty to her husband—become a symbol today of Hindutva
(the nature of being Hindu)?

To date, there has been a shared interest by many Indian women,
urban elite men, and the Indian government in improving the lot of
women. This is a legacy of the Hindu renaissance, the independence
movement, the constitution, the progressive idealism of the Nehru
era, various planning commissions, and legal reforms over the past
several decades. Now, though, there is a growing polarization between "secularists" and Hindu "militants." The former category
represents various groups who want to maintain the nature of India
as a secular state. Religious minorities prefer this position to pre-

vent the Hindu majority (82 percent of the population) from defining the nature of the state in Hindu terms. Marxists and socialists prefer it because they are hostile to religion and think it should be eliminated so that the country can progress. Still others do so simply because they are irreligious and materialistic or because they think that it is the only way to accommodate India's diverse groups. By contrast, the category of Hindu "militants" represents those who stand in the tradition of Hindutva. From the 1920s they have stood for a Hindu state, the prevention of conversions from Hinduism, the reconversion of Indian Muslims and Christians to Hinduism, and a ban on cow slaughter.[42] The Rashtriya Swayamsevak Sangh (RSS), with its militarized corps of volunteers, has stopped short of agitating for a Hindu state but certainly wants Hindu power. Subsequent Hindu parties such as the Jana Sangh, the Vishva Hindu Parishad (VHP), and the Bharatiya Janata Party (BJP) have furthered the Hindu cause.

In the more recent past, the Hindutva platform has also been increasingly labeled Hindu "fundamentalism."[43] Today aspects of Hinduism are being selected to provide a more explicit sense of what it means to be a Hindu. The Hindutva platform has also been labeled Hindu communalism. While communalism has been attributed to inherent conflict between religious communities, it has more recently been argued that such religious communities themselves had internal divisions. Communalism arose more as a response to economic competition and a crisis of identity than an inherent conflict between religions that managed to live together peacefully in some historical periods. Communalism, it has been argued, arose first among the middle classes in the colonial period. With economic stagnation, the collapse of traditional status systems, and the loss of identity, the middle classes began to compete for scarce resources. Frustration, identity confusion, and the sense of relative deprivation led to a volatile climate where a religious issue such as the protection of cows or music played in front of a mosque could provoke extreme violence, though the real conflict was over government jobs, political positions, and educational opportunities.[44] Communal tensions were exaggerated during the independence movement when Muslims and Hindus tried to improve their bargaining position with the British for future power. Thus, there were both economic and political components to communalism.

Increasingly, liberal Hindus who have backed the secular state are becoming concerned about loss of Hindu identity. The growing polarization between "secularists" and Hindu "militants" came to the point of overt clash in the fall of 1990. The final straw was the perception on the part of many Hindus that Prime Minister V.P. Singh increased reservations—appointments in the government and universities for Scheduled Castes (SC), Scheduled Tribes (ST), and Other Backward Classes (OBC)—simply to increase his voting bloc with the disadvantaged of society in order to rescue his minority government (the Janata Dal). At the Red Fort, on Indian Independence Day, he "appealed to the Scheduled Castes and Muslims by repeated references to Ambedkar and by declaring Prophet Mohammed's birthday a public holiday."[45] That such action would pit the SCs and STs (who together are 22.5 percent), OBCs (27 percent), and 10 percent poor[46] (thus 59 percent of the population) against the upper castes and break the Hindu majority into two enemy camps— with shades of a Marxist proletarian revolution—alarmed even liberal Hindus.

Because it was difficult to protest the issue of increased reservations for fear of alienating this large population, Hindu leaders defused the problem by turning the nation's attention to the Hindu demand that the mosque on the site of Lord Rāma's birthplace at Ayodhya be moved and a Hindu temple built there instead. Hindus had for some time been agitating to change the mosque to a temple; while there have been several reasons for this, it was foremost a cause célèbre for Hindu identity and power. When Hindus rallied and converged on the mosque at the end of October 1990, at least twelve died and thousands were injured. The security forces assembled for the confrontation refused to stop the crowds, thereby demonstrating their sympathy for the Hindu cause. In the days following there were severe communal riots between Hindus and Muslims throughout the country. The central government—first that of V. P. Singh and then (several months later) that of Chandra Shekhar—fell in the aftermath.

In the election of May 1991, tragically interrupted by the assassination of Rajiv Gandhi, the BJP made significant gains, though the sympathy vote after Gandhi's death brought Congress back to power and P. V. Narasimha Rao as prime minister. This sympathy vote "was to a large extent caused by women voters."[47] In this election, well-known swamis such as Chinmayananda ran for BJP seats and the Jagadguru Śaṅkarācārya Saraswati Mahārāja blessed the crowds on campaign routes. Several stars associated with the teleserial *Rāmāyaṇa* also ran for office. One was Dipika Chikhalla who played the role of Sītā. People came "for a real-life darshan of the telegoddess."[48] The ruling troika of the BJP was said to be two men, Atal

Behari Vajpayee and Lal Krishan Advani, and one women, Rajmata
Vijaya Raje Scindia. The latter "symbolises the shakti of Hindu
womanhood: Durgā and Rani of Jhansi rolled in one. She is an un-
compromising *Hindutva* advocate capable of touching emotional
heartstrings."[49] Campaign paraphernalia captured the new religious
mood. T-shirts said, "I am proud of my cultural heritage" or had a
lotus symbol. Women's bangles had "Sita-Ram" inscribed on them.
A new term had even been coined: "Scuppies," referring to saffron-
clad yuppies with their jeans and Gucci shoes. Now that it has become fashionable to identify with the BJP, it is timely to explore
several possible scenarios—a "reformed secular state," a liberal
Hindu state, and a conservative Hindu state—and what may happen to women as a consequence of each.

WOMEN AND A REFORMED SECULAR STATE

Indian women of various religious communities and women's
groups have been insisting on a uniform civil code to replace the
personal (family) law of the different religions. But the issue of a uniform civil code involves more than the issue of legal justice for Indian women. It is central to the growing debate among Hindus over
the continuing viability of the Indian secular state. Many liberal
Hindus are now saying that a minimum requirement to keep the
state secular is a uniform civil code; it is a test of loyalty to the state
to have a common law. In this connection it is worthwhile to remember that the issue of rebuilding the Hindu temple at the birthplace of Lord Rāma had begun seriously when the Hindu militant
party, the BJP, reacted to the Congress I's Muslim Women's Bill
(1986) following the Shah Bano controversy.

These are the details of the controversy. Shah Bano, a sixty-two
year old woman, was paid two hundred rupees (about twenty U.S.
dollars) per month as maintenance after she separated from her
forty-six year old husband, Mohammad Ahmed Khan (a lawyer).
When he stopped paying, she filed suit before a magistrate court under section 125 of the criminal procedure code to have him pay five
hundred rupees per month. Her husband then divorced her and paid
her a settlement or *mehr* of three thousand rupees, claiming this
fulfilled his obligations under Muslim personal law. Although the
lower court and the provincial high court gave her maintenance, the
case made its way to the supreme court when her husband refused
to pay more. On April 25, 1985, the supreme court upheld the right

of Muslim women to maintenance if destitute and not remarried after a divorce, according to criminal law which, it argued, is applicable uniformly to all citizens (although it had not been applied to Muslims on certain issues such as this one). It examined relevant sections of the *Qur'ān* (chapter 11, surahs 241 and 242) and concluded that this ruling was not against Muslim scripture. It also referred to article 44 of the constitution, which called for a common civil code and noted that "a common civil code will help the cause of national integration by removing disparate loyalties to laws which have conflicting ideologies."[50]

Although there had been several similar cases before, no one had referred to the *Qur'ān* or the need for a common civil code. These two references alerted the All India Muslim Personal Law Board, the Jamiat-ul Ullema-Hind, and the Jamiat-ul Islami which immediately protested the ruling. Shahida Lateef—despite her sensitivity to the concerns of the Muslim community[51] to maintain identity by controlling personal law (one of the few areas over which they have jurisdiction)—notes that Muslim conservatives immediately condemned the supreme court judgment. They mobilized Muslim organizations and the Urdu press to protest and provoked fear by suggesting that the minorities' freedom of religion was in danger because the supreme court had bypassed the traditional Muslim exegetes in their interpretation of the *Qur'ān*. Although Muslim liberals tried to counter the conservatives, they were not well organized. In the process the interests of Muslim women, which provoked the confrontation, were ignored, though Muslim women themselves began to organize to secure more rights. Even though it was obvious to many that the *Qur'ān* had not been violated and even though other Muslim societies had made similar reforms, the conservatives maintained their pressure until the government backed down. The Muslim Women's (protection of rights in divorce) Act was introduced in Parliament in 1986.[52]

Without going into the details of this bill,[53] suffice it to say that the government still legislated on Muslim law and that it even introduced new items not in the Shariat (for example, having the *waqf* boards support indigent women when relatives fail to do so). For both Muslim women activists and for the Hindu community at large, this bill seemed to violate articles 14 and 15 of the constitution. According to the former, the "State shall not deny any person equality before the law" and according to the latter the state shall not discriminate on the base of "religion, race, caste, sex or place of birth." The government decided to woo the conservative Muslims partly because the government had lost a Bihar by-election in November 1985; it wanted to shore up the Muslim vote by appealing to the conservatives who could deliver it through their organizations. "Because of the controversy over the Ram Janmabhoomi/Babri Masjid issue it was easier to play the politics of fear, particularly since the government's conduct of and intervention in minority issues had never been considered objective enough to inspire confidence within the community."[54] For Hindus the bill represented the government's unwillingness to secure everyone "equality before the law" (article 14) and to refrain from discriminating against any citizen on grounds of sex (article 16). It also showed the government's unwillingness to press for a uniform civil code as promised in the constitution (in the directive principles of state policy, article 44): the state shall endeavor to "secure for the citizens a uniform civil code throughout the territory of India." Finally, it seemed to indicate that the government was supporting a religious minority instead of heeding the aim of the constitution and the wishes of the majority.

Lateef, however, challenges some of these assumptions. She argues that the constitutional concept of secularism has been used both to legitimate religious and caste interests, and to criticize them. The cooperation of the government and conservative Muslims on the Muslim women's bill is an example of the former, for they used the concept of secularism to enact communal legislation and block application of the secular criminal code to all Indian women, arguing that the code was against majority Muslim opinion and the diversities of India had to be recognized. Hindu parties on the right also used secularism to argue for a uniform civil accord and against special treatment for a minority religion. Secularism can be used in so many ways, says Lateef, secularism itself needs to be debated. Does it really pose a threat to the minorities? Is the government objective in their treatment? Lateef suggests that until the government stops using Hindu religious symbolism, it will be perceived as promoting the interests of only one community and being anti-Muslim, thus playing into the hands of the conservatives who play on Muslim fears of cultural absorption.[55]

Having made the Muslim case for considering a reformed secularism—the need for a serious analysis of whether a uniform civil code is indeed a threat to the minorities and the need to eliminate any governmental bias toward and symbols favoring Hinduism—Lateef concludes by summarizing the woman factor in the Shah Bano episode: "Few examples could have demonstrated with such immediacy the paucity of Muslim woman power in India, or the marginalization of their concerns both by government and by the Muslim conservatives, as the Shah Bano case . . . ; among Muslim conservatives and the community in general not even a token attempt was made to treat women as partners to be either consulted or helped."[56] The saga of the Shah Bano case is not yet over. Some divorced Muslim women have filed an appeal in the supreme court against the bill; they argue that it violated their constitutional rights.[57]

Christian men, too, have been unwilling to change Christian personal law. As of 1990, divorce, for instance, was still regulated by the Indian Divorce Act (IDA) of 1869 and the Indian Christian Marriage Act, 1872. Under this colonial legislation a husband can divorce his wife with an accusation of adultery (no proof necessary). A wife, however, has to prove incestuous adultery; bigamy with adultery or marriage with another woman; rape, sodomy, or bestiality; or adultery with desertion without reasonable excuse for over two years by her husband. Because of the moral connotations of adultery, courts would deny a woman custody of her children. The IDA, moreover, does not recognize that a divorced woman has a right to maintenance (though a judge can demand a husband pay one-fifth of his income). Finally, the existing law stipulates that the property of an adulterous woman must be divided between her husband and her children.

When reform was first attempted in the early 1960s, Roman Catholic leaders in particular rejected it as interference in their internal affairs.[58] Emil D'Cruz reflects the view of the Christian minority (more precisely, the views of Christian men) and solidarity with the Muslim minority. He argues that progressive members of minority religions want a uniform civil code but find it difficult to argue for one. They think that "Hindu reactionaries" promote the code more as a power play to dominate other groups than as a sincere support of the code itself. First, D'Cruz suggests that it is one thing for the majority community to put its own house in order (with legal reforms of untouchability, suttee, child marriage and dowry) and quite another thing to reform a minority community (such as trying to change the Muslim Shariat). Second, he thinks that because of the communal riots caused by partition and the deep distrust between Muslims and Hindus, the state should refrain from interference in minority affairs. On the contrary, Muslims should sort out their own problems according to their own timetable.[59] Therefore, D'Cruz is against government insistence on a uniform civil code. While he uses the example of the Muslim community, he is really arguing for all minorities. He does not want government interference in Christian personal law; the instigation and definition of changes must be left to the individual religious minorities. D'Cruz uses several questionable arguments. If reform is needed by a certain set of criteria, it is needed irrespective of the religion. It is unfair for one group to have to change in the name of progress, but not other groups in society (for by definition there will be some loss of traditional identity in the process). Or if the more progressive group eventually reaps the benefits of education, skills, and so forth, it is unfair for the traditional group to cry discrimination (as often happens). Moreover, when communal violence after partition was instigated by both Muslims and Hindus, it is unfair to blame mistrust on Hindus today.

Be that as it may, Christian women are unwilling to leave the matter of reform to church authorities. Women's attempts at reform failed again in 1988 and 1989. Representatives of many Christian women's groups and other women activists met in Bombay in January 1990 to press for reforms of Christian personal law. Debate was held on the Joint Women's Programme (JWP) bill that would liberalize divorce laws by introducing mutual consent and maintenance in accordance with the standard of living. Press reports indicate the politics involved. While women argued that there should be a nonsexist, secular family code in India, Prime Minister V. P. Singh avoided the issue by saying that the communities themselves must demand a uniform civil code. Since male Christian leaders had so far not backed women's demands, Christian women were frustrated and incensed because they had fewer rights than Hindu women. But they also thought that Hindu "fundamentalist" organizations were not sincerely interested in improving the situation of women and were using the issue of a uniform civil code for their own political purposes—that is, criticizing the secular government and the minorities for their inaction and collaboration.[60]

According to the directive principles of the constitution, the state must take measures to understand the problems faced by women in social and economic development and take special measures, if need be, to correct the situation. Whether this meant "affirmative action" for women as for Scheduled Castes, Scheduled Tribes, and Other Backward Castes was a matter discussed in the mid-1970s. In the 1974 ministry of education report called *Towards Equality: Report of the Committee on the Status of Women in India*, it says:

"The minority argument cannot be applied to women, women are not a community, they are a category. Though they have some real problems of their own, they share with men the problems of their groups, locality, and community. Women are not concentrated in certain areas confined to particular fields of activity. Under these circumstances, there can be no rational basis for reservation for women"... . A note of dissent was, however, recorded by three members of the Committee who are eminent in their professions. They argue that, although they are committed to the principle of equality and therefore would oppose the idea of reservation except for SC/ST, "an unattainable goal is as meaningless as a right that cannot be exercised. Equality of opportunity cannot be achieved in the face of tremendous difficulties and obstacles which the social system imposes on all those sections whom traditional India treated as second or even third class citizens." The dissenting note points out that, despite legal changes, the actual condition of the mass of women has not materially changed in the decades since independence... . Thus, according to the dissenters, what needs to be done is to widen the ranks of women in legislative bodies so that they do not stand alone in their struggle against social and cultural forces which have held them in bondage. This enlargement of their ranks could be achieved through reservation.[61]

The question of affirmative action for Indian women was raised again in the early 1990s. Prime Minister Chandra Shekhar (V. P. Singh's successor), for instance, used the idea of reservations for women as a campaign promise:

A genuine gender-based critique of the reservation movement has been noticeably absent from the nationalist press. But that does not mean that progressive women do not care about this issue. In fact, part of the government's election promises was a commitment to reserve seats in educational facilities and government jobs for women also. So the struggle of women is integrally tied to the success of the broader reservation movement.[62]

The reservation controversy in India may come to embroil women as well. They will have to think through the morality of what to do when birth rather than need is sometimes the basis for special consideration, and is institutionalized in a reservation system making few willing to give it up when conditions have changed and when those once in need begin to compete on the basis of merit but lose out to those enjoying reservation opportunities.

A Uniform Civil Code

The issue of a uniform civil code is both substantive (an issue of law) and symbolic (an issue of identity). As we have seen, the gender factor is at the interface of tradition and modernity as well as secularism and communalism. Indian women of various religions such as Hinduism, Islam, and Christianity generally want a uniform civil code. Nevertheless, this consensus is now in danger of breaking down. Increased agitation for a Hindu state has as its corollary agitation against Muslims. So Muslim women may well side with Muslim conservatives. In fact, says Amrita Chhachhi:

The same divisions affected women in the early women's movement and national movements. In their struggle for suffrage, education and legal rights, both Hindu and Muslim women attacked the system of seclusion. However, as communal divisions intensified, Hindu feminists began to see purdah (seclusion) as a custom brought to India by Muslim invaders and a cause for the fall in women's high status in the Golden Age, and Muslim women, fearing that they would be swamped as a minority in an India ruled by a Hindu majority, began to defend passages in the Quran about female modesty.[63]

Though many liberal Hindus, both men and women, want a reformed secularism and a uniform civil code, they may decide that this is not enough to hold their loyalty to a state whose secularism is increasingly disliked because it is perceived to be antithetical to Hindu values and identity. Accordingly, even liberal Hindus, women and men alike, may join forces with conservative Hindus in working toward a Hindu state. It has been pointed out, for instance, that "Hindu communalist bodies like the Shiv Sena and the RSS have issued statements demanding a common civil code in the interests of national unity. What they mean by national unity is clear from their other statements. RSS chief Balasaheb Deoras, said on November 9, 1985, that the main purpose of the RSS is Hindu unity and it believes all citizens of India should have a 'Hindu culture.' "[64]

This possibility has activists and staunch supporters of secularism on political alert. Kishwar has been quick to support the cause of minorities. Regarding the Shah Bano case, for example, she declared that the "judgment . . . obsessively dwells upon 'Muslims' and 'Muslim personal law,' "[65] when in point of fact other religious communities are hardly egalitarian in their treatment of women. Rather, the issue "has been picked up vociferously by various self-appointed reformers amongst the Hindus to whip up the most blatant kind of anti-Muslim hysteria, using the plight of Muslim women as a banner. Once again, women are being used by men of different communities to settle scores with each other."[66] It is not incidental, argues Kishwar, that Muslims are economically and socially a disadvantaged community in India. She argues that just as British reformers were more interested in criticizing the plight of Indian women than reforming their own British law in England to improve the position of women, so also Indian reformers today who advocate a uniform civil code often ignore the fact that the legal rights of Hindu women, not to mention actual implementation of the law, is far from satisfactory.[67]

Kishwar reminds us that Hindus themselves are still governed by Hindu personal law in marriage, divorce, and succession. There have been reforms, but there are still many problems. One is the discrimination against daughters in inheritance. A second is that fathers are automatically the "natural" guardians of legitimate children over the age of five. A third is that Hindu marriages are not legally registered (which makes bigamy possible). Thus, Kishwar points out the urgent need for a uniform secular code applicable to everyone (not an extension of Hindu personal law as it now exists); all citizens should have the right to abide by it. She suggests that women themselves need to take the lead in designing such a code to ensure the equality of men and women, and to make sure that minority women are fully involved in the debate.

Liberal Hindus are quick to point out, however, that "The Congress, since before Independence, has had a political alliance with orthodox Muslims and specifically with those associated with the Jamiyyat-ul-Ulamā, an organization of Muslim clerics. The Jamiyyat's cooperation with the Congress has involved a political bargain in which the Ulamā have given their support on the assumption that the Muslim personal law (Shariat) would be maintained, as would endowments, mosques, and other institutions as aspects of Muslim culture."[68] To Hindus, then, the issue of a uniform civil code is larger than the issue of women's problems. It belongs to the political arena as well, for it symbolizes the government's concessions to minorities for votes. Refusal to be citizens under one law and refusal to heed the call for change through legal reform, moreover, symbolizes for many Hindus the separatist tendencies of Muslims or at least their lack of genuine commitment to Indian nation-building and modernization.

Liberal Hindus may be willing to renew the secular state, but the secular state would have to include a universal common code. The renewed secular state would likely pay lip service to the equality of religions (*sarva-dharma-samabhāva*) and the state's support of all religions (what we may term "positive secularism")—since this form of secularism was found through much of Indian history. Drawing on ancient Indian views of the state and concepts of tolerance, Radhakrishnan, in his *Recovery of Faith*, said: "Secularism as here defined is in accordance with the ancient religious tradition of India. It tries to build up a fellowship of believers, not by subordinating individual qualities to the group mind but by bringing them into harmony with each other. This fellowship is based on the principle of diversity in unity which alone has the quality of creativeness."[69] Elsewhere he writes: "Secularism here does not mean irreligion or atheism or even stress on material comforts. It proclaims that it lays stress on the universality of spiritual values which may be attained by a variety of ways."[70] The state was to support all religions although one could be emphasized (according to the religious persuasion of the ruler) as long as there was no feeling of relative deprivation on the part of others.

WOMEN AND A CONSERVATIVE HINDU STATE

In connection with the idea of a uniform civil code, it should not be forgotten that when Nehru tried to reform Hindu law through the Hindu code bill of 1951, he was opposed by conservative Hindus and some well-known nationalists. They made it an election issue and managed to have it abandoned, although the Hindu Marriage Act and Succession Act were eventually passed in 1955. In fact, the battle had been long and vociferous. The issue polarized men and women. From 1944 there was a series of inconclusive debates with Congress split. Women in Congress, however, were united across party lines:

This was referred to by members in parliament as a "tyranny of women." Sitaramayya regretted that "half a dozen lady members can drag us by the heels and make us take up this bill." Every clause of the bill was opposed, including the one that abolished polygamy. Members in parliament called the bill "anti Hindu and anti Indian." The cry of "religion in danger" was raised. Massive demonstrations against the bill were staged in different parts of the country and outside parliament. . . . The most vehemently opposed clause was the one that gave daughters a share in property. Because of this opposition, daughters were finally excluded from a share in ancestral property. Supporters of the bill regretted that by the time it was passed, it had been so amended as to be of very limited benefit to women.[71]

Given this history, it is not surprising that those who have called for a Hindu state have also called for the repeal of the Hindu marriage act.[72]

It has been observed of many developing countries that economic development affects men and women differently: men as a group gain, women lose. More and more women are searching for jobs to pay for their dowry and to help maintain a middle-class standard of living for their families. Taking India as a whole, Chhachhi demonstrates that trends since the early part of the century are not promising for women. Women's jobs in textiles, mines, and plantations have declined as men take them over. Most of women's paid jobs have been in those industries where labor is done in the home. (Now men are even competing for these jobs, which are generally poorly paid.) With the green revolution, the number of female agricultural wage-laborers has grown, though they are generally seasonal workers and their wages have declined to half that of male laborers. The number of female cultivators has declined because they have lost land. With growing unemployment, women are usually the first to be laid off.[73] Development projects have too often been designed for men or to further men's interests.

Sujata Gothoskar updates this report in a recent article for *Manushi*.[74] She observes that a reason for the shift by employers in the organized industrial sector to a nonunionized work force is because it is less expensive and more flexible. "The earliest victims of this preference have been women employed in the industrial organised sector."[75] One excuse made by industry for pushing women out has been the protective legislation making employers provide maternity benefits, creches, and safeguarding women from hazardous jobs. Another has been the shortage of jobs and the prestige attached to working with machines. Whereas machination should have helped women qualify for more jobs because strength was not so important, in point of fact it has lessened women's employment, since it was women who did the heavy work prior to industrialization. It is only educated, middle-class women in fields such as transport, communications, and financial services who have seen employment grow substantially.

The rise in the economic level of rural India has been expressed in traditional rather than modern status terms: as family income rises, women are withdrawn from the work force and confined to the home. The traditional notion of *strīdharma* (the behavior, duties, and values of women such as chastity, loyalty, patience, self-sacrifice) defined the status of the family (*kula*) and caste (*jāti*). One common way for a *jāti* to move up in the caste hierarchy was to imitate the behavior of Brahmins. This process was called Sanskritization or Brahmanization because it involved cultural assimilation to Hinduism as defined by Sanskrit texts and performed by Brahmin priests. This meant imitation of the conservative Brahmanical norms of womanhood—low marriage age, dowry, seclusion, and banning of remarriage for widows. According to Chhachhi, "the emergence of a rich peasant class has led to the withdrawal of women of this section from work in the fields. However, this has not meant an improvement in the status of these women. Seclusion only serves to hide the labour women perform within the household, which sometimes increases as a result of hiring in wage labour. In any case, this process does not result in any increase in women's economic control over resources and property or decision-making."[76]

In an age of anti-Brahmin movements throughout India and extensive legal reforms to change the traditional Brahmanical view of womanhood, it is ironic that seclusion and dependency of women is coming into vogue once more. This is especially the case in rural areas where wealthy lower and middle castes are using traditional methods of attaining upward mobility. The status of the family increases if women are not educated and do not work outside the home. It is possible that both cultural and economic factors contribute to this pattern: Sanskritization, in fact, may be a way to legitimate the removal of women from the competitive job market or prevent their entry into it in the first place. The statistics of female seclusion in north India are striking (Harayana 72.6 percent; Uttar Pradesh 46.4 percent; Maharashtra 16.7 percent).[77]

Reaffirmation of medieval Brahmanical or Hindu values through Sanskritization may also affect women in other ways. One traditional Brahmanical value, for instance, has been the desire for sons. In my opinion, it is likely that this idea developed (1) to compensate for the physical vulnerability of male fetuses and infants who die more frequently than their female counterparts; (2) to ensure reproduction and bind men to the care of women and children through male identification with biological offspring of the same sex; and (3) to maintain patrilineality and inheritance through the male line.[78] The goals were given religious legitimation by asserting that a man would go to heaven after death only if he had a son to perform the śrāddha rituals. Another Brahmanical value was that the daughter was to be given in marriage with gifts (kanyādāna). This gave rise to the practice of dowry, making female children an economic liability. The corollary of needing sons and giving dowries was avoiding daughters. Social scientists have long observed that there are many more men than women in India (in the 1991 census, as noted previously, it is reported that there are 929 females per 1,000 males); this suggests that the desire for sons and the avoidance of daughters is widespread in some families or groups. Exactly how this sex ratio occurs has been a subject of debate.

One possibility is infanticide—a practice that is categorically prohibited by Hinduism. In some communities female infanticide seems to be rising at the same rate as dowries. In the impoverished, martial Kallar caste of Isilampatti taluk (in the Madurai district of Tamil Nadu), for instance, it is estimated that there have been nearly six-thousand female babies poisoned to death over the last decade. "Males now constitute 52 per cent of the Kallar population whereas 10 years ago they accounted for only 48 per cent. And 70 per cent of Kallar children below the age of 10 are now boys. Ten years ago that figure was 50 per cent."[79] The dowry system took root in this community only twenty-five years ago when a dam was built bringing irrigation to this area and increasing prosperity. Today many Kallar are again impoverished and can no longer afford to pay dowry. But instead of eliminating the practice of dowry, they are eliminating female children.

Another way to get rid of daughters has been by neglecting their nutrition and health care. This leads to early death or poor health and stunted growth, often making it later difficult for the grown women to give birth, leading, in turn, to their death in childbirth.[80] Now, though, there is a new, more efficient method of sex selection. In the 1980s, modern, technological methods of sex selection were introduced into India from the West. The traditional socio-religious preference for sons was made possible by amniocentesis to determine the sex of the fetus, followed by aborting the fetus if it was female. *Nature Magazine* reported that out of 8,000 abortions in the wake of amniocentesis, 7,997 were of females.[81] Hospitals and clinics quickly realized the commercial potential of this technique. Roadside advertisements in Maharashtra told people to pay five-thousand rupees now, save fifty-thousand later in dowry. By 1982 it had become a national issue. Although it was debated in Parliament and all parties protested, the public campaign fizzled after six months. In 1985–1986, however, it was revived in the state of Maharashtra. At this time, small clinics were opening even in rural areas. The profile of women using the technology was also changing:

> The first to be attracted to the technique were communities (like the Marathas, Marwaris and Lewa Patils) in which dowry is rampant and where sex stereotyping is rigid. Today amniocentesis and subsequent abortion of the "wrong sex" has gained the acceptance of upper castes and the white-collared middle-class people, who used to be quite fussy about abortion. According to an experienced doctor, there is a growing enthusiasm for sex-determination tests among these people after one or at the most two daughters, as against the rich middle-class who take many more chances.
>
> Today, if you sit in any local train in Bombay, you will see at least one advertisement for pre-natal sex-determination. Huge display boards and pamphlets and evening paper advertisements confront you, as if telling you that the day of low-key activity and controversy are over. . . .
>
> On analysis of 118 cases from a clinic in Bombay showed that 12% women had one living son and 10% women had not more than one living daughter (i.e. those who have none or just one daughter). Out of the 172 cases studied in another clinic 11.6% of the mothers had one son and 16.2% not more than one daughter. Meanwhile, a leading population expert is also reported to have encountered cases of women aborting their first or second pregnancies of the wrong sex. From this it is clear that amniocentesis is used not only for minimising the number of daughters, but also for increasing the number of sons.[82]

Whereas the earlier campaign had focused on the problem as a women's issue, which, in the words of one activist, was a "fashionable thing to do," the political organizers of the protest decided on the second round to make it an issue for both men and women. It was a human rights issue, a health issue, and an issue for democracy. The government of Maharashtra, after considerable debate and agitation, responded with the world's first law on sex selection: the Maharashtra act no. 15 of 1988. As of 1990, some other states and the national government were contemplating legislation. Activists had a sense of urgency regarding national legislation. If the practice of sex selection became established in the Hindi-speaking heartland of northern India—it already had the lowest sex ratio in all of India due to traditional methods of sex selection—there would be even fewer women than men.

More efficient sex selection is one possible outcome of reaffirming traditional Hindu values, especially in the rural areas. Conflict over dowry is another. Even in parts of south India where dowry had never been practiced, it is starting to occur due to the upward mobility of certain castes (as had happened with the Kallars mentioned above) and their emulation of northern Sanskritic practices. Despite the antidowry campaign of the past decade, dowry has actually spread.[83] Dowry consists of property given by the bride's family, in cash or kind, ostensibly to the bride but (aside from jewelry which the bride keeps) really to the bridegroom's family as a condition for the performance of marriage. It can be used to exploit the bride and her family. Harassment, denial of conjugal rights, and the bride's death (either by murder or suicide) have all been associated with conflicts over dowry. Amendments in 1984 to the Dowry Prohibition Act of 1961 make the "taking, giving or demanding of dowry and the abetment of taking or giving of dowry" a substantive offense punishable by a minimum of six months and up to two years in prison, plus a fine of Rs. 10,000 or the amount of the dowry, whichever is more."[84] Improved legislation may check the practice and abuse of dowry. But even improved legislation may be no match for other pressures encouraging it.

While dowry has been closely tied to Hindu marriage practices in the past—hence the danger of reinforcing it with a renewal of Sanskritization—it is now also associated with the enormous economic changes occurring in modern India. Industrialization has led to a general increase of wealth in society, more consumer goods, and a burgeoning middle class. For a family seeking avenues to economic advance, dowry provides an opportunity for easy wealth—assuming, that is, there are more sons than daughters in the family. "The increase in dowry has to be seen in the context of rising consumerism (commodities and bank loans are advertised openly for dowry, the competition to get men with jobs in the organised sector (a new form of hypergamy), which is also a form by which certain men are accumulating seed capital to set up new businesses or investments. There have been cases of men marrying two or three times each time collecting a dowry and murdering the wife."[85] If trends such as Sanskritization in general and sex selection and dowry abuse in particular are already taking place (and spreading to other religious communities), they may become far more problematic in a conservative Hindu state. Their effect on the lives of women is worthy of consideration.

Suttee

What else could happen if traditional Hindu values are reasserted in a conservative Hindu state? Even suttee (along with other forms of self-willed death for both men and women) may once again come into vogue, perhaps in a more politicized form spearheaded by Hindu women themselves. Students have recently earned esteem and martyr status over the reservation issue when they offered their lives (*ātmadāna*). So have the *kar sewaks* who lost their lives at Ayodhya when they stormed the mosque on the site of the proposed temple to Rāma; urns of their ashes have been paraded through the countryside so that others could be blessed by the sight of auspicious martyrdom for Hindutva. If wives of such martyrs were to die as suttees, their self-sacrifice might be considered a contemporary expression of a medieval Hindu ideal. It is evident, moreover, that many Hindus are so annoyed with the constant polemic against the religion because of suttee—despite its virtual disappearance—that they may be ready for another approach: defiantly reclaiming the ideal on their own terms. What better way, traditional Hindu women may ask, than *to freely choose* martyrdom for Hindutva?

In the past few years, there have been a few efforts to revalorize suttee. One of the main arguments is that suttee has always been a voluntary ideal, not a homicide or a suicide. Another is that female chastity has been the basis for the strong Hindu family over the centuries. This is to be esteemed when compared to the breakdown of the family in the West. Finally, it is argued that if other religions acknowledge suicide, self-willed death, Hindus should not be ashamed if Hindu women voluntarily choose to die for their ideal.

An example of such reasoning is found in the petition of Smt. Girdhar Kanwar, a widowed relative of Roop Kanwar who performed suttee in Deorala, Rajasthan, on September 4, 1987:

It is argued that Roop Kanwar's Sati was absolutely voluntary. Thus to argue that Sati is categorically homicide is an affront to Hinduism. Then, too, in the past the State did not interfere in the religion; rather, the ethical norms were formulated by the religious leaders. In the path to liberation called Bhakti, people had the freedom to choose any symbol for the deity, virtue, and the power of the supernatural. Woman was one such symbol. She was even worshipped in image form in temples.

This worship also had its sociological aspect. The unity of wife and husband was central to marriage. The chastity of women created confidence in men regarding their paternity. On this basis family solidarity was based and gave to Hinduism its firm foundations through the centuries. Indeed, the symbol of living Hinduism was Sati, which literally means the chaste wife. Because of the concept of reincarnation and the idea that the bond of marriage extended to future lives, the idea of the abandonment of the body for reunion was integral to these beliefs.

If other religions have not spoken out explicitly against suicide (e.g. Christian scripture) or have even practised self-willed death as in Jainism, they should not condemn forms of self-willed death in Hinduism. Moreover, since the Suicide Act . . . abrogated the criminality of suicide and many other countries no longer legally view suicide as a crime, Sati should not be viewed as a crime and Sati as the chaste woman should not be replaced by the free-sex and broken families of the developed nations.[86]

Other Hindus have made similar arguments. Bharatiya Janata party leader Mrs. Scindia, for instance, publicly defended suttee as a voluntary act. "Mrs. Scindia said that the Indian Constitution recognised an individual's right to faith and 'Sati' formed a part of the Hindu faith. 'No woman wishing to be a Sati after her departed husband could, therefore, be deprived of her right to that faith,' she asserted."[87] Women's groups were quick to protest. The national conference on women, religion, and family laws, for instance, denounced the justification and glorification of suttee made by Vijaya Raje Scindia, the BJP vice-president at the time, and pointed out that communal groups by praising this practice were really using women for their own political goals.[88]

In January 1990 I discussed the issue of suttee with scholars at the Institute for Oriental Study, Thane (near Bombay), who were re-examining the whole history of suttee. They showed me over forty eyewitness accounts by the British and other non-Hindus of suttee and how all these cases except two were reported as voluntary (contrary to the characterization of suttee in Regulation 17 of 1829, during the British Raj, as culpable homicide). They were also quick to point out that (1) the Bombay high court has ruled in 1986 that Indian citizens possess the constitutional right to commit suicide, and (2) Western countries now seem to be in favor of active euthanasia based on the idea of freedom of choice, therefore, suttee should also be accepted *if it is the woman's own decision.* I pointed out the danger that women could be socialized to accept the idea of suttee, thus preventing it from being really voluntary. It was answered that Westerners could be socialized to want active euthanasia, especially if society is either unwilling or unable to subsidize extensive health care for the growing number of elderly and AIDS patients. I was shown a translation of an article entitled "Samvad" by Dr. Baliram Sadashiv Yerkuntawar.[89] He argues that Congressites, socialists, communists, Gandhians, Muslims, Christians, and now Sikhs have constantly attacked Hindu ideals. The Hindu Code Bill, says Yerkuntawar, was foisted on Hindus with utter disregard to the opposing views of Dr. Rajendra Prasad, Dr. Radhakrishnan, and others. Finally, he claims that the government has been totally contradictory in its treatment of the Muslim woman's bill and the suttee episode of Deorala: on the former they backed down because of Muslim pressure; on the latter they took an aggressive stance *despite Hindu pressure.*

Suttee is thus said to be an issue of freedom of speech. When I asked Hindu scholars sympathetic to the position of Yerkuntawar if their aim was simply to set the historical record straight or if they really thought a return to the practice of suttee should be an ideal for Hindus in 1991, they differed in their response. Some thought rewriting history would be sufficient vindication; others thought it should be a matter for real Hindu women alone to decide. In support, some Hindu women of Thane wrote the following letter to the *Times of India,* in February 1989, to protest feminist reaction to the recurrence of suttee:

[They] should not pose to be holding a brief for all women of India and the approach towards men in this country. The position of women in socialist countries like China, U.S.S.R., Vietnam, Cuba and Eastern Europe, is extremely pitiable and disgraceful. Even the West, which claims to have "liberated" women have fettered women with drug-addiction, alcoholism, and have made them libertine and even lewd. It will be a worthwhile study for [the protestors of suttee] to know how many young girls, possessed with the fever of 'liberation' phenomenon, have fallen victims to smoking, alcoholism and sensualism and have developed a hatred towards males. Such advocates of liberation described above, are free to pursue their own life style but they should not interfere in affairs of those women who want to marry and lead a compatible life with their husbands. Only women who enjoy a life of "conjugal love" alone can understand and appreciate the psyche of "Sati" and not women for whom marriage is a "slavery," and a "burden."[90]

Before leaving the topic of suttee, I must point out that a renewal of suttee, should it occur, may also be influenced by economics and regional politics. Rising expectations for a better life are accompanied by a breakdown of traditional obligations. In the past, widows were perceived as liabilities since their families had to continue supporting them. Today, this is even more true. Instead of renouncing all possessions, comforts, and taking only minimal food, widows now expect equal treatment. And because they are also entitled to some inheritance under modern law, widows may be subject to the avaricious designs of in-laws and encouraged to perform suttee. After the suttee of Roop Kanwar, Madhu Kishwar and Ruth Vanita wrote in *Manushi:* "what was essentially a women's rights struggle has been distorted into an issue of 'tradition' versus 'modernity,' a struggle of the religious majority against an irreligious minority" (1987, 16). On the contrary, argue Kishwar and Vanita, the suttee of Roop Kanwar was a completely modern event; the village where it took place is an advanced and prosperous village with a high literacy rate (70 percent), electricity, televisions, and motorcycles. They observe that it was young, urban, and educated men belonging to the regional elite who politicized the suttee by giving it the flavor of a rally with slogans in order to unite the internally divided Rajput community and capture it as a vote bank.

The political dimension of that suttee incident has also been explored by Lourens P. van den Bosch.[91] He notes that the newer suttee temples are built and supported by rich merchants who seem to be emulating the royal rulers and warriors of former times. Accordingly, the phenomenon is related to upward mobility; in this case, however, the imitation is not of the Brahmins but of Kṣatriyas who competed throughout history with Brahmins for supreme status:

> The ancient hallowed values and institutions which were once especially supported by the royal rulers and the warrior class, are now promoted as well by new economic dominant groups—rich merchants and captains of industries—belonging to the third estate. From this point of view it seems to me that the Marwari Agrawal community originating from Jhunjhunu tries to obtain prestige by constituting itself as a protector of values which were once especially connected with the dominant Rajputs and deeply rooted in traditional folk religion. The relation of their ancestral shrine in Jhunjhunu with the legend about the merchant's wife, Narayani Devi, who immolated herself as a *sati*, may therefore be regarded as a legitimation of their aspirations. The fact that many Rajasthani politicians have visited the Rani Sati temple in the (recent) past to pay tribute to the mighty goddess shows that the shrine was acknowledged by them as an influential sacred centre, which might serve their political interests as well.[92]

If this were the case several years ago, such political suttees could become even more common in the future given the highly politicized religion of Hindutva. On the other hand, it could be argued that even speculation on the possible revival of suttee as undertaken here—when only a few incidents have actually occurred—is but another example of using suttee (along with the other problems connected with traditional *strīdharma* and Sanskritization) to instigate yet more attacks on Hinduism. And it could be argued that this will only destabilize Hindu liberalism and move many progressive Hindus toward the conservatives.

If a conservative Hindu state were to emerge, several other developments may occur. Because the family is the locus classicus of Hindu identity and its key institution, emphasis on the Hindu family would probably be renewed. While some have claimed that the joint family has remained strong, others see changes afoot in the urban areas. In *Women and the Law*, T. N. Srivastava notes: "Whatever may be the reason, the problems related to marriage, separation and divorce are now on the increase."[93] According to one study,[94] the concept of the nuclear family is more popular with female college students than is the traditional extended family, though the latter still shows few signs of decline. According to another study done in the city of Indore (Madhya Pradesh),[95] divorce is becoming more common in the educated and middle classes. When the number of divorces was analyzed by caste, they were most numerous among Brahmins, once the most conservative caste, and especially among Maharashtrian Brahmins. (The latter can be explained by the fact that Maharashtra is one of the most liberal provinces.) The other major change is the breakdown of the arranged marriage system in urban areas:

Less than a decade ago, the middle class contented themselves with soulful, long distance glances. Couples trundling down snowy slopes to Kishor Kumar's music was the stuff dreams were made of. Some of that fantasy has now become flesh. Young people in the cities are dating at every level, especially the middle classes and lower income groups. The virtual apartheid between the two sexes in conservative families has begun to give way. A sexual glasnost in breezing through, sending young clerks, stenographers and receptionists out in pursuit of romance.

But it's romance on the sly. Dating is still taboo for most lower middle class parents, although a few have become more flexible about the time their daughters return home. . . . Many girls are seeking relationships before marriage—preferring to defer marriage . . . why the sudden crush for courtship? The widespread phenomenon of dating in this social strata is a reflection of the changes in urban middle class society. The information explosion—more explicit films and TV programmes, video cassettes which range from powder blue porn to the real stuff, the emergence of kiss-and-tell magazines—is one of the catalysts for this new openness. Helping things along is the telephone, the new instrument of middle class love. But the engine of change is undoubtedly the woman. . . .

There was a time when good girls didn't work. But today, "there is a social sanction for young girls to bring home money." . . . With the leap in the number of working women, the citadels of tradition are crumbling. Economic freedom has brought with it other kinds of freedom—and opportunity. Work-ties lead to love-ties. Work also provides an alibi for being out of the house.

Usually, economic hardship or the inability of parents to arrange marriages, compels girls to date in the hope of finding

husbands. . . . Young girls [are] asking for contraceptive
advice. . . . Young girls are looking for thrills because they are
bored or in search of affection.[96]

There is a danger, of course, that the combination of liberal divorce
laws, women's education, and economic independence may be per-
ceived by conservative Hindus as contributing to the breakup of the
Hindu family. In an earlier call for Hindu state[97] by the conservative
Mahasabha platform, a request was made for repeal of the Hindu
Marriage Act which liberalized divorce.

There has also been a refusal to entertain changes in the law to
give women equal inheritance rights. Hindus often take pride in the
great stability of Hindu families compared to those of the West; they
explain the latter as reflecting the decline of Western civilization.
As a result, they may be tempted to remove liberal divorce laws and
refuse to reform inheritance in view of a similar threat to Indian civilization. And they may try to bolster the Hindu family by emphasizing the traditional duties of a woman (strīdharma) such as
loyalty to the husband, self-sacrifice, and forbearance in the manner
of a Sītā; this would distinguish Hindu ideals of society from what
is viewed as Western decadence. Ironically, it may be rural non-
Brahmins who—through their own interest in Sanskritization and
upward mobility—would impose the old Brahmanical model on urban renegade Brahmins in a conservative Hindu state. Once again
we are reminded of the fact that, in other developing countries,
threats to the family, which appear to undermine the fabric of society, have been heeded by traditionalists, women as well as men.
When decline of family life is accompanied by competition for jobs,
many men want women to leave their jobs and return to the family.
This happened in North America during the great depression and
after World War II. Along with a growth of fundamentalism, it
happened more recently in Egypt. It would not be an implausible
scenario for India as well, with or without a conservative Hindu
state. The secularists in industrial and postindustrial societies have
yet to demonstrate how complete freedom of the individual can be
combined with the continuity of family life generally conceded as
important for the raising of children.

WOMEN AND A LIBERAL HINDU STATE

A third possible outcome of the current political turmoil is a
liberal Hindu state albeit one that recognizes the freedom of other
religions within certain limits. Western scholars have generally not

been willing to entertain any idea of Hindu political action, much less a Hindu state. One of the few exceptions has been Klaus Klostermaier, a prominent scholar of Hinduism who has also had a long relationship with the Christian community in India. While bemoaning the growth of communalism, admiring Hinduism's past history of tolerance, and still hoping for accommodation in the present crisis, he voices sympathy for the Hindu cause in his article "Truth and Toleration in Contemporary Hinduism."[98] He argues that Hinduism has always been viewed as a way of life; more than just myth, ritual, and doctrine, it affects other aspects of existence such as economics, politics, and law. Despite the fact that various Hindu communities have different versions of this way of life, they have managed to live together peacefully and productively over the centuries. Although the various sects and schools of philosophy encouraged tolerance, this did not lead to compromise with truth, the ultimate value and ideal to be lived. Public institutions and personal mores, says Klostermaier, must be shaped by such truth. For Hindus, protection of cows belongs to such a view of truth, unlike the practice of killing and eating cattle by Christians and Muslims; cows deserve protection by public institutions. Because Hinduism has made the major contribution to the "truth" of Indian languages, philosophy, art, literature, music, statecraft, scholarship, and religion, argues Klostermaier, Indian culture is largely Hindu-inspired. If one identifies with the cultural heritage of India, one must accept that this heritage has a Hindu tinge:

> A community has a right to defend its culture, especially if it perceives its central values to be threatened. . . . Hindus and Hinduism cannot be kept out from the major decisions affecting the culture and society of contemporary India. It would be unrealistic to expect the members of the majority religion not to express themselves on matters which they consider of vital interest. . . . To the extent to which a large group of people with a common cause and purpose—be it religious or other—wields a certain amount of political and economical power, "communalism" cannot be eradicated and there is no reason why it should be. Similarly religious revival—in our case *Hindu jagaran*—is, in and by itself, something positive. It becomes a threat to society only if it uses its power to suppress others.[99]

Hindus supporting both India as a secular state and the reform of Hinduism have been sensing a growing crisis of values. In the words of one scholar, there has been a gradual decline in the political ethos of the country from (1) Mahatma Gandhi's goodness politics, Vinoba's saintly politics, and Nehru's pragmatic idealism to (2)Indira Gandhi's ultramachiavellianism, Rajiv Gandhi's amoral politics with its link to business and criminal elements,[100] and V. P. Singh's and Chandra Shekhar's vote-grabbing. While the former group could still relate to Hindu values, such as nonviolence and tolerance, the latter cannot. Machiavellian and amoral politics is increasingly perceived as antithetical to Hinduism, the majority religion of the country. Due to this crisis of values, even liberal Hindus are beginning to entertain the idea of a Hindu state. Their secular critics argue that all religions must be treated equally; to impose one religion on a country is undemocratic. But it has also been argued that every nation needs to have some common bonds, a common purpose, and a shared notion of the common good; otherwise, by definition, there is fragmentation.

Even when the American constitution created a separation between church and state, the Christian majority gave an underlying consensus of values, as did American civil religion. It served to unite the majority of Americans. It was assumed that immigrants would be "Americanized" in some way, though they could still proudly call themselves Italian Americans or Chinese Americans. Even if the old view of assimilation is increasingly challenged, the fact remains that a nation, by definition, must be more than the sum of its different communities. Unification need not be homogeneity. But it must be something that gives meaning, depth, and purpose to the majority of citizens. At the very least, most citizens must see their identity reflected in that of the state and the values it espouses. Otherwise, they will try to change the nature of the state—either democratically or by force. One would expect a liberal Hindu state to continue to associate itself with Hindu reforms for women, because Hindus, both men and women, since the nineteenth century, have been leaders in the reform movement and because Hindu women have been leaders in the women's movement during the fight for independence. If Hindus remain loyal to this tradition (sometimes termed neo-Hinduism), they may keep or improve existing legislation. But it is virtually certain that they will insist on a uniform code bill, since that has been the recent Hindu cause célèbre.

When we think of liberal Hinduism and women, we would do well to pause and remember that even Hindu religious leaders have been spontaneously redressing the position of women in the past century. In the medieval period, a number of women saints, such as Antal and Mirabai, took the extreme step of avoiding or stepping out of marriage, which was the sine qua non of the Hindu woman's life, to pursue a path to liberation. Their act was highly individualistic and did not become institutionalized as an alternative for other women; nor did these saints become gurus or *ācāryas* in the sense of having disciples and founding a system of thought. With the nineteenth-century reform movement, though, this began to change.

Ursula King traces this development with special reference to the Ramakrishna order. She looks specifically at Ramakrishna (the saint), Sarada Devi (his wife) who headed the order after his death, and Vivekananda (his disciple) who encouraged women to become *sannyāsinīs* in order to propagate Hinduism.[101] She also discusses various women such as Sister Nivedita, Gauri Ma, Sudhira Basu, and Sarala Mukhopadhyaya associated with the Ramakrishna order or its later branches. When King broadens her perspective to survey other developments associated with women ascetics in modern Hinduism, she detects several departures from the past. One is women's study of Sanskrit and the Vedas, and the performance of Vedic rituals (formerly forbidden to women) in the Arya Samaj, the Sarada Devi Mission, the Kanya Kumaris Sthan, and Vinoba Bhave's Brahma Vidya Mandir. Another is the symbol of the divine mother, which first served to rally neo-Hindu apologists and nationalists, and then was viewed as actually embodied in women ascetics such as Sarada Devi, Sati Godavari Mataji, Anandamayi Ma, and the Mother of the Aurobindo ashram in Pondicherry. "Particularly intriguing is the new emphasis on women ascetics as the bearers and proclaimers of Hindu spirituality."[102]

Let us take the example of Anandamayi Ma. Anandamayi Ma was one of the most popular religious figures of modern India; in 1987 the government of India even issued a stamp in her honor. Her popularity was established by the hagiographic process (with its claims of divine conception, phenomenal birth, and extraordinary childhood) and by the idea of collective sainthood (the homologization of her life with that of previous luminaries such as Caitanya and Ramakrishna through establishing parallels, or the connection of her life with contemporary gurus such as Paramahamsa Yogananda, and Swami Chidananda). Anandamayi Ma considered herself the incarnation of the Goddess Kālī; others did as well. It is reported that once, during *pūjā*, devotees saw her transformation: her "fair complexion had darkened, her eyes became fixed and enlarged like those of the goddess Kālī in her clay image . . . after some time she was covered with flowers of different colours. The effable beauty and majesty of her countenance filled every heart with awe, wonder and homage."[103] But Anandamayi Ma is also viewed as the embodiment of other Hindu deities such as Viṣṇu or Śiva. Finally, the connection of Anandamayi Ma with other religions such as Islam is established through stories of her visions of the subtle bodies of Arab *fakirs* or her recitation of the *Qur'ān*. For her, God is one, though known by different names. Anandamayi Ma was sympathetic to the poor, for she herself had experienced poverty in her early life, and she periodically stepped out of caste exclusivism and Brahmanical orthodoxy to affirm the universalism of religion through blessing people of all castes and eating with outcastes. That this saint was viewed as the embodiment of *strīdharma* (the norms of womanhood) and remained within the sacred institution of marriage, thereby upholding Hindu tradition, also contributed to her popularity among orthodox Hindus:

> Although a wife, she herself was without child and like the Goddess, or should we say "as the goddess (who is virtually never associated with children) she, Anandamayi Ma, was the Mother of all. It may be said that just as incarnations (*avatāras*) of old came when *adharma* (injustice) threatened the values of society, so Anandamayi Ma appeared on the historical stage at a critical moment for feminine justice. . . .
> That Hindu men had been blamed for the plight of the 19th century Hindu woman created the polarization of their maleness and "Hinduness," and they, too, were ready to see the Hindu ideal reasserted beyond the opposition of male and female orientations. The *modus vivendi* for this spiritual step was to view woman as incarnation of the Great Deity, who was none other than Hindu woman as ideal wife.[104]

There were other innovations by Anandamayi Ma. She established ashrams and played the traditionally unprecedented role of guru, although she preserved a semblance of orthodoxy by refusing to initiate disciples herself. Finally, her popularity was sealed through her connection to the Nehru family; Kamala Nehru frequently visited her; this, in turn, led to a connection of Anandamayi Ma with Prime Minister Nehru and Mahatma Gandhi, though the men did not become disciples. Indira Gandhi (daughter of Kamala and Jawarhalal Nehru) often visited Anandamayi Ma after her mother's death, though she never formally became a disciple, perhaps because she was more secular than her mother or perhaps because she felt she could not take this step as prime minister. In any case, that the seat of temporal power represented by the women of the Nehru family was connected to this woman saint enhanced immeasurably Anandamayi Ma's reputation just as traditional saints in previous centuries enhanced their's through some connection to a king. "We suspect that Anandamayi Ma knew full well that her spiritual message was in tune with the grand project of national integration led by her political friends. Her role was to make sure that Hinduism maintained its elasticity for its role as good citizen in a modern nation state. Over the years she acted as the ambassador of Hinduism. After independence she was received by many state governments or officials. . . . She always spoke for Hinduism but never at the expense of any other religion or the secular state."[105]

Yet another development is the fact that major Hindu teachers have passed their spiritual mantle on to women. According to Linda Johnsen, the new wave today is women, for major Indian gurus have passed on their spiritual mantle to women:

Ramakrishna passed his to his wife, Sarada Devi; Paramahansa Yogananda to the American-born Daya Mata; Sivananda to the Canadian Sivananda Radha; Upasani Baba to Godavari Mataaji; Swami Paramananda to his niece, Gayatri Devi; Swami Lakshmana (Raman Maharshi's premier disciple) to the rebellious young Mathru Sri Sarada; Dhyanyogi Madhusudandas to Asha Ma; and Siddha Yoga master Swami Muktananda to Gurumayi Chidvilasananda. This is a dramatic shift. . . . In the past century, some of India's foremost spiritual giants have acted to redress the gender imbalance in their tradition, even when it has meant coaxing reluctant female disciples into the limelight.[106]

There are also cases where orthodox Hindu leaders have initiated women as ascetics and spiritual teachers: the Sankaracarya of Kanchipuram, for example, initiated the woman Jnanananda as *sannyāsinī* and guru.[107] Despite the fact that this initially shocked many Hindus, an important precedent was set. Another significant departure from the past is the fact that some women spiritual figures are now initiating disciples on their own. This new wave may grow stronger in the future. The key to religious expertise has traditionally resided in knowledge of Sanskrit, the language of the religious texts. While this was once a Brahmin, male expertise, it has been extended to anyone interested, with the development of Sanskrit departments in universities. Today university study of Sanskrit is almost always undertaken by women (since its prestige has fallen and male students head for status and money-making professions such as engineering, business management, and science). In fact, it is now jokingly called an *apauruṣeya* subject, which puns on the double meaning of the term as both "nonhuman" and "not male." (Apauruṣeya once was a descriptor of revelation in the sense of being "nonhuman;" now it is a descriptor of the fact that men are no longer involved in the transmission of Sanskrit learning.) When the current generation of Sanskrit male priests and ritual experts dies, the next generation may have to be women if they alone possess the expertise.

CONCLUSION

The nineteenth and twentieth centuries have seen major changes for Hindu women in the family, the work place, and the public religious domain. More and more families have their Draupadīs (minus four of the five husbands, of course). And more and more religious orders have their women gurus and disciples. If a Hindu state were to come into being, many precedents for a liberal approach to women's issues can be found. It is true that much still remains to be done before the life of the ordinary Indian woman is influenced by the new laws and opportunities. But it is also true that Hinduism has had its reformers—both men and women, both religious leaders and ordinary people—who have taken bold steps toward change. When this record is completely ignored, Hinduism is stereotyped by socialists, Marxists, Muslims, Christians, and feminists (not to mention by Westerners generally from the British Raj to contemporary North American journalists) as the tradition of suttee, female seclusion, and dowry-deaths.

Naturally, Hindus think the stereotypes are unjust. In fact, such accusations are already alienating many liberal Hindus from the idea of a "reformed" secular state. They may well join those working toward a Hindu state. To bring it about, though, they would have to join with those of a more traditional ilk.

The agitation to rebuild the temple to Lord Rāma in Ayodhya continues. On December 6th, 1992, the Babri Masjid (mosque) was stormed by two hundred thousand Hindus and totally destroyed in six hours by picks and shovels while thirteen thousand government paramilitary troops looked on. A temporary shrine to Rāma was installed at the site. In the aftermath of this event, there were riots between Hindus and Muslims throughout India with almost two thousand killed (one hundred and eighty in Bombay alone) and thousands injured. (Even in foreign countries temples and mosques were destroyed by Muslims and Hindus respectively.) Prime Minister P. V. Narasimha Rao expressed disappointment at the razing of the mosque and ordered the arrest of BJP and VHP leaders. After a court order, the worship of Hindu images at the makeshift temple was allowed. In the wake of the destruction of the mosque, letters to the editor filled Indian newspapers. Some argued for separation of politics and religion; others for rebuilding the mosque; and still others for building a temple to Rāma. In the meantime the government said it would build both a temple and a mosque side by side. And it survived a no-confidence motion by the BJP.

For Uma Bharati—the BJP member of Parliament who once stood in the tradition of Hindu liberalism but who has become increasingly conservative—rebuilding the temple at Ayodhya represents Hindu pride: before the mosque was razed she said, "The masjid should be moved with all due respect and the temple built on the site, the way Sardar Patel renovated the Somnath Temple. No patriotic person, no Hindu, will stand for less, or be pacified with a memorial or a garden in that spot."[108] After it was razed, she was jubilant. Ayodhya also represents the call for a Hindu state. The issue becomes what *kind* of a Hindu state may ultimately emerge.

Whatever scenario—continual communal strife, a reformed secularism, a conservative Hindu state, or a liberal Hindu state—may be played out in the future and whoever is on center stage (Draupadī, Sītā, or a divine mother in human form) the issue of women is sure to be part of the Indian dharma. This discussion shows that the position of women in modern India has been closely related to economic forces—availability of jobs, desire for dowry as a way to augment a family's financial resources, the related phenomenon of sex selection through abortion of female fetuses after amniocentesis or female infanticide, and seclusion related to upward mobility as a corollary of the green and industrial revolutions. The position of women has also been related to political forces. We noted how the non-Brahmin movement took up the cause of women, in part as a way to settle old scores with Brahmin men. We saw how Marxists and socialists after independence saw the treatment of women as the Achilles' heel of religion and consequently attacked religion in the name of progress. And we observed how the issue of women has figured prominently in the communal tensions between Hindus and Muslims.

Despite the economic and political vicissitudes, there has been considerable expression of solidarity among women. British women rallied to the cause of Indian women despite the opposition of British men. Muslim, Christian, Hindu, socialist, and Marxist women have had strong alliances on many issues, though this seems to break down when women of a religious group think that the group's religious identity is being fundamentally challenged. Indian history in the last century has shown that women have rarely been the pawns of men, but have taken the initiative on women's issues and have organized themselves. Most of the time this has not involved direct confrontation with men. Rather, both traditional and nontraditional men have been directly involved in reform movements. Certainly, criticism by political opponents on the issue of women was an important part of the dynamic for men's participation in reforms. But it is also evident that a sense of justice and idealism inspired many men who supported the women's movement after the "consciousness raising" about women's problems in traditional society.

The recent growth of fundamentalism and communalism on the part of various religious groups in India, however, means that the advances of the last century for women may be endangered. Chhachhi draws our attention to the fact that modern development schemes that are responding to a new awareness of women's rights and entry into the labor force have weakened traditional controls over women, especially in the family. The breakdown of the patriarchal order is often perceived by men as threatening. When this is combined with an economic crisis and loss of jobs, men turn to fundamentalism as a way to legitimate traditional controls over women and to secure inheritance rights, land, and jobs for themselves. Sometimes it is the men in the family who enforce these rules, and sometimes it is the village elders who monitor women's labor, keeping them out of paid jobs, away from travel related to employment, and returning them to seclusion in the domestic sphere or to low-paid jobs that men do not want.

Chhachhi also suggests that men are reacting to pressure from the women's movement. As women's awareness of abuses such as dowry murders, rape, and abortion of female fetuses after amniocentesis increases, they are speaking out and agitating. Fundamentalism as a call to return to traditional religious values could be a way of reinstituting patriarchal control over the household. Men also turn to communalism, says Chhachhi, as way to gain a competitive economic edge with other religious groups. She notes that communal groups have paramilitary organizations that are male-dominated, if not exclusively male. They provide a way for young middle-class men to have a sense of manliness. The Hindu organizations, for instance, were first developed during the colonial period to counteract the emasculation of Hindu men by the British. The antidote for this emasculation was hypermasculinity. One of the easiest ways to express this hypermasculinity was to subject women to men's control. That women developed new strengths in the fight for independence also inspired a hypermasculinity in men as antidote.[109] Hypermasculinity may be increasing today as a response to current economic and political crises.

Because the British represented a common enemy for Indians, men and women alike, during the fight for independence, Indians were united to fight for a common goal (except for those Muslims who envisioned a separate state). After independence, however, the opposition between men's interests and women's interests has slowly grown. Unless the idealism of lokasaṅgraha can continue to inspire and unite both men and women of various religious groups for a cause beyond immediate self-gain, it is likely that polarization between religious groups and between men and women will become an increasingly common feature of Indian society. It is possible, for instance, that the debate over the reservation policy may change the inter-caste of lower-caste "uplift" character of the contemporary women's movement (as illustrated by Mhapasekara and Kishwar's work). Men and women may begin to see the debate around reservations quite differently. It is conceivable that a high-caste woman, for example, may not oppose reservations for backward castes, while her husband would. Or possibly the idea of reservations for Backward castes is one of those "progressive" ideas that ultimately would have negative effects on Backward-caste women as it is presumably mostly men who would get the positions (as happened in economic development projects). While backward-caste men would gain higher status, security, and wealth, their women would not, and the gap would widen between the perspectives of men and women.[110]

The American author Richard Neuhaus, in his book The Naked Public Square,[111] has argued that an attempt to prevent religious conflict by a strict separation of church and state can lead to a vacuum at the center of national life which may be taken over by the worldview of secularism that is indifferent if not hostile to religion. This, in turn, provokes fundamentalists into bringing religion back into the public square and restoring some sense of identity to the majority who still consider themselves religious. In the process, however, the liberal nature of majority religion has been destroyed and along with it the willingness to reform traditions and to protect minorities. It is striking that Klostermaier has alluded to such a scenario in India. He, too, observes that when religion is denied its role of shaping public life, it may become fanatic, fundamental, and communal. "Religions cannot abdicate their interest in the life of individuals and communities, they cannot be kept out from the marketplace, where not only economic decisions are made but where also policies affecting the conscience are debated and shaped."[112] The liberal spirit of many Hindus on various issues—including those related to women—is still alive and well despite the battle lines being drawn. The major questions are whether these Hindus can sustain the liberal banner in an age of increasing polarization and what will be the political outcome when society becomes polarized. A reformed secularism or a liberal Hindu state may be difficult to attain given the economic and political forces afoot that threaten the gains by and for women over the past century.

Nancy J. Barnes

WOMEN IN BUDDHISM

In the last hundred years, the peoples of Buddhist Asia have suffered a wrenching confrontation with Western civilization—its ideas, its institutions, its technologies, and its invading presence. In many countries local political authorities were ousted and replaced by representatives of European colonial powers, social and economic structures were undermined and thrown into chaos, and traditional religious institutions were insolently challenged by the militant missionaries of Christ. Prolonged struggles for national independence, wars, and Marxist revolutions have brought an end to direct Western control in Asia in our century, but the impact of Western ideas and of Western-inspired modernization continues to be a central fact in the lives of today's Asian Buddhists. Not for a thousand years, since Islam swept across Asia from Iran to Indonesia, has Buddhism suffered such a massive dislocation. In those days, where Islam penetrated, Buddhism soon perished.

In modern Buddhist Asia there have also been casualties in the contest with Western ideas. Cambodia and Tibet have suffered most catastrophically: there Buddhist clerics have been massacred and Buddhist institutions decimated by Asian revolutionaries inspired by the thought of Marx, Lenin, and Mao Zedong. Confrontation with Western ideas has not always ended in disaster for Asian Buddhists, however. The confrontation has acted as a catalyst too, which has pushed Buddhists to reexamine and reinterpret their own traditions, and to mount creative responses to the West and to Christianity.

Those responses have been diverse. Interest in the study of Buddhist scriptures and Buddhist history has been revitalized among clerics and laity alike. In tandem with the rediscovery of their own traditions, some countries have experienced vigorous revivals of Buddhism, which have brilliantly incorporated Christian methods of organizing and proselytizing. New Buddhist lay movements, and new concepts of leadership in Buddhist communities, have emerged all over Asia. Brand-new Buddhist sects have sprung up like mushrooms in many countries. Out of a growing awareness of the need to take responsibility for solving social problems, Buddhist groups have been formed specifically to address social needs. And in many of the great struggles for independence from colonial rule, which flared up all over Asia in our century, Buddhism became a rallying point and a symbol of national identity.

Now, since the end of World War II, Buddhists who were once bombarded with the propaganda of Western superiority have turned the tables on the West. With delicious irony, the revitalized Buddhism of Asia has come West and established itself in Europe and America with resounding success. All major sects of Buddhism are now represented in the West, and leaders from nearly every Buddhist country have journeyed westward to teach, attracting substantial followings. Moreover, Buddhism has regained a modest foothold in a few Asian countries where it had once flourished but had long since disappeared—in Indonesia, in Malaysia, and, most notably, in India, the land of its birth.

Buddhism is changing. It is now a truly international religion, whose members from all over the world communicate frequently and influence each other. The most significant changes have undoubtedly occurred in the composition of the leadership of the religion. In former times, monks dominated everywhere. But in the twentieth century, many laymen and laywomen have led reform movements in Asia and have become religious teachers there and in the West. Buddhist women, in particular, have finally found their voice and have stepped into the limelight as spiritual leaders, teachers, scholars, organizers, and shapers of a new Buddhism for the modern world.

RESTORATION OF THE NUNS' ORDER IN BUDDHIST ASIA

One of the most important issues modern Buddhist women have raised is the matter of the restoration of the nuns' order (*bhikṣuṇī saṃgha*, order of female mendicants)[1] in countries where it no longer exists, and its introduction where it never did find a home in the past. According to Buddhist scriptures, the *bhikṣuṇī samgha* was founded, along with the *bhikṣu samgha* (order of male mendicants or monks), by Gautama the Buddha early in his career as a religious teacher.[2] Nuns and monks lived as wandering renunciants seeking enlightenment and liberation (nirvana) from pain-bringing attachment to worldly life. Meditation and moral discipline was their path to liberation. Monks, and sometimes nuns, preached the Buddha's doctrines (dharma) to lay devotees, and were in turn supported by their donations of food, clothing, and other necessities. Buddhist monastic life was meant to be totally devoted to the spiritual goal of liberation. And so it was, in the Buddha's day.

The nun's order flourished in India for some centuries and then declined in numbers and activity. Meanwhile, the order had been established in Sri Lanka by Indian nuns around 250 B.C.E., and traveling Sinhalese nuns carried it on to China in 433 or 434 C.E., and later to Burma.[3] From China the transmission of the order continued to Korea, Japan, and Vietnam.[4]

Eventually the order disappeared completely, not only from India but from Sri Lanka and Burma as well. It has, however, continued to thrive in China, and also in Korea, Japan, and Vietnam to the present day. In China proper, the Communist government of the People's Republic of China holds Buddhism and other religions under tight restraint. Yet several thousand nuns and monks remain active there, and there have been a number of ordinations of new clerics during the past decade.[5] In Taiwan the nuns' order flourishes. Thus it is in China, and in the Chinese-influenced countries of the Far East, that the order of fully ordained nuns has remained intact, from the time of its establishment there in the fifth century to the present.

The order of fully ordained nuns never did spread to other Buddhist countries in Asia, however; it has never existed in Thailand, Cambodia, or Laos, or in Tibet or the Himalayan kingdoms of Nepal, Bhutan, and Sikkim, whose Buddhism was received from Tibet. But in those countries, and in modern Sri Lanka and Burma, there are women who have shaved their heads as nuns do and live as renunciants after having accepted the eight or ten basic precepts of the Buddhist devotee.[6] These women are called *dasasilmattawa* in Sri Lanka, *mae chi* in Thailand, and *thila shin* in Burma. Full ordination is not available to them and they are regarded merely as pious laywomen. Their social status has been low and their positions in society ambiguous. However, many devote their time to meditation for the sake of spiritual development. In this they contrast sharply with monks in modern Theravada countries, whose time is spent studying Buddhist scriptures or performing rituals for their lay followers.[7]

Most Thai *mae chi* donned their white robes when they were already elderly, and poor. Because they have no religious status according to Buddhist canon law, lay persons can gain no spiritual merit by giving them alms, as they do when they give to monks. So the *mae chi* remain ill-supported. Until recently little was done for them, and they lacked access to the social and economic benefits stemming from membership in a venerated religious order.[8]

Burmese *thila shin* have had a more auspicious history than the Thai *mae chi*, though their social position is also ambiguous. Attitudes toward them vary. Many of them are highly esteemed, particularly the eminent teachers and meditators among them, but they seem never to be afforded respect equal to that given the monks. They are adequately supported by their families and by lay donors, and can participate in religious ceremonies for which they earn fees. They are also encouraged to study Buddhist scriptures.[9] Thus, their situation is much better than that of the *mae chi*, but certainly inferior to that of the monks in their own country.

Women ordained in the Tibetan monastic orders, *ani*, have the rank of novice rather than fully ordained *bhikṣunī*. There have never been many of these *ani* compared with the very large numbers of monks, in Tibet itself before 1959 and now among Tibetan communities in India, Nepal, Bhutan, and Sikkim. In Tibet the *ani* could choose a life-style she found compatible, since rules for living the religious life were very flexible. Some *ani* lived in nunneries, some wandered about, others dwelt as hermits meditating in remote huts or caves.[10] Their lives were hard, they never had a status comparable to the monks', but many lived full and free religious lives, and still do in their new homes in India and Nepal. The pattern of their lives is very different from that of the Theravada renunciant women.

To establish or reestablish the nuns' order where it does not exist, it would be necessary to institute a valid ordination procedure. That could be done only by permitting nuns from China, whose ordination lineage is intact, to carry out the ordination. That is a problem, for Chinese Buddhists belong to the Mahayana division of Buddhism, which relies on scriptures different from those used by Theravada Buddhists, the dominant school in south and southeast Asia.[11] As Buddhist scholars know, although there are doctrinal differences between Mahayana and Theravada Buddhism, the rules for monastic life and for ritual procedures observed in the two traditions are virtually the same. Mahayana Buddhists have always used the old codes of monastic precepts called Vinaya,[12] formulated very early in Buddhist history by Theravada monastics and those of related pre-Mahayana schools. Mahayana Buddhists never composed Vinaya of their own. The Vinaya actually used in China belongs to an old Buddhist school closely related to the Theravada.[13] Thus, theoretically, it should be a simple matter to reinstate the nuns' ordination procedures in the Theravada lands of south and southeast Asia. However, the order of nuns could not prosper there unless it was generally accepted by the Theravada Buddhists of those countries, and very few of the monks, not to mention the laity and the poorly educated eight- or ten-precept quasi nuns themselves, understand that Mahayana and Theravada Buddhists share the same code of monastic discipline. On the contrary, most ordinary Theravada Buddhists believe that Mahayana Buddhists have completely corrupted the true tradition taught by Gautama the Buddha.[14]

Tibetan Buddhists are Mahayanists, although their practices differ from those of the Chinese. Tibetan religious leaders have had some doubts about whether the ordination lineage has actually remained unbroken in China since the fifth century.[15] But there are far fewer obstacles to the establishment of a true nuns' ordination for women of the Tibetan tradition than for those of the Theravada.

Ordination for the Buddhist nun or monk is a two-step process.[16] First comes the ceremony of "going forth" from lay life (pravrajyā). Children of eight years or older can "go forth" with the permission of their parents, but according to the Vinaya it is preferred that a prospective nun be twenty years old before taking this step.[17] The novice's head is shaved and she or he dons the yellow clerical robe. The novice who has gone forth acquires two teachers who teach him or her the vows to be taken (ten for the male novice, six for the female)[18] and give further instruction during the period of the novitiate. If a female novice is under twenty years of age, or is a woman who has been married longer than twelve years before choosing the life of a renunciant, she must undergo a two-year probationary period before she can take the higher ordination. No such specific restriction is placed on prospective monks. But neither women nor men can receive ordination as full-fledged nuns or monks before reaching the age of twenty.

The higher ordination is called upasaṃpadā. The novice, supplied with begging bowl and the fivefold nun's robes (the monk wears only three robes), goes with her two nun-instructors to present herself before the chapter of nuns. There must be at least ten nuns in attendance. Immediately afterward she must also present herself with her instructors before the chapter of ten or more monks. Nuns are required to receive *upasaṃpadā* from the twofold assembly of nuns and monks; monks are ordained only by other monks.[19] A series of questions is put to the nun about her fitness for ordination, and if she is judged acceptable the assembled chapters then confer ordination upon her.

It is already evident from this account that more restrictions are placed on women than on men in the Buddhist monastic order. In all, a monk is required to conduct himself in accordance with about two-hundred-twenty rules, which govern his ordinary comings and goings, but a nun is obliged to observe in principle "five-hundred rules." Although in actual fact the extant Vinaya of six ancient Buddhist schools list between two-hundred-ninety and three-hundred-eighty rules for nuns and not five-hundred, nuns' lives are definitely more closely regulated than those of monks. The harshest regulations imposed on the female members of the order are the "eight chief rules" (*garudhammā*), which require each nun to treat every monk as her senior and superior; that she go regularly to the community of monks to seek instruction but never instruct or admonish any monk herself; and that all the sisters' formal ceremonies be carried out in the presence of monks as well as nuns, including the setting of penances for erring nuns.[20]

From the earliest days of Buddhism, the nuns' order was subordinated to the monks', and the lion's share of patronage went to the monks in all Buddhist lands. Under such circumstances the nuns' order never grew as strong as the monks', and when hard times came it was the first to suffer.[21] The nuns' order disappeared from India sometime after the ninth century, from Sri Lanka in the tenth, and from Burma in the thirteenth, and apparently no effort was made to revive it. The monks' order also came perilously near extinction in Sri Lanka in the eleventh century, but the king had monks sent from Burma to keep the ordination lineage alive. Clearly the fate of the monks' order was deemed more important than that of the nuns'.[22] Monks have always held the positions of authority in institutionalized Buddhism, and they continue to dominate today. That is a major factor to be dealt with when considering the question of reestablishment of the nuns' order in all Buddhist lands.

Opposition by the Theravada monks of Sri Lanka, Thailand, and Burma to the reestablishment of the order of fully ordained nuns in their countries has sometimes been quite virulent. At the present time, many members of the Theravada hierarchy recognize that the issue needs to be faced and discussed, but the feelings of great numbers of ordinary monks are easily inflamed by any hint that the status quo may be altered.[23] A recent international conference on Buddhist nuns held in India (1987) provoked charges that the issue of the nuns' order is being inflated by strident feminists inspired by Western ideas.[24]

Conservative monks are not the only ones to oppose the reinstatement of the nuns' order, however. Many of the eight- or ten-precept women in the Theravada countries feel no need to become fully ordained *bhikṣuṇī*. Some are simply ignorant of the possibility; others weigh the advantages of their present freedom of action against the structured control by monks they would have to endure if they became fully ordained nuns.

Sri Lanka has experienced a major revival of traditional Buddhism during the last century, and the rise of the *dasasilmattawa*, or ten-precept women, to a new level of dignity is a part of that revival.[25] There are now about twenty-five hundred of these women, most living in groups in *ārāmayas* (monastic residences) established for them by lay supporters. They live disciplined lives, many have received a good education, and some preach in public to the laity or lead them in meditation retreats. The laity is well aware of their presence and generally respect the *dasasilmattawa* as persons genuinely dedicated to spiritual goals—in contrast to the monks who are regarded as far more worldly and self-interested. The prestige of the *dasasilmattawa* is growing rapidly.[26]

Because the *dasasilmattawa* are not fully ordained nuns, they are not subject to the rules which govern nuns in the old Vinaya books. They are in fact independent of the monks' order: because of their ambiguous position with respect to the *saṃgha*, they cannot be controlled and directed by the monks. Many *dasasilmattawa* consider themselves morally purer than the monks, and hardly wish to subject themselves to the monks' authority, as the Vinaya says they would have to do if they had the status of fully ordained *bhikṣuṇī*. There is real resistance from many *dasasilmattawa*, therefore, to reinstating the nuns' order.[27]

That their concerns are realistic can be seen from the cautionary example of the experiences of a contemporary order of fully ordained nuns in Japan. Nuns belonging to the Soto Zen sect of Buddhism engaged in a gruelling seventy-year struggle with the Soto hierarchy for the right to practice their religion as fully as the monks do, and to control their own institutions. It appears that even the limited rights accorded nuns by the Vinaya books were undercut by the Soto hierarchy. Before 1900, Soto nuns were uneducated, were permitted to live only in remote hermitages, could not participate in the Buddhist rituals for the laity, which were a major source of income for the order, and had no hope of attaining higher ranks within the monastic community. A few nuns set out to change their situation by working first to establish schools to educate themselves and their sisters. Then, in the 1920s nuns organized themselves and began to petition for such rights as initiating and training nun pupils, the opportunity for advanced study of Soto doctrine, the right to have convents in which to meditate, and the right to hold priestly offices in the chief Soto monastery-temples. The monks' resistance was bitter. It was not until 1970 that nuns finally achieved all their demands for dignity and responsibility equal to the monks', by having reforms made in the sect's constitution.[28]

The power relationship between nuns and monks within the order can obviously be problematic, and many Buddhist women would prefer to avoid it altogether. The idea that nuns must accept a position of permanent subjugation to monks is repellent to many Western women who are converts to Buddhism. Nonetheless there are a great many Buddhist women, Asian and Western, who want to see the *bhikṣuṇī saṃgha* reestablished worldwide, and who are working very determinedly to realize their goal.

Some Thai *mae chi* and Burmese *thila shin* favor full ordination for women, as do some Sri Lanka *dasasilmattawa*. But the main impetus behind the effort to restore the nuns' order undoubtedly comes from educated Asian women (and some men) who are well acquainted with Western culture and are familiar with modern Western ideas on the equality of women. Joining them are many Western women who have received the lower ordination into the Theravada or one of the Tibetan Buddhist sects and aspire to full ordination.

Many of the arguments made on behalf of reestablishment of the *bhikṣuṇī saṃgha* reflect Western modes of evaluating the problem.[29] Proponents see the absence of the nuns' order as a denial of a legitimate religious aspiration of Buddhist women. They argue that it must be revived so that women who are deeply drawn to the religious vocation and are devoted to Buddhism can live lives that are as wholly Buddhist as monks' lives are. Since their spiritual capacities are not inferior to men's, women should have opportunities that are equal to mens'; that is why, after all, the *bhikṣuṇī saṃgha* was originally instituted by the Buddha. That nuns in a restored bhikṣuṇī saṃgha could not have equality with monks is less important to these people than the reestablishment of an institution that would restore to all female renunciants the dignity and legitimacy that are their due. Stability and security would be regained as well, for bhikṣuṇī would also have surer access to reliable economic support from the Buddhist saṃgha, and from the laity who would perceive their gifts of alms to the bhikṣuṇī as acts that would earn them merit.

The agitation to restore the nuns' order itself provides an important focus for Buddhist women's desires to help mold contemporary Buddhism and shape its course for the future. It is an opportunity for Buddhist women to lead, an opportunity rare for women in the history of the religion. Many Asian and Western Buddhist women are more than eager to take up the challenge.

Many very prominent monk-leaders have already become convinced by the arguments of proponents of bhikṣuṇī saṃgha restoration, and by their own views of the possibilities for Buddhism in the modern world. The Dalai Lama has enunciated his support clearly, has encouraged women of the Tibetan lineages in their aspiration to full ordination, and has personally ordained several novice nuns. Other Tibetan leaders have done the same.[30] A number of Theravada monks who teach regularly in the West also support full ordination for women and have participated in ordination ceremonies in the United States.[31] It is the rank and file monks of Asia who are not yet convinced.

In all Theravada countries the reestablishment of the nuns' order remains a sensitive issue. The Westerners and westernized Asians who have agitated for it most vocally recognize that it must be handled with discretion. There are, after all, some fifty thousand Asian Buddhist nuns, and only about three hundred from the west.[32] The number of Asian Buddhist monks is far greater, and the total of those who now favor restoring the nuns' order is only a small fraction of it. It is the acceptance by the monastic orders of all Asia that must be won, and that of the lay population as well. Progress has been made. But the restoration of the bhikṣuṇī saṃgha to all Asian lands will undoubtedly require much time and much patience to accomplish.

LAY WOMEN: NEW PATTERNS FOR SPIRITUAL LIFE

When he established the saṃgha of monks (bhikṣu) and nuns bhikṣuṇī), the Buddha also established a saṃgha of laywomen (upāsikā) and laymen (upāsaka) who followed his teachings. Those layfolk who were most devoted to the teachings and most eager to follow the holy path while remaining in the midst of worldly life could undertake to observe five or even eight or ten of the basic rules for self-restraint found in the Buddhist scriptures.[33] They could observe these rules permanently, or for a limited period of time—a day, a week, a month. Lay people still do this, throughout the Buddhist world.

Lay people could demonstrate their dedication to the Buddha's teachings by observing the precepts, but in ancient times they had no thought of striving for nirvana in this life.[34] It was the monks and nuns who cherished that aspiration, and for its sake went forth from worldly life into the forest to meditate and discipline them-selves, and open their minds to a higher understanding. Upāsikā and upāsaka remained at home, and sought to acquire merit for themselves so that in a future existence they too could hope for nirvana. Merit is achieved through virtuous actions, especially by giving gifts of food, clothing, and other requisites to monks and nuns. The lay faithful have always been indispensable to the mo-nastics, for they are the source of their livelihood. Women have probably always made up the majority of the Buddhist laity in most countries, as they have for example in modern Korea and in China before 1949.[35]

In the past, lay Buddhists have readily left leadership of the whole saṃgha to the monks, even the many royal ladies and kings who lavishly patronized the religion. But things have changed in modern Buddhism: now it is often laywomen and men who take the lead and bring about the most far-reaching changes. They led the twentieth-century revivals of Buddhism in China and Sri Lanka, with the cooperation of reformist clergy; and they have developed new forms of Buddhist practice and new sects all over Buddhist Asia, especially in Japan and Korea. Laywomen and men also make up the vast majority of Buddhist practitioners in Europe and Amer-ica, and in those new centers of Buddhist activity a lay teacher is as likely to be the head of a Buddhist community as a monk.

One of the most fascinating phenomena in twentieth-century Buddhism is the astonishing emergence of a host of entirely new sects in Japan—the so-called "new religions." "New religions" be-gan to appear in Japan in the early 1800s and continued to prolifer-ate throughout the period of rapid modernization and adaptation of Western ideas in the late nineteenth and twentieth centuries. Espe-cially since the end of World War II the new religions have played a major role in Japanese society, and the membership of all the new religions now numbers several million.[36] Some are Buddhist in orientation, others Shinto. But they are "new" religions because they arose outside mainstream Buddhist and Shinto traditions. They interpret elements from Japanese religious tradition in new ways, and even combine inspirations drawn from Buddhism, Shinto, Confucianism, and Christianity. Most appeared suddenly, due to the revelatory experiences of a prophetic founder. These founders were often women.[37] Similar new lay Buddhist religions have appeared in Korea as well in this century, and women are also prominent in them.[38]

There is a tradition of female mediums and shamanistic diviners in Japan and Korea, which extends back long before the introduction of Buddhism to those countries, back even before the beginning of historical records. A female shaman would enter ecstatic trance and become possessed by a spirit or deity. She then became the oracle of the possessing spirit, who spoke through her mouth.[39] Many founders of new religions in Japan seem to have had experiences similar to the ancient shamans', and presented themselves to the world subsequently as prophets of their possessing deities.

In Japan there is also a (nearly) unique tradition of a lay clergy. Since at least the thirteenth century, when Shinran introduced the custom into his Jōdō Shin (True Pure Land) school, there have been married priests. The preference for a married priesthood eventually spread to other Japanese Buddhist sects.[40] Priests are ordained, but they do not withdraw from ordinary worldly life as monks and nuns do. They embrace it. The distinction between priestly and lay roles is thus blurred. In Japan, therefore, placing the leadership of a Buddhist sect in the hands of a layman is hardly a new phenomenon. But the exercising of such authority by laywomen is.

Women have founded several of the new religions of Japan, or have been the co-founders who have taken their partners' message into the world and built the new movement into a major religion with a huge following. After the founders' deaths, other women have then continued as the active ministers, counselors, and healers in the various religions; these women are the heart and the strong right arm of the new religions. But it is men who are the titular heads of most of the sects and who hold the highest positions. Moreover, after a female co-founder's death, her importance in the movement is often played down and that of her male associate is embellished. Thus a "history" of the religion is created that accords with its conservative values, which insist on male dominance in the religion, the family, and society.[41]

Though the new religions have no traditional priesthood, they do have leaders organized in hierarchical ranks. The important new Buddhist sect, Reiyūkai, for example, is composed of several branches, each with its leader, and the branches are made up of smaller groups with their own leaders. At the top of the pyramid is the current president of Reiyūkai, the son of the founder. Fifty-five percent of all branch leaders are men and forty-five percent women, but that ratio shifts completely in the lower leadership ranks: sixty-one percent of the lowest-ranking leaders, the group (*hōza*) leaders, are women. In family-centered Reiyūkai, as in other new religions, however, married couples often share leadership positions; and in many of these cases it is the wife who actively functions as leader although it is her husband who is nominally the head.[42] Branch and group leaders earn their ranks by proselytizing new members, and women appear to be far more active as proselytizers than men are. Leaders offer counseling to members, teaching them in a highly authoritarian manner how to deal with their problems, and women are sought out as counselors far more often than men are.[43] The counseling or "healing" of members' personal problems is the very foundation of Reiyūaki and other new religions, in fact, for it is this that draws new members tightly into the sect and wins their whole-hearted commitment. These women leaders are believed to possess great spiritual power; they can discern a person's true nature deep within, and so they are regarded as living Buddhas.[44] Men, on the other hand, are merely able administrators.

Why are women so prominent in the new religions? The chief reason is certainly that these are family-centered religions: not only are traditional family values the focus of attention and foundation of life in the new religions, whole families join the sect and center their lives around it. This happens normally through the conversion of one family member, most often the wife and mother, who then induces the rest of the family to join. A woman can thus be deeply involved in her religion and assume an extremely active role in it while remaining in her familiar domestic sphere, the place which is properly hers according to traditional Japanese thinking.[45] In fact, the new religions are highly useful to women who accept their traditional housewifely roles, for through them they can achieve new levels of prestige and influence within the family, by winning the loyalty and obedience of their children, and a degree of respect and cooperation from husbands and in-laws, which they might scarcely hope for otherwise.[46] The new religions provide women with the perfect outlet for their pent up energies and skills, while enclosing them in the warm embrace of propriety. In a word, the new religions fulfill the religious aspirations of women far more completely than traditional Japanese Buddhism, Shinto, Confucianism, or Christianity do.

Traditional Shinto belief insists that women are polluted and impure—a view reinforced in common Japanese thinking by the Buddhist notion that women carry greater karmic hindrances than men do, and are therefore at a lower stage of spiritual development.[47] The idea of the pollution of women was absorbed into Japanese Buddhism, in fact, and numerous restrictions were placed on women's involvement in traditional forms of Buddhist practice because of it. But in the new religions, there are far fewer pollution restrictions limiting women's participation.[48] The kind of freedom of action and advancement open to women in the new religions is a rarity in established forms of Buddhism.[49]

Nonetheless, women do not have an easy time of it, as members of the new religions see it. Because women are born with greater liabilities they have much more to endure and to overcome. But when a woman accepts her lot as a woman, fulfilling her duties as wife, mother, and daughter-in-law, her character deepens and her spiritual power expands immeasurably. Women are thought to be far closer to the spiritual, and to spirits, than men are; that is why they are preferred by suppliants in the new religions as counselors and healers.[50] Women who heal, and women who receive the messages of the spirits in Reiyūkai, Risshō Kōsei-kai, Kurozumikyō, Tensho-kotai-jingu-kyō,[51] and other new religions, carry on the traditional religious role of Japanese women as shamans and mediums. The absorption of this most ancient female religious role into the new religions is of course still another reason for women's prominence in them.

Although women may not win the highest ranks and titles in the new religions, since the traditional value of male dominance must prevail, they do gain real recognition and enjoy real power. But the paradox remains: the new religions' women leaders staunchly proclaim that "woman's place is in the home," while they fill conspicuously active and creative roles in a public sphere, which takes them far beyond the boundaries of ordinary family life. They have internalized conservative values and the most negative views of women's character,[52] and have nonetheless become active and strong individuals. How is this possible?

It is precisely because they have internalized all the negative views of women as polluted, inferior, greedy, jealous, attached to worldly things that women of Reiyūkai and other Japanese new religions have been freed to become active and creative. They accept the humiliation of their own femaleness, but they also accept the extremely important Buddhist idea that each person can attain liberation by her or his own strenuous effort. Since women begin at a great disadvantage, they must exert a huge effort to transcend their condition and reach the highest possible level. But when they do, they feel themselves genuinely liberated, and empowered to act. Others reverently look up to them as living Buddhas.[53] At one and the same time these women are "bound" in the traditional Japanese family pattern, and they are "liberated" from all its normal limitations.[54] This paradox is difficult for women outside the tradition to view with sympathy. One wonders, with Hardacre,[55] what the hidden emotional costs might be to these women, and to their daughters, of such self-denigration and even self-hatred. Yet there is no doubt that many women within the new religions have achieved a level of dignity and power that is scarcely imaginable for women elsewhere in Japanese society. They have found a way to make the ancient Buddhist quest for liberation work for themselves, in a new way and in a new context.

In the twentieth century, laywomen in Theravada lands have assumed new roles in their religion, also. In Sri Lanka, Thailand, and Burma, increasing numbers of Buddhist laywomen practice meditation regularly at meditation centers. Most of these centers in Thailand and Sri Lanka are in the cities, for it was educated members of the urban elite who were first attracted to the practice of meditation. Now, in Sri Lanka at least, village women of more traditional backgrounds are also joining the exodus to meditation training centers in their own areas. At these centers, both urban and rural, laywomen and laymen learn the techniques of meditation during intensive courses lasting a week or more, which may require up to twenty hours of meditation per day. Many return periodically to join meditation retreats and to reach higher levels of proficiency. The highly respected teachers at some of the better known centers are laywomen.[56]

As Richard Gombrich and Gananath Obeyesekere have pointed out, the widespread practice of meditation by the laity is the greatest single change that has occurred in Theravada Buddhist countries since the end of World War II.[57] The many, many lay Buddhists who are now practicing meditation regularly and seriously are demonstrating their belief that every Buddhist should seek her or his own salvation in this life. They are acting on their conviction that it is possible for a lay person to attain nirvana here and now. Nirvana is not just the business of the monastic. One does not need to renounce the world in order to reach the ultimate goal. Many lay meditators today in Theravada lands regard meditation as their basic religious practice, rather than the rituals that were the mainstay of lay religious life in the past. This is a truly radical change in the character of Theravada Buddhism, and in the balance of duty and authority between clerics and laity. Even more radical is the presumption of laywomen to take on the role of meditation teacher. Some—Achan Naeb in Thailand, for example—teach monks as well as lay people, a remarkable innovation.[58]

The practice of meditation had been neglected for centuries by the monks in Theravada countries, who gave their attention instead to the study of Buddhist scriptures and the performance of ceremonies for the lay faithful. But in Burma the traditions of Buddhist meditation seem to have survived better than in the other Theravada countries. Early in the twentieth century Burmese monks revived and reworked an old and once renowned meditation method called *satipaṭṭhāna* (the practice of mindfulness) or *vipassanā* (insight meditation). Beginning with concentrated attention on the process of breathing—mindfulness of breathing—the meditator reaches progressively deeper levels of insight into the nature of existence, and this brings liberation. It was this practice, as modified by the revered monk and teacher Mahasi Sayadaw, that was brought to Sri Lanka and Thailand, and then to Europe and America. It is the most favored Theravada meditation technique used now all over the world. Although Burmese monks first propagated *vipassanā* meditation, it was lay people who adopted it most enthusiastically—lay people and the *thila shin, mae chi,* and *dasasilmattawa,* the quasi nuns of Theravada Asia.[59] Lay appropriation of the practice of meditation, the means to their own liberation, is an expression of the reaction against the established Buddhist monastic hierarchy, which is a noticeable element in the modern reformation of Buddhism. Since laywomen and men plunged into meditation practice more readily than conservative monks did in Sri Lanka and Thailand, an unusual number of them have become accomplished teachers and are sought out by monks who have decided they are now ready to learn *vipassanā* meditation.

In Europe and in America, too, there are several *vipassanā* centers. Some are directed by Asian monks, but most are headed by Western lay teachers. A great many of these are women.[60]

BUDDHISTS AND SOCIAL ACTION: WOMEN
AND MEN WORKING TOGETHER?

The revitalization of Buddhism in the twentieth century has brought with it a call to engage in actions to benefit society. Although the idea is not entirely new in the history of Buddhism, it has been assigned a special urgency by many of the lay reformers of Buddhism in Asia today, and by new Western converts to the religion. Since modern social action projects involve clerics and lay people of both sexes, one might expect them to afford many opportunities for women and men to work together without the limitations imposed by old gender biases. This, however, has not been the case.

The idea that the Buddhist truly committed to her or his religion should also be committed to ameliorating social ills goes back at least two thousand years. Mahayana Buddhism, which arose in India around the beginning of the common era, proclaimed that all Buddhists should emulate the example of Gautama the historical Buddha, who himself was believed to have spent lifetimes sacrificing all he had for the benefit of others. Mahayana lay people as well as monks and nuns could follow the Buddha's path as bodhisattvas,[61] true children of the Buddha. The fundamental religious duty of the lay bodhisattva is generous giving, according to the Mahayana scriptures, and he or she is to take full responsibility for the physical and moral well-being of all those among whom she or he lives. Selfless living gradually perfects the lay bodhisattva who will ultimately attain the perfect wisdom of the Buddhas. Mahayana clerics are also expected to minister to the world, but after they have perfected their understanding, meditating in solitary retreats.[62]

This was the Mahayana ideal. No doubt the reality has often been less than that. In fact Mahayana monks and nuns have usually lived much like their Theravada counterparts. They dwell behind monastery walls separated from the lay world and care for the pious by preaching and performing rituals on their behalf, and sometimes educating their children. How lay people lived in Mahayana countries is largely unknown. The only certain records they left are of their donations to monasteries and temples, though popular literature also tells of occasional feasts that pious lay people offered to the poor or of roadside hostels they erected for pilgrims and travelers.[63] In modern times, we read of schools, orphanages, and disaster relief organized by laymen and women in China, and projects to aid the poor, the sick, and the elderly carried out by nuns in Taiwan, Hong Kong, Singapore, and Vietnam.[64]

The Theravada monk's ideal is different from the Mahayana cleric's, however, and a dilemma arises when Theravada monks are urged by modern reformers to involve themselves in social causes. For in Theravada lands, the traditional goal of religious practice has always been to lead a pure life, which is only possible in the seclusion of a forest retreat. It can certainly not be done amid the distractions of the modern secular world; it cannot even be realized in the village temple, where the resident monk is constantly called on to perform rituals for his parishioners' well-being. That is why the majority of Sinhalese village monks are not highly respected by the laity nowadays: for, although they perform an indispensable service, they are felt to have missed the ideal of the true monk, who silently cultivates his spiritual development, aloof from human society. In Theravada lands veneration of monks depends on their aloofness, on the fact that their lives are the opposite of the lay person's. How can a Theravada monk plunge into society, as so many reform-minded Buddhists, Asian and Western, say he must, and still retain the respect of the ordinary folk?[65]

Modern Theravada reformers argue that Theravada Buddhism has a venerable social ethic, just as surely as Mahayana Buddhism has. They trace it to the Buddha's admonition to his early disciples to "wander forth for the good of the many, in compassion for the world, for the welfare, for the good, for the happiness of gods and men."[66] But there is no doubt that much of the modern impulse to social engagement, for monks as well as laymen and laywomen, comes from the Western ideas imbibed by Buddhist reformers. The reformers have been sophisticated, educated individuals, and they are willing to modify tradition for the sake of goals relevant to modern life and reformist agendas. The average Sinhalese or Thai villager, however, wants to venerate exemplary monks who live lives of spiritual purity. Who could they look up to if all the monks became social workers?

Sinhalese men who felt drawn to the religious life and at the same time to a life of commitment to the betterment of human society invented a new role for themselves, that of the *anagārika* or "homeless one." The *anagārika* accepts the ten precepts of the pious layman and the novice monk and lives abstaining from sexual contacts, but remains in the world engaged in work for society's sake. Anagārika Dharmapala, the great nineteenth-century religious and political leader, was the first to adopt this role.[67] He hoped that many would follow his example. Few have.

The role of fully ordained renunciant has not been available to Sinhalese women, as we have seen. Thus, Modern women who wished to devote their lives to religion have also had to invent a new role for themselves: that of the *dasasilmattawa*, the ten-precept women.[68] Beginning around 1900, laymen and laywomen took up the cause of the *dasasilmattawa* who were living as female renunciants without the sanction of the monks' *saṃgha*. These lay patrons established residences for them, and some, like the Buddhist nationalist H. Sri Nissanka, wanted to have them trained to perform useful services in society. They were to become teachers and nurses, like Roman Catholic nuns, and go into neighboring villages to carry out social work of various kinds. Nissanka and the other lay people who joined him in his project were well-educated members of Sri Lanka's urban elite, leaders of society, familiar with the best and the worst of Western culture. They were also well read in Buddhist literature. They, like many Westerners attracted to Buddhism, wanted to link the personal quest for liberation to the acceptance of responsibility for curing social ills. But the *dasasilmattawa* in Nissanka's "nunnery" at Biyagama had little interest in social work. They had taken the precepts in order to follow the true renunciant's vocation. Their ideal was that of the forest monk; they wanted to meditate in solitude away from the distractions of village life.[69]

The *dasasilmattawa* have had their way, at Biyagama and at many other forest residences on the island. They are now recognized and respected by most of the laity as true renunciants. Ironically, it is because they live aloof from social concerns that they have earned the reverence of the common people. They have had to struggle for independence from control by upper-class lay reformers, and lay attempts to channel their religious vocations. The reformist, urban, educated laity have been leaders of the Buddhist revival in Sri Lanka since it began in the nineteenth century, however. Though they did not succeed in keeping the *dasasilmattawa* under their control,[70] they have continued to seek ways to mold the quest for liberation into a social ethic.

Sarvodaya is a lay society founded in 1958 and still directed by A. T. Ariyaratna, formerly a science teacher at a Colombo (Sri Lanka) high school. Its governing board is made up of educators and other members of the country's urban elite. But Sarvodaya is a movement engaged in community development in rural Sri Lanka, and it tries to foster a model of development consonant with Buddhist doctrine.[71] Sarvodaya organizes teams of volunteers to set up work camps in selected villages where they will work with the villagers on large-scale local projects: building a road, digging a new well, establishing a new cottage industry. Volunteers and villagers living and working closely together for the duration of the project are expected to be awakened by the experience. The volunteers make a gift of their labor, which captures the true meaning of the fundamental Buddhist virtue of giving, according to Ariyaratna. Selfless labor develops the volunteer morally and awakens the mind—it is not that she or he attains enlightenment here and now, but an awakening that is a step on the path. The villagers on their side are to awaken into self-sufficiency, self-respect, and prosperity.

Volunteers—there have been hundred of thousands of them— say their lives have been changed by the experience, and several villages have certainly been benefited. But critics like Gombrich and Obeyesekere question whether Sarvodaya can really effect major changes in society. What Ariyaratna has succeeded in doing, however, is to introduce a "profound vision of involvement in the world, expressed in Buddhist terms" into Sri Lankan society. This is an ideal that Gombrich and Obeyesekere believe represents the high point of the entire Buddhist revival in Sri Lanka.[72]

Sinhala women have been very prominent in the Buddhist revival in their country for the last century, and in efforts to effect social change. Women have volunteered for Sarvodaya labor projects, and women villagers have of course been involved as well. Sarvodaya has led in the contemporary reinterpretation of Buddhism that "regards social development and social equality as the fulfillment of the Buddhist ideal."[73] In light of all this, it is odd to read Ariyaratna's catalog of duties that a woman owes to her husband. A wife, he writes, should "consider [her] husband as a god and do herself everything to look upon him with affection." She is to devote herself exclusively to household affairs, children, and relatives, and leave other matters to her husband. This is a model of middle-class domesticity, which Ariyaratna is ready to impose on the rural peasantry as well.[74] But as Gombrich and Obeyesekere point out, the notion that a woman should regard her husband as a god is not a Buddhist idea at all. It is not found in any Theravada scripture, and furthermore it was never a part of Sinhala peasant life. It is a *Brahmanic* ideal, which Ariyaratna has borrowed from ancient India's Hindu law books. Although Sinhala Buddhist reformers began by wanting to revive the best in their own religion and restore it to strength, Sarvodaya now advocates a new subservient role for women that is based on foreign values. This surprising idea about how to improve Sinhala society runs counter to Buddhist models and would signal a major social change if implemented.

Thai monks have also organized community development programs in their country, with the support of the government. The programs are designed to improve conditions in villages in the more remote areas of the country, particularly the border regions of the extreme south, north, and northeast. Some programs train local monks in rural development, public health, sanitation, and so on, so that they can provide practical leadership for projects in their own villages. Others send teams of monks and laymen to distant areas to construct bridges, roads, and schools.[75] In contrast to the Sarvodaya projects in Sri Lanka, however, which are organized and carried out almost entirely by laymen and women, the Thai programs are administered and carried out mostly by monks. Laymen participate in only a few programs, and laywomen scarcely at all. The absence of women in projects run by monks is consistent with restrictions on contacts between women and monks, which are so rigorously observed in Thailand. The spheres of religious activity for women and men in Thailand are neatly separated.[76] There, as in the Sarvodaya movement in Sri Lanka, the question of Buddhist women's role in social programs remains unresolved.

Thousands of Western women and men have converted to Buddhism, most of them since the end of World War II. To them, steeped in the old idea of Christian charity and the new desire for "social relevance," a religion that requires its clergy to remain aloof from worldly life seems unnatural, incomplete. Westerners who convert to Buddhism, whether at home or in Asia, usually expect practical results from their practice of meditation. They expect a personal transformation that will empower them to act effectively in the world, with compassion, wisdom, and energy.[77] In the 1960s and 1970s, "effective action in society" often meant political action.

Western Buddhists joined countless other Americans and Europeans in the movement against the war in Vietnam. Western Buddhist involvement seemed especially apposite, since it was Buddhist monks, nuns, and lay people in South Vietnam who spearheaded the nonviolent protests against the government of President Ngo Dinh Diem and his American supporters, which grew into a national movement to end the civil war in their country. Vietnamese Buddhism had seemed moribund early in the twentieth century, but, like Buddhists elsewhere in Asia, Vietnamese Buddhists reawakened to their own tradition as the struggle against the French colonial power intensified after World War II. When the dictatorship of President Ngo Dinh Diem replaced the French and sought to violently repress the Buddhist religion, the antigovernment feelings of masses of South Vietnamese people coalesced around the beleaguered Buddhists who at first were struggling only for the freedom to practice their religion. Consequently, the Buddhist movement quickly expanded into a strong national political movement, the single noncommunist voice of opposition to the government in the country. It was an extraordinary act of protest by the Buddhists, which riveted the attention of the Vietnamese and of people around the world on the Buddhist cause.

On June 11, 1963, the elderly monk Thich Quang Duc sat in lotus position on a street in Saigon, poured gasoline over himself, and ignited it. Deep in meditation, he remained tranquil and unmoved as his body was consumed by flames. In the next four months, seven other Buddhists followed his example—five monks, one layman, and a nun, Ni-cô Diêu Quang, who immolated herself on August 15 near Nha Trang.[78] Suicide was undoubtedly the most powerful means available to the Buddhists to awaken the nation and the world to the situation in Vietnam, and it worked. Although the government remained recalcitrant, in November Diem was overthrown by a military coup. But the civil war against the communists went on, so the Buddhist-led movement, now very strong and well-organized, redirected its energies toward bringing about an end to the war. Buddhists sought to influence public opinion in the United States and Europe, at the United Nations, and in the other Buddhist countries in Asia, and they succeeded. Ultimately they could not achieve their goals of a return to a freely elected civilian government and a negotiated end to the civil war. But the Buddhists of South Vietnam did become a principal catalyst for the creation of a modern international religious movement with political and social concerns, out of the ancient religion of renunciation.

Buddhists are embroiled today in civil strife in Sri Lanka and Tibet. Tibetan monks, nuns, and lay people struggle for political independence and religious freedom against a much stronger power, the government of the People's Republic of China. The Buddhists of Sri Lanka, however, are the majority group, and they are immersed in a bloody contest for power with the minority Tamil-speaking population, which is Hindu. Since regaining their independence from the British in 1948, Sinhala Buddhists have reclaimed the dignity and power stripped from them during centuries of colonial rule, and they and their political leaders have identified national interests with the Sinhala language and the Buddhist religion. Prime ministers since 1956 have been aggressively Buddhist, but have found it difficult to manage the demands of Buddhist extremist groups. S. W. R. D. Bandaranaike was assassinated by disaffected monks in 1959. His widow, Sirimavo Bandaranaike, who succeeded him as prime minister in 1960, lost the confidence of her Buddhist supporters over the issue of making Buddhism Sri Lanka's national religion, and was voted out of office.[79]

Sinhala nationalism in fateful combination with deteriorating economic conditions in the country has increasingly embittered Sinhalese and Tamils against each other, and has finally erupted into outright warfare. Now, thoroughly repelled by the latest waves of horrendous brutality of Sinhalese against Tamils, some Buddhist women and men have begun to publicly reassert the basic Buddhist values of loving kindness and tolerance, and are trying to extract the Buddhist religion from the deadly web of Sinhala nationalism. Lay Buddhist organizations have sought to intervene with the government to restore the peace and harmony which they say once prevailed between the two groups. Meanwhile, Sri Lanka's present agony reveals the darkest side of modern Buddhism, and the low point of the Buddhist revival there.

Despite the current spectacle in Sri Lanka of an alliance between the Buddhist religion and narrow political interests, many Buddhists of various nationalities continue to build an international Buddhist movement which will promote world peace. Beginning with Anagārika Dharmapala's founding of the Mahā Bodhi Society in 1891, there have been several attempts to bring about closer cooperation between Buddhists from all countries, and to create an international Buddhist movement. Newer international Buddhist organizations, such as the World Fellowship of Buddhists (founded 1950) and the World Buddhist Saṃgha Council (established 1966), not only bring members together to discuss matters of specifically Buddhist interest, they attempt to help build world peace by "spreading the Buddha's message of compassion and wisdom against violence and materialist thinking devoid of moral values."[80]

Japanese monks and nuns of the Nipponzan Myōhōji sect have traveled throughout the world and have built more than seventy Peace Pagodas in the last several years. Nipponzan Myōhōji is one of the many Buddhist "new religions" generated by the Nichiren sect of Japan, but unlike the Japanese new religions discussed earlier, this one is made up of ordained clerics who wander the world attending peace and antinuclear demonstrations and building pagodas as Buddhist emblems of world peace. Local women and men, whether they are Buddhist or not, join them in raising the shining white-domed pagodas. Although these Japanese monks work for a progressive goal and pursue a religious vocation with an unusual twist, they at first had trouble meeting one new challenge: they found it difficult to accept their women co-workers as anything like their equals. Now, however, Western women who work with them in the United States report that the monks' sexist attitudes are changing, as they share tasks with women and learn to respect their contributions.[81]

Real cooperation between men and women, and mutual respect as they work together as Buddhists for social and political goals, is what one hopes for. Often that is not what happens. Nonetheless, in today's world Buddhist women are making contributions on many levels in their communities. They are not likely to retreat to the sidelines again, whether or not they meet resistance from conservative Buddhist men.

WOMEN AS LEADERS, EAST AND WEST

In the past, men dominated Buddhism, and today they still do. But one of the most heartening things about modern Buddhism is that women are stepping to the forefront at all levels of Buddhist activity. They are working and they are leading, and, happily, they are doing it with the cooperation of many Buddhist men. In our century at last, outstanding women in Asia and in the West are working with men to shape the practice and development of Buddhism. Some are spiritual leaders and religious teachers who have attracted crowds of followers. Others are movers and shakers—they organize, they administer, and they consciously work for change. Still others are the keepers of the records: they are scholars and teachers who tell the world about women's Buddhism and interpret Buddhist doctrine and history from a woman's point of view. All these women are breathing a fresh life into the old religion; they are helping it to change.

Spiritual Leaders and Religious Teachers

Of all the major Buddhist traditions and national groups, women have always been most prominent in the Tibetan tradition. That is not to say that Tibetan women have found ready access to the religious life, or that their lives in religion were easy. There have been some very famous female tantric adepts, such as Yeshe Tsogyel, whose biographies have been preserved.[82] But most Tibetan women who chose a religious vocation lived obscure and often trying lives as *ani* in nunneries, or as unknown wanderers or mountain hermits.

One of the few modern Tibetan women whose accomplishments have been recorded was Ayu Khandro, a great tantric adept who lived from 1839 to 1953.[83] One of her last students, Namkhai Norbu, who now lives in Italy, decided to write her life story; otherwise she would have remained unknown outside the circle of her own disciples, as countless other women tantrics and nuns have done. Ayu Khandro was born in eastern Tibet to a family of traders and herders. She had an aunt who lived a solitary life as a religious practitioner, with whom she went to stay as a child. She felt strongly drawn to the religious life also, received initiation in her teens into tantric practices, and wished to devote her life to meditation and spiritual development. Her parents, however, arranged a marriage for her into a wealthy family, and she had to accede to their wishes. But three years later she became seriously ill. A lama (Tibetan Buddhist teacher) explained to her husband that the illness had come about because she had interrupted her religious practice against her will, and if she did not return to it she would die. Ayu Khandro's husband was very cooperative: he helped her return to her aunt for further religious training, and continued to support her practice for the rest of his life.

Ayu Khandro passed several years traveling throughout Tibet, alone or with other tantrics, studying with various teachers and perfecting her practice. She received instruction from numerous lamas during her long life and was initiated into an extensive repertoire of tantric meditation practices. She came to be known as a woman of exceptional accomplishments. Many students, both male and female, went to seek teachings from her in the tiny mountain hermitage where she spent the last sixty years of her life in retreat. By the time she died she was known as a living Vajrayoginī ("adamantine female yogi"),[84] a fully realized being, a female Buddha.

Ayu Khandro was not a nun, although some women who practiced with her were. A contemporary of hers, Ani Lochen, was both a nun and an outstanding religious teacher with many disciples. One, Lobsang Lhalungpa, has written of her exceptional "inner development, inner experience and attainment" which were so great that she seemed to emanate an "awesome power that permeated" her pupil's entire being.[85] Ani Lochen and Ayu Khandro were two of the greatest Tibetan women teachers of recent times, but there have been others. It is our good fortune that scholars, lamas, and ordinary Buddhists are now taking interest in these remarkable women, and telling the wider world about their attainments. In their own time, their influence was limited to a few of their own countrymen and women. Thanks to their disciples' written records, however, they may now affect a wider circle of individuals interested in Buddhism.

There are a number of other noteworthy women religious teachers in Asia today. Sister Sudharma, one of the most important leaders of the *dasasilmattawa* in Sri Lanka, taught Buddhism in a girls' school and then in a college for over twenty years before retiring to the forest to meditate and lead a life of renunciation. She has so far established fourteen monastic residences for *dasasilmattawa* to which she accepts students from all over the world, and she also administers a retirement home for aged *dasasilmattawa*.[86] The lay teacher Achan Naeb heads a large network of meditation centers in Bangkok and central Thailand, where she teaches both lay people and monks.[87] Daw Panna, a *thila shin* in Burma, follows the model of her grandmother and heads an important monastic residence and school for women renunciants.[88] Venerable Bhikṣuṇī Tae-heng Se Nim, a Korean nun of the Chogye lineage, is the founder and spiritual head of seven Han Ma Um Zen centers in Korea and America. She has some twenty thousand lay followers in Korea and a growing number in the United States.[89] Venerable Bhikṣuṇī Hiu Wan is a scholar, painter, and Chan (Zen) master in Taiwan.[90] Rengetsu was another artist-nun, of nineteenth-century Japan, who influenced many through her spiritual example and her generosity to others, as well as through her art.[91] And there was Satomi Myōdō, a Soto Zen nun, who died in 1978. She is important not as a teacher but as an example to others of extraordinary fortitude in the pursuit of her spiritual goal.[92]

There are now a great many Western women too who have earned reputations as superior teachers. When Buddhism was first brought to the United States at the beginning of the twentieth century, it was taught to Americans by Asian monks, who were later succeeded by their Western male disciples. More and more women converted to Buddhism from the 1950s to the 1970s, however, and now there is a generation of highly respected women teachers, such as Ruth Denison who heads the Desert Vipassanā Center in California near Palm Springs and conducts meditation retreats throughout the country. Maurine Stuart received dharma transmission, or permission to teach Zen, from her Japanese teacher, Soen Nakagawa, and also the title of Roshi (Zen master). Her meditation center was the Cambridge (Massachusetts) Buddhist Association.[93] Both Denison and Stuart have taught men as well as women, but they have been particularly valued as sensitive teachers and as role models by their women students.

There are dozens more women teachers in America and Europe, but the first of them was Jiyu Kennett Roshi, abbess of Shasta Abbey in northern California. British-born Jiyu Kennett Roshi is the only female head of a Zen Buddhist monastery in the United States. She founded Shasta Abbey in 1970, after having been ordained a *bhikṣuṇī* in the Chinese tradition in Malaysia and training under Koho Zenji at the Sōjiji Zen temple in Tokyo. The Sōjiji is one of the main Soto Zen training centers in Japan. Jiyu Kennett was invited there by Koho Zenji, the renowned head of the temple, for training, and she became the first woman in several centuries to be publicly admitted into it as the equal of the male clerics.[94] She was the official "priest" of her own Soto temple in Japan before some of her American followers invited her to establish a temple on the other side of the Pacific.

At Shasta Abbey, men and women train together and are treated as equals. The routine is the same for both sexes, the garb, and ordination. As Kennett Roshi points out, the Japanese word for "monk-priest" has both male and female forms, and when you translate the feminine form as "nun" you are imparting a Christian coloring to the way of life, which is not accurate.[95] At Shasta Abbey there is no place for arbitrary gender distinctions, for, as Kennett Roshi asserts, having a deep religious experience—*kenshō*, or enlightenment—inevitably requires becoming both male and female, knitting the genders together, and going beyond distinction-making. Women are held back from spiritual attainment, she says, by the niggling sense that they *are* as inadequate as so many others have told them they are. When a women looks within herself, as Kennett Roshi has, and recognizes herself as whole, she will never again feel inadequate. "As soon as we *know* we have full rights," she declares, "they're going to give them to us anyway." The key to equality in the world out there is, in her view, the recognition of the spiritual equality of all by the individual women and men who follow the established religions. "When men know that spiritually we are the same as they are, they will have to judge us on our merits and our ability and not on what someone said thousands of years ago." That will apply in all aspects of life, but it must all start inside individuals, and inside the great religious traditions.[96]

Movers and Shakers

Western women were instrumental in bringing Buddhism to their own countries. They were among the movers and shakers who made things happen. It was Mrs. Alexander Russell who, with her husband, a wealthy San Francisco businessman, first invited a Japanese Roshi to the United States to teach Zen to Americans. That was in 1905.[97] Elsie Mitchell played a similar role in the late 1950s in Cambridge, Massachusetts. With her husband, she organized a meditation group and a Buddhist library, which became the Cambridge Buddhist Association. One of the first Zen centers for Westerners in the country, it was headed by Maurine Stuart Roshi until her death in 1990.[98]

Ruth Fuller Sasaki was also instrumental in supporting and directing an emerging Zen community, in New York City: the Buddhist Society of America, founded in 1931, and now known as the First Zen Institute of America. Ruth Fuller Sasaki's career in Buddhism took a unique turn, however: having married the institute's Zen master, Sokei-an Sasaki, she moved to Japan after his death to immerse herself in Zen study, was ordained a priest of the Rinzai sect at Daitokuji temple in Kyoto, and became abbess of her own temple in Japan.[99]

Like Ruth Fuller Sasaki, the British graduate of Oxford University and long-time resident of India, Freda Bedi, elected to serve the causes of Buddhism in Asia. After the fatal Tibetan uprising against the Chinese occupation had forced the Dalai Lama and so many other Tibetans to flee to exile in India in 1959, she helped establish a school for young lamas in New Delhi. Later she was ordained as a Tibetan novice nun (*ani*), and founded the Mahayana Buddhist Nunnery in Dalhousie, India.[100]

One of the most influential Western women now active in Asia is Ayya Khema, who founded Parappuduwa Nuns' Island in Sri Lanka in 1984.[101] It is a place to which women from Sri Lanka and from all over the world may come to practice meditation and study the Buddha's teachings in English. Some take the ten precepts as *dasasilmattawa*, some take only eight precepts, and others choose to remain ordinary laywomen. Sri Lankan laywomen helped her establish the residence, and the government provided the land. Women run the island retreat. Ayya Khema has established two Theravada monastic teaching and retreat centers in Australia and one in Germany, where both women and men meditate and train. She also travels to other countries giving short courses in meditation.

Her name means Khema, the venerable lady, and is the name of one of the Buddha's early female disciples. She was born in Berlin in 1923, fled the Nazis with her family to China, became a U.S. citizen after World War II, lived on a farm in Australia, married, and had two children. She studied *vipassana* meditation with a series of Theravada masters in Burma, Thailand, and Sri Lanka, and was ordained as a *dasasilmattawa* in Sri Lanka in 1979. In 1988 she took ordination from Chinese nuns and monks, and is now Venerable Bhikṣuṇī Khema.

Ayya Khema has attracted much attention among the English-speaking upper classes in Sri Lanka by way of her public lectures and television appearances. She is one of the most articulate advocates in Theravada lands for the reestablishment of the *bhikṣuṇī saṃgha*. She has helped make the cause of the education and training of *dasasilmattawa* and the growth of the order an important issue for Buddhist women. She views the absence of an active order of Theravada *bhikṣuṇī* as a loss to the world as well as to Buddhist women who aspire to the religious life. She observes that women have a special capacity for loving and nourishing life, which needs to be incorporated into the teaching of Buddhist spiritual values. As spiritual leaders, women could help harness the destructive urges that today threaten the survival of the whole world. Modern women are realizing their own self-confidence and independence everyday, and many of them have already demonstrated their outstanding abilities in many fields. They should be allowed to take their rightful place as spiritual leaders beside men.[102]

Ayya Khema has a keen sense of the responsibility the religious person bears to society. She favors the active engagement of Sri Lanka's *dasasilmattawa* in teaching, hospital work, and other social services. She called for a women's peace corps in Sri Lanka in 1982, to aid in the development of the country, for, as she says, one must not "eat the rice of the country in vain."[103] In her willingness to see the *dasasilmattawa* actively working in society, she is allied with Sinhala lay Buddhist leaders who are her main supporters in the country.

Most Sinhala *dasasilmattawa*, led by Sister Sudharma and others, prefer the life of renunciation, and do not see eye-to-eye with Khema. The *dasasilmattawa* are said to disagree with her also about the wisdom of reestablishing the *bhikṣuṇī saṃgha* under the inevitable supervision of the *bhikṣu saṃgha*.[104] Her messages on social responsibility and on the role of women as spiritual leaders reach beyond the boundaries of Sri Lanka, however, and are being listened to by many throughout the world.

An ally of Ayya Khema in the struggle for the reestablishment of the *bhikṣuṇī saṃgha* is Dr. Chatsumarn Kabilsingh, a Buddhist scholar and professor at Thammasat University in Bangkok.[105] She is founder and contributing editor of NIBWA, the *Newsletter on International Buddhist Women's Activities*. It is an important forum for Buddhist women and others to exchange ideas, and an invaluable focal point around which women can rally and identify themselves to each other as Buddhist women. Dr. Kabilsingh is active in many other Buddhist projects, and has traveled widely in Asia attending conferences and bringing Buddhist women's groups into contact with one another. She was one of the organizers of the international conference on Buddhist nuns held at Bodh Gayā, India (the place of the Buddha's enlightenment), in 1987.

Dr. Kabilsingh studied at Visva Bharati University at Santiniketan, India, and at McMaster University in Canada. Her mother, Venerable Bhikṣuṇī Voramai Kabilsingh, who was once a teacher herself, became one of the first Theravada women to receive full ordination as a *bhikṣuṇī*, from the Chinese *saṃgha* in Taiwan in 1972. She is now head of Thailand's only nunnery for *bhikṣuṇī*, Wat Songdharma Kalyani in Nakhon Pathom. Chatsumarn Kabilsingh wants to see more nunneries established so that women committed to the ordained life can devote themselves to the study of Buddhism, and so that laywomen can come to the nuns for instruction in the religion and help with family and social problems. Thoughtful and educated Buddhist women in Thailand and elsewhere want to involve themselves in solving social problems and improving prospects for the world's survival, but the opportunities for doing this, in a Buddhist way, are limited for women at present. Establishment of the *bhikṣuṇī saṃgha* everywhere would open one important avenue to women, Dr. Kabilsingh believes, and would have significant repercussions on the lives of other Buddhist women as well.

Dr. Kabilsingh recognizes that there is more support for her ideas abroad than at home at the moment, but hopes that today's universal Buddhist movement will inspire changes in the more conservative societies. Thai monks, particularly the younger ones, are gradually changing their views about the *bhikṣuṇī saṃgha*, she says, but women who earnestly desire ordination should not wait for their permission. Instead, women should seek ordination abroad, then establish *bhikṣuṇī* communities at home, and become living proof that they are beneficial to society. The movement would certainly spread, and the monks would be won over and offer ordination to the *bhikṣuṇī* in the Theravada tradition. As Dr. Kabilsingh sees it, it must be educated women from the more privileged and influential classes who take the lead in seeking ordination. They must also be the ones who support and champion the movement. They and sympathetic men from their own social circles understand the issues, and they have influence to bring about change.[106]

Through NIBWA and her many other publications, her teaching, and her international activities, Dr. Kabilsingh is working very energetically to bring about fundamental changes in Buddhist women's lives in Thailand and in the whole world. There are others like her in Asia, such as the Japanese nun Kojima Kendō who spearheaded the effort to transform the situation of nuns in the Soto Zen sect at the end of World War II.[107] Because of women such as these, Buddhism is changing rapidly in our modern world.

Keepers of the Records

In times past, few records were kept of what Buddhist women did, nor did they leave many traces of their own lives.[108] Today, however, there are many women scholars and teachers in Asia and in the West who are chronicling what Buddhist women are doing today, and researching the history of what Buddhist women did in the past. Most of the published research on Buddhist women has been produced by women, beginning with Caroline A. F. Rhys Davids and Isaline B. Horner in England during the first half of the twentieth century. The original work of many of these scholars is cited in the bibliography to this chapter. Moreover, the subject of women in Buddhism is coming to be regarded as a legitimate one for investigation by the male scholars who still dominate Buddhist studies, and some of them have written seriously on it. There are also some special publications on women in Buddhism, such as NIBWA and *Kahawai Journal of Women and Zen*, and a new international association of Buddhist women called Sakyadhitā, which will compile information on Buddhist women, promote further research, and foster communication on issues important to women in Buddhism today.

It was women scholars who first made the subject of women in Buddhism respectable. And now, in their published work and in their classroom teaching, they are interpreting Buddhism for others from women's points of view. Along with women spiritual leaders, they are shaping the perception of Buddhism while helping build the reality of a new Buddhism, which will be different from the old because of the prominence of women within it.

CONCLUSIONS

Modern Buddhism is in process of change. The most significant change is the leading role that women, both nuns and lay, and laymen have assumed. Their active involvement arises from the realization that the fundamental Buddhist directive—that each person must seek her or his *own* liberation, here and now—is indeed a mandate for all Buddhists, not just for monks. The old distinction between the status of lay and cleric is being rejected by many, giving scope to new possibilities for practice and leadership. Now, lay Buddhists are often the ones who are serious meditators rather than the monks, and laywomen and laymen even offer meditation instruction to the *bhikṣu*. New identities are being forged in modern Buddhism, too, such as that of the *dasasilmattawa* of Sri Lanka who are neither nuns nor laywomen but somewhere between, and who have earned general respect for their commitment to practice and for the purity of their lives. And entirely new Buddhist sects have sprung up, with new balances of power between lay and cleric, and women and men. Modern Buddhist women and men take their religion seriously, and they take full responsibility for their spiritual destiny upon themselves.

The new developments in Buddhism have come about because Asian Buddhists have reexamined their own traditions and revitalized them with new insights. Such rejuvenating scrutiny of old traditions has occurred from time to time in Buddhist history, but this modern reinterpretation has been evoked by the waves of painful confrontations with Western culture, which Asian peoples have endured in the last hundred-odd years. Now ideas and values are indeed being borrowed, but by both sides, and the triumphant Buddhist march westward is one of the hallmarks of the vigor of the modern religion.

Women are important participants in the newest developments in Buddhism, and in the critical analysis of Buddhist and Western values, which hopes to blend the best of both for the sake of a better world. It is appropriate therefore to end this chapter with a brief summary of some thoughts of two Western Buddhist scholars, Anne Klein and Rita Gross, on how this might be accomplished.

Feminist historians of religions often judge the Buddhist record on the treatment of women to be good, compared with most of the world's other major religions. Buddhist doctrine, particularly the key Mahayana doctrine of emptiness (śūnyatā), meaning the indissoluble interrelatedness and interdependence of all that exists, requires that the practitioner transcend distinction-making between female and male. Moreover, the practice which leads to liberation is open to all, and women's spiritual capacities are understood to be no different from men's. The understanding attained by the enlightened individual is not limited by worldly biases. Yet, as Anne Klein observes,[109] in Buddhist societies where for centuries substantial numbers of people have been honestly cultivating the realization of emptiness (Tibet, for example), there seems to be no clear causal connection between that fact and specific social developments affecting women. Outside the relatively closed circle of active practitioners, whether clerics or tantric adepts, women appear to be no more highly regarded or better off than in many non-Buddhist societies. This is a disturbing incongruity. Prevailing attitudes and social patterns in such countries are obviously shaped by various factors other than Buddhism. Is it possible nonetheless that in our modern world Buddhist insights could somehow be used to alter social patterns to the benefit of women, and to the benefit of all beings?

The Judeo-Christian-Islamic religious traditions of the West have been used to support dualistic thinking, which defines persons and experiences as being in opposition to one another. Catalogs of characteristics are assigned to male and female, which then stand to each other as opposites. On the positive side are placed male characteristics, and men are the ones called capable of effective action, while women are considered passive and uncreative. As feminist critics of the established religions have discerned, the impact of such thinking on Western societies has been comprehensive and devastating for women. Rita Gross[110] reminds us of the "profoundly misogynist tendency in western culture" which women cannot afford to forget by assuming it is a regressive characteristic that has now been overcome in our progressive age. If we want to make changes in our own Western societies, and nurture peaceful solutions to international problems, we need new models.

There is a need, in the West as well as in the East, "for a religiously, personally, and communally practical model that accounts for differences—male-female, divine-mundane, subject-object, active-passive, and so forth—without placing them in opposition."[111]

For the patriarchal style of thinking of the Judeo-Christian-Islamic traditions emphasizes conflict or contrast between autonomous individuals, organizes all things in authoritarian structures, and insists that action and progress can be born only from the opposition of autonomous individuals. Buddhist nondualism, the understanding of emptiness as the relatedness of all things, offers a possible model, as a foil to the dualistic, patriarchal style of thinking.

The Buddhist doctrine of emptiness and nondualism, which is the ground of the tantric meditations Klein describes, does not present opposition as a necessary component of effective action, or absolute autonomy as a necessary condition of psychological health. Religious experiences transform the tantric practitioner by transcending her or his own negative emotions. The power of selfish action, for example, is transformed by practice into the power of passionate helpfulness, which is directed outward toward others. This inner transformation is not a matter of conquest, nor does it evoke the desire to conquer other beings "out there."

Dualistic thinking implies antagonism and exclusion rather than embracing: there is always something "out there" which is perceived as opposed and therefore threatening. The Buddhist doctrine of nondualism, and the practices designed to foster the experiencing of it, can generate visions of action and altruism within a nondualistic, nonoppositional, embracing framework. Feminist thinkers have valued connectedness rather than separation and opposition, and they have identified many of the social problems resulting from the patriarchal style of thinking. Klein and Gross assert that it is now time for Buddhists and feminist thinkers to blend their insights and intellectual skills, and borrow from each other's strengths. From this joining of forces it should be possible to establish powerful alternatives to a dualistic outlook on our complex, tormented modern world.[112]

Miriam Levering

WOMEN, THE STATE, AND RELIGION TODAY IN THE PEOPLE'S REPUBLIC OF CHINA

Except for a brief period in 1957 and from 1960 to 1963, the period from 1949 to 1980 was severely difficult for religious groups and religious people in the People's Republic of China. It is fair to say that the government rendered four of the five recognized religious groups—Buddhists, Taoists, Protestants, and Catholics—simply unable to foster the religious life of their members. Religious groups were forbidden to collect money to support priests and ministers, while most Buddhist, Taoist, and Catholic monks and nuns were forced to start factories in their monasteries or to return to lay life (Welch 1972, 42–61).

Since in the case of Buddhists, Protestants, and Catholics there were large constituencies abroad who were interested in the fate of their co-religionists in China, for foreign policy reasons a certain very controlled and limited level of functioning was permitted until 1966: a few houses of worship were kept open as showplaces, and a few leaders were available for foreigners to visit (Welch 1972, 178, 201–10, 452–55). Atheism was taught in the schools (Wei 1989, 61) while religious groups were forbidden to practice their religion anywhere but in designated worship halls, lest they infringe on the rights of the nonreligious.

In 1966 the Great Proletarian Cultural Revolution began, and young people and leftist cadres carried out a nationwide attack on religion. Many of the remaining religious leaders were thrown in jail, religious texts were burned, images were smashed or defaced, and the remaining places of worship were closed and used as factories, schools, and residences. Ordinary people who were known to be religious lived in fear of destructive visits from the Red Guard in search of Bibles or Buddha images, and many were forced into reeducation programs which deprived them of their freedom and used up all their savings. Most of the few Buddhist and Taoist monks and nuns who remained in monastic life in 1966 were forced to return to lay life.

Since 1979 Party and government policy toward religion has changed quite dramatically. Religious groups are given some of the rent on the property they once owned, and the government has given money toward the restoration of a certain number of places of worship to the religious groups, offering help with resettlement to factories and residents of former churches and temples, and money to the religious groups for refurbishing the buildings.

Not only have buildings been restored, but religious groups have been allowed to set up educational programs to train a new generation of leaders. Ordinary people are not so afraid to attend services of worship or to participate in pilgrimages, Taoist communal purificatory rites, or other religious practices. Since 1980 there has been sufficient relaxation of government and party control to allow meaningful religious preaching, education, practice, and community to reappear in China (Goldman 1986).[1] And in some cases— most notably among Christians, but also among Buddhists, Taoists, and in the realm of popular religion—they have reappeared with a surprising energy and liveliness, and a startlingly broad appeal.

These changes have made it now meaningful to ask the question of what roles women have been playing in this revival of religion in China. At this crucial moment of rebirth it is important to ask whether women and men are unthinkingly replicating in the newly revived religions the gender ideologies and arrangements that characterized these religions in the past, or whether new gender ideologies and arrangements are now becoming a reality in religious communities in China.[1a]

WOMEN IN CONTEMPORARY CHINA

To understand the world of possibilities that women who are active in religious groups in China can contemplate, we need first to understand the history of the Communist revolution and the Communist government and its impact on women's lives.

Some have argued that commitment to the Communist revolution itself, and to its distinctively Chinese version of Marxist-Leninist ideology, was for many a religious commitment, while the experience of political struggle for radical social change was for some a religious experience. Others have argued that the Chinese Communist Party sought to create a pseudo religion in place of religion, through "the deification of Mao and the Party, the study of Marxism-Leninism, and the rituals of criticism and public confession of political sins" (Goldman 1986, 148). Whether or not it is useful to think of the Chinese revolution as a religious phenomenon, it does represent an attempt to bring about a new moral order, and to bring about dramatic changes in the worldview of the Chinese people, as well as in the fundamental economic and power relationships in Chinese society.

The Communist Party's revolutionary strategy was threefold. First, the Party sought to withdraw credibility from the traditional Chinese worldview and its moral order, its religious (cosmological and ethical) framework, already under attack by the intellectuals of the nineteen teens and twenties (called the "May Fourth" period) (Barlow 1989, 2). Second, the Party sought to take advantage of aroused nationalist sentiments during the war with Japan, by portraying themselves as the group that was actively resisting the Japanese occupation (C. Johnson). Finally, they sought to institute a process of class struggle and land reform which would destroy the power and privileges of the landlord class, awaken the political consciousness of poor peasants, and win their allegiance. They sought to establish a new moral order which would regard as important the wrongs suffered by the lower classes of society, and redress those wrongs. They sought to establish a new moral order in which the labor of workers and peasants would receive the highest value, and the orientation toward profit and the individual family's accumulation of wealth typical of the bourgeois classes would be seen as morally defective, since it leads to exploiting others for one's own gain.

One of the stated goals of the Communist Party and of the revolution was to end the oppression and suffering which the economic and social systems, sustained by the traditional "Confucian" ideology, caused women (K. Johnson 1983, 35, 40–41; Wolf 1985, 26). The revolution allegedly sought to free women to play larger roles in economic production and in politics (K. Johnson 1983, 54). The revolution also promised that under its new laws women would enjoy more freedom, equality, and power in their families (K. Johnson 1983, 45, 54–55). The extent to which women will be able to find their own fulfillment within religious organizations and activities in China will depend in part on the degree to which the

Communists have succeeded in changing the fundamental structural conditions of women's lives as well as the ideologies of personhood and gender that underlie them.

The Family System of Late Imperial China

In the traditional social order, women were required to leave their families to marry into a family of a different surname living in a different village. Decisions about the marriage were made by the parents on both sides; in most cases the bride and groom did not know each other prior to the wedding. Women were exchanged between two families in a transaction in which dowry and bride price were important elements. Much of the symbolism of the wedding emphasized that the wife could not go home to her natal family. The husband's family could send the wife back to her parents, in which case the wife would be disgraced and her parents seriously inconvenienced. The wife could not seek divorce. A woman who was not needed or could not be supported by a family could be sold.[2]

Women's work should be inside the home, including domestic handicrafts, but not outside the home. In many parts of the country, particularly in the north, rural women did not work in the fields. Women who were forced to support themselves by working outside the home had few options: work as domestic servants, or as prostitutes. Women were responsible for child rearing and housework. Women were less able than men, work should be gender-segregated, and women's work was of a lower order than that of men. Women should not be leaders, or be publicly consulted about politics or community decisions.

Women should not be autonomous. In the famous formulation, they should obey their fathers, their husbands, and their sons. In the case of sons, however, the need for obedience was clouded by the importance of age in determining one's place in the family hierarchy, and the closely related principle of filial piety, which commanded children to obey their parents.

The concept "woman" as an independent entity over against "man," possessed of her own interests, which may be in conflict with those of the men in her life, and entitled to her own independent agency and to means toward the fulfillment of her interests, was not a part of the discourse of traditional China, or of republican China outside certain small Western-influenced intellectual groups (Barlow 1989). A person was understood to become a person by filling roles within a hierarchical family and social structure; gender was only one determinant of what roles one will assume. Thus a woman was not thought of as the actually or potentially autonomous subject of her life, as an individual first and foremost, but rather as a daughter, a daughter-in-law, a mother, a mother-in-law, having her existence in her relationships with parents and children and in-laws, within a family with which she often identified.

The family system, with its gender hierarchy, was rationalized through cosmological belief and regularized through Confucian ritual (K. Johnson 1983, 1). Everything in the universe is marked by an interaction or a particular combination of yin and yang. "Everything exists in a state of constant flux with its opposite which is not only its complement but is necessary to its identity. . . . Both men and women as physical beings contain a measure of both yin and yang" (Anagnost 1989, 320). However, women were associated with yin, the passive, life-receiving, receptive, in ways that men were not, and likewise men were associated with yang, the active, life-producing, aggressive.

Even though the harmonious functioning of both was required for real productivity, beginning in the Han dynasty (220 B.C.E-201 C.E.) it was seen as appropriate that yang, being morally superior, should dominate yin. And where yang and yin combined, the good outcome was thereafter most often symbolized as yang. Yin and yang became grafted onto a theory of human nature in which yin was recognized as the source of emotions, and thus "the cause of confusion and evil," while yang was identified with the rational faculties, and with the highest Confucian virtue, *ren* or benevolence (Overmyer 1980, 158). Gender, though, was not an absolute determinant of whether one was yin or yang in a given situation. There were situations in which a woman stood higher in a given hierarchy than a man, in which, therefore, in a sense they were positionally yang to the man's yin (Barlow 1989, 10).

But the general association of women with yin created a danger for a woman exercising the power or claiming the privileges of higher rank or class (Anagnost 1989, 321). When a woman gains extraordinary power for one of her sex because she is capable, or when she dominates males in her family, then she is in danger of being portrayed as sexless, or lacking the virtues of her sex. Her use of power is easily delegitimated by pointing to her sex—she is that unnatural thing, yin in power.[3] Stories of women in power are often stories of their abuse of power.

While women's roles were limited during the period of imperial rule to domestic work, childbearing, household handicrafts, or prostitution, things had begun to change well before 1949. During the Republican period (1911–1949) many women moved out of the home into industrial production, professions such as teaching, social work, and medicine, student activism, and politics (Honig and Hershatter 1988, 1).

Two Family Crises. This traditional gender and family ideology and the patriarchal family structure it supported came under severe attack during the Republican period by all groups of urban intelligentsia interested in strengthening the nation through cultural change. A family system that was so oppressive of women was an embarrassment to a modern nation, and most modernizing political groups agreed that it should be changed. The tragic fates of women in the traditional family became sign and proof of the moral bankruptcy of the "Confucian" ideology of the old order. Educated young people after the May Fourth Movement of 1919, whether Communists, nationalists, or feminists, all sought the reform of the family system. Women were not the only sufferers in the traditional family: young men also sought power to make decisions about their own marriage partners and careers (K. Johnson 1983, 25–29; Barlow 1989, 9).

But just as the urban youth were seeking to change the old family system, poor men and most older women in the countryside were seeking to restore stable, viable families along traditional models. Due to famines and political disruptions, conditions in the countryside had become so harsh that men could not afford wives, and mothers of men could not expect the help of daughters-in-law and grandsons. Instead, women were widely being sold or abandoned by men who could not afford to keep them (K. Johnson 1983, 29–35).

The Revolutionary Period

When the Communist Party took its army to the countryside and began organizing peasants to take part in the revolution in its rural peasant base areas, the party soon found itself in a conflict. On the one hand, the party had promised that family reform and the liberation of women would be integral to the revolution (K. Johnson Johnson 1983, 85). Educated women who had become Party activist such as the famous writer Ding Ling, expected it (Barlow 1989, 39-40; K. Johnson 1983, 72–75). There were some younger women in the countryside who wanted support against the oppression by husbands and parents-in-law in their marriages, as Jack Belden's powerful account of a young wife's liberation from oppressed wife and daughter-in-law to cadre in "Goldflower's Story" indicates (Belden 1949, 275–307; K. Johnson 1983, 79).

On the other hand, poor peasant men were needed for the army, and to carry out class struggle and land reform, and poor peasant men did not want marriage reform. Most men in the countryside who had families had paid a lot in bride price to get wives; they wanted economic help to be able to keep them, not easier divorce through which they could lose them (K. Johnson 1983, 46, 55–56). And older women who had finally created within the patriarchal family a fulfilling and reliable "uterine family" of sons, daughters-in-law, and grandchildren, did not find the idea of free choice marriages and easy divorce for women very appealing (K. Johnson 1983, 34, 49). Even young women must have preferred family life, however oppressive, to the alternatives. Women forced out of families were powerless, and were likely to have to sell themselves to men as prostitutes or virtual slaves to avoid starvation (K. Johnson 1983, 32–34). A feminist agenda or any kind of advocacy for women against the prerogatives of their husbands and parents-in-law threatened the success of the revolution (K. Johnson 1983, 51–89).

Gender Ideology. Furthermore, to achieve liberation for women, the category "woman" would have to be introduced into political discourse, identifying a new political subject. Women would have to be understood to be individuals with interests and rights that might place them at odds with the interests of the men in their families. In the countryside these were definitely foreign ideas. Tani Barlow (1989) argues that "woman" as a term in a discourse which posits "woman" as over against "man" was a fundamental category in the nineteenth-century West, but when introduced by Western-influenced feminists found little resonance in China:

> Qing [dynasty (1688–1911)] China did indeed derogate women and privilege men. Yet male dominance was never enforced by a strictly binary discourse permitting only two polar perspectives, male and female (9). . . . Male and female, Confucian subjects always appeared as part of something else, defined not by essence but by context, marked by interdependency and reciprocal obligation rather than by autonomy and contradiction (10).

The "something else" was of course the family and the society, which offered to women and men subject positions in a set of intersecting hierarchies: age, generation, occupation, rank, gender, and class. Gender limited the range of positions women could occupy in the occupational hierarchy, and gender hierarchy dictated that within persons of the same age, generation, rank, and class, women would rank lower than men; but a woman of a higher rank, age, generation, or class could demand deference from a man whose position was lower. Barlow (1989) points out that roles in family and society were understood as participation in reciprocal (though unequal) relationships.

The most fundamental relationships, or *lun*, through the rhetoric of which social order was expressed, were those between ruler and subject, father and son, and husband and wife. A woman was a daughter, a daughter-in-law, a wife. One's performance of these roles constituted one's self, and was the standard by which one judged oneself. As Barlow (1989) says, "Engenderment relied most heavily on the *li*, the ritual, governing how the parts of the *lun* [that is, dyadic relationships] should act in relation to each other. Gendered subjects were the effect of *li*, the highly graded, absolutely specific technical knowledge of proper behavior. . . . Knowing how to behave as a person in a given range of contexts was continuous with being that person" (11).

Thus, when the Communist Party undertook to raise the status of women in the countryside, local cadres, who saw not "women" but "wives" and "daughters-in-law," did not see that much needed to be changed so long as family units were being treated fairly (K. Johnson 1983, 76). When in land reform women were given individual titles to land, which feminists in the Party thought would give women some degree of economic independence, local cadres usually handed the deeds over to the husband as the family's financial manager (K. Johnson 1983, 110; Wolf 1985, 19). When later women complained that it was unfair that in collectives women were paid less for the same work, male cadres could not understand their complaints, since family units composed of one man and one woman were being treated fairly.

Class Struggle. Confronting these difficulties, the Chinese Communist Party and later the Chinese state never abandoned their commitment to the liberation of women, but chose to mobilize women and men on class issues rather than on issues specific to women (K. Johnson 1983, 80). Women in China were classified for the purposes of class struggle according to the class background of their fathers and husbands, such that a woman who had never actually had control over property, or even a say in the disposal of her own person, would be classed as belonging to the landlord class if her husband belonged to that class (K. Johnson 1983, 40). As Marilyn Young (1989) notes:

> In a country that defines itself as a dictatorship of the proletariat, the contradiction of women's doubled identity [of gender and class] (and often consequent invisibility) makes their relationship to the state of vital importance. Uniting with the men of their class almost always means the disappearance of those concerns that are specific to their gender. Uniting with women of other classes on the basis of gender ignores real class divisions and is, or was, ideologically suspect. Unable, then, to marshall sufficient social force to act on their own behalf, without independent power or leverage, women are placed in the position of depending on what Judith Stacey has called the "public patriarchy"—the state and the party—to a greater extent than other groups in the society (254).

The Party organized a Women's Federation to mobilize women. But the Women's Federation, which had the potential to be a force that could raise women's consciousness of their own oppression and their own power to liberate themselves, has never been allowed an independent development. It has been kept carefully subordinate to the Party, so that the thoroughly male-dominated Party could decide what issues women should give their energies to (K. Johnson 1983, 77, 81–82).

In general, any kind of effort to mobilize women around women's issues or family issues has been seen as a dangerous splitting of women's efforts from the main thrust of the revolution, which has always been understood as class struggle. Since women thus belonged to many classes, any effort on behalf of women as women was likely to be seen as "bourgeois feminism" rather than as political action based on a pure Marxist class analysis.

Successes and Failures. The Party has at various times envisioned an end to abusive relationships within the family. The Marriage Law of 1950 proclaimed equal and easy access to divorce, and freedom of both men and women to choose their marriage partners (Wolf 1985, 144–45).

But in many areas local cadres have not tried hard to protect women from abusive relations. In the countryside parents still make marriage decisions, but with a greater input by the young people involved. Unless they go to high school, as only a small minority do, young people have no easy ways of meeting or getting to know each other before being engaged (Wolf 1985, 166). In the city, the Marriage Law of 1950 has been more successful: the young people play a much more active role in choosing their own partners (Wolf 1985, 163). And despite its recognition that divorce and an independent way of making a living is the weapon that women have against an oppressive family system, the Party has not made divorce readily available to women (K. Johnson 1983, 213–14). In the countryside, decisions about divorce are made by local cadres, who sometimes harass and criticize women who seek divorce, and in any case exercise considerable discretion (Wolf 1985, 163–64). Cadres generally seek to preserve families, even when it is clearly at the expense of women (K. Johnson 1983, 214). The New Marriage Law of 1980 makes divorce possible when neither side has love left for the other, and the divorce rate has risen again after a long lull since 1953 (Hareven 1987, 71). But it is still very low, particularly in the countryside: Wolf heard of only three divorces in the families of three hundred urban and rural women that she interviewed (Wolf 1985, 164).

The Party has also occasionally sought to make matrilocal marriage and intravillage marriage more acceptable. The 1950 Marriage Law supported village exogamy; in the 1980 revision this clause was quietly dropped (K. Johnson 1983, 209). In the Anti-Lin Biao, Anti-Confucius Campaign of the mid 1970s, matrilocal marriage was promoted (K. Johnson 1983, 197–98). These changes would allow women to remain in the village in which they already have established networks, instead of moving to a village where all the people in power are friends and relatives of the husband. Intravillage marriage also would benefit men, who in the cases where this has happened often have had to pay less in bride price for women in their own villages (Chan 1984). Two recent studies have found twenty percent of marriages occurring within the village or brigade (Wolf 1985, 167; Parish and Whyte 1978, 171).

The Party has sought to end expensive wedding ceremonies, bride price, and dowry. But none of these practices has been eliminated (K. Johnson, 209–13; Wolf, 158–62).

The Party has also sought to end the adopted-daughter-in-law form of marriage. Until recently one could have confidently written that this had been eliminated. Now there is some question raised by the fact that quite a few more male births are being registered than female births. Some of the missing girl babies may be being adopted by other families as future brides.

The Party has largely succeeded in ending the selling of girls and women, though in the wake of the economic reforms of the 1980s there has been a resurgence of such cases. Foot binding has ended, however, even in remote villages.

In all these areas of family and marriage practice, there have been gains, but in most of these areas there have not been thoroughgoing or widespread changes. Scholars argue that the Party, given the choice, has always backed off pursuing women's liberation with the kind of thoroughgoing campaign that would be needed to get changes made. The closest thing to an effective campaign was that which lasted for a few months in 1953 in support of the new Marriage Law of 1950. The Party itself admitted that it had largely been a failure, and did not renew it (K. Johnson 1983, 138–53; Stacey 1983; Wolf 1985).

Women and Work. When challenged to deliver on the promise of women's liberation, the Party has argued, as had Friedrich Engels, that when women come to take an equal part in productive labor, their position in the oppressive family system would naturally change (K. Johnson 1983, 88–89). It is indeed in the area of mobilizing women's labor outside the home that the Party has directed the most effort and had its greatest success, from the time of the revolutionary bases in the countryside to the present (K. Johnson 1983, 87). Official propaganda has fostered the idea that women are capable of the same kinds of work as men. Drawing more fully on women's untapped labor potential was crucial to the success of the revolution, as men were drawn off into the army. It was crucial also to later efforts toward economic expansion, for example during the Great Leap Forward period in the late 1950s.

But except in a few communes and factories, the Party has not seen to it that women had the kind of support (crèches, nurseries, canteens, sewing cooperatives) that would enable them to participate equally in the "productive" labor force (K. Johnson 1983, 172–73). And in fact women do not have equal access to jobs with good pay or good benefits, or to education, nor is there widespread practice of equal pay for equal work (Wolf 1985, 56–111).

The Party has sold the idea that women should participate equally with men in productive labor and in political life. The problem is that the Party has never really made this possible in China—as indeed it has never really been made possible in any other modern state. Women are not getting equal pay for equal work, and they are not being chosen for the best-paying categories of jobs, or promoted equally with men (Wolf 1985). Their earnings rapidly fall behind those of the men in their age cohorts (Wolf 1985, 66). And with the exception of the Great Leap Forward period in the late 1950s, no sustained effort has been made to relieve women who work full-time from the expectation of bearing unequally the burdens of housework and child rearing—what feminists call "the double day."

Another approach, taken for example during the Cultural Revolution, has been to locate the cause of inequality in the realm of ideas: feudal ideas on the part of men and rural peasants. This meant that gender-based inequality was attacked ideologically, but the structural basis of inequality (the double burden, the fact that in rural areas women marry out of their own villages) was not addressed (Young 1989, 255; K. Johnson 1983, 178–93).

Indeed, some scholars speak of a new Party and state-sponsored familism, in which the restoration of traditional family codes in the context of a restructured family for the purposes of the state is more important than women's liberation per se. What the Party has really done is to make an effort to raise the status of wives, daughters, and daughters-in-law within the "New Democratic" (yet still patriarchal) family:

> Where the rural peasant family made the father-son relationship sacrosanct, the Communist government propagandized for filial obligation to mothers and to the nation, the *guo*, through the mother-and-father. It recuperated into theory the cultural codes of filial subordination, the emphatic preference for immediate relationships, and the pattern of social construction of personal identity through participation in social dyads. . . . The post-Liberation People's Republic of China might be represented by the following formula: Husband is to wife as parents are to children and the state is to its citizens. [Barlow 1989, 16]

The Cultural Revolution Period. The Cultural Revolution period from 1966 to 1976 was in some ways good for women. First in the Anti-Lin Biao, Anti-Confucius Campaign, which is now seen as falling within the Cultural Revolution period, the issue of equal pay for equal work was explicitly raised (K. Johnson 1983, 194–207).

Second, the slogan "Politics in Command" meant a conscious, ongoing effort to expand women's public, political roles as well as economic ones. "After the initial stage of the Cultural Revolution when Revolutionary Committees were being established at all levels and Party Committees were being reconstituted, local authorities were directed from the top to increase the number of women on these bodies" (K. Johnson 1983, 185). Not only were more women mobilized, but young women in particular suddenly enjoyed considerable freedom and mobility (Young 1989, 255). Indeed even prior to the Cultural Revolution there had been success in getting more women to become politically involved, first through the Women's Federation, then through the land reform struggle, when party cadres encouraged women to come to meetings and to speak up (K. Johnson 1983, 108).

At the same time, though, the great emphasis during the Cultural Revolution on "Politics in Command" meant that women must not protest their double burden of a full-time job plus all the housework—failure to get all these things done meant that one had not really dedicated herself to the revolution, she had not really placed politics in command (K. Johnson 1983, 146–88). Any complaint made one suspect of bourgeois individualism (K. Johnson 1983, 184). And except during the Anti-Confucius Anti-Lin Biao Campaign, a woman who complained about unequal pay for equal work could be accused of placing material rewards, rather than politics, in command (K. Johnson 1983, 184).

Thus in practice what often happened in the countryside was an unplanned consonance between traditional "feudal" mores with respect to women and leftist denunciation of "bourgeois" individualism and personal freedom (Young 1989, 255).

Rural Leadership. The Party has not done what would be necessary to enable women to gain leadership positions in the countryside, even though at times the Party has urged rural cadres to give more leadership positions to women. This is at least partly because the Party has not really pushed on this matter. But it is also because the Party has seen the barriers to women's liberation and advancement as ideological rather than structural. For example, the Party has not recognized that women are held back from equal access to political participation and leadership positions by village exogamy and patrilocality in marriage, which prevent them from getting the kind of political base and real membership in their villages that men have because they remain in the same place with the same male network from birth (K. Johnson 1983, 189; Wolf 1985, 86–87).

It has been shown that where there are rural women leaders, they are usually women who have not married out of the village, and who are sisters or other blood relatives of leading men (Diamond 1975, 25; Wolf 1985, 87).

The Deng Xiao-ping Era of Economic Reforms

Since 1978, economic reforms have reshaped the lives of women. In the countryside, agriculture has been decollectivized and households have become the basic unit of production. Peasants have been encouraged to engage in sideline production, private markets have flourished, and the government has raised the prices it pays for farm produce. Agricultural work has largely been left for women to do, because it can be more easily combined with household and child rearing tasks, while men have sought other more lucrative jobs. These new policies and arrangements have increased women's opportunities to earn income (Honig and Hershatter 1988, 4), but in many places they have created a greater disparity between the income of women and men. They have also reinforced family authority (Wolf 1985; Stacey 1983, 271–72; Anagnost 1989).

In the cities, industrial enterprises have been given expanded powers to hire and fire, and have been held responsible for their own profits and losses. Under great pressure to make money, many have decided to hire men rather than women, allegedly because women need pregnancy leave, might press for day care facilities, and are less reliable workers because of their responsibilities at home (Honig and Hershatter 1988, 5). Behind these specific reasons lies a general belief that men are more capable than women. The educational system has been expanded, but at the same time entrance qualifications at all levels have become more restrictive (Honig and Hershatter 1988, 5). Here again a gender gap is evident in the widespread practice of requiring higher entrance examination scores for girls than for boys (Honig and Hershatter 1988, 21).

In the gender ideology of the 1980s and 90s what we have seen is a reaction against the Maoist gender ideology of the Cultural Revolution period (Honig and Hershatter 1988, 7, 25). Marilyn Young observes that the Maoist approach to the problem of women:

Rejects a biological determinism, embraces a concept of universal humanity, but the "universal human," the class conscious revolutionary, is male. Social change can be a product of the transformation of human attitudes; the "feudal" human attitude that needs to be changed is that women are seen as women, as different from men. So the solution is not to see them as women. At the level of material reality, of course, they will continue to bear and rear children and be responsible for their usual chores. At the level of ideology, though, this implicit aspect of their identity can be put aside. In the public realm they are to be seen as men. . . . The new woman [is to be] a kind of socialist androgyne: for public purposes a man, at home a loving wife and mother; genderless in public, chaste wives and selfless mothers in private. [Young 1989, 256; see also Andors 1983]

This Maoist idea that it is possible for a woman to be just like a man has been rather decisively rejected in the post-Cultural Revolution period. The "iron girl" model put forward in the Great Leap Forward, and again in the Cultural Revolution—namely, women who can do the same work as men, be as strong as men, accomplish the same revolutionary tasks as men—is now discredited. Now, men comment in the press that no one would want to marry an "iron girl," that these are "false boys" that should not be held up as a model for women, and that women have their own virtues, such as gentleness and emotional sensitivity, that should be valued (Honig and Hershatter 1988, 23–26).

But the men who are asking for women's special strengths to be valued are not asking for them to be valued *in the world of male work*, to be seen as virtues in cadres or managers, for example. Thus the definition of normative human being which women still have to meet in the most valued work places remains male (Young 1989, 261).

Gender-based division of labor is now assumed, or urged, as natural. Women are said to be naturally better at jobs requiring fine handwork, like embroidery, which also pay less. Women are naturally better at language. Women are naturally not good at science, or at higher education, or at mechanical or technical work, or engineering, or tractor driving. Women are naturally suited to child rearing, cooking, and sewing. Women are not promoted to be supervisors, for there is wide agreement that women make poor bosses (Wolf 1985, 68–76). The gender ideology that sees women as weaker and inferior workers, and supports gender-segregation in occupation based on ideas like "women can't learn a technical job" persists despite clear empirical evidence to the contrary (Honig and Hershatter 1988, 14–15; Wolf 1985, 82–85).

Honig and Hershatter report that media articles teach that girls are less capable than boys. In fact, the media convey a message to adolescents that biology dooms women to physical, intellectual, and emotional inferiority. As women reach puberty they should expect to lose ground to boys in all areas. The standard of value against which women should measure themselves always is male strengths, and by these standards women fall short. Also, media writers warn young women to expect obstacles to success: the persistence of "feudal ideas" in society mean that young women will be given fewer chances to succeed. But, the press says, nevertheless individual women should struggle against these impossible odds and try to succeed as best they can (Honig and Hershatter 1988, 14–31).

But as foreign feminist observers and the new creators of gender ideology in the Chinese press agree, it will not work. The feminists argue, though, that the problem is structural, not biological. As long as women are responsible for home and children, "they can no more fulfill the goals of the four modernizations equally with men than they could those of the preceding revolutionary period" (Young 1989, 261).

It has not been suggested in the 1970s, nor in the 1980s, that the sexual division of labor in China should be restructured so that society can benefit from the talents and contributions of both men and women. Nowhere is it suggested that men as well as women should care for children, cook, shop, wash, clean, and work full-time.

Rather, what is suggested is that women should expect less fulfillment and success in the world of work, and devote their energies to taking care of household matters and creating a restful home so that their husbands can give their all to their work and succeed in the work place. Women and men are complementary, gender polarity is to be honored, and women are to be instrumental to the realization of Chinese development, but now through their feminine gentleness and support for their men (Young 1989, 262). There has been a definite revival of the "virtuous wife and good mother" model. The press in the 1980s wrote frequently about women who displayed the qualities of "virtuous wives and good mothers" (Honig and Hershatter 1988, 173–81). "In stories about model fiancees and wives, attitudes about female virtues remained consonant with those of the imperial era, unchallenged by the public discourse that has challenged so much else in new China" (Honig and Hershatter 1988, 31).

These "modern" ideas about women in China fit well with traditional views. Marilyn Young (1989) notes: " 'Socialist spiritual civilization' . . . with respect to women . . . sounds remarkably like traditional Confucian morality: both subordinate the interests of the individual to that of the family. And the family is, in both, the province of the male head of household" (265). Wolf (1985) concludes that the state desires to weaken the power of the old family system, but simultaneously desires to promote the small domestic unit, which is often today the "stem family" consisting of two generations of couples and the unmarried children of the younger couple. This small family serves economically and socially necessary functions (188).

In fact, though, it is probably only in the rural areas that the family retains a good portion of its power over the lives of women and young people. Based on her extensive interviewing of women in rural and urban areas, Margery Wolf (1985) concludes that "in urban areas the state has more direct control over the futures of young people now than does the family." With respect to the ancestral rites that sustain the family ideology and reproductive practices that assure the family's future, the state has succeeded in making "not doing things the old way more attractive than doing things the old way" (246). By contrast, "rural China is still dominated by the family," both by the domestic group and by the ideological family of male relatives who live in the same village or collective:

> Ancestor worship is no longer carried on in the lineage halls, for they have been converted into granaries or stables, and the domestic ancestral tablets were burned during the Cultural Revolution. But many of the homes I interviewed in had pictures of deceased relatives, incense sticks, and makeshift bits of religious paraphernalia. Funerals . . . are again becoming elaborate, with mourning clothes and Daoist rituals to help the deceased through the various stages of postlife existence. [Wolf 1985, 247–48]

On Qing Ming, the traditional day for cleaning the graves of ancestors, the family still treks off to visit family graves. Children "learn their place in the long line of relatives who were there before they were born and who depend on them to continue on in the years ahead" (Wolf 1985, 248). While in urban areas women and men both interact with a larger society in their work units, in rural areas the family is still very much the context in which women live their lives. Neither the father-in-law nor the mother-in-law is quite as powerful as he or she once was—the daughter-in-law gains face by going out to work—but for a young woman divorce is still impossible without ruining her life, and most young women still live in communities consisting of their in-laws' relatives (Wolf 1985).

Contradictions of the Present

Conditions of unemployment and underemployment in the new freer economic market make it possible for the government to hold out to women the old promise of socialist liberation—that their equality will result from their integration into the paid work force and the socialization of household chores and child rearing (Young 1989, 265). Educated women express frustration at finding doors closed to them when they look for work at universities, one of the joint venture enterprises, or other desirable work places (Honig and Hershatter 1988, 248–50).

Many women are perhaps glad to be allowed to be central in their families as wife and mother, even at the sacrifice of equality in the work place. It is not clear that women in the countryside have ever wanted canteens, crèches, and nurseries to replace them as cooks and child rearers within their families. They might feel that this would involve giving up entirely their position in the family only to gain what would still probably be a second-class position in the world of work (Stacey 1983, 211–16).

On the other hand, whether a woman can still find fulfillment through her "uterine family" in her prized role of mother of sons, as Wolf (1972) has argued that she has done in the past, is now open to question. Having only one child makes the role of mother rather more limited than it was in the past.

The recent post-Mao population policy that limits births to one per family has had an enormous impact on women, as women are often blamed, and even beaten, when they have given birth to a female child (Honig and Hershatter 1988, 5; Wolf 1985, 258). And the decision whether or not to comply with the one-child policy places women in an impossible situation:

If a woman's husband and his family decide that it is worth the economic risk, it is her body that must conceal the illegal pregnancy, her body that will be the target of the cadre's anger if his quota is exceeded, her body that will endure a forced abortion perhaps too late to be entirely safe. She will be treated as if *she* had made the decision to have this illegal child even though the same cadre who is condemning her may also have "guided" his own sons and daughters-in-law in their reproductive decisions. [Wolf 1985, 258]

One would think that pushing the one-child policy would place great pressure on the government and Party to bring about greater equality of opportunity for men and women. For families to be satisfied with one child, one would think that the status of women must become more nearly equal to that of men (Young 1989, 265). Yet in fact the period of the promotion of the one-child policy has also been the period of lessening of efforts toward greater gender equality.

Lack of Focus on Gender Issues. According to Honig and Hershatter, since 1978 women who have been presented as role models in the press were of four types: "tireless workers for economic reform, famous personages, daring heroines, and loyal wives" (Honig and Hershatter 1988, 26). In the case of those who are models of hard work for the four modernizations, they are not singled out for doing work that challenged the sexual division of labor, or for exhibiting strength equal to that of men. The content of the stories do not revolve around gender issues at all. Rather, they are praised for virtues expected of all workers.

The same is true in the case of the stories of famous athletes, writers, or actresses: accounts of their professional achievements "seldom referred to the effects of gender on their work choices or career success." In the case of the heroines, "virtually no emphasis was placed on the fact that the protagonists were female" (Honig and Hershatter 1988, 27). It is as though gender hierarchy or discrimination is no longer a problem, so people can be written about as workers, peasants, or family members without calling attention to gender relations as a significant factor that shapes their experience. Chris Berry points out that even in films in which, to the Western eye, the story could be interpreted as raising gender issues, the way the film is shot prevents the viewer from identification based on gender (Berry 1985, 42).

The Feminization of Evil in Post–Cultural Revolution China. During the Cultural Revolution, state-sponsored insistence on the participation of women in the public realm inevitably unsettled the status quo of gender relations or, more basically perhaps, the given hierarchy of power and authority. Women apparently had opportunities to gain power (Young 1989, 258–59; Honig and Hershatter 1988). In the years after the Cultural Revolution, female figures in current literary and film treatments of that turbulent period have been frequently depicted as essentially venal, authoritarian, or brutal (Young 1989, 260; Gu Hua 1983).

Marilyn Young (1989) suggests that although these fictional characters are, of course, contemporary reconstructions intended for current consumption, they may also in some measure reflect reality: perhaps there were such abuses of power by women during the Cultural Revolution period. If so, she suggests, "perhaps the behavior of women in power should be understood as a reaction against long-established constraints on women. Given the possibility of some portion of power, they seized it, exercised it with maximum force, even relished it, not as power to do something, but, in a manner hardly peculiar to women, as power over others" (260).

But whether or not such abuses by women existed, women are now taking a disproportionate amount of blame. The most obvious example is the way in which Jiang Qing, Mao's wife, is portrayed as chiefly responsible for the Cultural Revolution, due to her lust for power, while of her husband Mao it is only said that he "made mistakes." Perhaps it is true, as Young writes, that in China "abuse of power is most easily denounced when it has been feminized. Evil itself has been feminized, and the message to women is clear: there is something in the natural order of things that does not love a woman exercising public power" (Young 1989, 262–63).

Progress. But despite these current trends away from further progress toward gender equality, there are still ways in which women's lives in China today are better than the lives of their grandmothers.

As Barlow (1989) says, men now marry citizens, protected in some ways by the state, and daughters now grow up—in rare cases—to be officials, no matter how restricted their powers may be in comparison to those exercised by male colleagues. Many girls have at least some access to education. Girls no longer suffer the pain of foot binding. Fewer are sold, killed at birth, or allowed to die of starvation. Women take more part in the political process, and it is taken for granted that women work outside the home.

And, as Barlow (1989) notes, "gender has entered the primary relation of state and citizen, breaking all historical precedent" (16).

"Woman" as seen through the opposition woman/man has been installed as a political category, though a subordinate one. Thus, the government pushes for inclusion of women (at least token) in leadership groups. "Woman" as an ideological category persists, and "has an iconography familiar to all of us—women driving tractors, women teaching school, women building dams—and a rhetoric, 'women hold up half the sky,' that makes it attractive, self-congratulatory, and accessible, from time to time, to the oppressed daughters-in-law that it originally intended to represent" (Barlow 1989, 16).

THE RELIGIONS

The government of China recognizes what it calls "five religions" in China: Catholicism, Protestantism, Islam, Buddhism, and Taoism (sometimes written Daoism). These five have institutions and written traditions of doctrine and practice that render them amenable to national organization; four of the five have their origins beyond China's borders and arouse the interest of coreligionists abroad. In what follows, we will look at the public discourse of gender in the four of these in which Han Chinese (ethnic Chinese) participate: Catholicism, Protestantism, Buddhism, and Taoism. We will also look at what facts and impressions we are able to gather about women's roles and opportunities within these religions.

The officially recognized "religions" of course do not exhaust the subject of religion in China. There are other "religious" social phenomena in contemporary China, which affect the lives of a great many women. The most significant is probably traditional Chinese "familism" (centered on patrilineage and expressing itself through reverence for ancestors). How "familism" and its values have fared in China since 1949 is a question of great importance to women, which we have tried to address in the previous section. The Confucian tradition of thought and practice has recently surfaced again in China. And there is also the diffuse but powerful "folk religion," centered on the worship of gods by networks of local communities. The folk religion, of course, has female representations of deity, as well as worldviews and practices that affect women's lives. But in all these cases, there is simply not enough information available yet on which to assess women's participation.[4]

Catholicism

In 1949 China had about three million Catholics and a church almost entirely under foreign missionary control. French Catholic missionaries built French-style cathedrals and appointed French bishops for the Chinese church. Today, after decades of vigorous suppression, when foreign support was cut off and most churches— for ten years all churches—were shut down, bishops and priests thrown in jail, and Catholics attacked as agents of foreign imperialist powers, there are still at least three million Catholics in China (some would say ten million). Many belong to families—in some cases whole villages or communities—that have been Catholic for generations, since the eighteenth or nineteenth centuries.

Since 1981 the state has again allowed an official Catholic Church to function under its control, being permitted no ties with the Vatican, but allowed to reopen seminaries for priests and novitiates for nuns, to reclaim church buildings, and restore open worship. In an interview published in *Asia Focus* in January 1989, Bishop Zong Huaide, president of the Chinese Catholic Patriotic Association, the independent Catholic institution created by the state in 1957, and acting head of the Chinese Catholic Church Administrative Commission and the Chinese Catholic Bishops' College, said there were 1,100 priests (including nearly ninety ordained since 1983), 630 seminarians studying for the priesthood in twelve seminaries, fifteen hundred religious sisters (probably almost all ordained before 1957), three hundred novice sisters, 57 bishops, more than a thousand churches and twenty-three hundred chapels opened since 1981, and an average of forty thousand baptisms each year (MacInnis 1989, 264.) But a very large number of Catholics avoid Masses given by the priests of the official church and attend those given by priests of a large underground church. About this underground church we have much less information, but it probably has at least as many priests, bishops, and communicants as the official church. Some estimate that it has more than seven million adherents with 60 to 120 bishops and 200 priests *(Far Eastern Economic Review,* 5 July 1990, 39).

Foreign Christian visitors to China sometimes ask about the position of women in the revived official church. They wonder whether there are any plans to allow women to become priests or hold leadership positions, as one might expect in a church which since 1957 has no longer had ties to the Vatican and which finds itself in a more occupationally egalitarian society. So far it has been their experi-

ence that church leaders do not respond directly to this question, merely voicing their concern about the shortage of church workers of all kinds (Cone 1986).[5] It seems that the church is very much concerned to revive traditional Catholicism as it has received it—note, for example, that the official church uses the Tridentine form of the Mass—in Latin, in silence, and with the second gospel—which is now largely unused outside China (Chan 1987, 156).

It is possible that given the shortage of trained and ordained clergy, nuns and lay women leaders may play greater roles than women in the same categories in other countries (that is, than their lack of formal ordination might suggest). Margaret Farley (1991) reports:

> Left after the Cultural Revolution with few and very elderly ordained clergy, unable to provide instant theological training for many new ministers and priests, the church has had to encourage the participation of lay people. Finding itself reborn in a society where equality of women and men is nearer achievement than almost anywhere else in the world, the church has acknowledged that "women hold up half the sky" (the one saying of Mao that we heard from Chinese women everywhere) and " ... in the church, more than half the sky" (as we were told by countless women churchworkers). Needless to say, the Protestant church has addressed these issues more fully than the Chinese Catholic Church, but even in the latter the role of women has changed considerably, and the participation of the laity grows daily. [204]

Scattered reports provide corroboration. For example, in 1988 in Guilin, which as of that date had no resident priest, three former sisters, married and now retired from secular work, led prayers, taught catechism, visited in homes, and in the absence of a resident priest provided pastoral care (MacInnis 1989, 311).

For another example, China Daily reports that one small county in Hebei province has nearly ten thousand Catholics living in 74 villages who worship in 47 churches or smaller places with religious guidance from five nuns and four priests (Jan. 28, 1991).

One thing on which all agree is that the number of priests and nuns is totally inadequate to the needs of so many Catholic communities. Lay leaders, including "catechists," former nuns, and lay sisters or "virgins," women who did not become nuns but who never married and dedicated themselves to serving the church, play very important roles, preaching, leading prayers, and offering pastoral care short of the sacraments. Due to the shortage of priests, most communities see a priest only once a month or even more infrequently. The result is that hearing Mass or receiving other sacraments is rare, and the life of the Catholic communities is sustained more often by learning the catechism and meeting for prayer under lay leadership.

But despite Dr. Farley's encouraging impression, it must also be said that Chinese Catholics in their current training programs are continuing the gender segregated structure of the Roman Catholic Church, even though they might be seen as having an opportunity to do something quite different.[6] Not only are current priests all men, but so are the next generation of future priests being trained now. Despite difficulty in some areas in finding suitable male candidates for seminary training, women are not being considered, but instead are being trained as nuns. And it is the stated goal of the revived church to limit priestly functions to celibate male priests.[7] These policies doubtless reflect the loyalty of Chinese Catholics to their own church tradition, as well as the loyalty of many, both inside and outside the official church, to the Holy See and the universal church (or perhaps the unwillingness of some to alienate the Holy See). But one consequence of the way that the revived official church has pursued its rebirth is that the voices of women within the Chinese church are not yet heard abroad.

As to the training of nuns, the *Beijing Review* published a report from the magazine *New Century (Xin Shiji)* that in 1990 more than a thousand women students were enrolled in primary schools for educating nuns opened since 1980. The article went on to report that in 1990 Beijing produced its first class of educated nuns, a group of seven. Aged 23 to 28, they were chosen in 1985 on the basis of entrance examinations. Their classes included Catholic principles, Bible, English, Chinese, current affairs, embroidery, and physical training. They received a stipend of 40 yuan a month. The report stated that after graduation they would "further their specific professions in nursing, English, cooking and sewing" (27).

Another example, perhaps more typical, is the three new novitiates in Guangxi province reported in 1988. In Guilin there had once been fourteen Chinese sisters trained by missionaries. Two of those, in their nineties, remain in Guilin. In 1987 the novitiate was reopened there, with six novices, all seventeen years old. "Three former Chinese Sisters will teach and guide the novices in spiritual formation, while a layman in charge of the church will teach politics. They hope to find a priest to teach scripture. Until they get the old convent back, they will live in the church" (MacInnis 1989, 311).

In Liuzhou eleven novices in their twenties are taught by two old "Virgins" (lay sisters). The novices earn their subsistence by doing sewing subcontracted from a factory. In Wuzhou twenty-one novices are taught by three former sisters and an aging parish priest. They follow the same daily schedule as missionary sisters did in former years: rise at 5:15; morning prayers and meditation; Mass; breakfast; household duties; classes; noon prayers; one hour of rest; sewing work in the afternoon; visit the Blessed Sacrament at 5:00; prepare and eat supper; free time in the evening; evening prayers; and bedtime at 9:30 (MacInnis 1989, 311–12).

Mary, known in Chinese as the Holy Mother, is very important to Chinese Catholics, and inspires many pilgrimages. For example, an annual pilgrimage in May to her shrine (the Basilica of Our Lady) on Sheshan, an hour's drive from Shanghai, draws thousands of Catholic men and women from Shanghai and the central coastal region (MacInnis 1989, 272).

Protestantism

After 1949 Chinese Protestants formed a single united church based on the principles of self-support, self-propagation, and self-government, stopped accepting missionaries and funds from abroad, and tried to survive in cooperation with socialist revolution in China under the United Front. Most churches were closed, pastors could not be supported, and articles in the few remaining publications tended to be limited to announcements of the church's support for whatever political campaign the Party was launching at the moment (Whyte 1988).

During the Cultural Revolution the few remaining churches were closed or destroyed, Bibles were confiscated and burned, and even the most cooperative ministers and leaders were put in jail. Since 1979 these leaders have been freed, supervision under the Religious Affairs Bureau of the government (and the United Front Office of the Party) has been restored, and the government has permitted churches to be returned to the government-controlled Chinese Christian Three-Self Patriotic Movement Committee (TSPM) and the China Christian Council.

As in the case of Catholics, in the absence of churches many Protestants had formed networks of underground meeting places in their homes. While perhaps four million Protestants have returned to the reopened officially sanctioned churches, a larger number (the China Christian Council claims three million; some evangelical groups claim fifty million; one careful estimate in the service of neither group suggests sixteen million) continue to meet in the so-called house churches.

Some of these are explicitly separatist—that is, unwilling to affiliate in any way with the China Christian Council and the TSPM (Chao and Van Houten 1988). Underground house churches are free of government control of their theology and teachings. Some groups preach a highly eschatological theology or one focused entirely on miracles and on heaven, as well as a complete separation of Christian concerns from those of the society (K. H. Ting 1991, 402).

Protestant communities vary widely according to what overseas missionary groups or indigenous Christian movements had had the most influence in the region. The officially sanctioned church does not have large financial resources, and is not allowed to accept gifts from abroad, except through the Amity Foundation, which has accepted help with social service projects, Bible printing, and English teaching (Y. R. Ting 1991; B. Whyte 1988). The officially sanctioned church has been allowed to use its resources to open a limited number of theological seminaries, to send out a correspondance course to forty-five thousand rural church leaders who have been cut off from training, and to send a small number of seminary graduates abroad for further training (Woo 1988, 495). The non Three-Self churches have accepted clandestine support from evangelicals abroad.

Although most of the leaders of the church and the pastors are over seventy, and only a few are women, the China Christian Council, the officially sanctioned church, has worked toward establishing a future marked by a greater degree of gender equality. Nanjing Theological Seminary reopened its doors in March 1981 with 51 students enrolled in a four-year course, selected from more than seven hundred applicants. Twenty-nine were men, twenty-two were women. Since that time at least a third of the seminarians at Nanjing Theological Seminary have been women (G. Brown 1983, 175). In 1981 a three-year graduate course was added. One reliable observer says that half of the seminary students across the country are women (Jean Woo, personal communication, July 1991). Ge Baojuan reports that at the seminary where she teaches, Zhongnan Seminary in Wuhan, there are eighteen women students and fifteen men students (Ge 1991, 2–3.) A third of the students sent abroad are women.

There are a number of women on the faculties of theological seminaries, including Nanjing, though mostly not yet in the core theological sciences. One seminary was for several years headed by a woman (Towery 1987, 120–21). There are a number of women leaders at the national level, mostly former YWCA leaders.[8]

The fruits of this effort are seen clearly in the churches of many cities and towns. On the basis of a stay of some months in China in which she interviewed women church leaders, San Francisco Theological Seminary professor Antoinette Clark Wire (1989) writes: "Three Self and China Christian Council have been particularly active in the cities and one can see there the results of their policies of incorporating all cherished Christian practices, cultivating Chinese arts and wisdom, and not discriminating by sex, age and level of education" (193). James H. Cone, who on a visit to China inquired particularly into the church's progress toward gender equality, reported that the preacher at a service he attended in Nanjing was a woman who was one of the pastors at the church (Cone 1986). Antoinette Clark Wire (1989) writes:

> In city and town churches the women who take leadership
> roles are of two generations. Those trained before the revolu-
> tion or shortly thereafter are more often quite
> conservative. . . . These older women tell their stories in
> terms of the sins of childhood, naming the great Chinese
> preacher who converted them. Skills they gained in Christian
> schools and seminaries [usually in sex segregated training pro-
> grams] they have practiced in preaching and music leadership
> in many cities. In the early years they were sent out by their
> denominations, later they served in more indigenous spiritual
> groups, and now they are asked to assist in local churches.
> Their preaching is Biblically based . . . dogmatic and moralis-
> tic but with a strong appeal to God's love and forgiveness.
> Even well beyond retirement age—at 55-60 for Chinese
> women—they continue to preach and take special leadership
> in local Three-Self committees, choir directing, youth and wo-
> men's Bible study, and are known for organizing lively testi-
> mony services. These women were traditionally lay leaders,
> though a few have been ordained in recent years. Their major
> focus seems to be on the individual spiritual life of other
> Christians whom they serve. . . .
> The younger generation of women church leaders in the
> towns and cities have been trained in the 1980's and are just

beginning to teach and preach. Very few are now ordained because extended parish experience is expected first. Some have finished seminary training and work full-time in churches or are pursuing graduate study to prepare for teaching. But more are factory or farm workers whose gifts led them into preaching and who now seek training wherever possible without permanently leaving their jobs. . . . These younger women leaders are often already model workers in their factories and involved in neighborhood committees. It is their Christian faith that is new, not their social integration. Their Christian faith is focused by this social integration on God's love for all, on Christ's sacrifice for others, and on the Spirit of peace and cooperation that transforms family and community life. [193]

However, a somewhat different picture emerges if one looks to the countryside. On the one hand, as Wire (1989) writes, "the rural church is the place where women's leadership is most pronounced." Women are very active as leaders in rural Protestant "meeting points" (worshiping congregations, sometimes as large as a thousand people) or prayer groups in villages that are only infrequently served by a pastor. In many cases it was these women who kept such meeting points or prayer groups going whenever possible through the difficult Cultural Revolution period (Jean Woo, personal conversation, 1991). As Antoinette Clark Wire (1989) reports:

The commonplace about the church during the Cultural Revolution, when buildings and Bibles were confiscated, is that "only a few old women" were known as Christians. In some places they were ignored, in others they were put into reeducation classes where they were supposed to analyze their problem, were physically restricted and required to financially support their teachers. . . . Whatever the treatment, the sudden surge of interest in the church after the fall of the "gang of four" is witness to widespread respect for the integrity of these women. [192]

Since 1987 hundreds of these women leaders have come to Nanjing Seminary and now to other regional seminaries for one-year theological training courses, as part of what has been a major effort by the China Christian Council to improve the theological education of rural church leadership. The pilot program at Nanjing Seminary was begun and coordinated by a woman, Sister Jiang Peifen (China News Update July 1991, 5).

But, on the other hand, although these women have emerged as leaders, many are quite conservative theologically and socially, as are their communities. Faced with the need for baptism, for example, rather than officiating themselves, these rural women would more likely invite a pastor (male) from a city church to come and perform the ceremony (Jean Woo, personal communication, 1991). There are other signs that, as one would expect from the way in which rural women have not been able to attain leadership positions in society since 1949, the idea of women exercising formal authority as heads of churches and as leaders of religiously sponsored projects is not yet broadly acceptable. It can be feared that the leadership of women that developed under the conditions of the Cultural Revolution is unlikely to be reproduced in more stable times. For example, in post-Cultural Revolution church activities such as rural clinics and rural development projects sponsored by the Amity Foundation with overseas support, women apparently do not take or are not given leading roles. An American churchman sent to report on the work of Amity social service projects reported that while women are well represented on the national staff, at the county and township level leaders in the field were almost entirely men (L. Brown 1991, 617.)

The fact is that most Protestant Christians in China are theologically conservative, and many are conservative on the question of women in church leadership as well. In a field report on Christians in Zhejiang province, who number over a million,[9] Philip Wickeri (1990) reported that "Zhejiang Christians are generally conservative-evangelical. . . . They tend to see themselves as "apolitical" in their approach to Christian faith, and maintain a fairly traditional Chinese social outlook. Most Zhejiang churches, for example, will not accept a woman pastor" (576). To serve all the Protestants in Zhejiang there were in the spring of 1990 only ninety-nine pastors, mostly in their sixties and seventies. Only two of the ordained pastors are women. In the city of Wenzhou, which has an extraordinarily flourishing Protestant community of four hundred thousand there are 133 full-time pastors, including 23 newly graduated seminarians, and three thousand voluntary church workers. Wickeri was told that there were no women pastors, but that a third of the voluntary church workers, who were the backbone of the churches, were women (Wickeri 1990, 577). One longtime observer commented that the church in Zhejiang is the slowest in the whole nation to ordain women pastors, in marked contrast to the church in Shanghai, which has ordained women pastors for years (Woo, personal communication, July 1990).

Chen Tingting (1991), a recent graduate of Zhejiang Seminary, writes of her pains and joys as a new evangelist in the Christian Church of Linping township in Zhejiang province. Her dilemmas seem to reflect the tension created by two salient aspects of contemporary Chinese church life. On the one hand the church is a strong supporter of traditional family and gender-marked arrangements, concentrating in its preaching on the importance of filial behavior, of meekness and obedience in relations between mother-in-law and daughter-in-law—the story of Ruth and Naomi is a popular sermon topic. On the other hand the church is calling on women to take on new leadership roles—new both in the experience of the church and in the experience of the rural society—that make the fulfillment of traditional family and gender responsibilities very difficult. At the moment the state is also promoting traditional family structures and traditional household responsibilities and roles for women, in addition of course to work outside the home. Thus the traditionalist values of Protestants are doubly functional in securing them a safe place in society. Chen Tingting's exemplary behavior helps her family win the "model family" award, which helps them support their contention that Christianity is not antisocial or antisocialist:

> I am a woman, and a most ordinary one. I have a family which includes my husband, parents-in-law and a son. For generations we have been farmers and still depend on working on the land for a livelihood. Having chosen church work as my profession does not mean that I can give up farming. Nor can I neglect my duties at home as a filial daughter-in-law, a traditional wife and a mother. With the shortage of staff in the rural churches, I am responsible to lead three congregations. Many church meetings take place in the evenings. In addition to Bible studies and prayer services during the week, my ministry includes families—at the time of their weddings, funerals, and special thanksgiving services which are common in rural China to celebrate birthdays, or the completion of building a new home. In the past years I have [also] been asked to organize short term training classes for church volunteers. That involves much coordination of human and written resources, travelling to villages and "meeting points" (worshipping congregations, sometimes as large as 1,000 peo-

ple) throughout the county, making arrangements for classes to take place, and the recruitment and selection of students. Whenever I am not doing any of the above, I would be visiting church members in their homes, a very important part of my work, to listen to my parishoners, to understand their needs and to demonstrate that the church cares for them.

With this kind of work load, which I do enjoy, there is little time or energy left to take care of my own son, or to be constantly available to my elderly parents-in-law. The least but not last is my own need for quiet time for reflection, prayer, study and the search for guidance from God. . . .

Though my life may sound very overburdened with tasks, I am not overwhelmed because I do find so much joy in serving God. . . . In my province there is [sic] still no ordained woman pastors. It is generally recognized or even an accepted fact that women would have more difficulty leading a church. But it is not the case in my church. The elderly leaders have been exceptionally understanding. For example, during harvest time or the planting season when the task of farming is doubled or tripled in my family farm, they would make accommodations, so that I can do my share at home. The leaders in the church would frequently consider my responsibilities at home when they schedule meetings. They would adjust their schedule the best they can so that I have time with my family in the evenings. Their thoughtfulness has actually helped my relationship with my family. My husband used to complain, out of his lack of understanding. But now he is very supportive to my work. Whenever there is important work in the church he would volunteer to do more housework and encourage me to concentrate on the work I need to do in the church.

Of course serving God in rural China is not all smooth sailing. While preaching is one of my main tasks, it is more important to live it. . . . We are a witness to Christ not only within the church, but in our society at large as well. This year my family received a "model family" award in our village. This too is our way of witness in Socialist China: that Christians are good examples and good citizens demonstrating God's love in all that we do. [3–4]

The need for equal participation by men and women in practice and leadership, and the need to make it possible for women's voices to be heard in the church, are not topics about which national church leaders have yet taken many occasions to speak and write. A sign that this may be changing is a speech by Ms. Cao Shengjie, Associate General Secretary of the China Christian Council, given at the women's panel of a worldwide ecumenical conference held in Nanjing in May 1986. Cao reported to her largely foreign audience:

> Women's ordination is not a big problem now. We have women pastors all over our country. More and more church women are participating fully in many fields of church work. This is the bright side. But due to historical reasons, church women are on the whole less educated and lack training. Some are too timid, too shy to bear responsibilities, and in some church communities, hold to conservative ideas. Some older Christians still take women church workers as inferior to men. That is why women do much in the church, but not many women church leaders have emerged yet, on the national level anyway. I hope that women will be more represented in our China Christian Council and Three-Self Movement, so that our voices may get louder.

That Cao's recognition that there is an issue that needs to be addressed is shared by other leaders of the National China Christian Council is reflected in the recent establishment at its headquarters of a women's desk, headed at this time by Cao Shengjie (Jean Woo, personal communication, 1991). Even more striking is a recent statement by Bishop K. H. Ting, the leader of the national China Christian Council:

> Half of the population consists of women. Yet due to the long history of male-centeredness throughout the world, women have been taking a subordinate role. Even in the church Christians (including women) continue to read the Bible and to manage church affairs only from men's perspectives. Although there have been some breakthroughs in recent years, the potential for women's contribution is far from being developed, nor is it taken seriously by Christians (including women themselves). Can *Tian Feng* be instrumental in helping raise the status of women in the church, and in encouraging women to make their unique contributions to Bible study and theology?

This statement perhaps mirrors the influence on Ting's thinking of his women students who have been sent to Western theological seminaries for graduate study and have there encountered Christian feminist theology. It has a wonderful resonance within contemporary Western feminist theological discourse. Whether it has any of the same kind or degree of resonance within the discourse of the now very indigenous Chinese Protestant churches remains to be seen.

Taoism

Today's Taoism in China can be divided into two types: a monastic Taoist lineage, called Quanzhen, and a hereditary married male Taoist priesthood known as the Zhengyi lineage.[10] Quanzhen Taoism has now been revived in many monasteries large and small in the north and southwest of China; many of these monasteries house both women and men celibate monastics. Women monastics are known as *kundao* or *daogu*; men monastics are known as *qiandao* or *daoshi*; collectively Taoist monastics are called *daoshi*.[11] Zhengyi Taoists conduct Taoist ceremonies and in a variety of ways serve local and regional folk religion by embedding its rites in a Taoist cosmological context (Dean 1988; 1989). This tradition once had court sponsorship and was the predominant form of Taoism in China. It has ceased to be significant as an independent movement and is important now as a servant to folk religion. Its ceremonies are popular particularly in Shanghai and the southeast.

There are some indications that women once participated in Zhengyi ceremonies, but this seems no longer to be always the case: indeed, it seems more common that women are banned from the ritually defined sacred space at major Zhengyi rites (Dean 1989).[12] Quanzhen, on the other hand, since its origins in the twelfth century, has always included women in its lineages and practice on a remarkably equal basis (Despeux 1990; Tao-chung Yao, personal communication, August 1991). Since monastic Quanzhen is the only form of Taoism alive today in the People's Republic of China in which women participate significantly, we will focus on women's roles in Quanzhen.

The Revival of Quanzhen Taoism. Quanzhen, and indeed a particular subsect called Longmen, has been the form of Taoism whose revival has received the most support from the central government of the People's Republic of China. One reason perhaps is that it has less connection with popular religion, always seen as a danger to state power. Another reason may be that Quanzhen *qiandao* (monks) and *kundao* (nuns), since they have no families, are ideal for the task of guarding and maintaining the historically important Taoist sites and worship centers that the government now wishes to protect and exploit. The interests of the government and the interests of Taoists are in conflict: the government wants caretakers and tour guides; the Taoists are willing to work as caretakers, hotel and restaurant managers, and tour guides in order to resume communal life, carry out their meditative and yogic practices, and pass on their lineages and traditions. The challenge Taoists face is to achieve these goals in the face of limited resources, restrictive supervision, and heavy work schedules (Bokenkamp, personal communication, June 1991).

As in the case of the other religions classed among the "five religions," the government has set up a national Taoist association with headquarters in Beijing at a famous Taoist temple, the Baiyunguan. The national Taoist association publishes two journals, *Zhongguo Daojiao* and *Daoxiehuikan*. There is at least one woman on the editorial board of these publications, and a few women who write for them.[13] In addition, there are at least three women members of the executive committee of the national Taoist association (David Yu, personal communication, 1991; also Pas, personal communication, 1991). A small national training program lasting nine months or a year for novice *qiandao* and *kundao* is conducted in Beijing; the first four classes, of 24, 40, 38, and 47 students each, were for *qiandao* only; the fifth, a class of approximately forty, was for *kundao* only (MacInnis 1989, 210).[14]

In areas where Quanzhen has the potential to be active, or where major Taoist temples and sites exist that the government wished to reopen and protect, the government set up local Taoist associations. Monastery property has been returned to these associations, which in turn has supervised the reopening of Taoist places of worship and practice, and the construction of facilities needed by tourists. *Qiandao* and *kundao* are given monthly salaries by the Taoist association, which sells entrance tickets and collects receipts from hotels, restaurants, and shops run by the Taoist monastics and lay employees. Taoists at small sites with no tourist potential are encouraged to support themselves by farming.

So far, the government has not permitted any full ordinations of new *qiandao* or *kundao*, a sign that it is reluctant to allow Taoism, even Quanzhen Taoism, to revive (Hahn 1989). Young men and women with good educational backgrounds who wish to become novices must apply to the United Front Office of the Communist Party that supervises religious activities, and to the city or provincial Taoist association. The total numbers accepted are limited by the state; those chosen are assigned to monasteries by the supervisory organizations. There are many more applicants, particularly women applicants, than can be accepted (MacInnis 1989).

Local training programs for novices are being carried out in a number of places. In Sichuan at least *kundao* and *qiandao* participate equally in the training, and in not too unequal numbers. These programs last around three weeks, and at the very least teach new recruits how to chant the daily scripture recitations and the longer calendrical ceremonies. Longer training programs include Taoist history (Hachiya 1990). As with the other religions, Taoists are only allowed to conduct ceremonies on the premises of the monastery or temple. A number of activities considered superstitious are forbidden on monastery or temple grounds. These include divination, the selling of talismans, and so forth (Bokenkamp, personal communication, 1991).

The Lives of Kundao. Qingchengshan near Chengdu in Sichuan province is a good example of a historically important Taoist mountain monastic center which has been redeveloped as a tourist site. A steep but beautiful path leads up the mountain past a number of temples. The buildings on the mountain were not severely damaged during the Cultural Revolution. Oral tradition credits the late Premier Zhou En-lai with personally ordering its protection.

The Taoist association for this region has 105 members who are monastics: 41 men and 64 women. There are only two fully ordained people, one man and one woman. In 1988 the Japanese scholar Hachiya Kunio (1990) led an investigative team to China to visit Taoist sites, interview monastery officers and Taoist association officials at each, and report on the current state of Taoism in China. He found that, of the temples on the mountain, the largest and most important is headed by a man, while the two next most sizable and important are headed by women. Both *qiandao* and *kundao* live and work at all three, and other offices at all three are filled by both women and men. Drawing on his report, as well as other sources published in China, the following more detailed picture emerges of the lives of *kundao* on Qingchengshan.

Wu Yuan-chang is the head of the Jianfugong, the first monastery on the way up the mountain. She is 84 years old. She became a *kundao* at 19. In 1957 she moved to Qingchengshan, where she has been ever since (Hachiya 1990, 126, note 1). She is vice chairperson of the local Taoist association for Qingchengshan (Hachiya 1990, 133). She met with Hachiya's team and answered most of the questions. Questions about the business aspects were answered by Xia Ming-qing, a 30-year-old *kundao* who is given the title of "accountant" (124).

Wu *kundao* reported that twelve monastics live in Jianfugong, three men and nine women. Most are quite young; four are in their twenties. One layman also lives there. They support themselves by growing and selling tea and selling souvenirs. They also have a hotel, offering single and double rooms. They sell the wine produced at one of the other temples on the mountain. They take in several tens of thousands of yuan per year (probably in excess of the equivalent of U.S. $10,000). They do not have land on which to raise food.

They have very little time for the practice of the rituals of their tradition. They do not try to hold any of the big ritual celebrations of the year; these are held instead further up the mountain at the Laojundian at Tianshidong. Nor do they have any special ceremony on the first and fifteenth of the month, even though pilgrims are many on those days. Likewise, special services at the request of lay people are held further up the mountain at Tianshidong.

They get up at 5:30, and from 6 to 7 they recite the morning service. At 7 they have breakfast, everyone together in silence in the dining room, silently reciting a mantra. At 8 they all start work in the tea plantation, the shop, or the hotel. At 12 they have the midday meal. In the afternoon they go back to work. At 6:30 they have the evening meal, and at 7 go to the worship hall for a thirty-minute evening service. From 8 to 9 P.M. they study, sometimes individually, sometimes as a group. They read scriptures or study how to perform rituals. At 10 they go to bed. Seated meditation is done in the middle of the night in their rooms, the older ones tending to do it for longer periods than the younger ones. Some will do it for an hour, some for two hours, some all through the night.

Further up the mountain, at a thousand meters, Hachiya came to the most active monastery, ritual center, and tourist destination, the Tianshidong (Hachiya 1990, 132–56). Tianshidong is headed by a man, the *gao-gong*, who is eighty-one, but has several women officers, including a 34-year-old *kundao* who is the guest master. Here there were 22 monastics in residence, 11 men and 11 women. The monastics here get the best salary on the mountain, about forty yuan a month, in addition to food. Clothing and texts are provided once a year by the Taoist association. Income is from a shop, a hotel (the most important source), a restaurant, a tea plantation, and donations. The money from admission tickets goes to the Taoist association, not to the monastery.

This is the major temple at which the four great yearly festivals are held for three days each in the hall of the highest deities, the Three Pure Ones. There are two other festivals honoring founders of the tradition that are held in the hall of the Three Pure Ones for one day each. The festival honoring the first Celestial Master, Chang Tao-ling, used to be a very big affair; Hachiya was told that now only two temples in China, Tianshidong and Hemingshan, carry it on (Hachiya 1990).

On the first and fifteenth of the month there are monthly observances, which everyone unless sick attends, in the Yellow Emperor Hall. Four or five times a year special services are put on at the request of and for the benefit of laity. There are two types: the first is to help the souls of the deceased—this varies in length and can cost from 1000 yuan to 5 or 6,000 yuan. The second is to worship the Heavenly Worthies and to pray for prosperity and long life.

The daily routine resembles that of Jianfugong, except that an hour is given in the morning from 5:30 to 6:30 to the practice of their own individual training methods (breathing exercises [qi-gong], music, calligraphy). During the day they all work at their assigned jobs in the tea plantation, guarding the worship halls, or working in the hotel. After the evening service and dinner, which ends at 8, they can return to the individual pursuits they practiced in the morning. At 10 they go to bed.

The central practice of the Quanzhen tradition, seated meditation for the practice of "inner alchemy," is done at any time in their rooms. Hachiya was told that Taoist inner alchemy is a conservative tradition that is taught and practiced secretly. A master may have three disciples, and give each of them different instructions. Therefore practice is carried out in one's own room (Hachiya 1990, 136–37).[15]

Tianshigong is also the site of short-term training programs for novices; when Hachiya visited, there were 43 students, all monastics from all over Sichuan (Hachiya 1990, 137). On the day of the visit they were practicing chanting. The class schedule showed that the students were studying writing, calligraphy, acupuncture, history of Taoism, history of Qingchengshan, rituals, martial arts (Hachiya 1990, 144–45). Hachiya did not comment on their gender, but during my own visit there in the summer of 1988 a similar training program was in progress, and women students made up at least one-third of the class (Levering 1988a).

Hachiya's next visit was to Chaoyangdong, where 3 *kundao* live (Hachiya 1990, 158). Yin Ming-dao (age 75) is the head of the temple.

Yin Ming-dao is clearly knowledgeable about the specifically female practice of inner alchemy. Catherine Despeux, a French scholar of Taoist inner alchemy asked Yin Ming-dao, in October, 1984, whether there was any difference in Taoist practice between men and women. Yin Ming-dao reportedly replied:

> When we worship in the temple, when we chant sacred texts aloud, it is exactly the same [for men and women], there is really no difference. The difference is in the physical and meditative practice *(lian-gong)* [of inner alchemy]. What a [male] *Daoshi* practices is "making the white tiger submit" (that is, not releasing semen but circulating it back up the spine to the head). For a [female] *Daogu,* the practice is "cutting off the head of the red dragon" (causing the menses to cease). [Lai 1985]

Finally, Hachiya and his team reached a large temple near the top of the mountain, Shangqinggong (Hachiya 1990, 160). The head of the monastery here is a woman, Xiao Ming-xiao, age 70. She left home in 1939, and was fully ordained in 1943. The temple was returned to the Taoist association in 1986; at the time there were 7 monastics living in it. Income comes from a hotel, a restaurant, and a shop. There are 12 *mou* of land, on which tea is grown for sale, and vegetables are grown for the temple's own consumption. They have to buy most of their food. Profits are greatest from the restaurant. Of their income, 60 percent goes to the Taoist association.

A total of 12 *qiandao* and 12 *kundao* live here. Then there are two still in their probationary period. Three laymen live here too and share in the work.

There are 13 large festivals during the year, roughly one a month except for three in the first month and two in the ninth month. A special ritual is done in the morning service of the first and the fifteenth of each month.

This year only one service for the recently dead had been put on, at the request of a lay family from Chengdu; it lasted three days and cost 2,300 yuan. It took the monastics a month to prepare for this service, including preparing the documents. They also do "releasing the burning mouths" *(fang yan-kou)* services for all the dead.

Xiao Ming-xiao is apparently a woman of exceptional warmth and graciousness, ideally suited to the role of provider of hospitality, which in the current context of the Taoist revival so many Taoist women and men now have to assume. Hachiya's team reported that she kindly showed them all her ordination robes and paraphernalia (Hachiya 1990, 163–64). She is featured in an article in *Zhongguo Daojiao* in March 1987, entitled "Under the Leadership of the Qingchengshan Taoist Association All of the Taoists on the Mountain Work Hard to Make a Contribution to our Country's Four Modernizations" (Lai 1987). The article tells of the activities of Daoist men and women at Qingchengshan. The article fits the pattern found by Honig and Hershatter: it does not focus on the gender of the model women and men described:

The monks and nuns of Qingchengshan love the temple as their own home, for the sake of building up Qingchengshan they get up early and stay up late. Working very hard, their thoughts are on improvement. For example the abbess of Shangqinggong Xiao Zong-qing, sixty-seven, works very hard . . . ; she also makes "Taoist pickles," and is excellent at making vegetarian dishes [so that people are attracted to her temple to eat]. To build up Qingchengshan and make contributions to the "Four Modernizations," when she became the head of the temple, she realized that the busy guest season was approaching, but the quilts and mosquito nets and other furnishings that the guests would need were in terribly dilapidated condition. In order to make the guests comfortable, she donated her entire savings of many years, 9,630 yuan, and bought bedding and quilts and mosquito nets for the guests. She also painted and refurbished the interior and exterior of the temple. She treats guests with great courtesy, and cares about them more than she cares about herself. In the middle of the night in April of last year four travellers from far away with no reservations arrived with a small child, only to find that all the beds were filled, and there weren't even any quilts or coverings. When Abbess Xiao heard about this, she personally took them to her room, gave them her bed and her quilt. Several of the other nuns and monks followed her example and gave the guests their quilts, sleeping till morning wrapped instead in cotton overcoats. The guests were so moved that they said, "you nuns and monks are wonderful, treating your guests with such kindness, we feel so much warmth it's almost as though we were with our own family." Abbess Xiao has many times received that kind of praise from guests.

Special Practices for Women in Quanzhen. Historically, women enjoyed a relatively high status within Quanzhen Taoism. This is shown by the quantity of poems addressed to female adepts, and by the number of nunneries attached to this tradition (Pregadio 1991, 86–87).

Within Quanzhen Taoism there arose an "inner alchemy" literature specifically addressed to women, as well as a set of moral and ritual precepts specifically for women (Pregadio 1991, 87). There were nine precepts for Quanzhen female adepts, which were expounded as part of Wang Ch'ang-yueh's *Precepts for the First Degree of Perfection* compiled in 1656 (Pregadio 1991, 87). Slightly different rules are given in later inner alchemy texts for women. "The daily practice involved meditation and recitation of scriptures, including the *Lao-tzu, Chuang-tzu, Huang-t'ing ching, Ta-tung ching,* and *Tung-ku ching*" (Pregadio 1991, 87).

In the "inner alchemy" aiming at cultivating the vital force *(ming),* the practices are arranged into three basic stages, defined as transmutation of the Essence *(ching)* into Energy *(ch'i),* Energy into Spirit *(shen),* and Spirit into Emptiness *(hsu).* A "woman's *ch'i* resides in her breasts, or in a point between them called the Cavity of *ch'i.* . . . This *ch'i* produces secretions that become menstrual blood, the material aspect of the Essence in a woman's body" (Pregadio 1991, 89). The first stage of the practice is to avoid the downward dispersal of the Essence "by massaging the breasts, so that their secretions, rather than transforming themselves into blood, enrich the woman's natural endowment of *ch'i*" (Pregadio 1991, 89; see Despeux 1990, 245–53). "This results in the progressive diminution and final disappearance of menstruums [menstruation], a process called 'Decapitation of the Red Dragon' *(chan ch'ih-lung)*" (Pregadio 1991, 89–90).[16] A woman further practices to avoid the degradation of the "Pearl of Dew" naturally present in her body, and to "collect it when it is in full brilliance two and a half days before each menstruation" (Pregadio 1991, 90). Collecting the Pearl marks the completion of the first stage of the practice.

In the second stage, the Pearl is developed into an Embryo through the union of the adept's Spirit with the pure Energy that has been cultivated during the first stage (Despeux 1990, 269–73). This is typically described as the exchange of the essences of the heart and the generative organs. The pure yin essence of the heart, and the yang essence of the generative organs meet halfway during their respective descent and rise, generating the Embryo (Pregadio 1991, 90). Once generated, the Embryo is nourished for ten months through the method called "embryonic breathing," which circulates the inner breath through the five viscera (heart, spleen, liver, lungs, and kidneys). At the end of the ten months "Energy has been transmuted into Spirit, a Spirit with Yin qualities" (Pregadio 1991, 90–91).

The transmutation of this yin Spirit into yang Spirit is the object of the third and final stage (Despeux 1990, 275–81). Four phases mark this stage for a woman. The first, called "delivery from the womb," is the actual birth of the Immortal Child. In the second phase, "breast-feeding for three years," the Child is taught how to exit through the "heavenly gate" (the top of the skull). Then the Child receives further instruction on how to blend his light with Emptiness. Finally the Child, the refined and pure yang Spirit of the adept, rises to Emptiness (Pregadio 1991, 91). Pregadio argues that this yang Spirit is not simply masculine as opposed to feminine, but is the result of a transcending of the masculine-feminine yang-yin opposition into "a condition that can only be defined as yang . . . in the same way as, for example, entering the state beyond the life/death opposition results in Life (eternal or immortal life), and the light/darkness opposition is transcended in Light (a light that is not the antithesis of darkness)" (Pregadio 1991, 92).

The transmission of this tradition has not entirely died out among Taoist women in China. Daily recitations of scriptures by both men and women are continuing in Quanzhen monasteries, though sometimes they are omitted or abbreviated because of heavy work schedules (Steven Bokenkamp, personal communication, May 1991). Meditation continues as an optional rather than an organized practice done in the small hours of the night. Despeux (1990) found that the canonical nine precepts for women were still observed in a Sichuan monastery in 1984 (149). She also found women adepts who knew of and practiced the "inner alchemy" cultivations for women (Lai 1985; Despeux 1990, 183–85). Taoist women are not the only ones not allowing the tradition to die: in Beijing the Chinese Women's Publishing Company has recently published a collection of punctuated editions of some of the Taoist books on inner alchemy for women (Wang and Hsiao 1989).

Buddhism

Buddhism is a religion with monastic and lay followers. Those who are most serious about freeing themselves and others from the unhappiness due to attachment and desire are expected to leave the household life, seek ordination under a teacher who is a monk or a nun, undertake certain vows aimed at changing one's psychological patterns and behavior, and live a celibate life in community. Many Buddhists of course do not take such a radical step, but instead practice at home: they take lay vows, recite scriptures, make offerings to Buddhas, go on pilgrimages, and make donations to the monasteries to support the life of the nuns and monks, and to sponsor their ceremonies. All these activities earn merit which lay people may use to bring long life, health and prosperity to their living loved ones or a better rebirth to their ancestors.

Ordination in Buddhism requires the presence of ten properly ordained monastics (Welch 1967, 289). Historically, not only have Buddhists instituted different rules for men and women, they have kept men's and women's ordination lineages distinct. In Theravada Buddhist countries such as Sri Lanka and Thailand women's ordination lineages came to an end centuries ago. The Chinese have maintained an unbroken ordination lineage for women, and have always had large numbers of active Buddhist nuns (Welch 1967, 411–19; 1972, 406). Likewise, women have been the most numerous and probably the most active portion of the Buddhist laity, and have been vital as donors to both monks and nuns (Welch 1972, 406).

An important feature of Buddhist monasticism and its priestly functions is that nuns can perform all the priestly ceremonies that monks can perform, unlike Catholic nuns who cannot perform sacraments. Furthermore, to a very large extent, unlike Catholic nuns who have to summon priests to hear confessions, Buddhist nuns are autonomous in the performing of their own rituals and in the governing of the affairs of their own convents; except in the case of ordination, there are no occasions on which they have to summon, notify, or otherwise rely on monks for approval or consent. Thus the Buddhist monastic order for women has been one among a very few institutions in China in which women have been close to fully in control (Levering 1988b).

The twentieth century has been hard on Chinese Buddhism. The political and social upheavals added to the poverty and family disruption which caused many to give their children to convents and monasteries. But at the same time the same upheavals have made the monastery not a place to seek a secure life. This has of course been particularly true since 1949. Beginning in 1950, the new government classed monasteries and convents as landlords who had oppressed the peasants, and took away their land, returning to them only a small allotment if they were willing to farm it themselves (Welch 1972, 42–48, 68–73). The Party taught that monks and nuns were parasites (Welch 1971, 60–61), and some said openly that their goal was to eliminate the orders altogether (Welch 1972, 210). Donations to monks and nuns were strongly discouraged (Welch 1972, 62). Some monks and nuns tried to run factories on the premises as a means of livelihood, but in most cases the results were disastrous (Welch 1972, 50–61). The remaining rural monasteries and convents were lumped together into communes (Welch 1972, 65). Most monks and nuns returned to lay life (Welch 1972, 67–68).

A few monasteries and convents were kept as showplaces, commonly a convent and a monastery in each city, with monks and nuns who could put on rituals and answer questions when foreign guests from Buddhist countries appeared (Welch 1972, 452–55; 201–10). Only during periods of relaxation such as occurred from 1956 through early 1957, and again between 1960 and 1963, were numbers of local people observed attending ceremonies at Buddhist places of worship (Welch 1972, 65).

Meanwhile, Chinese monks, nuns, and lay leaders who sought to cooperate with the government organized a Chinese Buddhist association with its headquarters in Beijing. Monks and nuns were well represented on its national council, but lay people were in the majority on its executive committee (Welch 1972, 408). While a few nuns were elected to the council, they were far from being represented in proportion to their numbers (Welch 1972, 408, 410–17). In 1956 the Chinese Buddhist Seminary was established in Beijing, which graduated a scant 361 students in 10 years, and which until the present has admitted only men (Welch 1972, 156–59).

Beginning in 1963 attacks against Buddhism mounted, culminating in the Cultural Revolution that began in 1966, in which Buddhism was a major target of revolutionary struggle campaigns (Welch 1972, 340–63). Most of the remaining monasteries and convents were closed entirely. Those monks and nuns who were allowed to remain in their monasteries and convents survived by growing their own food, as for example in the Nanputo Temple in Xiamen (Amoy), a major center, where 30 monks stayed on at the temple during the Cultural Revolution, surviving on food raised on the property (MacInnis 1989, 136). Images were destroyed, and books and libraries burned.

In December 1978, at the Third Plenum of the Eleventh Congress of the Chinese Communist Party, government policy changed. Localities were directed to permit and even assist the reopening of a few major monasteries and convents in each city or region. The central government provided financial assistance for refurbishing or rebuilding damaged buildings. Buddhists are now permitted to accept large donations from Japanese Buddhists and from overseas Chinese to restore historically important sites and reestablish famous monasteries (Hahn 1989, 92).

Seminaries have been opened at a number of places to train novices, both men and women. At Nanputoshan in Xiamen, for example, there were 90 male and 65 female novices in 1988 in a two-year Buddhist academy on the grounds of the famous monastery. The abbot told a foreign scholar that there are many more women volunteers for the novitiate than men, and more of both sexes than the seminary has places for (MacInnis 1989, 139). Almost all the novices come from rural areas; in fact, there are none from the city in which the temple is located (MacInnis 1989, 138). Upon graduation they are free to go to any temple or monastery in China (MacInnis 1989, 136), or indeed abroad.

Nationwide, the abbot of Nanputoshan said, there are about a thousand men and women studying in novitiate programs for middle school graduates. For example, in Fujian province alone, in addition to the hundred fifty novices in training at Nanputoshan, the city of Fuzhou's Buddhist novitiate has a hundred women in three classes, while the city of Putien has sixty men. Beyond Fujian, for example, Shanghai has 50 men and 30 women; Suzhou has 60 men; Nanjing has sixty or seventy men. There are fifty women studying in a three-year program near Chengdu in Sichuan in what is perhaps the most ambitious of the seminaries for women. Beijing's top-level Chinese Buddhist Seminary has seventy men (MacInnis 1989, 138). Hong Kong Buddhists are supplying books and curricular materials for these new educational ventures (Levering 1989).

Ordinations are now being carried out again in China for both men and women monastics, on a considerable scale (Hahn 1989, 92).

One attraction of becoming a nun, apparently, is becoming a member of an international institution, the larger mainland and overseas Chinese network of Chinese Buddhist monks and nuns, which extends to Hong Kong, Singapore, Malaysia, Indonesia, Taiwan, and the United States of America. Younger nuns speak of overseas Chinese monks they have met, and the possibility of going abroad to serve in a Chinese Buddhist temple in Hong Kong or Southeast Asia (Levering 1989). The abbot of Nanputoshan told MacInnis that some who become monks and nuns hope to go abroad, and in fact many have done so. The government allows them to go if they have a valid invitation to serve a temple or monastery (MacInnis 1989, 136).

Chengdu and the Aidaotang: A Case Study. The city of Chengdu is the capital of the rich southwestern province of Sichuan. Sichuan was a main center of Buddhist activity prior to 1949, though it was much outranked by provinces in the lower Yangtze River region like Kiangsu and Zhejiang, which between them had in 1930 close to half of all the monks in China (Welch 1968, 246–51). Sichuan had a venerable tradition of outstanding monasteries, as well as the great pilgrimage center of Mt. Omei. Sichuan's proximity to Tibet made it a center in the twentieth century of interest by Han Chinese in Tibetan esoteric Buddhism (Welch 1968, 177, 199).

According to an internal report prepared by the Chengdu City Office for the Management of the Real Property of Religions issued in December of 1986, in 1909 in the city of Chengdu there were 273 Buddhist temples, 486 monks, and 111 nuns (25). Of the major temples in the city, Zhaojuesi had 150 monks and seven thousand *mou* of land. There were several other good-sized monasteries, including the Wenshuyuan with 100 monks, the Caotangsi with 70, and the Jinzusi with 200. The largest convent, the Aidaotang, had 50 nuns, but no land except that on which its buildings were built and the property of a few smaller affiliated temples. There were several other convents of moderate size, and about twenty small ones.[17]

By 1957 these numbers had dropped significantly. There were only 66 temples in Chengdu. Numbers of monks at major temples had dropped as well: Zhaojuesi, for example, had dropped from 150 in 1909 to 41 in 1957; Wenshuyuan had dropped from 100 in 1909 to 45 in 1957. The Caotangsi had 70 monks in 1909, and 33 in 1957. The Jinzusi had had 200 monks in 1909, but was not listed in 1957.

The number of nuns at Aidaotang had actually increased from 50 in 1909 to 57 in 1957. This probably reflects the tendency of nuns and monks to band together in the few remaining monasteries and convents (Welch 1972, 418). Most of the other convents had fewer than three nuns. But the report also indicates an increase in the number of nuns in the city, which in 1957 totalled 142.

During the Cultural Revolution, the report states, there was major destruction to the remaining monasteries and convents in Chengdu, all of which were shut down and converted to other uses. The convent Aidaotang was a good example:

During the Cultural Revolution the Buddhist images [at Ai-daotang] were destroyed, and the worship halls and buildings were occupied. Aidaotang was occupied by a lubricating oil factory, a book bindery, and a factory that made screens to put over dishes on the table to keep flies away. The nuns who re-mained were pushed into a small corner of the property; most left and found other ways of making a living. [32]

By 1986 the city government had decided to reopen two monas-teries, the Wenshuyuan and the Zhaojuesi, and one convent, the Aidaotang. The report states:

At the time of writing there are more than 60 Buddhist nuns in Chengdu, mostly living at Aidaotang, Jinsha-an and Juexiangsi.[18] . . . So that the nuns could have a place to carry out their religious activities, the city of Chengdu found land for the units occupying [Aidaotang] and assisted with their moving expenses. The national government gave 95,000 yuan[19] toward restoring Aidaotang, which had completely lost its character as a temple. At the time of writing it has already restored its temple-like appearance, the nuns have begun per-forming the morning and evening service daily, and quite a few overseas Chinese laywomen and foreign nuns come to worship. [3]

When I visited Aidaotang in 1988 it housed a number of older nuns, including old students of the abbess from before liberation, and a few younger nuns. Most of the older nuns had held secular jobs since the 1950s; their pensions from those jobs supported them now as nuns. The younger nuns received a salary. The Dangjia, the seventy-eight year old head of the day-to-day operations of the con-vent, commented that it was very difficult to find well-qualified young nuns. The job had to be made attractive to them by providing a good salary and living conditions. (I have also heard from other non-Buddhist sources that nuns and monks in China are now al-lowed to marry.) While I was there in 1988 quite a number of lay-women came to make offerings at Aidaotang, even though due to the ongoing reconstruction only a tiny side hall with an image of the Bodhisattva Guanyin was open for worship. The Dangjia told me that the nuns had been able to reclaim the building only because the head of the Chinese Buddhist Association, Zhao Pu-chu, had come to Chengdu personally to see to it that the local government carried through on its promise to transfer the property. In fact it had taken until 1988 for the nuns to be able to move in (Levering 1988a).

The group of older nuns I talked to were quite joyful about their return to monastic life. They chant the morning and evening service every day from memory. When I asked one who chanted it for me how she managed to remember it still after decades in secular life, she said she had chanted it every morning to herself before she got out of bed. They were very busy watching every move the contractors made to see no substitutions of shoddy materials and delays occurred. One nun in her sixties pointed out there were no nuns there between sixty and thirty, the new recruits all being in their twenties. She thought that it would be a number of years before the young nuns would be ready to assume the burdens which for now the old nuns must carry (Levering 1988a).

Long-lian. The abbess of Aidaotang is the Rev. Long-lian, now past 80, a nun who has been prominent in Buddhist affairs at the national level for a long time, and is now actively developing Buddhist education for nuns in Chengdu. She is well educated, a college graduate before becoming a nun, and a talented and accomplished poet and calligrapher. She is clearly the most widely respected scholar-nun in China, and has been cooperative with the government since the 1950s.

Long-lian's story, if not typical, does reflect the changes in this century in the opportunities and circumstances of women's Buddhist practice. She became a nun in Sichuan after having had some experience of the world. A nun who had known her since before liberation told me that as a young woman she had twice passed the government civil service examination to qualify to be the administrative head of a county, but had been refused the post because she was a woman, and then given a job as a secretary instead. This, said her friend, was the reason she had decided to become a nun. Her first teacher was a Tibetan teacher of esoteric Buddhism, which was popular in Sichuan in the decades prior to 1945 (Chün-fang Yü, personal communication, August 28, 1991). In Chengdu she was the leader and teacher of a group of nuns who were eager to learn and practice Buddhism in general and Tibetan Buddhism in particular. They walked miles from their own country convent to the big monasteries to listen to every sutra lecturer who came. One of these monasteries, Jinzusi, had become under Abbot Neng-hai a center for the translation and publication of Tibetan texts, as well as for the practice of Tibetan liturgy and meditation methods (Welch 1968,

199). The nuns were given quite rigorous training in meditation. For three months at a time they were not allowed to leave the gates, and they often had five meditation periods a day (Levering 1988a).

After liberation all this activity came to a halt. Long-lian left her position as abbess of a convent in Chengdu and moved to Beijing. There she became one of the leading nuns of the Tongjiaosi, a famous nunnery in Beijing that remained open at least into the late 1950s, when the nuns' unusually strict adherence to the rules governing meals was noted by a visiting Japanese scholar.[20] In 1955 Long-lian was elected to the national council of the Chinese Buddhist Association, on which she has served ever since (Welch 1972, 413). She contributes frequently to the journal of the association, and is said to have written a book on the Mādhyamika philosophical school of Indian Buddhism (Goonatilake, 117). By 1962 when she was reelected to the council she had moved back to Sichuan (Welch 1972, 409). She is said to have spent the Cultural Revolution in a nunnery on Sichuan's Mt. Omei, one of the famous Buddhist pilgrimage centers, where she and others survived by growing their own food (Goonatilake, 117).

Since the early 1980s Long-lian has been back in Chengdu working toward opening a seminary for nuns. In 1988 the seminary under her direction had forty students in a three-year course. English, Chinese language and literature, and other secular subjects taught by some of Chengdu's best teachers are offered alongside courses on Buddhist topics taught by Long-lian and others. The seminary has a small library, and meditation is taught (Levering 1988a). Long-lian hopes that the seminary can make a contribution to the cause of ordination for Buddhist nuns in Theravada countries. One year the seminary accepted thirty Sri Lankan women for training, and even had an especially comfortable dormitory built for the Sri Lankan women. Unfortunately the latter were prevented by the unrest in their own country from traveling to China (Chün-fang Yü, personal communication, August 28, 1991).

Long-lian's seminary is clearly one of the best educational institutions for nuns in China. When one compares the training and opportunities for study that she and her older students and colleagues had in Chengdu before liberation with those available for her younger students now, the differences are instructive. Before liberation fortunate nuns such as Long-lian and her followers studied in the old, broad but less systematic way, following courses of sutra lectures as best they could, picking things up gradually (Levering 1988a). Education in secular subjects was not offered. Today's stu-

dents study secular learning, which probably leaves them less ignorant about the larger world than their elders. They now study
Buddhist subjects more systematically, but perhaps in less depth
and from fewer and less qualified teachers. Practice disciplines such
as Buddha's name recitation, visualization, and meditation cannot
be pursued so intensively today for lack of time, for all nuns are expected to be workers. Nuns today cannot expect to live the highly
regulated life that included many practice periods which Long-lian
and her colleagues enjoyed in their younger days. Much still remains to be done to restore the basic financial, institutional, and
educational conditions necessary for the most serious forms of Buddhist study and practice.

The Buddhism of Laywomen. When I was in China in 1985,
1988, 1989 and 1992 I saw women actively taking part in Buddhist
lay activities at every end of the social scale. At Guangjisi in Beijing, the temple that serves also as the headquarters of the Chinese
Buddhist Association, I chanted sutras with a large group of middle-
aged and older urban women taking part in a dharma assembly lasting several days. At Fayuansi in Beijing I spent the afternoon with an
educated woman who had traveled many miles to seek out the guest
master, a quietly impressive monk, in the hopes of learning meditation (and *qi-gong*) from him.

One evening I was invited by a woman to join her family at a
service they were sponsoring for their recently deceased husband
and father, a high-ranking official. It was an elaborate nine-hour "release of the burning mouths" *(fang-yan-kou)* ceremony, chanted
beautifully by seven monks. The widow is a believer, and so is one
of her sons. The very bright, highly educated son who is a member
of the Chinese Academy of Social Sciences, wanted me to know that
he is not a believer.

In Shanghai, in Wenzhou and Ningbo in Zhejiang province, and
at Putoshan I saw groups of peasant and working women worshiping
and chanting sutras. In Hangzhou in late March I saw a most striking sight: everywhere in the temples and along the tourist routes
were blue-clad peasant women with red armbands, towels or ker-
chiefs on their heads, and yellow pilgrim bags slung over their
shoulders. These mostly older women were in Hangzhou on a pilgrimage to temples sacred to Guanyin, the feminine Bodhisattva, of
all Bodhisattvas the most beloved and most Chinese. The pilgrimage centered on Guanyin's birthday, the nineteenth day of the second lunar month. I was told that this was a relatively free period in

the agricultural cycle of the surrounding countryside. In one of the temples that are central to the Guanyin pilgrimage, Middle Tianzhusi, Buddhist nuns had gathered from all over the country to serve the pilgrims. They were offering not only religious ceremonies and altars at which to offer incense and candles, but also lodging during the pilgrimage. The women came carrying their traveling necessities in the yellow cotton pilgrim bags, which would be stamped with the seal of each temple they visited along the pilgrimage route.

Recently Chün-fang Yü has studied the history and current revival of this "spring pilgrimage," observing and interviewing pilgrims and members of what is now called the "religious tourism" business.[21] In the nineteenth century this pilgrimage and its associated pilgrims' fair were major events in Hangzhou. But it was not insignificant in 1987, when officials estimated that between late February and early May two million pilgrims had come to the city. On the day before Guanyin's birthday the Upper Tianzhu temple sold forty thousand entrance tickets. A cadre at the traffic control office said that the city had to limit the numbers who came, and estimated that during the four spring pilgrimage months thirty thousand pilgrims were admitted into the city every day. Hotel and innkeepers whom Yü interviewed reported that 80 percent of their pilgrim guests were women. Half were between 50 and 65 (most women retire at 50), with another 20 to 30 percent over 65.

Pilgrims come by boat or in chartered buses, usually spending two nights en route and two in an inn in Hangzhou. They keep a vegetarian diet, starting with the evening before they leave home. If they come with their husbands, they must sleep in separate quarters. They are led by group leaders who take care of practical matters. Some groups also have a spiritual leader who knows how to chant scriptures, sing pilgrimage songs, go into trance, become a spokesperson for Guanyin, and practice healing among fellow pilgrims.

Although the pilgrims freely say that the fun of an outing in the spring is one reason they come, they save sightseeing and shopping for the second day of their stay. On embarking from boat or bus they head straight for the Upper Tianzhu temple by foot, where they begin the round of temple visits, lighting incense and chanting scriptures before miracle-working images of Guanyin. After they return to the inn in the later afternoon, they relax by gossiping, exchanging stories about Guanyin, and singing pilgrims' songs together. The pilgrims say that having done this pilgrimage, they feel at peace, knowing that things will go well at home—the crops, the animals, the children's health.

Yü Chün-fang was able to collect a number of the pilgrims' songs. A favorite, which refers to details of the life story of the human incarnation of Guanyin called Miao-shan, goes:

> Guanyin Bodhisattva is as beautiful as a flower.
> Being a great beauty I have bare feet.[22]
> Mother gave me birth on the 19th of the second month.
> I ascended to Heaven on the 19th of the sixth month.
> Heaven above and earth below.
> Firstly I do not suffer the ill humor of in-laws.
> Secondly I do not eat food provided by a husband.
> Thirdly I neither carry a son in my stomach nor a grandson on
>   my arms.
> Fourthly I sit lightly on a lotus throne.
> Adoration of Guan-xi-yin, the Great Compassionate One.

It is interesting that what the women sing of in this song is not the profound compassion for which Guanyin is celebrated. Rather, it is the freedom of Miao-shan/Guanyin, who, determined to pursue a life of spiritual cultivation, managed despite the violent opposition of her father to avoid the fate of marriage and children, a fate to which all the pilgrim women have had to submit.[23]

CONCLUSION

It is hard to gather information about women in the "five religions" in China. Only Protestant women are writing about their own experiences; perhaps they are doing so because so many Protestant women (and men) in churches abroad are intensely interested to hear what they are experiencing as women. We have yet to hear from Catholic women, Taoist women, and Buddhist women about their own views of their lives and religious practice.

Honig and Hershatter report that the Chinese press is not interested in writing about women confronting the world of work *as women.* Articles are not written now, as they once were, about women encountering gender-related obstacles and challenges. Rather, the press writes about women working out problems in their personal life, about women fulfilling traditional roles, and about women and men as model workers. The very limited religious press has taken a similar tack. The Taoist journal *Zhongguo Dao-jiao*'s portrait of *qiandao* and *kundao* on Qingchengshan is a good example: it describes model workers, men and women going beyond the ordinary in inventiveness, dedication, and hard work to make Qingchengshan's hotels, restaurants, wine factory, and tea plantations a success. The Abbess Xiao is featured in this article not for her attainments in Taoist practice, nor for her effectiveness in passing the tradition on to the present generation of young *kundao*, but for her self-sacrifice in using her savings to refurbish the inn, and her warmth and hospitality to guests. No one has thought to write about how she arose to her responsible position in the Qingcheng-shan monastic system, or whether being a woman gave her a unique perspective.

Thus the kind of knowledge we would like to have of women in China's "religions" must await more opportunities for religious Chinese women to speak for themselves. It must await as well the kinds of extensive interview or participant observation studies that have not yet been possible.

What can be said at the moment is that there are opportunities in Catholic, Protestant, Taoist, and Buddhist institutions for Chinese women to practice their religion, as laywomen and as religious specialists. These opportunities are limited by the heavy work demands placed on women, and by government control, but they are nonetheless real. There are also opportunities for women to serve their religious communities. Women lay leaders served throughout the darkest days of the Cultural Revolution, and now continue to serve. Occupational and professional opportunities are offered to middle and high school graduates, as well as to old *kundao*, nuns, evangelists, and sisters. Comprehensive figures are lacking, but it seems that these opportunities are not quite as numerous for women as they are for men.

In the Taoist, Buddhist, and Catholic cases it is young rural women who find professional opportunities attractive. More apply than can be accepted. Many come from Taoist, Buddhist, and Catholic families of long standing, and are motivated in part by a desire to see their traditions continue. The work by which these women must support themselves and contribute to the economic development of the state is not unattractive, nor so different from the work they might otherwise be doing: working in restaurants, inns, and shops, light industry, sewing and cooking, mastering elementary knowledge of their religion, and its most basic forms of practice.

The wages are competitive. For young women who are unable to further their education beyond middle school, facing an overpopulation of young people and a very competitive job market, meaningful work as a *kundao*, a Buddhist or a Catholic nun must seem very suitable (David C. Yu, personal communication, 1991).

Young women who join Buddhist and Taoist monastic orders may have motivations different from those of their elders. But thanks to the efforts of now quite elderly religious women like Long-lian and to the efforts of interested persons in publishing houses and abroad, they still will be able to participate in at least some of the transformative systems of study and practice of those traditions. Whatever the motivation of those who encounter them, the transformative practices still do have power to transform.

Scholars like Margery Wolf have found that in society as a whole women do not have and have not had occupational and political leadership opportunities equal to those of men. In the countryside old ideas that women do not make good leaders persist, as do the handicaps of marriage into a community of strangers, and the burden of the "double day." In urban factories and agencies women are discriminated against in hiring and promotion. As Tani Barlow notes, it remains true that it is a common perception in China that "in most cases women are not as valuable as men" (Barlow and Lowe 1987, 192).

By contrast, religious women have established leadership by having taken the lead in many places in keeping religious activities alive during the worst periods of suppression. Women have established leadership by being willing to offer their talents to serve their religious traditions despite the personal risk incurred by being identified with religion. It is very probable that the women who have offered themselves are at least as educated, talented, and dedicated as the men.

The government too has supported the notion that women can lead in religion by insisting on at least a token representation of women on the highest religious bodies. The government has included nuns as well as monks and priests as representatives of religion in the People's Consultative Congresses at various levels. It has supported higher training for women in Buddhist, Taoist, and Protestant seminaries and Catholic novitiates, though not always quite on an equal basis with men.

It also can be said that feminine forms of the divine that express feminine powers and the contradictions of women's lives—like the Holy Mother Mary for the Catholics and the Bodhisattva Guanyin for the Buddhists—remain popular foci of faith and pilgrimages for lay people in China.

Persons interested in the relations between women, gender constructions, and religion in the West must continue in the Chinese case to look at the gender ideology and practice of the Chinese family and the state. The Chinese family and the state have always been important religious institutions in China. And while Chinese Communism is not a "religion," it is an attempt to put into practice in society a particular cosmological and moral order, one which is based on an analysis of the interests of different classes. Questions and issues concerning the personal moral order that women and men in America often discuss in the context of religion—the nature of men and women, the nature of marriage, acceptable reasons for divorce—these are questions on which the Party and the state are the arbiters, and on which discussion takes place not in a religious community, but in state-controlled media (Honig and Hershatter 1989).

It is equally true that any successful attempt to change the gender ideology and gender hierarchy in China will have to be led by the Chinese state. Religious groups will probably for some time not have the strength or independence to influence gender ideology as much as they can do in America. But religious groups in China have an opportunity now to model for the whole society a more inclusive, egalitarian order. Buddhists, Quanzhen Taoists, and some Protestants in fact are doing so to a remarkable extent. So far the China Christian Council is the only official religious body that has taken notice of this opportunity and publicly committed itself to furthering an egalitarian order.[24] They will have to work hard to see to it that revived familism (which on the whole they support) and the "double day" do not cripple their young women leaders. It will be hard to prevent patterns of gender hierarchy that persist in the larger society from coming to characterize their own institutions.

Barbara Reed

WOMEN AND CHINESE RELIGION IN CONTEMPORARY TAIWAN

The People's Republic of China succeeded in all but eliminating Chinese popular religion during the Cultural Revolution (1966–1969).[1] During the same period Chinese religious and philosophical traditions flourished on Taiwan (Republic of China).[2] The government itself promotes Confucian values through its educational system and conducts an elaborate ceremony to commemorate Confucius's birthday every September. And contrary to the expectations (and sometimes hopes) of many Chinese scholars, folk religious practices have adapted and thrived with the increasing industrialization and modernization of Taiwan in the 1970s and 80s. The "economic miracle" of Taiwan has brought wealth to the Taiwanese, who have used some of it to build new temples and expand old ones. Between 1956 and 1980 the number of temples in Taiwan increased about 113 percent (Ch'ü 1988, 5).

Chinese women's lives in Taiwan have changed radically in the last few decades. Women today are more highly educated, more likely to work outside the family, and have fewer children than in the past. In 1958 women made up less than one-third of the high school student population, but in 1987 they were about one-half the total (Social Welfare Indices, 10). Whereas in 1958 only about 14 percent of women were employed outside the home, the statistic for 1987 was over 37 percent (Statistical Yearbook, 26–27). The manufacturing sector employs the largest number of women, whose youthful willingness to work for low wages was a major factor in the rapid industrialization of Taiwan and its great success in exporting manufactured goods. Along with the radical social changes that took women out of the house and divided their attention between work and family, was a corresponding change in the number of children they bore: the 1987 fertility rate was only one-third that of the 1958 rate (*Statistical Yearbook*, 35).[3]

The social changes experienced by the Chinese in Taiwan have brought with them changes in religious values and activities. One clear example is ancestor worship, the heart of Chinese religion. Women have traditionally been responsible for the domestic ancestor rituals conducted before the ancestors' tablets. With industrialization and rural to urban migration, ancestor rituals have been greatly simplified and in some cases forgotten. Yü Te-hui and Wang Yu-ling see this abandonment of ritual as a possible prelude to the abandonment of values: "Although ancestors are the foundation of the Chinese mind, it is doubtful whether we can still maintain the idea of reverence for ancestors while the rituals of ancestor worship disappear day by day"[4] (Yü 1987, 45).

Many women in non-Western cultures struggle with the tension between their desire to identify with and support their own tradition, which is under seige by outside forces, and their desire to critique their own tradition from their experience as women. In Taiwan the issues surrounding the nature and value of "Chinese culture" is complicated because Taiwanese face not only the introduction of Western values but also the government sponsorship of what it considers to be the true Chinese culture. Since the government on the island of Taiwan has long been dominated by Nationalists who left mainland China after the communist victory in 1949, the Chinese culture which they propose is an idealized culture from mainland China rather than the regional, Taiwanese version of Chinese culture.

This article will discuss several Chinese women who have in different ways dealt with the tension between their old Chinese/Taiwanese religious/philosophical traditions and their new aspirations as women of contemporary Taiwan. Taoism and Buddhism have traditionally been alternative religions in the Confucian-dominated Chinese society. Chinese Buddhism continues to be an appealing alternative for devout religious women. Taoist religion, strictly speaking, is alive today primarily as the religion of the Taoist priests who master Taoist texts and rituals, and serve as ritual specialists for popular religion. The most pervasive traditions are Confucian philosophy and Chinese popular religion, which draws on Confucian, Taoist, Buddhist, and folk religious elements.[5]

The first two women discussed in this article, Lü Hsiu-lien and Lin Mei-jung, are intellectuals who critique the patriarchal moral and social philosophy of Confucianism. With its emphasis on the moral virtues of family relationships, especially filial piety (*hsiao*), Confucianism is identified as the primary force behind the restrictions placed on women as filial daughters, obedient wives, and devoted mothers. Neither of these women is a religious professional—one is trained in law and the other in anthropology. Their concerns with transforming society led them to call for the transformation of dominant Confucian traditions at the core of their society.

The rest of the women discussed here are participants in Chinese popular religion or in sectarian movements that have sprung from popular religion. These women seek from the gods and goddesses of Chinese religion something they did not find in the dominant Confucian ideology—a sense of fulfillment, of spiritual unity, of divine protection. Although popular religion contains Confucian elements as well as Taoist, Buddhist, and folk religious elements, we can see that the enormous variety of Chinese popular religion allows women great leeway in constructing their own self-affirming religious systems.

FEMINIST CRITIQUE OF CONFUCIANISM: LÜ HSIU-LIEN

Because of a strong commitment to transforming the patriarchal traditions in Taiwan, Lü Hsiu-lien has studied law in Taiwan and at Harvard University, written and spoken about feminist concerns, and participated in opposition political activities that led to her imprisonment. Her feminist criticism of Confucian traditions has inspired vigorous defense and sometimes personal hostility.

"But this is a tradition of thousands of years!" This is the response Taiwanese feminist leader Lü Hsiu-lien hears in response to her questioning of traditional Chinese male/female rituals, roles, and morality (Lü 1974, 99). Although anyone might appeal to tradition to defend male dominance, for the Chinese the power of such an appeal is greater due to the Chinese pride in the antiquity of their culture. The Chinese like to tell people that they have a seven thousand year history—therefore, "tradition" is not to be lightly dismissed. Lü, however, thinks the use of tradition as an "excuse" shows the weakness of what is invariably an irrational position. After all, autocracy and bound feet were part of Chinese "tradition." Lü asks, "Is 'tradition' an immutable golden rule?" (Lü 1974, 99). In her 1974 groundbreaking feminist work *New Feminism (Hsin Nü-hsing chu-yi)* Lü introduced Western feminist thought and activities

to her Chinese readers in Taiwan and then critiqued the Chinese
tradition from a feminist perspective.

In a survey of the history of women in Chinese society, Lü
traces the development of men's views of women as men's dependents and shadows dating from the Han dynasty (206 B.C.E.–220
C.E.) and as men's playthings dating from the Three Kingdom's period (220–265 C.E.) (1974, 26–27). She sees Confucians at the heart
of the traditional denigration of women. Confucian texts, Lü says,
see humanity and maleness as equivalent. Discussions of humanity
are actually discussions of men. Women are treated primarily in
special texts, the "Women's Four Books," which were written to
make them into second-class human beings (Lü 1974, 128).

Lü identifies four traditional Chinese views dealing with the
fate of women. These four views, inculcated in women for centuries, are the root of contemporary women's low position and lack
of self-confidence.

"Continue the Family Line" (ch'uan tsung chieh tai)

The most powerful, and in Lü's eyes most destructive, traditional Chinese value is the dominating importance of continuing
the male family line (1974, 29–30). Male heirs are necessary to carry
on the family name and the ancestral sacrifices. Male descendants
perform the funeral rites and ancestral rituals for their ancestors
that provide them with a comfortable and peaceful afterlife. Without male descendants and their ritual offerings, the ancestors'
spirits would be doomed to pathetic existences as hungry ghosts.
According to Confucian tradition, "There are three things which are
unfilial, and to have no posterity is the greatest of them" (Mencius
4A:26; Legge 1966, 725). In a patrilineal system posterity, of course,
means male descendants.

According to Lü, the overriding importance of this aspect of filial piety causes parents and society in general to "consider boys important and girls unimportant" (*chung nan ch'ing nü*). Lü sees this
as causing families to view their own daughters as commodities and
for their husband's families to view them as their own "tools" for
continuing their family line. There is a popular Chinese expression,
"married daughters are spilled water," which refers to the view that
women can never return to their natal families after marriage, that
no matter what happens they are the property of their husband's
family. Even some educated, supposedly progressive women demonstrate a strong preference for their first child to be a son. They deny

that it is because they consider boys more important, but say that if they have a son then they will feel relieved from the pressure to have sons (Lü 1974, 70). One woman told Lü Hsiu-lien that she wanted to increase the small number of her family in Taiwan, with the understanding that only sons count as family because they carry on the surname (1974, 72).

Lü sees several societal problems arising from this prejudice. Families see little point in educating someone who will benefit someone else's family. Instead of educating their daughters, they may force them to work in factories at a young age, or to work as bar girls or prostitutes in order to add to the family income (Lü 1974, 72). Daughters are expected to pay back their natal families for the expense of raising them before they enter their husband's families. The preference for sons also creates problems for family planning, a major concern for Taiwan as well as the People's Republic of China. Although Taiwan's population growth rate is now rather small, the high population density of the small island makes family planning important.

Lü wants to end the emphasis that Chinese society puts on continuing the male family line because it is the root of discrimination against women. In order to eliminate the issue of passing on the family surname, she proposes that children take either the mother's or father's surname. After much heated discussion, in 1985 revision of family law allows a child to take the mother's surname, but only if she has no brothers and she has the written consent of her husband (Chiang and Ku, 19).

Lü Hsiu-lien also proposes that women abandon both their husband's surname and the title "Mrs.," which "surround a woman's name and identity like a hat and shoes" (Lü 1974, 154). Marriage customs also must change to reflect the equality of men and women. In particular, the payment of the traditional dowry and bride price should end. According to Lü, the real gift that a bride brings to her marriage today is her talent. Dowries and bride prices are an outdated reflection of a patriarchal society (1974, 152–54).

There is some evidence that Lü's view of a "modern dowry" has been partially accepted by some urban Taiwanese (Tsui, 19). One mother reported to anthropologist Elaine Tsui the following retort to a complaint by her daughter's wealthy sister-in-law that her daughter's dowry was so small: "Do you know how much it costs to get a bachelor's degree? Besides, my daughter makes NT$500,000 (US$12,500) a year for your family. How could the face value of your own dowry match the total amount of her potential earnings in the future?" (Tsui, 19).

"Three Submissions and Four Virtues" (san ts'ung ssu te)

The second traditional view of women's destiny sums up women's moral life: the "three submissions and four virtues" (Lü 1974, 30). The three submissions of women's lives are proposed in the Confucian classic, *Li chi*. Chinese women must submit to their fathers and elder brothers prior to marriage, to their husbands after marriage, and to their sons in widowhood. Lü says that the "three submissions" is a magical spell comparable to the demon-subduing spell of the legendary Monkey King:[6] it makes women take submission as their reason for living from birth until death. It makes women into the shoes underneath men's feet (Lü 1974, 30).

Pan Chao (d. 116 c.e.), in her Confucian text *Instructions for Women (Nü-chieh)*, brought together the ideal of the "three submissions" with an ideal of the "four virtues" of womanhood: feminine virtue, feminine work, feminine deportment, and feminine speech (Lü 1974, 26). The substance of these "virtues," according to Lü, effectively ties up women's hands and feet, limiting their innate talents to merely adorning themselves and limiting their temperament to gentle submission, cowardice, and ignorance (1974, 30). By the end of the Ming dynasty (1368–1644) the understanding of feminine "virtue" was expressed by the phrase "the lack of talent is a virtue in a woman" (*nü tzu wu ts'ai pien shih te*) (Lü 1974, 28–29).

In opposition to the traditional feminine "four virtues" and talentlessness, Lü proposes that women "exhaust their talents" in all areas and that job discrimination be eliminated so that women can realize their potential.

"Men Outside/Women Inside" (nan wai nü nei)

Lü identifies the third traditional veiw of women's lot as the division of men's and women's realms of activity and influence (1974, 30). The *Li chi* set the ideal for the separation of men's and women's lives into separate spheres inside and outside the home: "Men don't speak of domestic matters and women don't speak of outside matters. Domestic conversations do not leave the home and discussions of the outside world do not enter the home." For Lü the ideal is not separation of men and women's lives, but rather equal participation by both men and women inside and outside the home (1974, 146–47).

"One-sided Chastity" (p'ien mien chen ts'ao)

Chastity is the primary moral virtue for women in some traditional Confucian texts and it is the fourth traditional view dealing with women's destiny discussed by Lü. Chastity became an ideal not only for wives but for widows too. Emperor Wen-ti (ruled 581–604) of the Sui dynasty prohibited the widows of upper-class families to remarry. By the Sung dynasty (960–1127) the nonremarriage of widows was glorified into the highest ideal for women. In the Ming dynasty (1368–1644) the government honored chaste widows with memorial arches, thus increasing the social pressure to remain chaste. Even engaged girls whose fiancés died were supposed to remain chaste and not ever marry (Lü 1974, 28).

As Lü sees it, chaste widowhood had nothing to do with romantic love, but only with public recognition and familial pressure (1974, 28). Of course, chaste widowhood was a luxury that only upper-class families could afford. Margery Wolf reports that in the Taiwanese village in which she did field work, a respected widow was one who stayed with her deceased husband's family, but the desire for male descendants allowed the family to ignore the ideal of sexual chastity if their daughter-in-law became pregnant. As Wolf puts it: "Virtuous widows among poor farm families were filial widows who stayed with their parents-in-law. Their sex life was not relevant" (Wolf, 201).

Lü Hsiu-lien cites the great Sung Neo-Confucian philosopher Ch'eng I's (1033–1107) startling rejection of the remarriage of poverty-stricken widows: "But to starve to death is a very small matter. To lose one's integrity, however, is a very serious matter" (*Chin-ssu lu* 6:3a; Chan 1967, 177). By the Ch'ing dynasty (1644–1911) girls whose reputations were compromised by male advances were expected to kill themselves as part of this glorification of chastity. Lü sees this as creating a society where women did in fact live and die for men (1974, 28).

If chastity is to remain a Chinese moral value, Lü proposes that it be a rational, two-sided chastity (1974, 140–41). In her short story "Chaste Widow Memorial Arch" (*Chen-chieh p'ai-fang*, 1985) she expresses most clearly what true chastity could mean for a contemporary woman. Lan Yü-ch'ing is a young woman pressed by family financial woes to seek work as a dancehall girl in Taipei. She chooses chastity not as a mere rejection of sexual activity, but as a means of maintaining self-respect. Lan Yü-ch'ing remembers the words of a woman whose lecture had a great influence on her:

Chastity isn't a kind of physiological manifestation, but
rather a psychological loyalty. . . . At the end the woman
writer summed up by saying that chastity should rise up from
the shackles of the Confucian teaching of propriety to become
character training, should change from being a forced restraint
to become self-motivated behavior, and moreover should expand from a one-sided female morality into a complete moral
principle for both sexes. [Lü 1985, 181–82]

Lü's main character Lan Yü-ch'ing embodies this ideal of chastity,
one that is motivated by love of self, rather than fear of social
disapproval.

To replace the four traditional views of women's destiny Lü proposes a "new feminism," which includes theory, belief, and power.
The theories of new feminism should be adjusted to contemporary
problems. The basic feminist belief is belief in a society of true
equality of men and women. Feminist power is needed to eliminate
the prejudices of patriarchal Chinese tradition and to build a new
society based on rationality (1974, 122–27). She calls on women to
"first be a human being, and then be a woman" (1974, 127–29). By
this she means that women should strive for the ideals and values of
full humanity first, and only then respond to particularly gender-
based roles and values. This is opposed to the traditional Confucian
tendency to see only men as fully human, and women in need of
separate and unequal morality and ideals.

DEAD CHINESE CULTURE VERSUS LIVING TAIWANESE
CULTURE: LIN MEI-JUNG

One young woman scholar has attacked the whole idea of a
dominant Confucian tradition. Lin Mei-jung, an anthropologist,
published an anthology of essays on religion, culture, and society
(Lin, 1989) more than a decade after the publication of Lü's influential *New Feminism*. Lin Mei-jung's specifically feminist essays are
by now less daring and less threatening to the status quo than her
critique of the Confucian-dominated Chinese culture from a specifically Taiwanese perspective. She opposes the "false Chinese culture" propagated by the goverment and others who favor cultural
and political unity with mainland China. Lin sharply contrasts this
false culture that is taught in the schools and glorified by the government with the multifaceted, living "Taiwanese culture" of the

people. False "Chinese culture" is exclusively Confucian, forgetting the Taoist, Legalist, and Buddhist traditions. "Taiwanese culture" is pluralistic, incorporating the traditions of aboriginal Taiwanese, the regional Chinese traditions of the early Fukienese and Hakka immigrants, and even the traditions of recent immigrants from the Chinese mainland (Lin, 135).

Lin also sees the false "Chinese culture" as an elitist culture of the intellectual class lacking the meaning for everyday life that popular "Taiwanese culture" contains. She believes that "Chinese culture" is used by the "Greater China chauvinists" (those who advocate unification of Taiwan and mainland China) to manufacture the appearance of the superiority of Chinese culture and the inferiority of Taiwanese culture (Lin, 135).

Taiwanese culture is a living tradition, which cannot be separated from the past, present, and future of the island of Taiwan. But the false Chinese culture on Taiwan has no land; it has only a past without a present or a future. As Lin sees it, Chinese culture on Taiwan is a dead culture, found only in museums and Confucian thought (135). Lin does not critique, and is not concerned with, the Chinese culture in the People's Republic of China, because she sees it as having a life of its own tied to the land and people there.

A final cultural difference noted by Lin is that unlike the Chinese mainland, Taiwanese culture is an island culture of people who have experienced immigration across the ocean and dealing with foreign cultures, people who have the courage to face present reality (136). Lin Mei-jung's pride in the courage and beauty of her own culture is mixed with sadness at watching its destruction by an elite, Confucian-dominated Chinese culture. She expresses this grief most directly through poetry. In her poem "Taiwan, My Mother" (T'ai-wan, wo-te mu-ch'in), she grieves for the dying of the Taiwanese dialect and Taiwanese culture, she grieves for the tearing out of Taiwan's heart, but in the end she still finds hope that her mother Taiwan will live (Lin, 129–32).

Although Lin Mei-jung loves her Taiwanese motherland and cherishes its cultural and religious traditions, she is not at all blind to its traditional obstacles for women. Her greatest criticism is of Confucian ideals that perpetuate inequality in Taiwanese society. In particular she has opposed the double standard that demands chastity for women (211–16) and the traditional view that without marriage women are nothing (207–9). She is particularly critical of government sponsorship of these Confucian ideals, such as Provincial Chairman Lin Yang-kang's promotion of chastity for unmarried girls (211) and the legal requirement that widows (but not widowers) wait at least six months before remarriage (Civil Code, 987; Lin, 250). By moving beyond a critique of Confucian culture to a critique of the government which finds much of its identity as the protector and promoter of that culture, Lin Mei-jung has put herself in a vulnerable position in a society whose power-holders have responded rather grudgingly to pressures for democratization.

WORSHIPING THE GODS AND SERVING
THE PEOPLE: HSING-T'IEN TEMPLE

Although most Taiwanese call themselves Taoists or Buddhists, the large majority of them participate in what can be best described as Chinese popular religion, a mixture of Taoism, Buddhism, Confucianism, and folk religion.[7] It is in this Chinese popular religion that Taiwanese women are most active. According to sociologist Ch'ü Hai-yuan, Chinese popular religion in Taiwan is becoming increasingly universalistic and individualistic (Ch'ü, 1988). The universalism is seen in the increased popularity of pan-Chinese deities (like the faithful military hero Kuan Kung, Shakymuni Buddha, and Kuan Yin Bodhisattva) and pan-Taiwanese deities (like the immensely popular Ma Tzu, a maternal goddess whose protection was sought by the Chinese immigrants who sailed from mainland China to the island of Taiwan). The greater individualism is seen in the increased popularity of individual as opposed to community worship. A striking example of both these trends is found in the throngs of women who worship in the popular Hsing-t'ien Temple in Taipei.[8]

Hsing-t'ien Temple is located in the midst of hectic, traffic-congested Taipei. It has branch temples in the nearby communities of Pei-t'ou and San-hsia. Hsing-t'ien Temple houses the red-faced god Kuan-kung, a deified military hero of the third century C.E. who has been worshiped throughout China. Although he is known as a god of war and of literature, his primary role for the worshipers at Hsing-t'ien Temple is as a healing, protector deity.

In general women in Taiwan, as in many cultures, are more religiously active than men (Ch'ü 1986, 73–76): they visit temples more often, they observe vegetarian fasts more often, they seek the services of fortune-tellers and spirit mediums more often.[9] The vast majority of worshipers at Hsing-t'ien Temple are women. They come to Hsing-t'ien Temple seeking aid for personal problems and family problems. Women are responsible for the well-being of their families and this leads them to seek religious help for them even if the family members do not themselves visit temples or worship gods/goddesses.

The rituals practiced at the temple are, for the most part, traditional rituals seen at most Chinese temples in Taiwan. However, at Hsing-t'ien Temple the setting is such that only simple religious rituals are encouraged; the socializing and chess-playing so popular at most Taiwanese temples are discouraged. Through the rituals women seek divine help and guidance. One popular ritual is *shou ching*, which is used to heal physical and mental illnesses caused by a frightened soul (Yü 1985, 26). At this temple this ritual is often performed by a temple volunteer laywoman who holds three sticks of incense and waves them in front of the person's body three times, around her head, and then waves them behind her back seven times. This ritual is repeated twice and then the divining blocks are cast to find out if the ritual has succeeded in making the person whole again (Yü 1985, 26–27).

In addition to healing rituals, there are also rituals through which worshipers may gain divine help in solving their personal or business problems. In order to receive specific messages from the god a worshiper silently says her name, address, age, and her problem, and then casts the crescent-shaped divining blocks. When the blocks land with one convex and one concave side up, indicating a positive response from the god, she then takes a numbered bamboo stick, which corresponds to a printed omen, which gives her the divine answer to her question (Yü 1985, 27). According to psychologist Yü Te-hui, if the divine response in fact comes true, then the devout believer has greater confidence in the efficacy of the god and an increased sense of divine protection. On the other hand, if the divine reponse is contradicted, then the believer sees herself as the reason: she was not sincere enough and thus decides to visit the temple even more often (Yü 1985, 27).

The personalized worship at Hsing-t'ien Temple gives worshipers a sense of security and a sense of being part of something beyond mundane life. One young woman experienced a powerful spiritual truth:

I was born and raised in a household that placed importance on worship. My eyes and ears were filled with respect for the deities since I was young, but I didn't pay too much attention to these things because I really didn't think that they existed.

What is strange is that I imperceptibly received an omen that I must enter their midst. When I was studying at university, my family was down on its luck because our business failed. My mother went to Hsing-t'ien Temple every month to pray, hoping and trusting that we could overcome this difficulty. Perhaps with my mother's devoutness we finally got through that period of inhuman days; moreover, our family situation finally began to gradually improve. Therefore, for over half a year I accompanied my mother to Hsing-t'ien Temple on the first and fifteenth day of every month. One day while I was placing incense sticks, suddenly there was a heavy power urging me forward to pay attention. I can't express that mysterious feeling. It was as if my whole body were full. No longer was I a solitary body—it was as if I discovered a source, telling me that this was only a beginning. That feeling continued for several days; sometimes I even felt like my mind was shining bright.

Having gone through several months of feeling my way through the darkness, I hoped to try again, hoping and trusting to again have that peaceful, moving feeling. Perhaps it was only an awakening which allowed me to discover that there are too many unfathomable mysteries that need to be pondered. Actually, now my footsteps tarry not only at Hsing-t'ien temple; I have been to many major temples all over the province. I am not intent on getting people's attention; I only hope that in the coming months I will again have an even deeper understanding. [Yü 1985, 30–31]

This educated young woman's eloquent expression of her search for spiritual truth is perhaps not typical of the experience of Hsing-t'ien Temple worshipers, at least in its articulation. She does, however, represent the possibility of discovering one's own spiritual truth amid the images and rituals of popular religion. Her testimony certainly counters the often-heard criticism of intellectuals of the superstitious beliefs of women worshipers.

A simpler, more concrete request for healing and protection is the concern of an old woman at the temple. She devoutly prays to Kuan-kung in behalf of her sick daughter:

Lord Benefactor! Please protect the Juan family's daughter. Since she was born her stomach and intestines have not been well, and the doctor has not been effective either. Today I have come to get a charm of incense ashes with the hope that your lordship will protect her, protect her well. [Yü 1985, 31]

Most of the volunteers who aid worshipers at Hsing-t'ien Temple are female, most of them over forty years old. For them the temple and its rituals have become central to their lives. There are approximately four or five hundred of these lay ritual specialists (Yü 1985, 33). They chant scriptures, distribute the sanctified incense ashes, and assist in the divination and interpretation of omens. This last task requires a fair amount of training. Because the turnover rate of volunteers is quite low, most of them are quite experienced in helping worshipers. Some women have served in the temple for ten or twenty years (Yü 1985, 34).

These devout volunteers are mostly women whose children are grown. They have found the sense of community, of sacred power, and of service to others offered by the temple to provide substance in their lives. Very old women stand for hours performing the *shou ching* soul-protecting ritual for people with illnesses, family disputes, business problems, school examination worries. They have taken the traditional concern for the well-being of family members and extended it to the larger society. As Yü points out, they also get daily confirmation of the truth and power of their own religious beliefs as they see worshipers return to thank Kuan-kung for his help by making donations or by repeatedly kneeling before his altar (Yü 1985, 35).

WOMEN IN CONTEMPORARY RELIGIOUS SECTS

Chinese sectarianism in Taiwan offers some of the same benefits to women found in the popular Chinese religion at Hsing-t'ien Temple: a sense of community, a chance for a special religious role, and a context in which to create spiritual meaning in their lives. As members of sects, women have an even greater sense of group membership and special religious status. David Jordan and Daniel Overmyer's study of Taiwan's spirit-writing sects offers insights into the lives of several women sect members. In their discussion of one sect, the Compassion Society, they note that almost half the offices in one branch were held by women (146–47). Although the greatest power apparently was in the hands of the hall chairman, a man who owned the temple and its land, women did achieve positions of importance in this branch hall of the sect (Jordan and Overmyer, 145).

The life of one woman leader, given the religious name "Phoenix Pencil," is especially interesting.

Phoenix Pencil became a wielder of the *chi*, the spirit-writing instrument through which the deities communicate with believers. Although the *chi* wielder is not the most prestigious position in the sect, it is the most important. As Jordan and Overmyer note, "since the activity of the hall is formally directed by divine command, manifested through the *chi*, the *chi* wielder must formulate and represent an image of divine will and divine action that is in accord with the member's expectations, tolerance, hopes, and interest" (147–48).

Phoenix Pencil, like many bright women born at the end of World War II, was denied the education that was encouraged for her brothers. She suffered the discrimination against daughters so strongly criticized by feminist writer Lü Hsiu-lien. As Phoenix Pencil reported: "Everybody valued boys and not girls. That was the old rural society. I went to school on my own. My father said that if I went he would cut off my legs. I went myself. I walked every day" (Jordan and Overmyer, 159). She was able to begin university, but quit when her father directly ordered her to quit and get married (Jordan and Overmyer, 159). In the Compassion Society she later found a fulfilling role for herself as a reader of spirit writing and later as a wielder of the *chi* spirit-writing instrument herself (160–61).

Women like Phoenix Pencil may be able to find meaning in positions of religious leadership in sectarian religion that are unavailable to them in community-based temple activities. The community-based temple festivals of Taiwanese Chinese religion still maintain a male hierarchy. In accordance with the separation of men and women into outside/inside roles, women have responsibility for domestic rituals and family well-being, while the men have the responsibility for community rituals and community well-being. The Taoist priests that serve as ritual specialists for temple festivals are male. The master of the incense pot (*lu chu*), who is in charge of organizing the temple festival, is a respected role that rotates among male heads of families (Sangren, 55–58). Women contribute their labors to the festivals, but do not fill official leadership roles. In the more individualized worship of Hsing-t'ien Temple and in the sectarian worship of societies such as the Compassion Society, we see women participating in more public roles of leadership and ritual expertise.

It is clear that Phoenix Pencil's activities in the Compassion Society relieved the loneliness of an isolated woman and fulfilled the intellectual aspirations thwarted by her father. The fact that she was the daughter-in-law of the owner of the temple certainly had something to do with her acceptance and success in the sect (Jordan and Overmyer, 164). It would be interesting to study the importance of male support for the success of women leaders in contemporary Chinese sects.

Jordan's interviews with three other women in the Compassion Society reveal the way women can make use of religious traditions in their own idiosyncratic way to find meaning and self-dignity (184–212). A 63-year-old woman (in 1976) with the religious title "Exquisite Fragrance," using the Compassion Society as her base, constructed a wondrous sacred world for herself through prophetic dreams and visions. Her dreams and visions gave this uneducated woman of limited means a sense of superior goodness and divine protection by the Golden Mother, the primary deity of the Compassion Society. Much of her religious life is independent of the Society, but the Society did provide for her important confirmation of her special status. According to Exquisite Fragrance, the Golden Mother wrote a verse for her through the Society's spirit-writing activity confirming and explaining her own dreams. She reported the Golden Mother's revelation as follows:

> You are like a piece of bamboo, for your heart is firm and merciful, and although people may harm you and cut you down, you do not fall because you have been practicing the Way. Until now you have been like this staff of bamboo. You have already grown to putting forth green buds and a bamboo head and the staff is long. If anyone should want to hurt you, he would have great difficulty in getting to you . [Jordan and Overmyer, 188]

In addition to her visions and the spirit-writing revelation, Exquisite Fragrance's life is full of miracles performed by the Golden Mother. She sees the Golden Mother's protection and punishment everywhere (Jordan and Overmyer, 190–94). Jordan found that Exquisite Fragrance and two of her women friends in the Society shared with each other their religious experiences, and thus formed a small informal subcult of their own (190).

Exquisite Compassion, one woman friend of Exquisite Fragrance, had her own visions "congratulating her on her sacrifices for her children and on remaining unmarried after the death of her husband, despite her economic difficulties and the economic motivation to seek a new husband" (Jordan and Overmyer, 200). Here we see visions by a sect member rewarding her for her adherence to the traditional Confucian ideal of chastity and for her sacrifices to fulfill the goal of continuing the male family line. In addition to participating in Compassion Society activities, she set up an altar to the Golden Mother in her own home and has a daughter serve as a spirit medium there (Jordan and Overmyer, 201). The Golden Mother is at the center of her life and has compensated her for the difficulties caused by traditional Chinese ideals of filiality and women's morality.

Another Compassion Society member interviewed by Jordan demonstrates how the Buddhist-derived concept of karma in Chinese religion can contribute to a contemporary woman's understanding of her fate as a woman. Ch'en Hsiu-hua was a sect member whose difficult life became meaningful through a revelation of her two previous lives and their karmic consequences (Jordan and Overmyer, 202–12). According to a revelation through spirit-writing, after a life as an extremely filial daughter, she was reborn as a son in a rich family. In this life he/she was an immoral philanderer and after dying at age thirty-two, his/her spirit appeared before the king of hell. The king of hell angrily said: "In your last life you did very well. This time I gave you an incarnation in a rich family, and you didn't contribute to the poor or relieve suffering; you spent your money on women and covered your body with gold. This is unsatisfactory. This time I shall give you an incarnation as a woman, as the daughter of the Ch'en family in Tainan, in Taiwan province. . . . You'll wed into a rich family, but you'll not enjoy what they have. That will be your fate. But although this is your current situation, do not despair. If you study the Way (Tao) then in the future you will be able to overcome the 'sea of troubles' and be reincarnated no more" (Jordan and Overmyer, 206). She reports her response to this revelation as follows: "I understood that it was my fate, forgot the troubles I had been through, and studied the Way with energy" (Jordan and Overmyer, 206).

In his analysis of this revelation, Jordan notes that the *chi-*wielder's organization of the traditional moral stereotypes of virtuous person and selfish wastrel "into a virtuous *female* and a wastrel *male* increases the probability of Hsiu-hua's identifying more strongly with the protagonist of the first than of the second incarnation story" (207). I think that we can also see a reflection of women's acknowledgment of social preference for sons: to be born female is a punishment and to be born male is a reward. Her knowledge of her previous lives gave her the ability to accept her fated suffering as a woman, but also gives hope for the future so that she does not fall into despair over her female fate.

Ch'en Hsiu-hua is also an example of how sectarian religion can fulfill educational desires usually denied to women. Although she had only six years of education, she became a copyist who records the spirit-writing of the Compassion Society. She studied on her own, copying verse texts. When she was first asked to act as copyist she had reservations, but agreed. She reported: "I burned incense to the immortals and buddhas and prayed that if they wanted to use me as a copyist they might send me inspiration (ling)" (Jordan and Overmyer, 211). She also reported to Jordan that following that prayer, the "God Who Manages Ritual" appeared to her in a dream and instructed her (211).

Ch'en Hsiu-hua found a literary role for herself in the sect. Her parents would not educate her, but her gods did. She found in sectarian religion ways to go far beyond the limited roles of filial obedience and submission defined for her by traditional Chinese views about women.

CONCLUSION: TRANSFORMING CONFUCIAN PATRIARCHY

Taiwanese society is still permeated with patriarchal Chinese traditions which prescribe women's roles and the roles of the men with which they must deal. As the foundation of Chinese social philosophy, Confucian values cannot be avoided. Confucianism permeates the legal code and the educational system. Confucianism defines the ideal family and the roles of its members. Whereas women are free to accept or reject other religious and philosophical traditions, they must in some way come to terms with dominating Confucian values.

Although Chinese women have found meaning and fulfillment in the family, it is doubtful that they have ever fully accepted the Confucian ideal for women and their role in the family. Surely few women have completely embraced the ideal of complete submission to father, husband, and son. Many women have found ways to transform the Chinese family defined by Confucian ideals to a form that serves their own interests. Margery Wolf has shown how women in rural Taiwan had their own understanding of family that was usually in conflict with the male lineage that they were supposed to perpetuate. She found that women used bonds of affection and loyalty to bind their children to them in their own "uterine families," which excluded husband and his family (Wolf, 32–37). Women created this uterine family for their own emotional and material support, because they recognized that their own interests were often in conflict with those of their husband's families. Whereas the Confucian teachings of filial piety, female submission, and chastity served the interests of the male family lineage, women used more personal and affective means to serve their own interests.

For meaning beyond the family, some women have turned to popular religion or sectarian religion to compensate them for the suffering they have experienced due to patriarchal views of women. A generation of women who sacrificed their own interests and educations for their families have occasionally found intellectual fulfillment and recognition for their talents in sectarian groups or lay religious organizations.

Ancestor reverence and filial piety have long provided an important source of meaning and self-definition for the Chinese, although women's interpretations of these ideals have often differed from those of men.[10] The importance of ancestor worship and filial piety goes beyond elite forms of Confucianism and permeates popular culture. Most Chinese in Taiwan, women and men alike, want to hold on to the ideal of filial piety. They do not want to fall into what they see as the American neglect of their parents and grandparents. Their view of the American lack of filial piety is, I believe, exaggerated. (People I talk to are invariably surprised to find out that my maternal grandmother lived with my parents for the last two decades of her life.) Recent studies have suggested that high school and college students in Taiwan still overwhelmingly approve of much of filial piety (Huang, 1989). About half the students completely agreed with the statement that "of all good actions, filial piety is foremost;" only a small percentage completely disagreed (Huang, 31).

An overwhelming majority thought that it was absolutely necessary to fulfill the obligations of filial piety toward their parents (Huang, 29). Men's and women's views of filial piety, however, do not completely agree. For example, another study showed that urban working women expected to contribute to the support of their own parents as a contemporary expression of filial piety, but their brothers and husbands believed that as sons it was their sole responsibility to support their parents. A few women in the study expressed the view that it is best to give money to their parents discreetly in order to allow their brothers to save face (Tsui, 21–22). Women seem to be adapting their understanding of filial piety to contemporary life-styles more quickly than men. More than ever now women are choosing to fulfill certain Chinese traditions and are transforming others. Although traditional social pressures still exist and patriarchal values are still reflected in laws,[11] with their greater economic independence women in Taiwan have greater freedom to determine their own relationship to Chinese religious and philosophical traditions.

There are some women doing the difficult work of articulating Chinese values in a way appropriate for contemporary Taiwanese society. Lü Hisu-lien has proposed a reformulation of Confucian ideals to foster the fulfillment of women's and men's lives both inside and outside the family. Lin Mei-jung has called for the freedom of regional Taiwanese culture to develp its own traditions liberated from the domination of government-sponsored, elitist Confucian ideals.

If the educated, economically independent women of Taiwan focus their energies on the reformulation of an egalitarian form of Confucianism, the results could be a fascinating. The role that popular religion and sectarian groups might play in such a transformation of society is unclear. They could serve as conservative forces by compensating women for some of the suffering they have experienced in patriarchal society and thus reducing reformist tendencies. Or they could serve as a means of transformation. Since sectarian groups are small and popular religion has no institutional organization, their power to reform society would seem to be limited. But given the proven ability of popular religion to adapt to social changes, it might take a very different form in a population of educated, working women.

Denise L. Carmody

TODAY'S JEWISH WOMEN

The watchword in both feminist and religious studies today is diversity. As historians, anthropologists, ritualists, and even theologians have studied the actual lives of religious women, they have found that race, class, historical context, nationality, and other factors all leave their mark. In addition, contemporary religious and feminist studies have run into the irreducible individuality of many women, especially those placed in unique circumstances or endowed with unique gifts. Thus, any authors attempting to sketch the patterns of women's religious experience in a given era or locale have to send messengers ahead to announce the modesty of their venture. At best they will be describing patterns that express the experience of a significant number of the population involved. At worst they will be retailing patterns that struck their own fancy but did not represent the majority of the population involved.

All the more so is this the case for those who attempt studies of contemporary religious women, who live in a time of rapid change. Many of the movements most important to contemporary religious women publish their projects and ideas by word of mouth and informal newsletters more than by books and formal articles. The international character of Judaism only adds a further complication, for who can document all that is happening in the former Soviet Union and Latin America, as well as in North America and Europe?

Faced with these difficulties, I have decided to concentrate on ideas and problems rather than facts and organizations. Some of the ideas seem fated, once one considers the historical shape of Judaism and its basic theological convictions. For example, Jewish women become aware of the egalitarian claims made by feminists seem bound to make gender a tool for reviewing their people's past. If the standard histories have neglected the female half of the race, and the female half is now considered as historical as the male half, then the standard histories need revision, to admit what can be retrieved of women's experiences and voices.

Similarly, if ritual is a major way that Jews remind themselves of their identity and shape their sense of where God may be leading them, then people sensitive to the rights and distinct experiences of women will inevitably concern themselves with adapting ritual to provide for women as well as men. One could say the same for theology. If theology deals with the mysterious counter-player who has stalked Jewish history and ritual, then a theology reflecting today's awareness of women's differences from men and the tendency of patriarchal traditions to neglect such differences will be brooding about the representation of women in the imagery used to name or invoke the deity.

I shall deal with these three areas—history, ritual, and theology—as concerns that cut across the diverse movements of contemporary Jewish women. For Jewish feminists (women or men trying to grant women equality with men as half the human race), these areas are all ripe for reform. For traditional Jewish women, who would not call themselves feminists, older patriarchal patterns may still rule, but often some awareness of the new global consciousness of women's past deprivations and present aspirations shifts those patriarchal patterns notably.

Prior to dealing with how contemporary Jewish women seem to be reconsidering history, ritual and theology, I shall reflect on some concerns that have surfaced recently in Israel. With the United States, Israel supplies much of the energy so evident in the efforts of contemporary Jewish women to bring their sense of religious faith and their sense of womanhood together in a mutually vivifying way. Most of my sources illustrating current Jewish women's work on history, ritual, and theology come from the United States, so the section on activities and concerns that have surfaced recently in Israel should be a good reminder that even though American Jewish women probably are the vanguard of Jewish feminism, in many other countries their sisters are struggling with similar problems.

Before moving to specific topics, however, it may be well to set the stage by reviewing two matters that shape the context or background of many Jewish women's aspirations today. One is the patriarchal tradition handed down by the past. The other is the conviction of feminists that women, for all their diversity, tend to have some needs and contributions discernibly different from those of men.

The tradition grounding the faith of Jewish women today stretches back into biblical prehistory, perhaps four thousand years ago. To call that tradition patriarchal is to underscore the predominance of men in formulating the beliefs and institutions that have constituted Judaism. Men are the main actors crossing the stage of biblical history, and men dominated the rabbinic culture that shaped Judaism in the common era. Certainly the Bible deals with women, sometimes describing famous women as heroic exemplars of faith, but the narratives and laws of the biblical writers generally reflect the bias we associate with patriarch cultures: men are the first definers of humanity and women are helpmeets or complements. Rabbinic Judaism, coming to predominance at the end of the biblical period and prevailing into the modern era, if not into the present, has sponsored a religious culture in which learning has been the badge of merit, and women have generally been excluded from learning.

Certainly such a bias was not unique to Judaism, but Jewish women have paid a special price for their exclusion from religious learning: virtually no entry to the precincts where the religious elite dealt with the questions shaping what it meant to be a Jew. Suffice it to recall that only three of the 613 religious injunctions laid out in the Torah (religious guidance or law) applied to women. Keeping such injunctions was the pride of the Jewish life. Not to be bound to such injunctions therefore was to be separated from many of the practical details and prayers that wove the fabric of daily faith. Certainly one could interpret the three duties incumbent on women—to prepare the Sabbath bread, light the Sabbath candles, and purify themselves in the ritual bath—as symbols swelling to embrace the whole of life (nourishment, illumination, purity), but in fact Jewish men have been the teachers and exemplars of holiness in most formal senses, while Jewish women have played on the margins. In the popular consciousness of both Jewish men and Jewish women, men have been the prime images of God and men's activity has been more surely religious.

The second factor crucial to understanding the movements and ideas of contemporary Jewish women is feminism. Whatever their degree of commitment to political programs designed to bring women into the mainstream of political and cultural power in their given nation, the majority of Jewish women nowadays are aware that patriarchy is neither inevitable nor just. Sometimes this awareness may be only oblique and inarticulate, but wherever women have any purchase on the issues of the present age, it is making a significant impact. Even the Jewish woman who belongs to no women's group and expresses no desire to change traditional religious ceremonies or ideas more often than not does so with an awareness of other options that would not have been available to her grandmother. So while it is true to say that women have always created defenses against the depradations of patriarchy, and that Jewish women have always found ways to express their conviction that they are an indispensible part of their community or people, the contemporary scene, in country after country, is distinctive because nowadays the majority of women are aware of the question of women's equal humanity and sensitive to the issue of how their equal humanity is or is not being honored in a given social context.

The women and movements that have most intrigued me, and so dominate my report on contemporary Jewish women, have been those that have put Jewishness and feminsim together to make a powerful dialectic. On the one hand, they are insisting that they do not want to be Jewish at the price of denying their gender or experiencing it to be shortchanged. On the other hand, they are insisting that they are Jewish, not secular or religious in any other mode. The two words, "Jewish" and "feminist," stand as mutually qualifying yet ineluctably joined. Sometimes one can speak of Jewish feminists. Other times one can speak of feminist Jews. On the whole, the terms demand equal emphasis. Criticize or slight the Jewishness and you will get a rebuke from the side of religious tradition. Criticize the feminism and you will get a rebuke from the side of sensitivity to gender rights. Criticize both, in the sense of asking both to bear on the identity of those asking what it means to be a Jewish woman today, and you will find yourself amid a wonderful ferment, full of diversity and pain, discovery and joy, and often wonderful creativity.

Lastly, I should note that while the creativity that has most beguiled me has played in liberal to radical religious and political tones, Orthodox Jewish women can show an equally intriguing blend of desire to be faithful to both their Jewishness and their femininity. Indeed, the phenomenon of women choosing a traditional, Orthodox life-style as a way to discover and develop their identity reminds us that the major terms we must employ (identity, wholeness, womanhood) can be found or validated in quite diverse ways. Thus the woman who finds the traditional law forbidding sexual relations during menstruation an enhancement of both her own dignity and her marriage has as rightful a claim on the attention of Jewish feminists as the woman who finds all such laws oppressive. To their great credit, the majority of the women on whom I have drawn are well aware of this fact and rejoice in it. Their sympathy extends to all women and all Jews, especially those working to improve the faith and lot of Jewish women.[1]

IMAGES FROM ISRAEL

Recently the *New York Times* carried this story with a by-line from Jerusalem:

> A group of Jewish women trying to hold a prayer service at the Wailing Wall were attacked today by rigorously Orthodox men and forced to flee when the police fired tear gas to dispense the attackers. Several women were knocked to the ground and one suffered a gash on her neck when a Hasidic man threw a heavy metal chair at the heads of the praying women. The Wailing Wall, which Israelis call the Western Wall, is the holiest site in Judaism. The 40 or so women infuriated the rigorously Orthodox men by trying to hold morning prayers while reading from a Torah and wearing prayer shawls. Orthodox men insist that women are forbidden even to carry a Torah scroll, and that only males have the right to don the shawls.[2]

Perhaps the key to understanding this story is the significance of the term "Orthodox" for the state of Israel. Whereas in other countries, most notably the United States, it is accepted that the Orthodox represent those who have rejected modern innovations (proposed by Reform, Conservative, or Reconstructionist movements) and deserve a respected place on the spectrum of Jewish belief or opinion, in Israel the traditionalists have gained a stranglehold on political influence. By linking the preservation of Jewish religious customs to the preservation or security of the state of Israel, they have gained enough popular support and political clout to dominate the laws and practices shaping religious life. Thus further paragraphs in this story suggest that the government has either sided with the Orthodox in their efforts to thwart women's innovations or been placed in the middle as the reluctant defender of the women's civil rights:

But Zevulun Or-Lev, the director general of the Ministry of
Religious Affairs, defended the Orthodox position, saying the
prohibition on women holding prayer services "is traditional
in Israel, and this tradition is law and can't be changed." The
police last week told the women that their prayer service
would be considered a threat to public safety and that they
might face arrest. At the women's last prayer service, in February, they were also attacked by Orthodox men. . . . Just after
7 A.M., as the women walked past soldiers guarding the gates
to the Wailing Wall plaza, an elderly Hasidic man with a
bushy beard began waving a prayer book and shouting, "Go to
the churches and pray there where you belong!" He was joined
by dozens of Orthodox men and boys in black hats and long
black coats. They cursed and screamed at the women and
linked arms, forming a human chain to block the women's
progress toward the wall. . . . After a few minutes, the women,
pale and clutching each other, moved forward as one until
they reached the short metal partitions separating the wom-
en's prayer section from the larger plaza facing the wall.
There, fierce scuffling broke out between the authorities, who
tried to clear the path, and the Orthodox men, who tried to
block it. The women stood by silently.[3]

Commenting on the efforts of Israeli women to move toward
equality with men, Galia Golan, a professor of political science at
the Hebrew University in Jerusalem, has sketched the background
of such conflicts as that played out recently at the Western Wall:

A third obstacle to equality is the religious establishment
which, like the army, holds a central place in Israeli society.
In a country which borders on theocracy, in which the convo-
luted political system allows the small religious parties to dic-
tate policy (by virtue of their ability to tip the scales in the
direction of one or the other of the two main political blocs),
the subordinate role of women in traditional Judaism takes on
an oppressive, official quality. All family law in Israel is in the
hands of the religious courts; for the Jews this means that all
questions regarding marriage and the dissolution of marriage
are in the hands of the Rabbinate. In the Rabbinical courts
women are not allowed to give evidence, there are no women
judges, and no women on the committees nominating the
judges. A husband must "grant" his wife a divorce—and

many are the cases of refusal, leading to years of suffering for the woman. The result of a woman being placed in this "suppliant" position may be the loss of her children (in any case the father has the right to custody of male children over the age of six) or grave financial hardship. Not satisifed with its already monopolistic role in the realm of marriage and divorce, the Rabbinate is seeking a broadening of its powers, that is, a legislative change empowering it to nullify civil marriage or divorce proceedings conducted outside Israel.[4]

Whereas in the United States women have been admitted to the rabbinate in Reformed, Conservative, and Reconstructionist circles, in Israel these branches of Judaism have no official standing. The Orthodox have successfully maneuvered to have them accounted deviant groups, so much so that the legitimacy of their children or the fully Jewish status of any of their members has been called into question.

The Hasidim, descendants of a movement begun in eighteenth-century eastern Europe by an ecstatic leader known as the Baal Shem Tov, tend to be among the most ardent opponents of any changes seeming to take Judaism toward accommodation with secularism. Despite the fact that many Israeli citizens do not consider themselves religious (as many Jews in other parts of the world do not), the Hasidim have worked with other Orthodox Jews to make the precepts of the religious law (halakah) binding in Israeli civil life. The result for women has been considerably less progress toward equality than the Zionist programs important at the founding of the modern state of Israel led women to expect. Thus Golan links the influence of Orthodox religious views of the family to problems women face in the fields of both work and family life:

> Yet family structures work against women's achievement of equality insofar as the society is not geared to accommodate working parents. The Israeli child's school day ends at twelve or one o'clock, necessitating part-time work for many women. Yet a person holding a part-time job (the vast majority of women in the work force) cannot get tenure at a university or achieve significant advancement in other professions. Flexible-time jobs are almost nonexistent, supervised after-school care for school-age children is rare, and daycare centers for preschoolers are insufficient and increasingly expensive. Household help sufficient to permit a woman to work outside

the home on a daily basis is scarce, very expensive, and not tax-deductible. Maternity leave is just three months and available only for the mother. Moreover, though the family is a hallowed institution, the woman's role within the family itself is a subordinate one. The woman's task is frequently—consciously or unconsciously—to serve the male members of the family (a tradition particularly strong among the Jews of "Eastern" origin). Wife-battering—by sons as well as husbands—is a serious problem. Only a few shelters for battered women, established privately by feminists and usually run on a shoestring, exist. The list of problems could go on and on, including, for example, cases of laws which have been passed, such as an equal pay for equal work law from the early 1950s, which are simply not implemented.[5]

Despite such problems, traceable at least in part to the Israeli religious establishment, notable Israeli women have found in their Zionist roots the basis for both pride in their femininity and political activism regarding Israel's preoccupying problem of coming to terms with its Palestinian population. Thus Shulamith Koenig, an Israeli feminist born in Jerusalem in 1930 of immigrants from Poland, writes:

Those of us who lift our voices in protest in Israel have decided that there is one thing on which we stand firm and will not move: the teaching of our prophets, the moral and ethical values of our lives. If the existence of the community contradicts the dignity of the individual, social commitment has no value. . . . How can we equate the dignity of the individual with Palestinian self-determination, with the inevitability of a two-state solution, with the realization that Israel can be democratic and Jewish, an enlightened state for the Jewish people who wish to live there, as well as giving full equality to its minorities? Those of us working for change in Israel have realized that we need to educate our young for such change. We know that a country is as good as its education. We have demonstrated in the streets. We have been called traitors. We have had tear gas bombs thrown at us. . . . In Israel there are over 8,000 women who signed . . . a manifesto to get our young men out of Lebanon. What happens in Lebanon or on the West Bank is not only tragic for the people of Lebanon and the West Bank. It is also a shameful tragedy for young Israelis who have to be there, and whose lives are distorted by the violence they perpetrate. . . . All my life I was very proud that I was a Jew, a woman, an Israeli, a mother. Today, there are times when I am ashamed. I need to work together with my sisters from around the world to find a way forward. My question is this: How do we stop humiliating one another? How do we turn from the experience of humiliation, and yet not go on to humiliate others? How do we break the cycle?[6]

This eloquent voice, filled with both love of country and pain at present injustices, strikes me as prototypically Jewish and feminine. From the tradition of the prophets that Koenig hallows comes the vibrant instinct that justice is the marrow of decent communal life. From the instincts of a mother comes the passionate concern to preserve life and dignity in the face of violence and humiliation. Joined, the two make a stunningly powerful appeal. In a Shulamith Koenig, it can seem, all the valiant women of Jewish history find the daughter that their best religious and feminine instincts longed to bring forth.

REINTERPRETING HISTORY

When Jewish women consider their tradition nowadays, they regularly follow the line of gender back into the past, to retrieve or imagine what the female half of their people experienced. Whether it be at the great moments of biblical history, such as when the covenant between Israel and God was forged,[7] or during the history of Jewish immigrants' struggles to find their place in the United States, the overriding conviction of feminist historians is that women were fifty percent of the actors and reactors creating the story of their people.

Perhaps the most interesting sector of Jewish history that feminists recently have been reviewing and reinterpreting is the biblical period. Jews have always considered this period paradigmatic: filled with lessons about the perennial nature of the covenant between God and the Jewish people. A particularly eloquent example of present-day imagination put to work on interpreting the experience of the mothers of Jews' biblical faith occurs in a recent essay by the novelist Cynthia Ozick on the book of Ruth. Ozick begins her essay by placing the image of Ruth in her own personal history, which has

been that of a daughter of Russian Jews come to the United States
with a rich heritage of religious sentiments:

> My grandfather's portrait had its permanent place over the
> secondhand piano. To the right, farther down the wall, hung
> the other picture. It was framed modestly in a thin black
> wooden rectangle, and was, in those spare days, all I knew of
> "art." Was it torn from a magazine, cut from a calendar? A
> barefoot young woman, her hair bound in a kerchief, grasping
> a sickle, stands alone and erect in a field. Behind her a red sun
> is half swallowed by the horizon. She wears a loose white
> peasant's blouse and a long dark skirt, deeply blue; her head
> and shoulders are isolated against a limitless sky. Her head is
> held poised: she gazes past my gaze into some infinity of lone-
> liness stiller than the sky.
> Below the picture was its title: *The Song of the Lark.*
> There was no lark. It did not come to me that the young
> woman, with her lifted face, was straining after the note of a
> bird who might be in a place invisible to the painter. What I
> saw and heard was something else: a scene older than French
> countryside, a woman lonelier even than the woman alone in
> the calendar meadow. It was, my mother said, Ruth: Ruth
> gleaning in the fields of Boaz.[8]

The point is that from girlhood Ozick experienced the characters of the Bible as heroes and heroines—larger than life figures
through whom one might interpret the trials and triumphs of any
Jewish life. Later, highly developed in literary and religious sensibility, she returned to the book of Ruth, on assigment to contribute to
a collection of essays on the Bible by Jewish writers, with a desire to
do right by the figure who had so enriched her childhood. The story
of Ruth, her mother-in-law Naomi, and her sister-in-law Orpah becomes for Ozick an occasion to wonder her way into the mysteries
of the Israelite God, the maker of the Jewish people. By meditating
on the experience of these literary women, Ozick arrives at some
burning retrievals of the singularity of Jewish monotheism:

> Her [Orpah's] prototype abounds. She has fine impulses, but
> she is not an iconoclast. She can push against convention to a
> generous degree, but it is out of the generosity of her temper-
> ament, not out of some large metaphysical idea. Who will de-
> mand of Orpah—think of the hugeness of the demand!—that

she admit monotheism to the concentration and trials of her mind? Offer montheism to almost anyone—offer it as something to take seriously—and ninety-nine times out of a hundred it will be declined, even by professing "monotheists." A Lord of History whose intent is felt, whose Commandments stand with immediacy, whose Covenant summons perpetual self-scrutiny and a continual Turning toward moral renewal, and yet *cannot, may not, be physically imagined?* A Creator neither remote and abstract like the God of the philosphers, nor palpable like the "normal" divinities, both ancient and contemporary, of both East and West? Give us (cries the nature of our race) our gods and goddesses; give us the little fertility icons with their welcoming breasts and elongated beckoning laps; give us the resplendent Virgin with her suffering brow and her arms outstretched in blessing; give us the Man on the Cross through whom to learn pity and love, and sometimes brutal exclusivity! Only give us what our eyes can see and our understanding understand: who can imagine the unimaginable? That may be for the philosophers; *they* can do it; but then they lack the imagination of the Covenant. The philosophers leave the world naked and blind and deaf and mute and relentlessly indifferent, and the village folk—who refuse the lonely cosmos without consolation—fill it and fill it and fill it with stone and wood and birds and mammals and miraculous potions and holy babes and animal carcasses and magically divine women and magically divine men: images, sights, and swallowings comprehensible to the hand, to the eye, to plain experience. For the nature of our race, God is one of the visual arts.[9]

Rereading the Bible with a contemporary woman's sensibility, Cynthia Ozick finds in Ruth's choice of the God of Naomi (the Israelite God whom Orpah understandably did not choose) the profound depths of montheistic audacity. Despite the fact that Ruth, whether or however she actually existed, never could have known about the God of the philosophers with whom Ozick contrasts the God of Abraham, Isaac, Jacob, Sarah, Rebecca, and Rachel, and that Ruth knew nothing about the claims for the incarnation of God consequent on Christianity, Ozick's reinterpretation of Ruth's choice and instinct rings true, because it goes to the depths of the Israelite intuition about the Lord who had to be One. Such a reinterpretation or retrieval or imaginative way of becoming a contemporary of a past heroine shows the great potential in recent feminist efforts to rewrite history so that it provides for a two-sexed humanity, rather than simply the story of eminent men.

Persuasively, many feminists using historical imagination the way that Ozick has done, argue that some stories are true, even though they never happened, while some stories that probably happened tell us little about the truth. Whether or not the story of Ruth actually happened, it carries to us the truth of a pagan woman's embrace of the whole being or situation of a woman she loved, and so of her embrace of that beloved woman's singular divinity. In making her choice, Ruth suggests the chasmic divide between the biblical God and the deities that people have to domesticate. Without a contemporary woman such as Cynthia Ozick, however, it is doubtful that we could see the grandeur latent in Ruth's choice.

Jewish women trying to rehabilitate a past that in gross perspective can seem oppressively patriarchal have gone to figures of rabbinic as well as biblical history, spurred by today's consciousness of gender to probe what the female sex of a character suggests about how she appears on the ledgers of Jewish accounting.[10] Rachel Adler, focusing on the traditions about the scholar Beruriah, wife of the great Rabbi Meir, finds that when one probes the significance of Beruriah's having been a singular woman, learned in the Torah and yet disgraced for having succumbed to seduction, the full outline of the bias of Jewish tradition against women looms into view. Viewed with a contemporary sensitivity to sexist prejudices, Beruriah becomes one of the many characters from the Jewish past carrying the potential to break the reader's heart:

> The legend of Beruriah is just such a story. Retelling it from the world in which we stand, we can see how character strains against context, how it shakes assumptions about what it means to be woman, a Jew, a sexual being. It is precisely this tension of character and context that makes the Beruriah legend anomalous. It is a story about a woman, although at the time of its formation, women seldom were held to have stories. Beruriah was viewed as unlike other women, although women were, as far as the storytellers were concerned, alike in all ways that mattered. And is it a true story? Say rather that the shards of truth are in it, but by the power of the Torah that it contains I hope to understand it and go on.[11]

Adler studies the story of Beruriah as a venture of the rabbis to probe what it would mean for a woman to be like them in learning. Pushing her sense that the legend of Beruriah brims with psychological overtones, Adler muses:

> Beruriah's story is thus imbued with profound ambivalence. On the positive side are Beruriah's brilliance, her special usefulness as a woman who vindicates rabbinic Judaism, and the uniquely appealing depictions of her relationship with her husband. On the negative side, Beruriah is viewed as a threat, a competitor, an arrogant woman contemptuous of men and of rabbinic tradition. This negative pole of the rabbinic attitude toward Beruriah, which culminates in the tale of her adultery and suicide, is filled with malignant power. It so pervades the legend retroactively that we cannot mention Beruriah's intelligence or accomplishments without adding, if only mentally, "But she came to a bad end." This mental reservation brings the iron bars of the rabbinic context crashing down upon the anomalous woman, indeed upon all women. . . . Ironically, this disreputable tale, often dismissed as a fabrication, testifies to the ultimate truthfulness of the legend. The answer to the question the rabbis posed—*What if there were a woman who was just like us?*—is that the institutionalized denigration, subordination, and exclusion of women would destroy her, and that in the process the keepers of the tradition would besmirch themselves and profane the Torah they sought to protect.[12]

Many feminist rereadings of history and legend, it follows, threaten to break the hearts of those who accomplish or hear them. To find that one's past actually sensed the injustices it was perpetrating but felt powerless to change the structures or perceptions responsible for them is to find oneself at the core of human darkness, sure to wonder about the fate of being a Jewish woman.

NEW RITUALS AND COMMUNITIES

Largely because they have been determined to create from the past a more workable present and future than that presented them in most Jewish congregations, numerous Jewish women have participated in new ritualistic communities—new groups where they might worship and help one another create a faith supportive of their womanhood. Sometimes the new communities have fitted into the general movement known as *havurah*, which has channeled the efforts of many Jews to create alternatives to the typical Jewish congregation (whether Orthodox, Conservative, Reformed, or Reconstructionist). At other times they have developed as ad hoc adaptations of a congregation affiliated with a major line. In both cases that I consider here, however, the new community has focused much of its energy and identity on rituals expressing the aspirations of Jewish women toward an equal share in their tradition and faith.

The all-female community of *B'not Esh*, a group assembling annually to work on Jewish feminism, repeatedly has found that its tensions and catharses tend to rivet upon ritual:

> That first year, tensions within the group came to the fore most dramatically (and unexpectedly) during the course of Sabbath *davvening* (communal prayer). Friday evening, we held a rather standard *Kabbalat Shabbat* [psalms and prayers said at dusk to welcome the Sabbath], during which the entire group became involved in spirited dancing and singing to welcome the Sabbath Queen. By the end of the service, however, while some members of the group were "high" with the power of an all-women's *davvening*, others felt alienated and angered by the fact that we had followed so closely the hierarchical, male-dominated, aspects of the liturgy. But these tensions were not articulated until the following morning, when we gathered for morning prayers, and were confronted by the fact that no one knew what to do. What began as a five minute-discussion turned into a two-hour session, during which almost everyone expressed strong feelings of alienation and exclusion, and many people were in tears. The group agreed that, rather than attempting the seemingly impossible task of creating a service that would "work" for everyone, each woman would bring what she most wanted to include and we would create a "free-form" *davvening*. Ultimately, although that service itself provoked confrontation, the combination of traditional prayers, meditations, contemporary feminist poetry, and body movement exercises worked: the group came together, and the *davvening*, however unorthodox, succeeded in giving spiritual expression to the diversity of the group.[13]

Perhaps the first thing to note is how quickly and clearly the tensions in this group came to expression when members of the group tried to pray together. The lesson may well be that prayer—address of God from the heart—is the most existential of religious actions and so potentially the most powerful. Sensing this, many Jewish women, as many women in other religious traditions, have been especially affronted by traditional ritualistic language that either excluded or depreciated them. As we see in the next section, ritual or liturgy immediately embroils one in theological issues, including so momentous an issue as the nature (sexuality) of divinity itself. For the women of *B'not Esh*, discussion has tended to flow into ritualistic prayer and out from ritualistic prayer. Because of their commitment to forming a community that could worship together, these women have had to confront such differences among them as their range of sexual orientations: straight, lesbian, bisexual, celibate; single, married; with children, without children, and so forth.

After discussing the political dimension of *B'not Esh*, the author of the article on which I am drawing returns to the central function of ritual:

Finally (though hardly least) in our process, is the role of ritual and music. I indicated that we had developed a number of rituals in and for the group; and that we had been able to draw on our spirtual power to heal and comfort one another in times of stress. Of course, our ability to do that is a *consequence* of our having *created* a community; but, at the same time, it also contributes in important ways to that process. Whenever we truly "meet" as a community—whether in *davvening*, in ritual, or in discussion—the community, itself, is strengthened. Music has been a crucial part of this process. We have in the group a number of musicians and performance artists, who have composed songs for B'not Esh which have become enormously important parts of our experiences together. The fact that the community can generate the energy and inspiration for beautiful music is empowering in itself; but the feeling in the room when all of us sing together cannot be described. Our spirituality, as a group, is not only political; it is, I have come to understand, intensely musical. And that has served as yet another strong bond among us.[14]

Another example of a group whose reforms of traditional Jewish rituals have proven central to its coalescing as a community is the Upstairs Minyan, a small Jewish congregation founded in 1965 at the Hillel Foundation of the University of Chicago. Although this congregation has been affiliated with Conservative Judaism, it has regularly been ahead of Conservative Judaism in opening its ceremonial life to women's participation:

> At the outset, women were confined mainly to doing English readings in the mainly-Hebrew service. Initially they began to do Herbrew readings and to be counted in the quorum required for worship; services were still led by men, however. Next, they began to lead regular Saturday morning services, to recite the blessings for reading the Torah, and to read from the Hebrew Torah scroll. Finally, women began to lead services and to read from the Torah scroll for the High Holiday services, which involved a much larger congregation composed mainly of people not familiar with the Upstairs Minyan and its innovations. A second area in which women were innovative deals with ritual accessories important to formal Jewish worship but not ususally used by women. Relatively early in the Minyan's history, women began to wear the prayer shawls and skull caps typically worn by men for Sabbath worship. Thirdly, the liturgical text of the Jewish prayer was sometimes changed to reflect the Minyan's increased sensitivity to the exclusion of women from traditional forms and a need to include them.[15]

When the author analyzes why women were able to make better progress in the Upstairs Minyan than they would have in the typical Conservative congregation, she focuses on learning. In large part because of its university setting, the Upstairs Minyan prized learning (mastery of both Hebrew and the traditions about chanting in Hebrew) even more than the typical Conservative congregation would have. As well, it offered training in Hebrew and musical tradition to all who wished to improve their knowledge. As soon as women availed themselves of such training, the major obstacle to their full participation or even leadership of Minyan services fell away. This was a congregation that prized learning—competence—more than any sexist traditions handed down from the past. Realizing that if they could present themselves as competent in the liturgical matters that were the community's heartbeat they could gain full participation, many women studied hard. Indeed, the entire Minyan became more fluent in Hebrew and better able to avail itself of the riches of the Jewish liturgical tradition expressed in Hebrew.

The fuller participation of women in the ritual life of the Upstairs Minyan led to some changes in the language of worship, but at the time of the author's writing the Minyan had yet to use feminine language or imagery for the deity itself. In reflecting on this fact the author raises some interesting questions about Jewish theology, perhaps suggesting that acquiring greater theological competence is the group's next challenge:

> The difficulty of producing a grammatically correct and literarily graceful redrafting of the liturgy using the feminine gender [for God] has so far deterred any attempts in that direction; no one wants to risk a superficial or hasty solution to such problems. A more philosophical reason is perhaps more important. The fact that the liturgy has been revised to include references to the biblical matriarchs wherever their male counterparts are alluded to but not to include female images of deity whenever male images are used, suggests preference for historical rather than theological concerns. As one member has put it, "We know *Jews* are male and female, and always have been. We aren't willing to make such drastic statements about God, because most of us are a lot more literate historically than theologically." Furthermore, Jewish tradition, at least in this century, has strongly encouraged this orientation.[16]

Is it fair to suggest that a raised historical consciousness tends to raise consciousness of sexism in traditional ritualistic usage, and that such raised ritualistic consciousness, in turn, tends to push theological matters to the fore, perhaps in intuitive realization that women will finally be equal to men only when their group's sense of ultimate reality provides for the female as much as the male? Such a linkage or logic is intriguing to contemplate, though most feminists would tend to make the relations among the components more circular than linear. At any rate, both *B'not Esh* and the Upstairs Minyan have found that their efforts to create communities committed to women's full sharing in Jewish life has entangled them in the reform of traditional rituals and challenges to traditional theology. By internal dynamics that in retrospect seemed inevitable, they have found their views of community, prayer, political action, and

God all impinging on one another, forcing them to realize that any significant reform to make women the full equals of men was holistic—a recasting of the entirety of their Jewish awareness.

THEOLOGY

Although the connections among history, ritual, community life, and theology become plain when one penetrates their circle, it is not unusual to find Jewish women highly developed in their sensitivity to one dimension but amateur or unreformed regarding another. For example, in an interview with the journal *Tikkun*, no less redoubtable a figure than Betty Friedan, the mother of the women's movement in the United States, proves to be quite traditional when it comes to the matter of the gender of God:

> I'm very quizzical about this Goddess stuff; I don't believe that there was a wonderful world where women were worshiped and that the Jews killed them off. Monotheism is what the Jews did. If God is seen as a male God, then that is a limitation. But you do not replace it by a female God. There is one God. And I, as a Jew, have no use for this Goddess-stuff. I have great use for how women theologians and rabbis are enriching the Jewish tradition by bringing rubrics that come from female experience, but the Goddess . . . "The Lord is One" is the basic truth here. . . . If female experience is to inform in a new way and enrich our values generally in any discipline, it should move us away from the either-or, polarized, win-lose, zero sum definitions that, to me at least, come from more linear male experience, and embrace the complexity of not either-or, but both. So, to say, "You had your God, that was a male God. Now we're going to have our Goddess"— that's ridiculous. That's not liberation.[17]

Marcia Falk, working to create new rituals for Jewish women, might agree with much in Friedan's reaction, but for Falk making explicit the feminine aspect of divinity is a high priority. As background, Falk associates herself with a broad trend among feminist Jewish theologians:

> Feminist theologians have called for new God-language; and in many circles, Jewish women have been emending the

prayerbook and even structuring whole new services to replace the traditional ones. Recognizing the enormous power of
God-talk to educate and shape our lives, feminist Jews in our
time are taking back the power of naming, addressing divinity
in our own voices, using language that reflects our own experiences. We do this because we take theology seriously and we
want to affirm ourselves back into the place from which, we
deeply intuit, we have been erased.[18]

As she has labored to create new blessings for the ritual occasions when Jews gather to pray and celebrate their community life,
Falk has come to appreciate the delicacy of the task of rendering
feminist theological insights into liturgical language. Yet in many of
her blessings nature and connectedness surface to replace older, patriarchal intuitions of lordship and transcendent power:

> I did not have to search long for a theological metaphor for
> this blessing [over the wine]: the image *eyn ha-hayyim*, which
> I had used in my blessing over bread, seemed fitting here, too,
> for wine, like bread, has its origins in the earth, and I knew
> that I wanted to connect this theological image with the im-
> age of *p'ri ha-gafen*, "the fruit of the vine," understood liter-
> ally, as part of the botanical world, and metaphorically, as
> representing human community. But when I looked at the
> verb connecting the two halves of the traditional blessing—
> *bore*, create—it seemed wrong. For *bore* means to "create" as
> the God of Genesis created, making, as the rabbis explain it,
> "something out of nothing"; and this image of creation did
> not feel true to the experience that my blessing was trying to
> evoke. Nothing in nature arises out of nothing; everything
> emerges from form to form, from seed to flower to fruit. So
> too, communities are not created full-blown out of nothing;
> they evolve gradually out of bonds sustained over time.[19]

The question of the possibility of a Jewish Goddess returns in a
study by Ellen Umansky that reflects on recent trends among feminist Jewish theologians. For example, Rita Gross, who has worked
on Hindu and Buddhist traditions, has suggested that Jewish theologians try to incorporate non-Jewish female images of the deity
into their reconstructions of Jewish theology:

> She suggests focusing on images of the Goddess as a coinci-
> dence of opposites ("She who gives and takes away"), as

capable, strong, and beautiful, as mother, giver of wisdom, and sexual being. Gross makes a careful distinction between experiencing the divine as Kali, Durga, Laksmi, or any other Hindu Goddess and using the symbolism of these and other Goddesses as a means of reimaging the Hebrew God. She is not, she maintains, "advocating mindless borrowing or wholesale syncretism." Rather, she advocates translating non-Western images of the Divine into images that, in form and content, can be identified as Jewish.[20]

Judith Plaskow, in Umansky's view, seeks to create a Jewish Goddess not by borrowing from Eastern traditions but returning to the roots of biblical experience:

> She reminds us that the ancient Israelites worshiped Gods and Goddesses, with the "exclusive worship of Jahweh . . . [the] product of a long, drawn-out struggle." Without arguing for a return to paganism, Plaskow boldly calls for a reimaging of the Goddess "through the lens of our monotheistic tradition." To acknowledge "the many names of the Goddess among the names of God," she writes, "becomes a measure of our ability to incorporate the feminine and women into a monotheistic religious framework. At the same time, naming women's experience as part of the nature of the deity brings the suppressed experience of women into the Jewish fold."[21]

One sees, then, that many Jewish feminists are wrestling with precisely the same two factors with which any theologians trying to square their tradition with present culture have to wrestle. On the one hand, they have symbols, language, rituals, laws, and other theological components handed down from patriarchal times and generally gilded with authority. On the other hand, they have the report of many contemporary women that these components of theological tradition no longer generate something living and adequate. For feminist Jewish theologians, the recent or present experience of women usually weighs at least as strongly as the usages handed down from the past. The major argument for this position is that by today's standards the past usages are simply unjust, if not outright deforming. Thus their authority has been fractured, and if women are to continue to prosper in Judaism the old systems must be replaced.

The work of replacement tends to mine several lodes, as we have already seen. One can glean hints from the biblical or rabbinic past and expand them into a full feminine dimension of the Jewish deity. As well, one can retrieve or reimagine the religious experience of past paradigmatic heroines such as Sarah and from that work out the voice with which present-day Jewish women might address the divine mystery. More speculatively, one can work out the implications of the Jewish conviction that monotheism relativizes or even abolishes all representations of divinity. One can reason, for instance, that since God cannot be captured by any language, Jews are always allowed to say of God anything not contradicting the divine goodness, power, and other key attributes. Thus, it is no more problematic to address God in feminine terms ("Goddess") than in male terms ("Lord"). The problems one faces are more matters of custom and group psychology than problems of theological propriety in a strict sense.

As a side benefit, one probably will find one's appreciation of the monotheistic instincts of Judaism growing. Because as one probes the reality of "God" with such new terms as "Goddess," that reality may again become original, alive, mysterious, as it was in the beginning, when people first tried to halt it for a moment with a human word, so that they might not be wholly speechless or terrified.

Theology, then, may be a capstone for the historical, ritualistic, and political work now transforming the Jewish identity of many women. In the measure that they take their efforts to purify Israeli sentiments regarding Arabs on the West Bank (or their efforts ro rework the traditional prayerbook, or their efforts to bring feminine experience to bear on the interpretation and construction of Jewish law) to the foundations indicated by such words as monotheism, covenant, and the other guardians of traditional Jewish faith, Jewish women should find their sense of their venture considerably enlarged. The fact is that all language and work, all struggle and contemplative rest, eventually exits into the ungraspable reality or symbolism of the One Goddess who comes to mind and heart when we keep pushing for origins, foundations, and consummating goals. If Jewish theologians are those best positioned to apply such a fact to the needs and hopes of Jewish women, they can be joined by any Jews serious about the traditions of their faith, prayer, and social commitment.

The Torah that has sustained Jews for millennia becomes sustaining for Jewish women today when they experience that it is not something closed or monolithic, but rather a blessed venue for encountering the creative source traditionally called God. Indeed, all of the traditional names for God—Lord, Judge, Holy One, and so many more—are capable of shedding light on the task of the Jewish women who want to claim their full heritage, because all suggest that only divinity is the final measure of the unmeasurable hopes that divinity itself stirs in the human breast.

Rosemary R. Ruether

CHRISTIANITY AND WOMEN IN THE MODERN WORLD

To write the story of women in contemporary world Christianity in a single chapter of a book on women in world religions today is a staggering task. There are 1,620 million Christians in the world today or 33 percent of the world's population. Catholicism accounts for more than 900 million of these Christians and Protestantism (including Anglicans) for 400 million. Another 300 million are Orthodox or belong to other Christian groups.[1] It is fair to say that women are more than half of these Christians and in many cases make up 60 to 75 percent of the active churchgoers.[2] In each of the hundreds of countries around the world, Christian women's lives are being shaped both by their societies and by some variety of the Christian church.

To write the full story of the varieties of Christian women's experience, shaped by these dual forces of church and society, is obviously impossible in one chapter. The story would be different for each country and would vary greatly with the various Christian denominations in each country. Nor is it legitimate to write this story only in terms of the United States, complex as that story would be. Some of the most dynamic churches today exist in areas where Christianity is expanding, such as Africa and Korea. It is necessary to recognize at the outset that this is a global story, not simply a Western or North American one.

The research to do justice to this story is hardly available at the present time. In an effort to gain some introductory information on women in the churches of various countries I devised a questionnaire in the spring of 1988 and sent it to women church leaders in several countries of western Europe, Latin America, Asia, Africa, and Canada. I asked the women leaders for the following information:

1) The percentage of persons who are active Christians.

2) The percentage of women to men who are active churchgoers.

3) The main activities in the churches done predominantly or exclusively by women.

4) The amount of professional ministry done by nonordained women and the main areas in which they minister.

5) The situation of women's ordination: the history of women's ordination in the various churches in the country; the number of churches which now ordain women and the percentage of ordained women in those churches.

6) The percentage of women in theological education and the degrees they are obtaining.

7) The number of women teaching in theological schools, the areas where they teach, and whether they have full-time positions.

8) The extent of the teaching of women's studies in theological schools.

9) The networks of feminist theological studies outside the theological schools and how many people are involved in them.

10) The main issues that feminist theologians are addressing in the country.

Some countries, such as Canada and Germany, sent rather full information on all these topics, but most of those who replied said that such information was not fully obtainable. The basic research had not been done. At best they could reply with sketchy impressions. Several church women were grateful for the questionnaire and said they hoped to use it to try to gather such information in the future, but it was not available to them at this time.

In this chapter I will focus first on the story of women in the Christian churches in North America, the United States and Canada. This is the area where the fullest information is available to me. It is also the area where there has been the earliest development of feminist theology and where there is a considerable number of women in theological education and in ordained ministry. The patterns found in North America have been somewhat the "pace-setters" for changes going on elsewhere in women's status and role in the churches.

U.S. feminist theology is the major theological export from the United States to the rest of the world. It is read throughout Europe, particularly in Scandinavia, Germany, and the Netherlands, and is being translated into the major European languages. It is also being circulated in Spanish in Latin America and being read in Africa and Asia, particularly in the areas where English is well known, such as Korea and India.[3] Yet in all these areas the reading of North American feminist theology is only a first step toward these women beginning to make their own contextualizations of feminist theology for their own cultural and social situations. Feminist theology is becoming increasingly global and multicontextual.

After sketching the changing situation for women in the U.S. and Canadian churches, I will provide an even sketchier picture of emerging feminist theologies and the changing status of women in several European countries, and in some countries of Asia, Africa, and Latin America. I regret that I was not able to gather much material on Africa or any on eastern Europe and the Middle East. The ancient Christian traditions of Orthodoxy and Oriental Christianity are assumed to be immobile on questions of women, but even there women are stirring. So this account can only be introductory, at best, but it will make clear that the revolution in women's consciousness in Christianity is global.

THE CHANGING STATUS OF WOMEN
IN U.S. SOCIETY AND CHURCHES

In the United States feminism in the church and in civil society was born at the same time and as part of the same movement. In the 1840s the involvement of U.S. American women in the abolitionist movement began to spark an awareness of the legal bondage of women. In that period women's legal status was defined by a tradition of English common law that denied women autonomous legal standing as citizens. The younger unmarried woman was regarded as being under her father's authority, while the married woman was seen as "disappearing" into the corporate headship of her husband who represented both himself, his wife, and his children before the law.[4]

Women could not vote, run for political office, make contracts, or enter into any legal relations in their own name. Their legal standing was that of permanent minors, although the older spinster and the widow had a certain anomalous standing as legal persons since they had no male "head" to represent them. According to a legal fiction, a widow could be recognized as "head" of her family as representative of her husband in absentia.[5]

Women's access to education and to employment was severely restricted. No college or university admitted her to its degree programs and even high school education was limited for women. Oberlin was the first college to open to women (1833). But even there women were seen as falling under St. Paul's restrictions against public speech and thus were not allowed to speak in class. The first female valedictorian had to have her speech read for her by a male classmate.[6] More colleges began to open to women in the 1870 and 80s, and most state universities were open to women by 1900, although the older prestigeous universities of the east coast— Yale, Harvard, and Princeton—did not open to women until the 1960s.[7]

Even as universities opened to women, women found their access to graduate professional education restricted. A few medical schools, law schools, and even theological seminaries were open to women in the late nineteenth century, but their presence there was not encouraged.[8] The real story of increased enrollment in professional graduate education for women would take place in the late 1960s to 1980s.

In the mid-nineteenth century many areas of skilled employment, which women had exercised on the basis of informal on-the-job training, were closing to women as these jobs became professionalized and so demanded specialized education, formal credentials, and licenses. This was particularly true in medicine where women had predominated historically as the doctors for their families, with skills in midwifery and herbal home remedies. The professionalization of medicine increasingly sought to rule out alternative forms of medicine exercised by women and others without established credentials.[9]

Thus the situation of U.S. American women in the 1840s to the 1860s was one of great contradictions. On the one hand, women were losing some of the professions they had formerly been able to exercise. The beginnings of industrialization was also starting to draw working-class and immigrant women out of the home into factories, such as textile factories. With industrialization the productive work that women had done in the home would gradually shrink as more and more such items would be purchased rather than produced at home. Yet women were severely restricted in their legal rights and their access to many types of employment was shrinking. It was this contradiction between women's shrinking "sphere" of work in the home and her lack of access to education, work, and legal rights in the larger society that sparked the women's rights movement of the nineteenth century.

In this struggle of U.S. women to gain access to education, professional employment, and legal rights, the Christian churches played an ambivalent role. On the one hand, clergymen were the major obstacle to women's expanded access to public rights and leadership roles. St. Paul's dictum that women should keep silent was understood by the Christian clergy, not simply to refer to the pulpit, but to any visible and vocal role in public society. Patriarchy or male headship over women in both the family and in the larger society was understood as the divinely mandated "order of creation."[10]

Yet the churches were often the places where women first gained access to an enlarged leadership role and experience beyond the family. Women organized fund raisers, education, revivals, and charitable outreach for their churches. From this experience as leaders they began to expand to found women's missionary societies and movements for social change in areas as diverse as nursery schools, moral reform (prostitution), temperance, prison reform, and suffrage.[11] These experiments in organizing and public speaking continually increased women's demand on the political institutions, to grant them full citizenship, and on the churches, to grant them full membership, with voting rights and ordination.

In the first women's rights convention in the U.S.A. held at Seneca Falls in 1848, these parallel demands on church and state were evident. Women voiced their grievances both against social systems that denied them access and against churches and theological ideologies that justified this subordination. In their demands for change, the women asked both for voting rights and for the right to ordination in the church, or, as they put it, "a speedy overthrow of the male monopoly of the pulpit."[12]

The first women to be officially ordained in a Christian denomination was Antoinette Brown in 1853 in the Congregational Church. Brown was a graduate of the collegiate and theological courses of Oberlin College, the first college to admit women to its theological program. She served briefly as pastor of a Congregational church, but soon dropped out of active ministry, not because of her gender, but because she found she could no longer accept and preach the orthodox Calvinist theology of predestination and the damnation of the unconverted. She would return to ministry in the Unitarian Church forty years later when she was in her seventies.[13]

But the mainline denominations were slow to follow this beginning of women's ordination. Some theological colleges were open to women in the 1870s to 1890s but the numbers of women enrolled remained very small, about 5 percent, until the 1960s. New nonor-

dained professional roles began to open to women, particularly deaconesses, foreign missionary work, and Christian education. The
few women who went to theological schools were mostly preparing
for these nonordained ministries.

In the 1880s these first graduates of theological colleges began to
challenge their churches to grant them ordained status. The Methodist Episcopal Church considered this demand at its 1880 general
convention and rejected it, deciding even to revoke the lay licenses
to preach that had been granted to women. A few small denominations opened ordination to women in the late nineteenth century:
some Congregationalists, Unitarians, Universalists, and The Methodist Protestant Church. But mainline Presbyterians, Methodists,
and Lutherans rejected women's ordination in this period. Only
gradually, in the late nineteenth and the first half of the twentieth
century, did women even gain full lay status in these denominations—that is, the right to be a voting lay delegate to local and national church conventions.[14]

In 1921, after almost a century of struggle, U.S. women won the
rights of full citizenship, the right to vote, and to be elected to political office. This final victory of women's suffrage signified far
more than the right to the ballot. For the first time since the rise of
patriarchal legal systems at least four millennia earlier,[15] women
were acknowledged to be autonomous legal persons in their own
right, able to represent themselves in legal, political, and economic
relations. This is the foundation of a revolution in the status of
women in all modern societies. But the full realization of the implications of this revolution for millennia-old social customs has
been slow in coming.

The churches, which had so long justified women's lack of civil
rights as ordained of God, made little movement in response to this
change. Many Roman Catholic bishops of the United States had actively taken a stand against women's suffrage in the years before the
amendment.[16] They reacted to the winning of the vote for women
by organizing the National Catholic Women's Council, under the
direction of the bishops, with a view to harnessing Catholic wom-
en's vote to the bishop's conservative agenda for the family and society. Catholic women of the National Council were to be the
episcopal mouthpieces against contraception and divorce, and in
favor of women's traditional roles in the home.[17]

Conservative Protestants also opposed women's suffrage and
saw it as a threat to the traditional patriarchal family and social order. They responded to the winning of the vote by tightening restric-

tions against women as lay preachers, which had been common in evangelical revival circles, and by intensified advocacy of women's subordination as the divinely mandated order of creation.[18] This effort to promote the "total woman" against the threats of women's expanded roles in society would continue into the present, as conservative evangelicals responded to the new feminist movement of the late 1960s and 1970s.[19]

The more liberal Protestant denominations made little overt changes in their views of women's ordination in the 1920s. The liberal journal *The Christian Century*, in an editorial published in 1923, while supporting women in ministry in principle, nevertheless appealed to women not to seek jobs in ministry lest they undercut the pay of male ministers.[20] The depression of the 1930s heightened these male anxieties about how women's new job opportunities might deprive men of employment. It became a kind of "gentlemen's agreement" of most corporations and businesses, officially sanctioned by regulations of the American government, that the male "breadwinner" should have the priority in job opportunities.[21]

The 1930s saw women lose opportunities for employment in areas such as librarianship and primary and secondary school teaching where they had made advances in previous decades. Women virtually disappeared as physicians and university professors. During World War II there was a temporary turnaround in the message to women to confine themselves to home and family, and leave paid employment to men (better paid employment, that is; for women have never been prevented from entering low-paid, drudge labor). With the young men off to war, American government and business actively solicited women for employment in the heavy industry necessary for the war effort.

During the war years it became a patriotic duty for women to become welders, truck drivers, or mechanics in industries that built ships and planes. Universities also sought women students to fill the empty desks left by college-age males. Even churches, more in Europe than in the United States, opened pulpits to women rather than leave churches without ministers. But after the war there was a concerted effort to return women to their traditional roles as homemakers.[22]

In the latter half of the 1940s, government and business propagandists reversed their public messages and told women that it was now their patriotic duty to leave their jobs in order to make them available to the returning soldiers. Popular psychology filled the magazines with the message that children needed full-time mothers (not fathers). Women, it was said, greatly endangered their child's psychological development by working.[23] The new consumer culture propagated the "feminine mystique" of the suburban housewife, happy and fully engaged in a round of meticulous housecleaning, child care, and hostessing for her husband.

The discontents of women of the middle classes with this restricted horizon of life, not to mention the real needs of women who needed to work to support themselves and their families, were smothered under this barrage of propaganda. In the mid-1960s these discontents would burst their bonds of silence in a new feminist movement that would seek to take up the struggle for women's full rights in society that had been repressed for a generation. Betty Friedan's 1962 book, *The Feminine Mystique*, would give voice to the frustrations of many suburban housewives with the lives dictated by the official ideology of the happy wife and mother, content with her polished floors, well-scrubbed children, and successful husband.

Again, as in the 1840s, a major upheaval in the status of blacks in American society would become the spark that also lit the feminist movement. Black men had been granted the vote and citizenship status by the 14th amendment to the American Constitution, only to be deprived of the exercise of these citizenship rights by the Jim Crow laws of the 1880s. Women had been denied suffrage by the same law that granted it to black males by the deliberate use of the word "male" as a qualification for citizenship in that amendment.[24]

Having been granted citizenship in 1921, women had experienced forty years of varying strategies to be persuaded that they, nevertheless, should voluntarily choose a life of homemaking and economic dependency on their husbands. Women who flocked into the civil rights movement and then the peace movement of the 1960s had the occasion, once again, as in the 1840s, to compare their own restricted roles to that of blacks, the most subordinated racial group in American society.

These women of the 1960s gained experience in political organizing and were inspired by the heady visions of "participatory democracy." But they soon found that the men who extolled these visions for black and white men did not include women in their perview. Black civil rights leader, Stokely Carmichael, made this contradiction crudely obvious with his reply to the question about the position of women in the civil rights movement. "The only position for women in the movement is prone," he opined, in what he presumed to be a joke. But this statement was quickly recognized by movement women as an expression of the male chauvinism of movement men.[25]

A new feminist movement was born out of the civil rights movement. U.S. American women began to explore the forbidden horizons of sexual and reproductive rights. They began to flock to medical and law schools, and to seek expanded employment opportunities higher up the economic ladder. They revived the equal rights amendment that had been dormant in Congress since it was first introduced in 1921. U.S. women would spend ten frustrating years trying to pass it, only to be defeated by rightwing, antifeminist reactionaries, spearheaded by conservative churches.[26]

The new feminist women also discovered that they had lost their earlier feminist history. The memory of their grandmothers and great-grandmothers, who had fought for the vote, education, and jobs in the first feminist movement of 1848 to 1921 had been largely erased from the textbooks of American history. They set about to rediscover their foremothers and to reclaim their history. Thus women studies was born and began to organize to reshape the academic curriculum of the colleges and universities.

This reborn feminist consciousness of the mid-1960s would have an immediate impact on the churches and theological education as well. Since the churches and male clergy played a major role in the civil rights movement, the new feminist consciousness being born from the civil rights movement turned its demands for change simultaneously on civil society and on the churches. Churchmen, who were stalwart advocates of full membership in society for blacks, would be challenged by the women of the civil rights movement for their lack of advocacy for women's ordination and full membership in the church.

This new feminist address to the Christian churches would find the liberal denominations ripe, if not ready, for such changes. In 1956 two major denominations, which had resisted women's ordination since the 1880s, the Methodist Church and the Presbyterian Church U.S.A., changed their regulations to admit women to full clergy status. The reasons for this momentous change in 1956, prior to the new birth of the feminist movement, are obscure. The reasons probably lie, not so much in one cause, as an accumulation of causes. For seventy years women had played exemplary roles in home and foreign missionary service and had returned to challenge the church for its failures to grant them full clergy status.

Some denominations, which had ordained women in the previous century, such as the Methodist Protestants, lost the ordination of women when they merged with the Methodist Episcopal Church to form the Methodist Church in 1939. But the members of the former denomination were dissatisfied with the outcome of the merger vote and continued to press for full clergy rights for women. Finally, the contradiction between women's right to vote and hold political office in civil society and their lack of such rights in the church pressed home upon the consciences of liberal churchmen.[27] The Lutheran and Reform churches in Germany and Scandinavia were also discussing the ordination of women in the mid-1950s, reflecting their experience with women pastors during World War II.

Yet despite this basic shift in their historic policy of forbidding ordination to women, this change was slow to make an impact upon these denominations in the United States. For a decade many Methodist and Presbyterian women remained unaware that they could go to seminary and become ordained. The clergymen who voted for this change did not foresee the revolution they were creating. Most expected the numbers of women interested in ordained ministry to remain small.

Only with the birth of the new feminist movement in the mid-1960s did there arise a new consciousness among Christian women that would begin to sieze and develop the new opportunities that had been quietly opened for them a decade earlier. After 1970 the numbers of women in theological seminaries began to increase steadily, faster in the schools of denominations that ordained women, but also in Catholic and conservative Protestant seminaries that still denied this right to women.

By 1972 the number of women in seminaries accredited by the American Theological Society (which now included Catholic seminaries) rose to 10 percent. By 1987 it had jumped to 27 percent, or some 15,310 women enrolled in these seminaries in that year nationwide.[28] Since this figure includes seminaries of churches that do not ordain women and which had few or no women, this meant that the seminaries of liberal denominations had risen to a 50/50 gender split in enrollment. In some seminaries, particularly in the United Church of Christ and the Unitarian churches, the number of women enrolled exceeded that of men.

THE FEMINIST REVOLUTION IN U.S.
AND CANADIAN CHURCHES

The 1960s and 70s saw a continual expansion of the number of U.S. and Canadian churches that ordain women, as well as a steady increase in women ordained in these denominations. According to 1986 statistics on twenty major U.S. churches, there were 11.5 percent of ordained clergy that were female. The percentages of women ordained in each of these denominations is instructive. How "clergy" is defined clearly makes a lot of difference in the access of women to this status. Sixty-two percent of the Salvation Army leaders were female (3,220 out of 5,195).

Holiness churches, which traditionally draw their ministry from those with personal charismatic gifts, also have a high percentage of women listed as clergy. The Four Square Gospel Church, founded by a woman charismatic preacher, Aimee Semple McPherson, had the next highest percentage with 19 percent, or 666 women clergy out of a total of 3,482. The Church of God and the Assemblies of God also had significant percentages of women clergy with 14 percent each. Very liberal churches also showed high percentages, with the Unitarian-Universalists having 27 percent (308 out of 1,140) and the United Church of Christ 14.5 percent of 1,460 out of a total of 10,071. The Disciples of Christ, one of the denominations to begin to ordain women in the nineteenth century, listed 11 percent of its clergy as female. The Episcopal Church, which only began to ordain women in 1976, had surged ahead in ten years to 10 percent or 796 out of a total of 7,887.

But mainline Protestant denominations, who think of themselves as having a large number of women clergy, in fact, remained among those denominations with well under ten percent. The United Methodist Church with about 33,000 clergy in full connection listed in 1989 2,096 ordained women in this status or a little over 6 percent. In that year, the Presbyterian Church U.S.A. had 7 percent women clergy, or 1,519 out of 19,514. The American Lutheran Church and the Lutheran Church in America, before their merger in 1987, had 4 percent and 5.6 percent female clergy respectively. The American Baptists had 5 percent. These figures were not higher than some of the churches thought to be more conservative, such as the Moravian Church with 6 percent and the Mennonite Church General Conference with 9 percent.[29] The numbers would expand for all those churches between 1987 and 1992. For example, in the new Evangelical Lutheran Church in America that emerged from the merger the numbers had grown to 8.7% of the total by 1992. United Methodist Clergy women were 12% of the total in 1992.

The Canadian churches follow a pattern similar to that of the United States. The United Church of Canada, a union of Congregational, Presbyterian, and Methodist churches, have ordained women since the union in 1936. In this merger the earlier Congregational tradition of ordaining women was able to bring the nonordaining churches into harmony with its practice at the union. In 1989 there were 491 ordained women clergy in the United Church, out of about 3,891 or 12.6 percent.

However, the United Church also maintains a diaconal ministry whose members are regarded as members of the order of ministry and equal in clergy status, salary, and benefits to presbyters. Diaconal ministers serve many small parishes. There are 141 female diaconal ministers, and 167 female lay professional and lay supply ministers, bringing the total of female pastors to 799 or 15.5 percent of the total.[30] The Anglican Church of Canada began to ordain women in 1976, the same year as the American Episcopal Church. In 1989 they had 241 women priests and deacons serving in 29 dioceses, in parish ministry, and in university, hospital, prison, and armed forces chaplancies (8.76 percent of the total number of ordained clergy).[31]

In order to have a full picture of how equal women actually are in ordained ministry, one would have to have data on the number of these ordained women with pastorates, their rank in these pastorates, salary, and size of churches; also the number and rank of women in church administration at the regional and national levels. This sort of information is presently unavailable to me. But it is important to note that mainline churches generally have little understanding of how the question of women's ordination functions in Pentacostal and Holiness churches which they think of as conservative "sects," but which often have large churches and a high percentage of women in the clergy. Such churches have sometimes had female founders and have long had women hold office with the title of "bishop."[32]

The attainment of the title of bishop has particular significance for those historic churches that regard themselves as preserving episcopal "apostolic succession" back through the Latin Middle Ages to the monarchical episcopacies that arose in early Christianity. Churches who use this title of bishop, but without a threefold definition of ministry, have more readily granted women this title. The United Methodist Church has advanced women to district superintendency and then to the office of bishop. The first woman bishop of the United Methodist Church was Marjorie Matthews, elected in 1984.[33] The United Methodist Church has elected eight women to the episcopacy, with six still serving in 1992.[34]

The Lutheran churches of Germany and Scandinavia, although they began to ordain women as priests in the 1950s and 60s, elected a woman to the episcopacy for the first time in 1992. The Evangelical Lutheran Church in America also elected a woman bishop that same year. So it was a somewhat startling development when the American Episcopal Church, which only began to ordain women in 1976, decided to ordain a woman bishop in 1989. Barbara Harris, a black woman, was elected and ordained suffragan bishop of the diocese of Massachusetts in that year.[35] Anglicans in New Zealand have also elected a woman bishop, Penelope Jamieson.

Since the Anglican Church has been particularly strong in asserting its preservation of the historic episcopacy, and has sought recognition of that fact by the Roman Catholic and Orthodox churches, this elevation of a woman to the episcopacy sent shock waves through the world Anglican communion. Anglo-Catholics were particularly distressed, claiming that this would shatter all hopes of recognition of Anglican orders by these traditional churches. Pope John Paul II also attempted to caution against this step on the same grounds. However American Episcopalians decided that full justice to women should not be postponed in the name of a questionable possibility of recognition of Anglican orders by an increasingly conservative, and overtly antifeminist, papacy. Finally, in November, 1992, the Church of England itself finally voted for the ordination of women to the priesthood (women were already serving as deacons in the Church of England).

However the story of the increasing numbers of women in theological seminaries and in ordained ministry is only the first part of the feminist revolution in the Christian churches. The second stage of this drama has to do with how this increasingly "critical" mass of women as students and clergy has begun to make an impact on the substance of the Christian faith, the way it is symbolized, organized, and understood.

As long as women are present as theological students and as clergy in only token numbers, they can do little but survive in an anomalous role, attempting to be accepted as able to study and minister "like men." Only when their numbers increase to the point where their presence becomes normal, rather than exceptional, is it possible to consider how the presence of women changes the content of a tradition that had previously regarded women's absence and silence as normative.

As women's numbers increased to 20 percent and more in theological schools in the 1970s, women students felt strong enough to organize as women and to demand feminist courses in the curriculum and the hiring of women professors who could teach feminist studies. In 1989 most theological schools have at least one full-time woman professor and at least one course that addresses feminist perspectives on Christian thought. Many seminaries, particularly liberal seminaries with a high percentage of women, have a far larger number of women professors and have integrated feminist studies into a fuller relation to the total curriculum.

United Methodism's thirteen seminaries represent a "mainstream" pattern in a church that ranges from fundamentalist to liberationist. In 1988 its enrollment of women students ranged from Gammon and Duke, with 25.9 and 33.9 percent women in its student body, to Iliff, Garrett-Evangelical, and Boston School of Theology with 52.6, 53.5, and 55.2 percent. The total number of women in United Methodist seminaries in 1988 was 1,088 or 40.9 percent.[36]

In 1987 there were 53 full-time and 44 part-time women faculty in United Methodist seminaries. With 279 total full-time faculty, women were 19 percent. Garrett-Evangelical in 1993 had eight women faculty out of a total of 28 (28 percent), four tenured full professors, including a woman Dean of Faculty, one tenured associate professor and three untenured.[37]

The development of feminist studies in theological education typically evolves through several stages. The first stage generally takes the form of an omnibus course on "women in Christianity," which attempts to cover all time periods and several fields (Bible, history, theology, pastoral psychology). It is often taught by a woman marginal to the regular faculty. At Garrett-Evangelical the first feminist course was taught by Dr. Rosemary Keller in 1975, at a time when she was still an adjunct faculty member. It attempted to cover a sweep of women's history in the American Protestant church.

The second stage of feminist studies allows for a more established and recognized role in the curriculum. Women professors are hired who are able to develop and teach feminist courses as part of the offerings in selected fields. Such women often are also engaged in primary research and writing in women studies in their fields. Thus at Garrett-Evangelical Rosemary Ruether and Rosemary Keller regularly teach courses on women in American and European church history and are recognized scholars, publishing in those fields of history.[38] Dr. Phyllis Bird regularly offers a course on women in ancient Israel and is currently authoring two major monographs on aspects of that topic.[39]

At Garrett feminist studies courses have been offered in all fields of the curriculum; Bible, history, ethics, theology, pastoral care, Christian education, church administration, preaching, and worship. The Association of Chicago Theological Schools, a consortium of twelve theological seminaries in the greater Chicago area, with two Catholic schools and ten Protestant schools, cross-lists women's studies courses at these seminaries. For the academic year 1989–1990 twenty-seven courses in women's studies were listed and in 1992–1993 twenty-two courses were listed. All these courses are elective, rather than required.

An optimum stage of feminist studies will be reached in theological schools when feminist studies are not seen simply as an elective to be taken by a feminist minority of the student body, mostly female, but is mandated to reshape the foundational curriculum. As long as foundational teaching in Bible, theology, history, ethics, and the other fields continues as before, with male experience and imagery as normative, feminist studies will be seen as "optional" rather than a demand laid on the whole church to reshape its normative tradition in order to correct a historic "heresy" of gender bias.

In a few seminaries, such as Garrett-Evangelical, women faculty and their published work are being integrated into the foundational courses in several fields. The basic methodology and content for teaching these courses is being rethought in order not just to include but to transform the tradition through the presence of women's experience. But this third stage is not yet present in most theological seminaries. Even at those where it takes place, this happens only sporatically. When a woman professor is in charge of a foundational course, she may try to transform the basic content and method of that course. A sensitive male teaching the course may integrate some feminist books into the readings and perhaps offer a "feminist" guest lecture, but will not deeply transform the content and method. A less sensitive male will continue androcentric teaching as usual.

Thus feminist studies in theological education are still mostly at the first or second stage of development. An enormous amount has been accomplished in twenty years. There are now recognized scholarly books and articles in great numbers in every field. One no longer has to invent a field with virtually no bibliography, but has an emerging "canon" of scholars and books on which to draw. Doctoral students can now draw on this work to write dissertations on feminist theology, feminist hermeneutics, feminist ethics. Yet the transformation is incomplete until all professors and students find it necessary to grapple with the feminist transformation as a reform of the normative tradition.

Women doing feminist studies in theological education often find the openings at established institutions too restrictive. They feel a need for fuller exploration of feminist consciousness and research in an atmosphere where it is normative, not marginal. So feminist scholars have reached out to form networks among themselves. For many feminist scholars this has taken the form of feminist caucuses and sections within the established professional societies, such as the American Academy of Religion, the Society of Biblical Literature, the Pastoral Theology Association, and the Society of Christian Ethics. Since most women scholars have neither the time nor the resources to attend many such national meetings, building a feminist network within the professional society of their field allows them to be in touch with both networks at the same meeting. The network of feminist scholars generated particularly through the women's caucus of the American Academy of Religion was the framework for the emergence of the first journal on feminist research in religious studies, *The Journal of Feminist Studies in Religion.*

There have been many regional and national conferences on various aspects of feminist theological studies, although, so far, a professional society has not emerged that can sponser such meetings regularly. There have also been several attempts to create alternative programs of feminist theological education, such as the Women's Seminary quarter at Grailville (1974–1978) and the Women's Theological Center in Boston that has run as a one-year program accredited through Episcopal Divinity School. In Washington, D.C., WATER (Women's Alliance for Theology, Ethics, and Ritual) has been able to survive as a noncredit program that offers feminist lectures and workshops. So far women lack the resources to create autonomous, degree-granting institutions with a feminist perspective, but have had to attach themselves to the margins of established institutions or else operate without academic accreditation.

Once women have finished their theological education, are ordained, and assigned a job in the pastorate, what impact does their presence have on the ministry and the understanding of Christian faith by those in the pews? From my experience of running a program on women in ministry, with women in pastoral ministry as supervisors,[40] it seems that most women in ministry are in their first or second assignments. They are still at the bottom of the profession in status and seniority, and have to prove themselves as equally competent to do the traditional kinds of ministries done by their male predecessors at that church. Even women with strong

feminist consciousness (not by any means the majority of those being ordained) often have to settle for simply doing well the traditional things, rather than making feminist innovations in language,
liturgy, and programs.

There are three main areas where feminist consciousness is
making an impact on local churches, but only in the beginning
stages and often with much resistance. This is in the areas of inclusive language, clergy-lay relations, and new liturgies. Inclusive language is probably the most discussed but poorly understood area of
feminist initiatives for change. This begins with a recognition that
male generic language for humans is illegitimate, and one must
speak of the human members of the church in a way that make the
presence of women visible, rather than masked under words such as
"brothers," "sons," and "men."

But the questions of inclusive language have many layers. A
more profound change of consciousness takes place when male generic language for God is questioned. This demands fundamental
rethinking of patriarchal theology. Many churches willing to entertain the inclusive language issue stop at changing male generic to
neutral generic language for God—that is, from Father to Parent, or
from Lord to Sovereign. This has the effect of creating a more abstract image of God, thus losing the intimacy of metaphorical language. Most people in the pews dislike such changes for reasons that
they have difficulty sorting out.[41]

Deeper change in God imagery must take us into an open inclusion of female imagery, not simply a neutering of male imagery.
There needs to be an examination of the root metaphors of power
relations that shape our experience of the divine. This will call for,
not simply exegetical committees, but mystics and poets who can
reincarnate our vision of God in new cultural forms; forms more
conducive to mutuality, less symptomatic of power relations of
domination and submission.[42]

Since women, in their socialization and social presence, have
not incarnated dominant power in the same way as men, they often
do not feel comfortable exercising the same kind of paternal authority as male clergy, nor are they easily accepted as exercising such
authority. This can take either the form of timidity and feelings of
inadequacy, perceived by others as incompetency, or it can take the
form of a self-confident effort to reshape the model of ministry in
relation to the community. A more conscious feminist minister will
seek to reeducate her lay community to cease to be passive recipi-
ents of ministry and become active sharers in the ministry of the

church. Thus the presence of female clergy becomes an occasion to reclaim a more participatory understanding of ministry as shared gifts of all members of the community, rather than the patriarchal active-passive mode of clergy-lay relations.[43]

Again, as in theological education, a stage seems to be reached in the feminist transformation of the local church where the institution is unable to imagine or accommodate a more holistic new vision. Feminists in the Christian churches grow frustrated with the token changes allowable in their established parishes and begin to reach for alternative feminist-defined, worshiping communities. These have come to be known as "women-church."[44]

Women-church is basically a feminist base Christian community which seeks to provide a gathering where feminist experience can be fully expressed, in worship, in study or reflection, and in action. It may take the form of everything from an occasional study group to an intentional community. For some women it is a complete alternative "church" over against a patriarchal church which does not nourish them at all and to which they feel no commitment. For others it is a parallel community that nourishes a new possibility which they then, in turn, seek to incarnate in established church institutions on the local level or through church boards, societies, or religious orders.

The extent to which women of women-church see this as a reform of the historic church, or a new church discontinuous with the old, has much to do with how much openness they experience for such initiatives in established church bodies. The future of the feminist revolution in the churches will be determined by the balance between these two alternatives.

WOMEN IN CHRISTIANITY; EUROPE, ASIA, AFRICA, LATIN AMERICA

In this section I will summarize, in an all too-brief and sketchy fashion, some of the information which I have gathered on women in Christian churches in western Europe, Asia, Africa, and Latin America in late 1988 and 1989. I will discuss this under the basic headings of women in theological education as students and as faculty, women in ordained ministry, and networks of feminist theology. I will suggest some of the distinct concerns that emerge in various regions as Christian women contextualize feminist issues in different cultural realities.

Women's presence in world Christianity in all continents can be seen as a broad-based pyramid, in which women are present in large numbers at the base and increasingly small numbers as one moves up the hierarchical ladder. In the various countries for which I received fairly complete replies to my 1989 survey (Germany, Holland, Norway, France, Scotland, Ireland, Argentina, Korea, the Philippines, and India[45]), the numbers of Christians vary greatly, from Ireland, where 98 percent regard themselves as Christian, to India where all Christians together are only 2.5 percent of the population.

In traditionally Christian societies in Europe, there are declining numbers of people who regularly attend church.[46] In Germany, where 42 percent of the population were listed as Protestant and 43 percent as Roman Catholic, 62 percent of Protestants did not attend church at all; 22 percent attended with some regularity. In Norway with 90 percent as nominal church members, mostly of the official Lutheran Church of Norway, 10 to 15 percent were active participants. Roman Catholicism generally retains a higher number of members who attend regularly, but even their numbers are declining. In Ireland 95 percent of the population is claimed as Roman Catholic, but in working-class areas the number who attend mass regularly have declined to less than 50 percent. In Argentina 75 percent call themselves Roman Catholics and 5 percent Evangelicals, with 30 percent as active participants.

Areas where Christians are recent converts, such as Korea with 30 percent Christians, have a very high percentage of those who not only attend Sunday services, but prayer meetings and Bible studies during the week. Sub-Saharan Africa is rapidly emerging as a predominantly Christian area. According to 1980 statistics, almost 70 percent of Africans are Christians. About 40 percent of these are Roman Catholics and 55 percent are Protestants, including the growing number of African indigenous churches, and 5 percent are Orthodox (mostly Ethiopians). Most African Christians also are regular church attendants (about 90 percent).[47]

Both in areas where there is a high percentage of attendance and in areas where there is low attendance, women predominate as active churchgoers. In Germany, France, Norway, and Ireland, women are 60 to 65 percent of the active churchgoers. In Korea, India, and the Philippines, women are 65 to 70 percent of the active churchgoers.

Women also do the overwhelming majority of lay, voluntary service. In Germany voluntary work connected with social services is 94.5 percent female, and Sunday school teaching is 90 percent female. Volunteer ministries such as Sunday school, fund raising through bazaars, flower arranging, cleaning altar linens, visiting the sick, and outreach to the poor is done almost entirely by women in both first-world and third-world churches. New volunteer lay roles have begun to open up to women in Catholic churches, such as readers and communion servers.

In both the Protestant and the Catholic churches there are lay professional ministries that are entirely female, Roman Catholic nuns and Protestant deaconneses[48] (a ministry invented for Protestant women in the late nineteenth century and also usually demanding celibacy). Teaching, pastoral and social work, and even some preaching is done by deaconesses. Nuns have done much of the catechetical teaching in parishes and in Catholic schools at the lower levels, as well as nursing and the running of charitable institutions, such as hospitals, orphanages, and old-age homes.

Large numbers of Catholic women have chosen to become nuns during periods of time and in countries where there were few other vocations open to women other than marriage. In western Europe and North America the numbers of women in religious orders have declined rapidly in the last twenty-five years, less due to a crisis in vocations caused by Vatican II reforms than simply the fact that many other paid professions are now available to women.[49] In some Asian societies, such as India, however, there are still fairly few professions that offer security for women, so a large number of Indian Catholic women continue to go into religious orders.

In India there were in 1988 sixty thousand Indian women in indigenous and international congregations of women. These religious women do all forms of church work except that which relates directly to the sacramental office. They run large and small hospitals and other charitable institutions, such as orphanages and old-age homes. They also run many schools, particularly those that teach girls, mainly on the primary and secondary levels. Evangelization, health, teaching, and social services are largely in the hands of nuns. Nuns control the resources of these institutions. Laywomen may also be employed, but with a lesser status.

In the Catholic system there is a female hierarchy that places nuns as church-supported professionals over laywomen who often do volunteer work. In many areas nuns are more powerful than local priests, since they run the major social, health, and educational services. In many traditional cultures, such as that which still prevails in India, males cannot visit women in their homes, so only women have access to home visitation to women. This pattern makes a distinct female ministry to females essential to the work of the church.[50]

Protestant women in India inherit a large network of social, health, and educational institutions that were built up by female missionaries. As lay professionals these Protestant women run schools for girls, hospitals, hostels, and other institutions. However, in Protestant churches control of financial resources and decision-making about these resources generally remain in the hands of the male clergy. An exception to this is the YWCA, which has been an important institution in providing administrative and job training for Protestant women in Asia and Africa. In these countries, the YWCA generally does not have sport facilities, as in the U.S.A., but rather provides housing for working women, job training, employment training, health and educational services. Because the YWCA is an autonomous international Christian organization, not under any church, it allows women control of its resources and valuable leadership experience. Many Asian and African women leaders, both in the church and in society, have emerged from work with the YWCA.

While women predominate as active lay members, and as lay volunteers and low-status lay professionals in the churches, their numbers dwindle in better paid lay professional work on administrative levels. Thus while women may do the overwhelming majority of the catechetical, health, and social work of the churches, the overview of these institutions at the diocesan or church headquarters level is likely to be assigned to a male lay professional or a clergyman. When a lay professional role rises in status and salary, more men apply. Thus in Germany the role of parish assistant used to be volunteer or poorly paid, part-time work, and was entirely done by women. More recently it has risen in status and salary. In 1986 34 women and 31 men were parish assistants full-time, and 18 women and 5 men had this work as a part-time job.

Traditionally women were excluded from ordained ministries in all Christian traditions. Throughout the world ordained ministry is now open to women in some Protestant denominations, although not to Roman Catholic and Orthodox women. The United Church of North India accepted women elders when it was first formed in 1924, and, in Scotland, Congregationalists ordained the first woman in 1929. In Japan the United Church of Christ ordained its first woman in 1932. In France the first women was ordained in the

Protestant Reformed Church in 1938. In Norway the first woman ordained was a Methodist, Agnes Nilsen Howard, in 1938. In the mid-1930s Jorgelina Lozuda, a member of the Disciples of Christ, was the first women ordained in Argentina. The bishop of Hong Kong ordained the first woman priest in the Anglican communion in 1944, but her ordination was rejected by Canterbury and she resigned from holy orders. In Korea Methodists ordained the first woman in 1955.

More established state or "folk" churches were generally behind these free churches in allowing women ordination. Women were ordained to the priesthood in the Church of Sweden in 1958 and the Church of Norway in 1961. The Church of Scotland ordained its first woman in 1968 and full ordination was granted to women in the Germany state churches in the 1960s.[51]

As in North America, the numbers of women clergy remained small until the new feminist consciousness of the 1970s and 80s began to encourage more women to go to theological schools and to seek jobs in the pastorate. In the German state churches (Lutheran and Reformed) there were 256 ordained women in 1964 (1.9 percent) and 2,153 ordained women in 1988 (11.9 percent). However, if all women employed as pastors, including the nonordained, are counted, women were 30 percent of parish pastors employed by the churches in Germany in 1988.

In French Protestantism 40 percent of the ordained clergy were women in 1989, but many are clergy couples in which only the man has an official appointment. His ordained wife serves as unpaid assistant. In the Lutheran Church of Norway there are 150 ordained women (5 percent), but only 50 in full-time positions in parishes, mostly in the second or third level position, rather than the head pastor. In Scotland also about 5 percent of the clergy of the Church of Scotland are female, and most of these are assigned to small, closing churches. In Argentina where Protestants are less than 1 percent of the population, women were ordained in six denominations in 1989, with a total of 21 ordained women in the country (about 10 percent of the clergy of their churches). In Nicaragua the Baptist Church ordained its first clergy woman in 1993.

In Korea with a fast growing Christian population, only two churches ordain women; the Methodist Church (third largest church) and the Presbyterian Church of the Republic of Korea (PROK; fifth-largest church). The Methodist Church had in 1988 60 ordained women (1.5 percent), but only in 1990 no longer required women to retire from ministry when they marry. The PROK has fourteen ordained women (2 percent). A large amount of ministry in Korean churches is done by nonordained lay pastors. The Presbyterian Church of Korea, the largest church and one which does not ordain women, employed 950 nonordained women as lay pastors. The PROK had, in addition to 14 ordained women, 104 nonordained female lay ministers, and the Methodist Church employed 367 laywomen pastors. The Presbyterian Church of Korea United, with no ordained women, had 300 female lay pastors. These nonordained women work primarily in Christian education and home visitation.

Even where women are ordained, they seldom have the top pastoral leadership in a parish. They tend to be given either subordinate ranks in multistaff churches or hardship positions in poor urban or rural areas. Where positions are defined as part-time, these are likely to be done by women. Lay women without clergy status continue to do the preponderance of the low paid or unpaid work of the churches.

In Europe, as in North America, the numbers of women are increasing in theological education far more rapidly than in their present share in the ordained ministry. In Protestant theological faculties in Germany there were 703 women theological students (17.6 percent) in 1973. This figure has increased to 5,203 (38.6 percent) by 1985. Thirty-two percent of women students went beyond the first level and took the advanced theological exam in 1987. In Norway women were a third of the theological students studying at the three theological faculties of the Church of Norway, although none had yet finished the doctoral degree.

In the nine major Protestant and Catholic theological faculties of Holland in 1988 women students were 42 percent. They were as fully represented in Catholic as in Protestant schools. At the Catholic University of Nijmegen, women theological students were 46 percent and at the Catholic Theological University of Amsterdam they were 52 percent. Women at these theological schools go on to the doctoral level in lesser, but still substantial, numbers.

By contrast there is a major difference between theological education available to Catholic women compared to Protestant women in third-world, traditionally Catholic, countries. In Argentina a few women attend the two Catholic seminaries, while the Ecumenical Protestant seminary enrolls 30 percent women students, as does the seminaries of the Baptists and the Christian Alliance. In the Philippines there is a major difference between seminaries that educate priests and pastoral institutes that train nuns and laity for social and catechetical ministries. In 1988 there were only 2 females about of 151 students at the University of St. Thomas, and 11 out of 270 students at Maryhill School of Theology, while there were 35 percent women at the East Asian Pastoral Institute, 50 percent at the Loyola School of Theology, and 80 percent at the University of San Carlos. Only one of these schools, St. Thomas, offers the doctorate, and one woman has obtained this degree as of 1988.

In Korea, where the ordination of women has not been encouraged by the Protestant churches, few women are in the master's program. Women are present in larger numbers in theological studies on the bachelor's level where they prepare for nonordained roles.[52]

However, even in western Europe, there are far fewer women as teachers on theological faculties than as students. They are present in the largest numbers as doctoral teaching and research assistants. But at the instructor level, they are much more likely to remain in part-time positions or to be slotted in second-rank positions, such as the teaching of biblical languages. In the highly competitive and exclusive club of the full rank professors, there are few women.

However, a few women are entering these professional ranks in western Europe and even in the third world. In Germany in 1988 at all theological faculties together there were 5 female professors, 3 Privatdozent, and 1 Honorar-Professor. There were 22 women employed as teaching or research assistants. In France there were 1 women professor out of a faculty of 20 at the University of Strasbourg, and 3 out of 21 at the Protestant Theological Institutes of Paris and Montpellier. In the Norwegian theological faculties there were 7 women teaching full-time, but only 1 at the professorial level. In Scotland there was 1 woman professor at St. Andrews theological faculty and 1 in the theological faculty of the University of Edinburgh.

The nine theological faculties of Holland have between two and nine female teaching faculty each, a total of 40. Most of these teach at the instructor level and 60 percent (24) are part-time. However in Holland feminist theology or women's studies in theology has emerged as a recognized and required theological subject at the foundational level (kandidaatsfase), a topic to which I will return later. Several of the women instructors in each of these faculties are employed to teach this subject. Only the University of Nijmegen has a full university chair in feminist theology and recognizes this as a major subject for doctoral work, although the possibility of including it as a subject within a major field, such as dogmatic theology, is available at all these universities.

In Latin America one or two women are teaching at most of the Protestant theological schools and even some of the Catholic ones. Some are teaching major subjects, rather than being confined to the traditional female areas of music and Christian education. The first such woman to teach theology with a feminist perspective was Beatriz Couch at the ISEDET (ecumenical) in Buenos Aries. In Brazil several leading Catholic feminist theologians hold teaching positions: Maria Clara Bingemer and Tereza Cavalcanti at the Pontifical Catholic University in Rio de Janeiro, and Ivone Gebara at the Theological Institute of Recife (which was closed in 1990). Elsa Tamez, a Methodist New Testament scholar, and three other women teach at the Latin American Biblical Seminary in Costa Rica.

In Korea there were 20 women teaching at the major Protestant theological seminaries, but almost all are lecturers, part-time, and teach subjects such as languages, writing, or Christian education. In the Philippines, Maryhill School of Theology employed 2 full-time and 4 part-time women faculty. Several of the other theological schools have at least one woman, part-time.

Women faculty are even more rare at the Indian theological schools. The Tamilnadu Theological Seminary at Madurai employs a German women, Gabriele Dietrich, who teaches social analysis. Prasanna Samuel is one of the first women to be employed in scripture. She is ordained and teaches at the Gurukul Theological College in Madras. Sarah Grant teaches part-time at the Papal Seminary in Pune.

If women are scarce as teachers in theological colleges, feminist theology as a subject is even less well established. Only in Holland has this subject been recognized as a regular subject required of entry-level students, as well as being available as an area of doctoral research. In Germany it is only occasionally taught at university-connected theological schools. In 1988 the University of Frankfort theological faculty agreed to offer a course of lectures on feminist theology every other semester, and there was a summer term course in 1988 on women and images of women in Church history.

In Norway there is interest in this subject in all three seminaries and some courses on women's studies and feminist theology are taught regularly at the theology faculty of the University of Oslo. In France it is hardly taught at a university level, although in the faculty of Montpellier a series of eight lectures on feminist theology was offered in 1989. In Scotland it is not regularly taught, although each of the two women professors have their own specialized research in this area, which they bring into their lectures.

In Argentina Beatriz Couch attempted to establish feminist theology as a subject at ISEDET in the late 60s and 70s, and failed to do so. A visiting feminist scholar, Dr. Mary Hunt, taught this subject there in 1980–81, and this has been the basis for a continuing student demand for such study. In 1987 the students organized their own course on feminist theology. In Korea women's studies courses are occasionally offered as electives. In the Philippines it has not been offered at the graduate level, although there are strong women's study courses in some women's undergraduate colleges, particularly at St. Scholastica's College which has its own Women Studies Institute.

In India the Jesuit college Vidyajyothi in New Delhi has occasionally employed Indonesian feminist theologian Marianna Katoppo to teach a short course in feminist theology. Gabrielle Dietrich has offered women's studies courses at Tamilnadu Theological Seminary; United Theological College in Bangalore has offered courses on women in the church, taught by a male professor and his wife.

However, in Europe and the third world university-based courses are a minor part of the development of feminist theological reflection. Most of the development of this subject is taking place outside the universities and seminaries in autonomous networks of theologically trained women working in social and pastoral ministries. There are hundreds of such networks, ranging from groups of students at a particular theological school, who have their own study group, to groups in local cities and regions, to national networks, continental networks, and intercontinental networks.

In Germany there is the network for feminist theology in the Evangelical Church of Hessen and Nassau, and another network that brings together mostly Protestant women from Germany, Switzerland, Austria, and the Netherlands. There is also a German protestant group of about 60 women that have gathered on the topic of women-church, and a group of 30 feminist theologians who meet four times a year on academic subjects.

German Catholic women also have several feminist networks; *Feminismus und Kirche*, which meets twice a year (some three hundred members) on academic theological research, and *Knupf an* (network) that focuses on feminist social praxis. There is also a group of Catholic men and women that promotes women's ordination. Another group of women see themselves as rejecting biblical religion for matriarchal religion. They have a society for promotion of sharing of research named Haggia.

In Norway there have been several networks, such as the Christian Forum for Women's Liberation, that has promoted feminist discussion in the Church of Norway since 1974. There are also networks of women pastors and of feminist researchers that link Norway, Sweden, Denmark, and Iceland. In Scotland the Women-sharing group met three times a year from 1983 to 1989. In France the Group Orsay, begun by Protestant women, has regular meetings and also translates and publishes work being done in Holland, Germany, and North America into French in order to break the isolation of the French world from these developments.

In England, WIT (Women in Theology), meets several times a year for lecturers and conferences on feminist theological reflection. Catholic women have created the Catholic Women's Network to address their concerns, while also participating in WIT. In Ireland there is growing popular interest in feminism and about seven hundred people are involved in several networks that have held occasional conferences. Holland has student study groups at most universities, pastoral networks, and national networks. In addition to these national networks, the European Society for Women's Theological Research brings together women scholars from all western Europe every other year.

In Argentina the Centro de Estudios Cristianos in Buenos Aires sponsers a network of feminist theology that has met three times a year since 1988. In Korea there is the Korean Association of Women Theologians (three hundred members), organized in 1979, which addresses theological and social issues. A smaller network within KAWT, the Korean Association of Feminist Theologians, gathers thirty-five to forty women monthly for sharing academic research. In the Philippines, the Association of Women in Theology, established in 1978, focuses on pastoral issues of and with women. In addition, a small group of fifteen women theologians meet to discuss theological reflection from a feminist perspective and to encourage research and publication. The interfaith action organization, *Gabriela*, brings together forty-five thousand members in a hundred mostly grassroots, women's organizations.

In Japan there are two feminist theological networks, one that brings together Christian women (coordinated by the women's desk of the Japanese Council of Churches), and an interfaith network. Both groups are deeply concerned about peacemaking as a theological and spiritual issue. They have worked to oppose nuclear testing in the Pacific region and against Japanese remilitarization. The Christian groups also wrote and delivered a letter to the Christian women of Korea repenting of the sins of Japanese imperialism against the Korean people.[53]

In India there are a number of women's organizations that focus on social and pastoral issues, particularly work with very poor women. The All India Christian Women's Council (Protestant) and interfaith WINA (Women's Institute for New Awakening) have gathered conferences on feminist theology and sponsored research and publication. There are also local groups, such as Satyashodak (Searchers for Truth, Catholic) in Bombay, that work on issues of women and religion, and the promotion of women in the church and in society.

For Asia, Africa, and Latin America a particularly important initiative in promoting feminist theological reflection has been undertaken by the Ecumenical Association of Third World Theologians (EATWOT). After their meeting in Geneva in January, 1983,[54] where almost 50 percent of the delegations from the three continents, as well as western Europe and North America, were female, EATWOT voted to organize a women's commission that would sponser conferences of women on the national levels, continental levels, and finally an intercontinental conference. These conference were held in 1985–86.

This process began with women in several countries in Asia, Africa, and Latin America identifying and bringing together women on the national level. Then there were continental conferences. There were two continental conferences in Africa, one for Francophone African women in Cameroun, August 1986, and another for Anglophone African women in Harcourt, Nigeria, August 1986. Asian women from Hong Kong, India, Japan, Korea, Malaysia, the Philippines, and Sri Lanka gathered for the Asian Church Women Speak conference in Manila, November 1985. Latin American women gathered for their conference on theology from the perspective of women in Buenos Aires, October–November 1985.[55]

The intercontinental conference of Asian, African, and Latin American women met in Oaxtepec, Mexico, December 1986. The final documents of all these conferences, as well as a selection of the papers from each of them, has been published by Orbis Press, under the title *With Passion and Compassion: Third World Women Doing Theology*.[56] The continental networks built by these conferences continue to provide a basis for Asian women, African women, and Latin American women to meet and to conceptualize feminist theology in their contexts. Feminist journals are also appearing in these regions. Asian feminist women link together and publish articles, liturgies, and reports in the journal *In God's Image*.[57] In 1992 the Institute of Women's Studies of St. Scholastica's College in the Philippines launched the Asian Pacific journal, *Lila*, and a group in Chile began to publish the journal, *Conspirando* on feminist theology, spirituality and ecological thought.

What common themes link all this global work of feminist theological reflection? What distinct themes are emerging in different areas, as women contextualize feminist theology in distinct cultures and social situations? Since many of the same works of feminist theological scholarship, much of it from North America, have been read by these women in western Europe, Asia, and Africa, this provides something of a common base for discussion. In Germany authors such as Mary Daly, Rosemary Ruether, and Elizabeth Schüssler Fiorenza are available in German. In Korea this literature has been translated into Korean, while Indian women read it in English. In Latin America some of this North American feminism is available in Spanish.

But in each of these countries feminist theologians are rapidly establishing their own books and articles that are the basis of their discussion. The Germans, Swiss, Austrians, and Dutch share a growing feminist literature that links them together, but also cuts them off from French, Spanish, and Italian feminists. The French group Orsay, as we noted, is seeking to break this French linquistic insularity.

German and Dutch feminist theology is less likely to be translated into English than vice versa, so Anglophone women are in danger of remaining unaware of these European developments. Latin American women are rapidly establishing their own feminist theological literature. Thanks to publishers, such as Orbis Press, much of this work in Spanish and Portuguese finds its way into English for the North American audience.[58]

There are many common themes for feminist theology in all these regions. All have concern for feminist biblical hermeneutics and exegesis. In all regions there are feminist interpretations of basic Christian symbols; God-imagery, christology, anthropology, and the nature of the church. Catholic women add mariology to this list of theological symbols.[59] Ethical issues, especially around sexuality, reproductive rights, and violence to women, concern all these feminists. Most link feminism with peace, economic justice, and ecological harmony.

For all Christian feminists there is an overarching concern for the promotion of women's full personhood in both the church and society, and a general agreement that this demands more than integration of women into these social systems as they are. These systems must be fundamentally revisioned and reorganized for both women and men in order for women to achieve their rightful place in society and their full human development.

Since feminists in all these regions believe that their theological reflection must begin with their experience, these issues become contextualized in quite distinct ways. Thus, although all Christian feminists assume that there is some core biblical message that can be correlated with the liberation of women, over against patriarchal tradition, this is dealt with quite differently in various contexts. These differences probably have as much to do with the educational milieux of the women than with their different national cultures.

From my reading it seems that women operating on a popular pastoral level are content to make relatively easy correlations with Jesus and the gospel as liberating for all people, therefore also for women, over against patriarchal ideology and practice.[60] But, when women have to compete in university settings where the complexities of historical-critical biblical exegesis is a highly specialized skill, this correlation becomes much more problematic. For university-based feminists in the German, Dutch, and Scandinavian world, feminist hermeneutics is a major preoccupation.

This concern to establish a scientifically valid biblical hermeneutic, that can show in what ways women can or cannot claim the Bible as the basis of feminism, seems to trouble Protestant women more than Catholic women. Yet the leading writer on feminist hermeneutics of the New Testament is the German Catholic Elizabeth Schüssler Fiorenza, who teaches at Harvard Divinity School.[61]

This Protestant-Catholic difference in focus on biblical hermeneutics may be cultural, rather than strictly confessional. French and Hispanic Protestants are more like Catholics and German Catholics more like Protestants in the way they do exegesis. Women of Latin culture seem to lay hold of whatever biblical symbols that they can reclaim metaphorically as feminist, without being as concerned with establishing the precise historical-hemeneutical bridge between the biblical world and their own.[62] This style perhaps also reflects popular Bible reading from a liberation perspective developed in Base Christian Communities in the Latin Christian world.[63]

University-based feminist theologians have different interests from Christian feminists operating on the popular, pastoral level.

Particularly in Holland, where feminist theology has become something of a required theological subject and has the promise, already realized at the University of Nijmegen, of being a major subject for study and research, there is great concern with conceptualizing how feminist theology fits into the general theological curriculum.

The feminist group at Nijmegen University, *Feminisme en Christendom*, has formulated the concept of "bipolarity" to describe their view of the best relation of feminist theology to the theological curriculum. Bipolarity means that feminist teaching, study, and research must both have its own autonomous base in the university to pursue all theological topics from a feminist perspective, but must also be related to each of the fields of theology, such as biblical studies, dogmatic theology, pastoral psychology, church history, and ethics.

For most feminists, the heart of feminist praxis has to do with challenging and changing systems of sexual and bodily violence to women. Rape, incest, prostitution, pornography, objectification of the female body, denial of reproductive rights, and wife-beating are found in all patriarchal societies. But there are also distinct issues of sexual violence in different cultures and social situations. French feminists, who work closely with African immigrant women's groups, cite female sexual incision as a concern, while Indian women include dowry-deaths on their list of issues of violence to women.

Korean women see Kisaeng tourism as a major issue. Kisaeng tourism is businessmen's vacation deals in the Pacific region that include female sexual services in the package. Philippine feminists also see prostitution, particularly that connected with American military bases, as well as diseases spread by sexual contact with American service men, as major issues.

Although the restraint of militarism and promotion of peace concern all feminists, each see these issues in their national and regional context. For example, Korean feminists have connected antimilitarism with the removal of American nuclear weapons stationed in their country and the opening of dialogue leading to national unification. National unification has become a synthesizing theme for Korean feminists, around which they link all the areas of domination and oppression of their society; of men over women; ruling class over working class; exploitation and destruction of nature; colonial and imperial domination of Japan and the U.S.A. over Korea as a colonized region, and the splitting of North and South Korea as an expression of the global split of capitalism and communism. National unification, in their view, demands an overcoming of all these types of splitting, the liberation and reharmonization of the entire Korean community with itself, in relation to other nations and to the earth.[64]

For many Christian feminists worldwide there lurks on the edge of their discussion a suspicion that biblical monotheistic religions themselves are a patriarchal cultural distortion. Feminism, it is suggested, harks back to a prepatriarchal or matricentric culture that existed before the rise of patriarchy. However this theme of matriarchal religion takes distinct forms in different contexts. In Germany matriarchal feminism is a distinct subgroup of religious feminism, harking back to earlier European interests in pre-Christian European religions.

However, such matriarchal feminism is deeply troubling to other German Christian feminists concerned to overcome anti-Judaism in European Christianity. Idealization of Germanic paganism over against biblical religion is dangerously reminiscent of romanticism and its exploitation by Nazism.[65] Some matriarchal feminists have scapegoated Judaism as the basic "cause" of the overthrow of "good" matriarchal nature religion by "bad" patriarchal monotheism.[66] Anti-Judaism is a major topic for these Christian feminists concerned to answer charges that feminism is anti-Semitic.[67]

In many Latin American countries pre-Christian religious culture has not disappeared, but is available among indigenous people, although suppressed under European cultural hegemony. In Peru, for example, the myths connected with the Inca mother goddess, Pachamama, has become a theme for revisioning divine imagery in a way that not only relates men and women, but also humanity with nature, more harmoniously.[68] Some Korean feminists have also made links with popular shamanism and have seen this religious culture as one they can creatively appropriate.[69]

However, this feminist reclaiming of pre-Christian and non-Christian religions of national cultures is easier when these religions have lost their male leadership and power. This allows Christians to idealize elements in these religions as containing holistic alternatives to patriarchal hierarchy. However, where the male leadership and authority of these religions is intact and known by women to be part of the problem for them in their culture, this Christian feminist reclaiming of other religions is more ambivalent. Although such feminists may want to make a more interreligious synthesis of their national cultures, they must differentiate patriarchal from feminist elements in these other religions, as they must do for their Christianity.

In Africa, male theologians have sought to reclaim elements of African traditional religion; its emphasis on a community across generations, including the dead, the spirit world, and the unborn, its sense of a divine presence pervading nature and humans as one community, and its rites of passage marking the life cycle, as positive elements for an indigenous African Christianity.[70] African feminist theologians, such as Mercy Oduyoye, have cautioned against the tendencies of these African men to idealize indigenous cultures, ratifying anew its ways of oppressing women; for example, clitorectomy, sewing up the vagina, polygamy, and purity taboos.[71]

Korean women are strongly critical of Korean men who wish to integrate Confucian with Western culture, seeing Confucianism as the chief root of patriarchal domination in their culture.[72] Indian Christian women have no reason to idealize either Hinduism or Islam as helpful for women, although they are also very clear that the Christian belief that Christianity liberated Indian women is problemmatic. Several Indian Christian feminists declare that Christianity, while liberating in its authentic message, has come to India in forms that reinforce, rather than change, traditional Indian ways of subordinating women.[73]

Although feminists generally connect feminism with economic justice for women, this is seen differently in western Europe than in the third world. The statement of the Dutch feminist project of Nijmegen University rejects the idea that feminism is a branch of liberation theology.[74] They see feminist theology as pointing to much deeper and older patterns of oppression than these modern economic and national liberation movements.

Not all European feminists would agree with this discounting of solidarity with national, economic, and racial liberation, however. Other Dutch feminists have entered into solidarity with third-world movements[75] and are connected with work with oppressed migrant peoples in their societies. These involvements direct European (and North American) feminism into solidarity with liberation movements of oppressed people, men and women. This emphasis on interclass and race solidarity is also found in the French Orsay group that works with women's groups of oppressed African and Asian migrant laborers.[76]

In the third world, which is still emerging from European and North American colonialism and neocolonialism, it is generally accepted that feminism arises within and as a deeping of national liberation, seeking to free the whole national community from international domination, class domination, and sexism. Feminist theology for third-world women is the "irruption within the irruption" of an oppressed and dominated people.[77]

However, third-world women are also very aware that third-world socialist men trivialize feminism as a "bourgeois North American deviation" that should be of no concern to third-world people, female or male. Male liberation theologians have tended to ignore or resist this intrusion of feminism into their concepts of the liberation of the "poor." In Latin America, Elza Tamez and other feminists have established dialogues with Latin American male liberation theologians in an effort to force them to reflect explicitly on the relation of their liberation theology to the oppression of women.[78] Korean women speak of themselves as the "minjung of the minjung" (the oppressed of the oppressed). But they have found little resonance with their feminist concerns among male minjung theologians, and thus have decided to organize separately from them.[79]

This lack of reciprocity between third-world feminists and male liberationists has forced third-world women to struggle with how class and national liberation is related to women's liberation. Third-world feminists generally believe that the two are interconnected, but how they see them as interconnected differs. For some, national and class liberation is the primary issue, with the oppression of women a subtheme of the liberation of the poor. Women are the poorest of the poor. Other women see sexual oppression as linking women across class and race, and pointing to a more fundamental gender oppression that underlies all other oppressions.[80]

Despite these differences of cultural and social context, feminist theology is clearly an international discourse about common themes of women's oppression in patriarchal societies, as this is reinforced by patriarchal religion. While it has been pioneered among Christian women, it is fast becoming an interreligious discourse, with feminist critique arising also among Jewish, Buddhist, and Muslim women. All these forms of religious feminism are asking what can be reclaimed from historic religious cultures for women, who, for the first time, are becoming subjects, rather than objects, of religious discourse.

For all these feminist women (and men) the critical question is what kind of spiritual culture can save us from destructive patterns of domination and violence that threaten, not only women, but ultimately all humans and the planet itself. How can we salvage use-able elements from the past to develop a new spiritual culture to reconcile men with women, to overcome injustice between economic groups, races, and nations, and to harmonize humanity with its planetary habitat? Religious feminism is, finally, about life itself, both about abundance of life for all, especially for the givers of life, women, who have been so long denied its full cultural fruits, but also about the very preservation and sustaining of life on earth.

Jane I. Smith

WOMEN IN ISLAM

Islam since its inception has maintained the claim of universality—a message and a way of life applicable and appropriate to all
peoples in all places and times. Now more clearly than at any other
point in the history of the Islamic tradition, this claim seems to be
manifested through the presence of Muslim communities literally
across the world. The Muslim population is estimated in the range
of one billion, approximately half of whom are women representing
a great range of cultures, racial-ethnic identifications, interests, attitudes, and aspirations.

While it may be rather daunting to attempt to generalize about
Muslim women, it is nonetheless true that certain themes emerge
with some regularity when one looks across the Islamic world. The
very universality that Islam espouses means that there is a common
base of understanding about traditional roles for women that forms
a backdrop to contemporary responses and movements. And
whether one identifies the recent resurgence of Islamic consciousness as fundamentalism, traditionalism, revivalism, or any of a
range of other isms, the fact is that tensions are high as Muslims
struggle with and attempt to reconcile the affirmation of their heritage with the challenges of the modern world and the ongoing legacy of Western imperialism. Muslim women in all societies are key
to these discussions, both subjects and objects in a very important
and continuing debate about what it means to be a Muslim at the
end of the twentieth century.

Rather than summarizing the issues of these debates, or trying
to sketch broadly the legal and social circumstances of Muslim
women in general, I have chosen to try to open a small window on

four contemporary Islamic countries: Egypt, Saudi Arabia, Iran, and Pakistan. By looking at some of the issues that concern women in these four representative but very different areas, we may begin to see both commonalities and distinctions in the ways Muslim women want—and are allowed—to define and affirm their rights, their opportunities, and their identities.

EGYPT

Contemporary Egyptian society in many ways provides a focus for matters that women are facing across the Muslim world. One finds there a great range of responses to issues of women's rights and responsibilities, education, work opportunities, and appropriate dress. The traditional strength of Egyptian women is displayed in the vehemence with which they address the question of what it means to be Muslim in the modern world, whether their responses embrace a conservative religious position or press for new interpretations of freedom and equality for women.

The twentieth century has witnessed the rise of two movements that both parallel and, in many ways, oppose each other. They are, to use simplistic but convenient labels, feminism and fundamentalism.[1] Beginning at the end of the last century, early feminism was part of Egyptian response to Western colonialism and the drive toward national independence. It was primarily a movement of the urban upper middle and upper classes, identified in the early part of this century with such organizations as Huda Sha'rawi's Egyptian Feminist Union and Doria Shafiq's Daughters of the Nile Society. Much of their program after independence focused on social welfare efforts for lower-class urban women. Muslim women's feminism came to the fore again in the 1970s and 80s in a somewhat redefined fashion, and characterizes the perspectives of those who are members of such groups as the now banned Arab Women's Solidarity Association.

What is popularly called fundamentalism emerged as a conscious response of Muslim women toward the middle of this century and became much more visible after the 1967 and 1973 Arab-Israeli wars. It was manifested long after early feminists in the 1920s began the process of liberation by removing their veils, and after the system of segregation had in effect ended and women were both increasingly educated and a significant part of the work force. Many factors contributed and continue to contribute to this movement, including a desire to reject Western influence and what is perceived as flagging Western morality, a response to Zionism, the huge influx of population from rural areas to urban Cairo, and a desire for leadership in what is seen as a worldwide renaissance of Islamic consciousness. As larger numbers of middle- and lower-middle class women have availed themselves of free university education, there has been a resulting glut in the labor market. The reappropriation of traditional Islamic values in which women are justified in home activities has served to ease that pressure somewhat.

While the very process of higher education has put many women in contact with fundamentalist groups, others less well educated have drifted into such associations by joining small local groups often connected with mosques. Earlier in this century the adoption of a more conservative religious position by women generally was strongly influenced by males in their families. If that has not totally changed, it is true that such a stance is now recognized as a woman's free choice, influenced as much by her female friends and associates as by her husband or male relatives. The reaffirmation of traditional Islamic values—the place of women in the home, the role of women as wives and mothers, and the limitation of appropriate subject matter for study and of professional activities to what is appropriate for women—often is accompanied by external forms of identification such as new kinds of clothing. This clothing is generally called Islamic dress, or *al-ziyy al-shar'i*.

A number of variations of style come under the general rubric of Islamic dress. It really means clothing that is modest, and may refer to anything from a calf-length skirt and long-sleeved blouse or jacket to a loose ankle-length dress, usually of a light but not bright color. The key ingredient is the essential hair covering, which may be a scarf arranged so that no hair is exposed or a more elaborate wimplelike headdress, which outlines the face and drapes down the front and back of the dress. Some version of this kind of clothing is extremely common in the urban areas of Egypt today. Occasionally worn, although much less frequently, are the full face veil or *niqab* and dark gloves, leaving all parts of the body covered save a slit for the eyes. Women wearing the *higab* (literally veil, but used to refer to Islamic dress without the face veil) are called *muhaggabat*, while those who opt for full covering are called *munaqqabat*.

A great many reasons are cited by Muslim women for the adoption of Islamic dress.[2] Some feel that what they would call the "immodest dress" of many Western women is part of the general integration of the sexes that is at the heart of rising Western immorality. One often hears the claim that the very wearing of Islamic dress is liberating in that it allows women to participate in public life protected both from possible molestation and from a misunderstanding of their motives. Most would say that Islamic dress is their consciously and freely adopted symbol of identification with a religious system to which they wish to express a deep commitment and allegiance. For many young Egyptian women the decision whether or not to wear the *higab* or *al-ziyy al-shar'i* is a very difficult one. They feel that once having taken the step, it would be difficult and embarrassing to reverse it. The adoption of stylish forms of modest dress by some women has contributed to what had been called the "faddishness" of the movement. This in turn has led to concern on the part of the Islamic religious establishment that in some cases conservative dress is being used for the wrong reasons.[3]

Many Egyptians who do not adopt the *higab* are deeply respectful of those who do. Others look on it as anything from foolish to the result of mass psychology deadening to the hopes of Muslim women for full participation in society. Women who courageously removed their own veils in the early part of the century look with horror at what they see as the backward movement supported by many of today's young women. Nawal al-Saadawi, former minister of health and outspoken advocate of women's rights, feels that those who adopt the *higab* are the brainwashed victims of a masochistic slave psychology.[4] No less enthusiastic about some forms of Western women's dress that exposes parts of the body, she and others see both options as yet again forms of patriarchal oppression. These women, who represent a minority perspective in Egypt today, blame Islamic fundamentalism for denying women the power and rights that are theirs within a rightly interpreted Islamic system. The problem is not Islam, they say, but a patriarchy that is reinforced and perpetuated through the fundamentalist brand of Islam.

One of the areas subject to ongoing discussion in the context of what are claimed to be Islamic norms and values is that of women and work. As was noted, higher numbers of educated Muslim women (the ratio of men and women students in Egyptian universities is less than 2:1) mean that more women are prepared for employment. The fundamentalist movement in one sense has provided the opportunity for women to enter the work place (through wearing appropriate dress) at the same time that it has underscored the importance of women fulfilling their natural roles as wives, mothers, and homemakers. Professions that necessitate close contact between men and women are strongly discouraged and the abundant literature on the subject details the kinds of occupations that are more or less appropriate for women. The reality for many women who work in Egypt, as in other Islamic countries, is that they end up with what amounts to two full-time jobs (since men do little around the house), that new duties are not accompanied by new rights, and that no new responsibilities are assumed by males to correspond to these new duties of women.

Egyptian women, in fact, have long been represented in many aspects of the work force, and recently they have been joining in increasing numbers (primarily, of course, out of economic necessity). Among Cairo's middle and lower classes, it is increasingly common for women to work outside the home. The question remains how this reality can be reconciled to an ethos in which women's professionalism is not valued in the same way that a man's is, and in which conservative Islamic groups are putting a great deal of pressure on families to have a woman work only if there is no other financial alternative.

One aspect of this concern has to do with the understanding of different roles for women and men, and the perspective of many conservative Muslims that women are incapable of assuming true leadership positions. This had very interesting repercussions when Benazir Bhutto was elected in Pakistan as the first female leader of a contemporary Islamic government. Conservative Egyptian religious leaders communicated to Pakistan's president that for Bhutto to be prime minister went against Islamic principles and tradition (some even cited women's physical weakness as prohibitive of the ability to lead in government). Other Egyptians defended her position as prime minister, saying that it was appropriate so long as she was not the president or true leader. And still others pointed to the election of a Muslim woman as a hopeful sign that what they saw as the tyranny of fundamentalism was perhaps coming to an end in the Islamic world.

Related both to the issue of women's rights and to the rise of Islamic fundamentalism in Egypt is the extreme problem of population growth (2–3 percent per year, one of the highest rates in the world) and the fact that in Egypt some 99 percent of the population lives on about 4 percent of the land. President Hosni Mubarak has engaged in serious attempts at population control, but these are regularly countered by the conservative religious establishment. The mufti of Egypt, highest ranking religious authority, has been accused by some of his colleagues of collaborating to support government propaganda when he encourages family planning as Islamic.

Some see efforts at population control to be part of a long-standing Western imperialist plot to curtail the numbers of Muslims in the world. For the time being the reality seems to be that Muslim women in Egypt, as in many other Islamic countries, will continue to be expected to produce as many children as possible, and to balance motherhood and family care along with whatever responsibilities they may assume in the larger community.

SAUDI ARABIA

Question: "What does it mean to say that men are the final authority within the Muslim family?"

Answer (by a Saudi woman in a private conversation with the author): "Precisely that. And if the woman can't find a way, either by herself or through his family or her family or their children, to convince him to change his mind, that is the end of it. The first responsibility of a Muslim woman is to obey her husband. The trick here, of course, is in learning the ways in which to get him to change his mind. Women are good at that, but in a nice way. They are very strong as personalities and have an enormous influence on all the men around them. Their attitudes about what they want to do and should do are simply different from those of most Western women."

It may be helpful to keep this response in mind when looking at the situation of Saudi women today. On the one hand they appear by Western standards to remain under what many would call very repressive conditions. On the other they are key players in what clearly is a changing social situation. But underscoring it all, as is the case for most Muslim women across the world, is the fact that their aims and their methods and their responses "are simply different from those of most Western women."

The tensions are real and inevitably growing for Saudi women and Saudi society in general. The country is deeply Islamic and dedicated with what in the past few years has seemed to be an increasing vigilance to its interpretation of the basic values of Islam. This means that the husband is indeed the head of the family structure and that the sexes still remain segregated at least in the public domain. It also means that the woman who does choose to work outside the home—and the numbers of such women, while still low, are growing—must in effect inhabit two worlds that are quite radically different. On the one hand she may be a teacher, a doctor, or some other kind of professional contributing to the advancement and betterment of society. At the same time she is required to be veiled and to observe strict rules of propriety in relation to men. She cannot drive or generally travel on a public conveyance unless accompanied by a man (bus companies in a few large cities have seats reserved for women), and she still inhabits a world in which males are the decision-makers.[5] Yet most Saudi women, while eager to have increased educational and professional opportunities, defend Islam as a religious and a social system. They work toward accommodation with rather than reaction against the restrictions that the Islamic system places on them.

Perhaps the most startling change for women in Saudi Arabia, and clearly the key to other developments, has been the recent rise in their overall level of education. Before 1960 women did not have access to formal education in any public way. A few families sent their girls to Quran schools or private institutions, or in unusual cases hired tutors in the home. In 1963 King Faisal announced that the 'ulamā' (learned doctors of Islam) favored the opening of schools for girls and proceeded to establish the first such school. Since that time the numbers of young women engaged in public education have risen dramatically. Higher education in all state schools and universities in the kingdom is free. Unlike state-supported education in a country such as Egypt, however, all learning in Saudi Arabia takes place in segregation. Young men and women attend separate institutions with separate faculties and administrations. (An occasional exception is made to the rule that women are taught by women, such as when a blind male teacher is engaged at a women's institution or males instruct over closed-circuit television.)

It is not hard to imagine the difficulties that such a segregated system creates: inadequate numbers of women teachers for girl's schools and faculty for their higher education, a shortage of educational facilities, problems in administrative communication because male and female administrators do not meet in person for discussion, and the like.[6] Nonetheless movement continues, and there are five women's universities in the kingdom as well as separate campuses for women in some men's universities. The recent reaffirmation of Islamic values and attendant concern that women not be compromised has led to a reversal of the earlier policy that allowed Saudi women with scholarships to study abroad at higher levels. While some Saudi women do travel privately for education, government scholarships are no longer given for that purpose.

Increased educational opportunities for women, as well as the country's need for workers, quite naturally have served to draw more women into the professional labor force. Of course there are strict definitions of what is appropriate work for women, the most acceptable occupations being in education and educational administration, the health field (women are doctors, but traditionally have considered nursing to be menial), liberal arts, and the social services—fields in which they can operate without being in the public domain or interacting with men. The economic growth of the country and the expansion of segregated educational facilities have created a strong impetus for more women to be employed outside the home.

It seems clear that even the more conservative Islamic voices in Saudi society are in agreement that women should be given the opportunity to work. The question becomes one of balancing appropriateness against both need and desire. Islamic law is cited both by those who would stress the importance of women's roles at home and advocate that they work only in very restricted circumstances, and those who see the participation of women as essential to the development of the country (much like Egyptians in the early part of the century) and as a way to reduce what has been a necessary reliance on a foreign labor force.[7] Among the new professions for women about which there has been considerable controversy are banking, journalism, and ownership of various small establishments such as beauty salons. Many of the activities permitted in the 1970s were curtailed in the 1980s under pressure from the religious establishment. The oil boom for Saudi Arabia has meant that women (who by quranic stipulation control their own money) are investing in businesses, real estate, and other profitable ventures. Much of the debate about women and work is carried out in the daily press, followed avidly by educated Saudi women.

It is clear that increased educational and professional opportunities for Saudi women are bringing about changes—and often difficulties—in the traditional structure of family relationships. Many men while theoretically in favor of women's employment are uncomfortable with what they feel to be the disapproval of their friends and families, and thus forbid their own wives to work. Child care is an obvious problem. Even getting married may be increasingly difficult for women who are educated (some young men are threatened at the prospect of an educated wife), or for whom the *mahr* or bride price is so high that most men cannot afford to pay it. Many women choose to continue their education before marrying, whereas men often prefer to marry younger women without waiting. And the rise in the number of professionally employed women has been paralleled by an increase in the divorce rate and the resulting situation of more single women in society.

Even apart from households in which professional engagement for women is in question, there have been important changes in recent years. While formerly the husband's mother was in charge of the house, this responsibility is increasingly being assumed by the young wife. Homes that used to be spacially segregated tend now to be more integrated, often reflecting more cooperative family planning between husband and wife. (This may be due to some extent to the fact that spacial segregation is increasingly expensive.)[8] Birth control methods, though generally frowned upon by the *ulema*, are used more frequently, and there have been some changes in terms of education and supervision of children. Increasingly mothers are involved in family decisions. And many women are more vocal in insisting that their husbands strictly observe Islamic restrictions pertaining to the taking of more than one wife.

To some extent these changes are superficial, however, and marriage along with education is a very high priority for Islamic women even when it is understood to be subject to the classical and still continuing restrictions for women. It remains the case that men are responsible for the behavior of women. One of the ways in which this continues to be manifested is in the insistence by most males that the women of their families be veiled. Here we do not have the phenomenon of a self-conscious and optional adoption of Islamic dress as with some Egyptian (and other) Muslim women, but the overall societal requirement of veiling as a continuing religious injunction. Unveiling in public is considered shameful both to the woman and to her family, and in general is not permitted in Saudi society.

Normally girls put on the "veil" or conservative dress at puberty. Traditional veiling consists of a kind of black cloak which is worn over a dress and hangs to the ground, with a thin scarf covering the head and shoulders. Younger women sometimes vary this by wearing a shorter garment over a full-length skirt or loose trousers or even a dress which comes below the knees. Even those who do not subscribe to this degree of modesty tend to cover their hair with some kind of scarf when appearing in public. Ultimately it remains the prerogative of the husband to decide the dress of his wife.

It is clear, then, that Saudi Arabia is a society in flux, and that the attempt to balance conservative and traditional (often identified as Islamic) values with the country's rapid movement into the modern industrial and technological world inevitably creates tensions and confusion. Women are no more certain of the directions in which they want things to go than are men, and with their sisters across the Islamic world both welcome educational and professional opportunities and fear that too rapid movement may lead to instability in the family and in society.

It seems difficult to imagine that a growing female work force can continue to function effectively under such restrictions as the inability to drive or (for the most part) to use public transportation. Issues of segregation and accessibility, decision-making, and the balance of opportunity, responsibility, and accountability loom as increasingly important matters for Saudi attention as the kingdom struggles to honor its Islamic heritage while it assumes its place among modern nations.

IRAN

The image of the Islamic woman most immediately evoked for the Western public may be that of an Iranian female locked inside her *chador* or cloak, sometimes holding a rifle as a symbol of her support for the revolution of 1979. The Western press has found her photographically irresistible—her picture often illustrates articles about contemporary Iran that do not deal specifically with women at all. While this is of course only one image among a great many representative of women in Islam, it is true that the *chador* provides a focus for understanding both the participation of women in the revolution and the reality of their situation since that time.

Critics of the Islamic regime of the Ayatollah Khomeini note that the shah, whatever his policies of repression for Iranian society as a whole, did effect significant legal reforms which helped improve the lot of women. The family protection law of 1967 (revised in 1975) implemented changes in such areas as polygamy, divorce, and child custody. Several things must be noted in this context, however. First, the great majority of Iranian women, living in rural areas, uneducated and not part of the paid labor force, remained more or less uneffected by these reforms. Recent decades actually saw a worsening of the circumstances of rural women due largely to economic ramifications of the shah's modernization policies, and little improvement in matters of illiteracy, early marriage, and overwork. Nonetheless—or perhaps because of these realities—there was little or no participation of rural women in the revolution.

A second reality in relation to the shah's reforms is that they were not appropriated by women as their own precisely because they were the prerogative of a monarch who was generally considered to be a despot. Iranian women have long shared a tradition of public protest and social action, but were not a recognized part of the decision-making which led the shah to ban the *chador*, promote higher education and better economic opportunity, and effect other changes for women. Many of those who opposed the shah did so not because they took issue with his program of reform, but because they opposed the means he used to implement it.

Women's opposition to the regime of the shah took a variety of forms.[9] Some women, especially those who had spent time studying in the West, brought a feminist perspective to the assessment of his role and methods. Others were strongly influenced by Marxism, many participating in underground cells and groups. Islamic revivalism with its religious critique of the shah brought many women into its fold. Intellectuals and activists objected to modes of operation that they found repressive and unacceptable. Thus a number of different causes were represented by the women who cooperated, in accord with their heritage of collective activism, in support of a movement which did bring about the end of the shah's rule. The irony, of course, is that their fragile union swiftly crumbled under the reality of the new regime. It soon became clear that virtually none of the ends for which they had collaborated—except the demise of the shah himself—was to be realized under the ayatollah.

The *chador* thus symbolizes both the collaboration and the disillusionment. To those who see it specifically as a mark of conservative Islam, it is difficult to understand why many women who were pressing for changes that certainly would not lead to a fundamentalist religious ethos would opt to wear it at the time of the revolution. For them it was not a religious or pro-Islamic but a political antishah symbol through which all Iranian women could protest against injustice. To their disappointment and disillusionment, the very symbol was turned against them by the ayatollah when he decreed that under his Islamic government women were forced to dress according to the strict Islamic code. It became clear that the revolution was indeed a fundamentalist Muslim one, and that the *chador* represented the state's definition of a position repressive to women and symbolized by dress.

It did not take women long to react violently against the decree that the *chador* was mandatory. Meetings, rallies, and protests against the veil at the time of international women's day in 1979 led to a temporary retreat on the part of the new government on this issue. Along with the right to make their own decisions regarding clothing, women demonstrated in favor of the family protection law, the right to equal wages and for participation in government. It was not long, however, before the enforcement of veiling reemerged— since 1980 women in government agencies and other offices have been forced to wear it, and many women in other professions have lost their jobs for refusing to comply. It was declared illegal for women to demonstrate, and the reversal of rights for women and a clear lowering of their status in relation to men became the norm for the new regime. Since the revolution women have no longer been allowed to practice law or to participate effectively in the running of Iranian society. The family protection law was suspended and strict Shi'i Islamic law reinstated in relation to family matters. Women have been barred from participation in international sports. Coeducation has been banned and classes segregated; women have been refused certain kinds of technical training; married women no longer can attend high school (at the same time that the marriage age has been lowered for girls). Further steps have been taken to ensure compulsory veiling. Women have been given segregated seating in public transportation (or put onto separate buses). Men and women who are not related cannot be seen walking or talking together. In general, women have been denied many of the rights taken for granted for the better part of this century.

The enforcement of veiling has been both official and unofficial—uncovered women have been refused service in stores, discriminated against, and attacked by both men and by veiled women.[10] (Because of the impracticality of the chador it is now permissible to replace it with a kind of uniform consisting of a head scarf covering the hair and forehead, a knee-length tunic, and long pants.) Polygamy is encouraged, the minimum marriage age for girls has been lowered to thirteen, divorce is practically impossible for women to initiate. Legally, economically, politically, educationally, and socially, women have been forced to assume a subjugated status as they have been veiled, eliminated from the paid work force, and deprived of basic education.

It is obviously unfair to suggest that all those who favor an Islamic society support the excesses of the Khomeini regime. Many Iranian women today see that there have been a variety of forms of oppression under which they have lived in this century, ranging from feudalism and extremist Islamic fundamentalism imposed from within Iran, to Western imperialism and Marxism operating from without. They are searching for an alternative to the oppression for women that they see all of these representing. And they are looking to find this not in a rejection of Islam as they see expressed by secular feminists but within the Islamic system. Some of them, in common with many women across the Islamic world, are attempting to find a model for true Islamic womanhood taken from the early days of Islam and focused specifically on the role of the prophet's daughter Fatima. That model, and the resulting implication for their role as Muslim women, is part of the platform of the continuingly popular interpreter Ali Shariati.[11]

Nor is it fair to say that all Iranian women find the wearing of the veil an unmitigated hardship. Many of those who took part in the revolution were from the urban middle and lower-middle classes, and were caught in an uncomfortable transition from veiling to unveiling. For many of these women it is a relief not to have to suffer the tensions of moving between a world of family in which traditional dress is expected and the world of work where things are often very different. Following is an excerpt from a conversation recorded shortly after the revolution with a young girl of sixteen years, a domestic in an Iranian family north of Tehran. When asked why one should wear the veil, she replied, "It is the mark of modesty. In truth the greatness of the woman is in her veil. An unveiled woman has no value in Islam. God has created woman with her modesty, with her veil, so that she can attain a perfect personality." Somewhat more practically, and echoing an argument made in many Muslim countries in reference to modest dress, she commented, "The veil does no harm to anyone, and if you do not wear it, it is possible for men to follow you in the street."[12]

Regardless of how one interprets the facts of what has happened in Iran in the last decade—as the victory of an indigenous movement over a leader influenced by imperialist forces, as the triumph of fundamentalist Islam over secularism, as the victory of the lower and middle classes over the upper educated Westernized classes— for most Iranian women life has not been easy. The Ayatollah Khomeini until his death remained convinced that women are basically a cause of disorder in society and of seduction to men, and that therefore they must be kept from full societal participation for the good of the Islamic order. In some of his writings he affirmed the opinion that women are inferior in every way—physically, psychologically, intellectually, and morally.

The reductions in women's rights cited above as the immediate products of the revolution have not been reversed in the last ten years. Recent reports indicate the degree to which the rulings of the ayatollah have continued to hold. Western publications showing unveiled women are forbidden; cosmetics, perfume, and long fingernails are prohibited. Attempts to enliven the severity of the *chador* with colored scarfs or high heels are strongly discouraged. Morality police are vigilant in regard to women's dress, pulling down sleeves or slitting pant legs that are too tight. Iranian men, themselves repressed under the regime, take out their frustrations by further subjugating the women of their families. Women have suffered deeply under the pain of seeing their young sons taken to war and of having to maintain their households under increasingly difficult economic circumstances. Perhaps hardest to bear for many educated and formerly successful professional women is what has been called the "institutionalized inferiority" of Iranian women. No matter what the circumstance or who the individuals involved, a man always takes preference.

It remains to be seen whether the new regime will continue what can only be called the repressive policies, at least for women, of its predecessor, the Ayatollah Khomeini. In the meantime, however, commitment to Shi'i Islam in Iran remains strong on the part of most women and men. Efforts continue at interpretation of that system so that when political circumstances permit, more harmonious, equitable, and ultimately Islamic solutions can be found for the relationship of males and females in Iran.

PAKISTAN

Pakistan is a new state in the world of nations, created in 1947 when religious tensions in India led to a rupture of that country and Muslims carved out a territory in which they could share a common religious identity. Since then the country has struggled with issues of Islamization and modernization, and in continuing ways those issues have related to the roles and opportunities of women. The heritage of strong Muslim women's movements, traditions of sexual segregation, the reactions of an often conservative religious establishment, and the political maneuvers of Pakistan's leaders have combined to create a fluctuating and often frustrating climate for the women of the country.

For the most part the issues have been played out in the arena of the urban educated, and it is these women who have watched and agitated as they have seen their lives and futures manipulated in the constant struggle for power in the young nation. The fact is, of course, that the vast majority of the population lives in rural areas, and that to a fair extent life continues for those women much as it has for a very long time. The circumstances of rural women are radically different from those of urban women. They remain generally uneducated and illiterate, uninformed and unaware of many of the rights that are theirs under both Islamic and constitutional law, subject to the control of the males in their families. While working long daily hours they are not counted in the female labor force statistics because they are not paid for their work. This is a large part of the reason why the proportion of women in the Pakistani labor force is among the world's lowest.

And it remains true that while many of the urban women of the country are highly educated and professionally active, the country as a whole still operates under a system of sexual segregation that influences all of Pakistani society.[13] This system is generally referred to as purdah, whereby women are secluded and prevented from full participation in society and in the world of males. It has been identified as one of the major difficulties in the way of women's education and thereby the entry of women into the labor force. Not surprisingly, it has been the subject of a great deal of controversy in the last decade in Pakistan.

Concretely purdah has two ramifications, one in terms of dress and the other in terms of living accommodations. The conservative dress worn by women to protect them from the intrusion of male observation can be either a *burqa*, a kind of cloak that serves more or less completely to cover the wearer, or a *chador*, generally referring in Pakistan to a scarf or shawl worn over the head and shoulders. Whether this covering is so total that the only opening is an embroidered slot for the eyes or simply a wrap for the head and hair, it symbolizes modesty and a way of maintaining social distance from the male world.

The other dimension of purdah relates to the tradition of private living space for women within the home, called *chardewari* (literally referring to the four walls of the home), where areas are set off in which men are not allowed to enter. The reverse side of this protecting privacy, of course, has been the relegation of women to their houses and limitation of their open participation in society. This kind of physical purdah has been extended to provide protected areas for women in public places by such means as curtains on automobiles, separate compartments in public conveyances, partitioned areas for women in public buildings, and the like. An extension of this concept is the separate women's school or university, to which many Pakistani women today vigorously object. It should be observed that as is true with policies of segregation in many other Muslim countries, there is a way in which it is an economic luxury. The poorest classes in society simply cannot afford it, nor does it exist among peasant women.

The overall situation of women in Pakistan, as in other Islamic countries, has been greatly effected by the ways in which political parties and leaders have felt it necessary to move in order to stay in power. The nationalist movement of Jinnah, head of the newly created state of Pakistan, helped form a strong political awareness of the power of women as well as men. As was the case with Egypt earlier in this century and in many developing areas today, there was a clear realization that progress for the nation depends on the education and participation of its women. But this philosophy has always led to struggles—and continues to do so today—with the strong conservative religious ideology which wishes to perpetuate the system of purdah. In the 1970s specific programs of population control, education, welfare, health, and housing had obvious implications for women. Under the socialist regime of Zulfiqar Ali Bhutto (father of the Pakistani leader Benazir Bhutto) the emancipation of women was cited as a major component in Pakistan's development and movement toward modernization. Education, employment (including child care and job opportunities), and health care were all part of the Bhutto platform. Mrs. Bhutto was prominently featured as a way of garnering female support.

When General Zia al-Haq took over the government, supported in large measure by conservative ulama, things became much more problematic for the advancement of the cause of women's "liberation." Women were promised their just and reasonable rights, but purdah was again stressed. Education, if encouraged at all, was to be segregated. One of the most influential of the state ministers was Maulana Mawdudi, founder of the conservative Jama'at al-Islami movement and staunch defender of purdah as an essential ingredient in an Islamic state.[14] Zia himself did not actually institute any changes in the earlier platform for the participation of women in society, but neither did he provide the concrete programs by which these goals could be realized. Unlike the secularist Bhutto whom he succeeded, Zia was a pious Muslim and generally used the Islamic platform and establishment to consolidate his own political power. His campaign of Islamization inevitably courted those elements that oppose movements for women's emancipation and participation in society, and favor a system of continuing sexual segregation.

Throughout Zia al-Haq's regime women who had fought for, and achieved, advances in society in earlier days watched nervously in fear of losing those rights. In 1982 an event occurred which ignited the agitated response of women whose nerves were already raw, illustrating the conflicting and strongly held views that prevail on the issue of women. A leading Islamic scholar named Dr. Israr, a member not of the ulama but of Mawdudi's Jama'at al-Islami, advocated in his weekly television program the pensioning off and return to the home of all working women in Pakistan.[15] Business and professional women lost no time in reacting. A group of some eighteen women's organizations banded together to claim what they saw as the Islamically given right to work and demanded cancelation of the program. An opposition group of women, fully veiled, demonstrated for its continuation and claimed that the other women were not truly Islam-loving. Zia hoped to end the controversy by pointing out that Israr was not an authority, because he was not a member of the ulama (who, incidentally, may have agreed with Israr's position but deeply resented his claim of authority on religious matters). The debate raged with no real resolution. One of the interesting issues in connection with this debate is the degree to which a popularized interpretation of Islam can be both effective and inflammatory in ways in which pronouncements of the religious establishment may fail to be.

The tensions in Pakistani society continue.[16] Many persons feel that it is essential for women to be involved in the advancement of the state, and see that involvement to be predicated on the abolition of purdah, both structurally and in terms of dress. Separate education for boys and girls generally begins just before puberty, and often but not always continues into the university. Many women's organizations actively oppose such segregated education on the grounds that it perpetuates vocational discrimination and mitigates against the entry of women into a full range of employment possibilities. Numbers of educated women have increased, but very slowly. Studies show that while the vast majority of Pakistanis feel women should be literate enough to read the Quran and religious books, fewer go so far as to support the goal of formal education. Many fear that if educated their daughters will not want to be good housewives, will lose their modesty, will no longer be obedient, and will have difficulty finding marriage partners (although in some segments of society an educated girl is considered an asset in an arranged marriage).

Even greater resistance is voiced to women in the work force, which is why the television statement of Dr. Israr caused such controversy. And the same constraints on appropriate occupations for women that we have seen in other societies—if they are permitted to work at all—obtain in Pakistan. Teaching and medicine again are considered the most (perhaps only) appropriate vocations, primarily because they can be pursued in segregation from men. To be a doctor is generally acceptable, to be a nurse is not. Positions often occupied by women in other societies such as secretaries, clerks, and salespersons are filled by men. It is not surprising that most Pakistani girls who go to school take general education courses rather than pursue specific vocational training.

Liberals in many parts of the Muslim world hoped that Benazir Bhutto would be able to effect significant changes for women in Pakistan, especially in such areas as improving health facilities and providing better educational opportunities. Ruling this complex young nation, however, proved to be beyond her capacity. Severe financial problems, the continuing opposition of many religious conservatives who challenged her right as a woman to rule a Muslim country, her own lack of political experience as well as charges of nepotism in her government let to the bloodless end of her regime with the elections of August 1990.

Bhutto's election as a female and a champion of women's rights was nonetheless a significant symbol for Muslim women, one that many would claim was fully in keeping with the model set by the wives of the Prophet Muhammad, especially his beloved A'isha. The brief duration of her rule, however, must give significant pause to those who hope to challenge the traditionalist Muslim perspective that denies to a woman the opportunity to serve in a leadership position. The new regime in Pakistan has done nothing to improve the lot of women in that country.

CONCLUSION

While such a quick survey serves at least to give a general summary of some of the main problems and concerns of the women in these respective societies, it neither does justice to the specific areas under consideration nor properly represents the range of differing circumstances for women across the Islamic world. It does suggest, however, some major issues that are being addressed in quite differing political, socio-economic, and cultural situations in the Muslim world today. Women's rights (both Islamic and constitutional) are under constant debate, as are matters of seclusion and segregation, the relationship of women's circumstances to fundamentalist religious pressures, and the role of women in political struggles for independence and economic advancement.

Some countries such as Egypt have stressed the importance of women's education for the better part of the century (although only 39 percent of females at the secondary level are enrolled in school as compared with 64 percent of males). Others like Saudi Arabia have only recently begun to work toward this goal. It is clear that overall there is increased attention to the importance of education for Muslim females both as a right and a value in and of itself, and as an essential ingredient in the advancement of nations. As in many areas, it is also clear that enormous differences exist educationally for women in urban and in rural areas, a dichotomy that at least in the short run probably will become even more pronounced.[17]

Woven through debates on the importance of women's education are the themes of segregation and the appropriateness of certain subjects for study by females. These themes carry over into the major concern of women's employment in Muslim countries and the debate over which occupations are considered proper for women to pursue. In many countries shortages in the labor force are making it imperative for women to work, but the tide of traditionalism tends to mitigate strongly in limiting those opportunities. In many countries increasing numbers of women are engaged as wage earners, but they are limited primarily to such occupations as teaching and medicine.[18] The oil wealth of the Gulf states had led both to better education and to more work opportunities, although the conservative Islamic ethos has severely complicated the situation. Kuwait offers the greatest opportunities for women's employment,[19] and Bahrain with its economic diversification is opening new doors for female employment. Whether because of or despite Islam or government policies, women across the Islamic world are becoming more economically active. This does not necessarily mean, of course, that they are pressing for increased work opportunities. Many women would prefer not to work, doing so only because of economic necessities and happy that the extra money earned means a more comfortable life for their families.

Enhanced professional opportunity for women is not without its down side. Women in a number of cultures have come to realize that along with the societal and familial strains that occur when women work outside the home (including perceptions that men cannot support their families) is the reality of women taking on added responsibilities without the expectation that they will be able to do less in other areas of their lives. And the relationship of economically and politically active women to the advancement of the state adds further strains for many women. In Iraq, for example, women's liberation and full integration into society is a part of the Ba'th party platform. But reforms in personal status laws lag behind the political rhetoric, adding to the burdens of women. This is generally true across the Islamic world, and it means that these burdens will continue as long as there is no real resolve in the tension between needing women for national development and not being able to accord them full status in society because of socio-religious restrictions.[20]

As has been very evident in the four cultures surveyed, the question of women's dress is one of the most pressing concerns of Islamic societies today. Sometimes the government in allegiance with the religious establishment and seeking its support insists on women wearing "appropriate" covering (in Libya, to give one of many examples, Colonel Qaddafi has instituted a dress code for all women students through the university). In other instances governments are making every attempt to discourage the wearing of Islamic dress precisely because they fear the rising power of extremist fundamentalism. The Kuwaiti ministry of the interior prevents women who are driving cars from wearing Islamic head covering, at the same time (and no doubt related to the fact) that more women on campuses are appearing in conservative dress. Nowhere is this tension more evident than in Turkey, the country in which laws affecting women's status changed radically in the 1920s from Islamic to secular civil codes. Today controversy over the government's ban on students wearing Islamic dress at the universities has become a major ideological and political issue. (Discussion in Turkey centers primarily on the turban, a traditional head scarf tied at the neck and covering the hair and forehead.) Islamic conservatives say that the Quran dictates the wearing of the turban, preferably with a kind of long loose overcoat covering the body to the feet. The government's supreme educational council has recommended disciplinary action for any female students appearing in such dress. The debate has become a major one in the struggle between secularist ideology and Islamic revivalism in that country.[21]

As we saw in Egypt and in Saudi Arabia, the question of birth control is a matter of major concern to many Muslim families.

While a few of the ulama, if supported by state efforts, are saying that there is Islamic sanction for some preventive measures, the majority oppose any such control as un-Islamic. When young Iraqi men and boys were being killed in the war with Iran, the government waged a campaign stressing the role of women as mothers. Contraceptives were no longer allowed at the same time that men were encouraged to take second wives for the purpose of having more children. Clearly there are differences in men's and women's attitudes on the issue of birth control. In Tunisia, for example, where legislation concerning women is generally seen to be more progressive than in many other countries, a survey showed that far more women than men favored the use of contraceptives. Where official policy does not support the possibility of contraception more subtle measures are sometimes used. In Bahrain housing projects limit the number of bedrooms so that they are available only to families with two children.

One important theme to which little attention has been directed in this brief survey should be the subject of a separate and more detailed study. This is the series of way in which Muslim women in a variety of cultures have worked out their own ways of being religious, of developing rites and practices that are peculiarly female in the context of male-oriented societies. In some cases these practices may appear to be on the margins of Islam, such as north African visitation of saint's shrines or Egyptian *zar* (spirit healing) ceremonies. In other places women are actually seen as the vehicles for transmission of basic Islamic rituals.[22] Women's Islamic organizations are increasingly active in some countries, such as the Aisyihah movement (after the prophet's wife 'A'isha) in Indonesia, which serves as an organ for the development of Muslim women's understanding of Islam. In Egypt and other areas women are increasingly taking on roles as teachers of other women in Quran and Islamic tradition. While Islam generally disallows specific religious leadership roles for women such as functioning as an imam or formal leader of the prayer, in Indonesia even this function is being assumed by a few women.

Finally, a word needs to be said about Muslim women and the rise of feminism. It cannot perhaps be emphasized too strongly that whatever stand Islamic women may take on issues of education, employment, and equal opportunities in society, they have serious reservations about what they understand to be feminism in the Western context. For the most part they find it too individualistic, too removed from genuine cooperation between males and females, and too much tied to forms of Western colonialism and imperialism. "Sexual behavior that may strike an American feminist as liberated," said one young Tunisian woman, "may strike me as just another form of slavery, and a rather neurotic form at that."[23] Women in "secular" societies such as Turkey have long looked to Western feminism as the ground for a theoretical analysis of their own circumstances, only to be disappointed. The feminist movement of Western society has been known in Indonesia for many years, but far from being accepted in this more liberal Islamic society it is suspect as over bound to the particulars of Western culture. As each country and area needs to develop its own platform in light of its own particular issues, so many Muslim women are eagerly searching for a kind of response that they can claim to be feminist within the Islamic context.

It seems clear that there is a strong connection between enhanced fidelity to traditional religion, in this case Islam, and a lack of appreciation for many of the principles of Western feminism. What may be less obvious is that even those women most opposed to what they see as the repressiveness of Islamic fundamentalism (which they argue is not true Islam) are dedicated to understanding the possibilities for the liberation of women from within the Islamic context. A few lone voices among women who are culturally Muslim call for a rejection of the entire patriarchal system of Islam. Virtually all others affirm the validity of Islam as a divinely revealed plan for human existence both individually and communally. They represent a range of positions as to the ways in which Islam can be interpreted, especially insofar as it is prescriptive for women both legally and socially. But in general they are in agreement that the West and Western women have somehow lost touch with the principles with which to sustain ongoing relationships between men and women, and with which humans can live together responsibly and creatively before God.

Muslim women and men together are still very much in the process of working out ways in which to affirm their Islamic identity as members of societies and nations moving into a new century. The issues they face will not be quickly or easily resolved. Women are not only faced by a number of conflicting pressures and claims on their allegiance, but find themselves speaking to a number of different audiences—their husbands and families, their Islamic sisters, their Western critics, the clerics or government agencies responsible for determining many of the circumstances of their lives, themselves. There is little question that many women across the Islamic world are becoming increasingly aware of the rights that belong to them within the Islamic system, as well as of themselves as key players in the movements that will continue to redefine the Islamic way of life. The responses they give to their own changing circumstances may vary with the different situations to which they are called to respond, and they may change fairly dramatically in the next few years. But it is clear that whatever solutions are found to the issues that they face, for most women they will be discovered in conversation with other females as well as males in the Muslim community, and they will be—in one form or another—Islamic solutions.

Rita M. Gross

STUDYING WOMEN AND RELIGION: CONCLUSIONS TWENTY-FIVE YEARS LATER

In 1967, more than twenty-five years ago, when I first decided to write a paper on women in religion, I had no idea that I had stumbled onto the concern that would occupy much of my scholarly and personal life. Nor did I realize that I had located the most serious blind spot of contemporary scholarship, not only in religious studies, but also in all humanistic and social scientific disciplines. I knew only that I had decided on this paper topic because I was very frustrated and blocked as a woman seriously involved in Western religions, and I wanted to find out if "things were that bad everywhere." Therefore, for a required graduate course in primitive religions, I decided to write a paper on the role of women in Australian and Melanesian religions.

Researching and writing that paper was difficult but absorbing. Data were almost impossible to find, but the scholars all told me that in these religions, men are regarded as sacred while women are regarded as profane and unclean. Furthermore, women were said to have no significant religious life.[1] On the surface, I should have concluded that "things were that bad (or even worse) everywhere." Nevertheless, I could not help but notice that the actual data of Australian and Melanesian religions recounted myths in which women originally held power and taught men all the religious rituals. Only later, according to these myths, did men steal power and knowledge from the women.

The actual data also included numerous rituals in which men imitated female physiological processes, even though they also excluded women from participation in those rituals. Something seemed not quite to add up.

I concluded in my paper that indeed women did have a religious life, that they were important in the symbol system of men's separate religion, and that the conventional scholarly hypotheses concerning these data were somehow inadequate. Women clearly seemed to be evaluated as sacred, though in a manner different from men.[2]

That paper turned into more than I bargained for or dreamed possible. Its effects are still very much with me in my identity as an outspoken feminist scholar and theologian. Were it not for that paper, I doubt that *Unspoken Worlds: Women's Religious Lives*[3] would have been written. And I probably would have had a much smoother ride through graduate school.

When Mircea Eliade, for whom I had written the paper, returned it to me, he strongly urged me to continue these explorations into my doctoral dissertation. His rationale, so vividly remembered all these years, was: "You're seeing things in these materials that I, as a man, would probably not see." My immediate response is equally etched in my memory: "No, I want to do my dissertation on something important." Somehow, I did end up deciding to continue studying something about women and religion for my doctoral work. In those days, women studies as a field and focus was nonexistent and categories regarding women and religion were extremely vague; therefore, one could be studying something as amorphous and general as "women and religion."

At the dissertation stage, my initial paper turned into a critique of conventional history of religions methodology—a sacrosanct topic at the University of Chicago. That fatal move led both to difficulties with my faculty mentors, which nearly resulted in my being unwillingly exited from graduate school, and to my career as a feminist scholar. These events all stemmed, not from my decision to continue studying "women and religion," but from my asking a question of feminist methodology: Why had women and religion not been studied very much or very well previously? That question led me to methodological considerations and to the claim that, while the history of religions was quite concerned with *homo religiosus*, it did not seem to be much concerned with *femina religiosa*. That question, though it did not yet articulate the most basic feminist critique of conventional scholarship, was threatening enough to garner the reply that an intelligent graduate student should understand that the masculine covered and included the feminine, thereby obviating the need for any specific attention to women's religious lives. Though not without serious opposition, I eventually did receive a doctorate for the first dissertation on women studies in religion to be accepted by any major graduate institution.[4]

The reason to tell these stories is not because I am the protagonist in them but because they illustrate so well major issues and themes in the study of women and religion. Typically, in women studies in religion, the link between experience and scholarship is openly acknowledged, despite a bias that scholarship should be "objective." Discipline lines are blurred, as is the distinction between so-called descriptive and so-called prescriptive studies; feminist scholarship is often deliberately synthetic. Finally, risks are taken in this kind of scholarship. Especially when we were graduate students and young scholars, those of us who first articulated the voice of feminist scholarship took enormous risks. Even though many of us are now better established, we still routinely write articles and give presentations that make us feel vulnerable and exposed.

Experiences of alienation and frustration regarding my own religious heritage had led me to explore religion in a wider context. During those explorations, I felt a strong, but inarticulate, reaction that somehow conventional scholarship had not really looked at women accurately and adequately. These experiences of frustration with my own religion and with scholarship on religion ultimately resulted in a basic paradigm shift in my thinking. Eventually, I realized that I was so frustrated by scholarship on women and religion, and it seemed so inadequate, because such scholarship resulted from an androcentric model of humanity in scholars' minds. It became clear that when I responded that I wanted to do my dissertation on something important, not women, I too had been utilizing an androcentric model of humanity.

After many months, perhaps even years of conceptual struggle, it became clear that a fundamental paradigm shift was called for. A better, more accurate and complete model of humanity was desperately needed by all scholars. We needed to exorcise the androcentric model of humanity from our consciousness and replace it thoroughly and completely, once and for all, with an androgynous model of humanity. That paradigm shift I now regard as the central issue in the study of women and religion, as well as the most significant challenge and contribution of the women studies perspective. This challenge and this contribution affect all humanistic and social scientific disciplines as profoundly as they affect religious studies.[5]

The more one works guided by this dense web of interwoven experience and scholarship, the more one realizes that scholarship simply is not "objective." The feminist critique of conventional scholarship thus encourages one to state one's methodological and philosophical standpoint at the beginning of an article—still not common practice among scholars, but something greatly to be urged. Stating one's presuppositions clearly, especially one's presuppositions regarding the proper model of humanity, encourages one to recognize as inevitably value-laden dimension of scholarship. Consciously recognizing that it is impossible to avoid a normative dimension in scholarship, the scholar is encouraged to go further, to blend disciplines and to break down discipline lines that do not make sense. This is especially the case for the very thick line within religious studies that separates the history of religions—a descriptive discipline studying religion historically and cross-culturally, from theology—a constructive, normative, and critical study within a faith tradition. Often such feminist scholarship takes the form of using historical and cross-cultural materials creatively and constructively—that is to say, of blending history of religions and theology without confusing them.

Thus, in delineating conclusions about the study of women and religion after twenty years, at the personal midpoint of such study, several themes stand out. Everything depends upon the willingness to bring experience into scholarship and to take risks. Everything turns on the paradigm shift from androcentrism to androgyny. And everything points to blending the disciplines within religious studies, especially so-called theology and so-called history of religions, seemingly descriptive and seemingly normative concerns.

THE PARADIGM SHIFT: ANDROCENTRISM
AND ANDROGYNY

The fundamental challenge and potential of women studies in religion, as in other fields, is its delineation and critique of androcentrism. The tasks of laying bare the fundamental unconscious preconceptions of androcentrism, demonstrating their inadequacy, and providing a more adequate alternative are the most important and central contributions of the women studies perspective to the fields of religious studies and comparative religions. These are also the implications of feminism for most other disciplines.

Both the essential promise of women studies to induce a paradigm shift in scholarship, and the necessity of a phase during which the women studies perspective manifests as a separate focus researching lost or supressed data on religion, are results of the pre-vailing conventional mind-set of most scholars. That mind-set utilizes an androcentric, one-sex model of humanity. The women and religion movement criticizes that model of humanity as inade-quate and offers instead a two-sex, androgynous model of humanity. All these terms need to be defined.

Definitions of androcentrism could easily be multiplied. While abstract discussions are important, a simple example has great power. How many times has one read or heard the equivalent of the following statement: "the Egyptians allow (or do not allow) women to. . . ."? The structure is so commonplace that even today many of my students have no clue about what is wrong with such a state-ment. For both those who make such statements and for those who hear them without wincing, "real Egyptians" are men. Egyptian women are objects acted upon by real Egyptians, but are not them-selves "Egyptians." What, in more analytical terms, is behind this long-standing habitual pattern of speech? The androcentric model of humanity has three central characteristics, which, when stated bluntly, suffice to demonstrate both the nature and the inadequacy of androcentrism.

First of all, in androcentric thought, the male norm and the hu-man norm are collapsed and become identical. In fact, recognition that maleness is but one facet of human experience is minimal or nonexistent. As deBeauvoir states:

In the midst of an abstract discussion it is vexing to hear a man say: You think thus and so because you are a woman," but I know that my only defense is to reply: "I think thus and so because it is true," thereby removing my subjective self from the argument. It would be out of the question to reply: "And you think the contrary because you are a man," for it is understood that the fact of being a man is no peculiarity. A man is in the right in being a man; it is the woman who is in the wrong. It amounts to this: just as for the ancients there was an absolute vertical with reference to which the oblique was defined, so there is an absolute human type, the mascu-line. Woman has ovaries, a uterus; these peculiarities imprison her in her subjectivity, circumscribe her within the limits of her own nature. It is often said that she thinks with her glands. Man superbly ignores the fact that his anatomy also includs glands, such as the testicles, and that they secrete hormones. He thinks of his body as a direct and normal connection with the world, which he believes he apprehends objectively, whereas he regards the body of woman as a hindrance, a prison, weighted down by everything peculiar to it.[6]

Thus in androcentric thinking maleness is normal; in addition, it is the norm. Any awareness of a distinction between maleness and humanity is clouded over and femaleness is viewed as an exception to the norm.

The second major characteristic of androcentrism follows directly from the first. If the male norm and the human norm are identical, it follows that the generic masculine habit of thought, language, and research will be assumed to be adequate. So we might say that scholarship dependent on the androcentric model of humanity utilizes generic masculine language. As a result, research about the religions of other times and places as well as about our own religious situation deals mainly with the lives and thinking of males. It seems unproblematic to include only a few stray comments about women's religious lives as a footnote or a short chapter toward the end of the book. The generic masculine habit of language, thought, and research is so prereflective and so strong that many scholars are genuinely unaware that one has studied only part of a religious situation if one has studied only the religious lives and thoughts of men. The need to present a full account of women and religion thoroughly integrated into the account of men and religion simply is not perceived. The generic masculine "covers" the feminine, as I was told by my mentors when I first questioned the completeness of conventional understandings of *homo religiosus.*

The problem, of course, it that it really does not, which brings up the third, and perhaps most problematic, aspect of androcentrism. The third constituent of the androcentric outlook is its attempt to deal with the fact that, since men and women are taught to be different in all cultures, the generic masculine simply does not cover the feminine. The generic masculine would work only in a religious-cultural situation where there were no gender roles, either explicit or implicit. That situation, of course, does not exist, not even in modern Christianity or Judaism, to say nothing of the religio-cultural situations of other times and places more normally investigated by the historian of religions. Therefore, women per se must sometimes be mentioned in accounts of religion. At this point, adherents of the androcentric model of humanity have reached a logical impasse. Their solution to this impasse is the most devastating component of the androcentric outlook. Because they differ from the male (presumably human) norm, women must be mentioned, at least in a cursory fashion. But because they deviate from these norms, when women, per se, are mentioned, androcentric thinking deals with them only as an object exterior to humankind, needing to be explained and fitted in somewhere, having the same epistemological and ontological status as trees, unicorns, deities, and other objects that must be discussed to make experience intelligible. Therefore, in most accounts of religion, males are presented as religious subjects, as "namers of reality,"[7] while females are presented only in relation to the males being studied, only as they appear to the males being studied.

As a corrective to this situation, a basic reorientation of the scholar's consciousness is called for. We need a basic paradigm shift from models of humanity and modes of research and thought that perceive males at the center and females on the edges to modes that perceive both females and males at the center and reflect the essential "femaleness-maleness" of androgynous humanity. That would be a "two-sex" model of humanity, as opposed to a "one-sex" model of humanity.

The most important aspect of what I have called "androgynous methodology" or the "androgynous model of humanity" is this characteristic of being a "two-sexed" or "bisexual" model of humanity. This concept requires clarification, for what I have in mind when I speak of androgynous models or methods differs considerably from both conventional notions of androcentric "mankind" and from the unisexual and sex-neutral meaning of androgyny that is popular at the present time.

What I mean by androgyny as a two-sex model of humanity and why such a model of humanity is mandatory should be clear from what has already been stated. First, to present the matter colloquially and informally, we may look at the alternative to stating that "the Egyptians allow women. . . ." A scholar who really understands the inadequacies of the androcentric model of humanity and the need for a more accurate, two-sexed model of humanity would write that in Egyptian society men do "X" and women do "Y," or perhaps, in some cases, she might write that "Egyptian men allow Egyptian women to . . . ," thereby recognizing both that Egyptian men have patriarchal control over the society and that Egyptian women are nevertheless Egyptian human beings, not an extrahuman species.

Very simply, we are in need of a model of humanity that accurately reflects two basic facts. First, biologically, for the most part humans are of one sex or the other, with little overlap at the most obvious level. Second, and even more important, the two-sexed bi ology of the human species is augmented and enhanced, rather than minimized by culture, society, and religion, so that today in all cultures, there is more stress on behaviors proper to and limited to one or the other sex than would be required by basic biology. As a result, men's and women's lives are more separate and different from each other than is biologically dictated. No scholarship prior to the current women studies movement has come close to dealing adequately with the sheer massive unyielding presence of such sex-role differentiation in all religio-cultural situations, which is the major reason why all previous scholarship and theology failed so abysmally to understand women and religion.

Therefore, clearly, a model of humanity is needed that compels recognition that humans come in two sexes and that both sexes are human, at the same time as it forbids placing one sex in the center and the other on the periphery. Androgyny as a two-sex model of humanity, as the notion that humanity is both female and male, meets those requirements, while traditional androcentrism and the sex-neutral model of humanity both fail completely. (By way of brief definition, a sex-neutral model of humanity is one that minimizes sexual differentiation, that regards distinct maleness and femaleness as irrelevant, and that urges pursuit of a "common humanity." While one could debate the utility of such a model of humanity as a prescription for the future, it is obviously quite useless as a guide to descriptions of the past or present.)

Clearly, these guidelines have enormous implications for scholarship, as well as for curriculum development, teaching methods, and textbook writing. It is impossible to overemphasize the subtle, sometimes not so subtle, changes in one's understanding of the basics of one's discipline that result. In the remainder of this discussion, I will spell out some of these shifts for major facets of religious studies. In each case, whether the subdiscipline is usually thought of as a descriptive discipline, like the history of religions, or a normative discipline like theology, I will attempt to show the interpenetrations of values and "objective" descriptions explicit in feminist scholarship. When this interpenetration becomes obvious in feminist scholarship, it immediately becomes equally obvious in the more conventional forms of scholarship, philosophy, and theology that we were taught to regard as neutral earlier in our academic training.

The implications of this transition from androcentrism to androgyny for religious studies are especially clear and important in three major subdisciplines. First, I will look at some of the implications for my "home" discipline, the cross-cultural and historical study of religions. For this discipline, the reforms at the level of data-gathering, reporting, and organizing are important. These reforms may seem to be only reforms in descriptive techniques, making the discipline more inclusive and accurate. However, reforms in description and organization of data motivated by this paradigm shift have a normative base and often encourage more speculative and critical evaluations than one expects from conventional historians of religion. Second, some of the implications of this paradigm shift for ethical questions will be explored. In this case, the discipline might seem more clearly normative, but recognizing that accurate descriptions of women's experience are important for dealing with ethical questions blurs the line once again. When cross-cultural data are brought into the matrix of decision-making, the lines become even more blurred. Finally, some of the manifold implications of this paradigm shift for theology, or attempts to discuss ultimate reality, will be surveyed. In this case, the mix of descriptive and normative perspectives is especially profound. On the one hand, many people want to think that theology is somehow beyond the messiness of human norms, that it is somehow more "objective" than all that. Theology is also the discipline, par excellence, that prescribes for people. Yet, upon analysis, no discipline in religious studies is more subject to the vagaries of culture, of historical epoch, and of gender, the latter unrecognized by all conventional scholarship and theology.

CROSS-CULTURAL AND HISTORICAL STUDIES: GUIDELINES FOR ANDROGYNOUS SCHOLARSHIP

In the so-called descriptive disciplines of religious studies, such as comparative and historical studies, the paradigm shift from androcentric to androgynous models of humanity, logically and rationally, should be unproblematic and unthreatening. Logically and rationally, it should also be welcomed as an obviously needed corrective that helps comparative and historical scholars do more accurate scholarship about their chosen specializations. After all, the paradigm shift does *not* directily challenge the scholar's private lifestyle or value system, as it might challenge that of the ethicist or the theologian. Especially in some segments of the academic world, a distance between the values of the scholar and the values presented by his subject matter is regarded as proof of objectivity. Thus, it is more conceivable to imagine that a comparative or historical scholar could do fine androgynous scholarship while living privately as a sexist patriarch than one can imagine an ethicist or a theologian living out such a dichotomy between life and scholarship.

However, much more important in my estimation, is the obvious fact that roughly half of the subjects studied by the comparativist or historian, no matter what his private politics of gender may be, are women. This fact makes it patently ridiculous to claim that one has a good grasp of a culture or a historical epoch if one has not included half the population in one's studies. That the scholar is studying a patriarchal, male-dominant situation, which is usually the case, is irrelevant to the claim that one needs to understand the women in that situation to understand the situation. One can and should study their roles within male dominant situations and how they cope with their position in male dominant societies, which is often extremely interesting. So the comparativist or historian has no grounds for excusing himself from androgynous scholarship by using the claim that his culture or period "doesn't have any important women in it."

Nevertheless, surprisingly, comparative and historical studies are at least as resistant to androgynous scholarship as the more obviously normative disciplines. In fact, my informed impression is that they are considerably behind the ethical and theological fields in internalizing and integrating the paradigm shift into norms and expectations for good scholarship in the field. I am somewhat at a loss to explain this phenomenon in a way that satisfies me completely, especially since the closely allied discipline of anthropology seems more attentive to the importance of studying women.[8] Some of the reasons may lie in the relatively low percentage of female scholars, and the even smaller percentage of feminist scholars in these fields, especially in my home discipline of the history of religions, which always remains something of a lightening rod for me in assessing this whole area of scholarship.

However, I suspect that the deeper reasons have to do with the fact that scholars who work with the androgynous model of humanity in descriptive studies have, for one reason or another, been pushed into a *personal* transformation of values and lifestyle from patriarchy to egalitarianism. The subject matter dealt with by comparative and historical scholars combined with the smaller percentages of women and feminists in these fields makes it easier for scholars to avoid this *internal* transformation. Lacking the internal transformation, they see little point in recasting their understanding of their fields, *especially if they are relatively established and escaped the women studies perspective in their early career training.* I am sure everyone can point to many such examples with ease. This analysis, if correct, strengthens my contentions regarding the inextricable linking of normative and descriptive concerns in all subfields within religious studies. The values and outlook of the descriptive scholar *do* affect his scholarship and choices of subject matter.

When pressed as to why they do not do androgynous scholarship, some scholars take refuge in two interrelated explanations for their male-centered approach. A frequent defense is that "we just don't have the information, the data, about women's lives and roles, so we can't do the kind of scholarship you are asking for." Such an explanation may have merit in the case of some topics of historical research, but it almost never justifies androcentric methods of research in contemporary cross-cultural, comparative studies. If necessary, the field research should be done over, but in many cases, as I know from my own research, the scholar working with an androgynous model of humanity will find much information about women *in standard library resources.* That information has been largely overlook by scholars with androcentric glasses. Furthermore, it has been largely interpreted as evidence that women are unimportant, minor participants in a male-dominant society—two assumptions that often prove false when the data are subjected to androgynous reconstruction.

Given my experience with various topics in cross-cultural studies, I am always suspicious when a historian tells me that the resources to say something about women's experience and roles simply cannot be found. However, it is imaginable that such situations do indeed exist. Then, however, the historian has another obligation and another method of doing androgynous scholarship. The omissions in the historical record can and should be pointed out, and explanations should be offered in terms of who kept the records. Then, at least the reader would know what is not known, but would need to be known if we were to have a reasonably accurate portrait of the historical materials being studied. We would also know that the scholar did try to do his homework and was aware that women need to be included in an adequate study.

A more insidious justification for not doing androgynous scholarship often involves some version of the "great works" thesis: "It would be nice to include something about women, but we *must* study all the great works of the period, all the really central ideas of a society, and, unfortuately, none of them were written by women. And there just isn't enough time to include less important materials. So what am I supposed to do?" The fundamental absurdity of this position is best seen by hearing what it sounds like when said in the context of another, rather foreign society. One commonly reads descriptions of religious events that affirm that an important ceremony must be attended by "all except women and children." Though for years, I too did not notice such statements, now the reaction is to question how important the ceremony can be if only significantly less than half the society is involved.

It may be objected that in the context of studying rituals of a less developed society, such a statement does indeed reflect an obvious value judgment and choice, whether made by the scholar or the society in question. (The society may *declare* this to be an "important ceremony" despite or because of the fact that women and children are not involved. Or the scholar may *interpret* this as to be an important ceremony.) But, on the contrary, some would argue, when dealing with great intellectual works of "advanced societies," selection for quality cannot be avoided. Therefore, these choices, it is claimed, have nothing to do with sexist values. "All the important and influential religious thinkers and leaders were men. That's just a fact, not a reflection of the scholar's androcentric outlook." For generations, such reasoning prevailed in academia. But femininist historians have begun to make a very strong case that the *choice* of what is interesting or important my already be influenced by androcentric and elitist values. *Why* are kings, wars, popes, and parliaments more interesting or important than ordinary people, peace, mystics, and domestic technology? For example, Eleanor McLaughlin suggests that historians of Christianity might well temper their interest in the history of theology and of church institutions, which is all I remember learning about in my church history graduate courses at the University of Chicago, with study of the world of spirituality. "In this world of spirituality . . . *women* are found who speak and write, who made history and shaped a tradition."[9] Yes, men do dominate the history of theology and of church institutions. But it is a *judgment* and a *choice*, rather than an objective datum, to conclude that these subjects are what one should study in the history of Christianity.

In fact, what is at stake is the common androcentric and patriarchal assumption that what women do is intrinsically less interesting and less important than what men do. What changes when those assumptions begin to break down? The androgynous paradigm demands that scholars be interested in women and what they do in the same way that we have always been interested in what men have done and thought.[10] When that paradigm shift begins to take effect, the result is not merely more information tacked onto the picture one already has. *In almost all cases, one discovers that one has to repaint the whole picture,* which may be why many scholars resist the paradigm shift. It is much more troublesome to repaint the picture than merely to fill in some details in a blank corner of the canvas.

For example, I have found in my own work on aboriginal Australian religions that many commonly made generalizations simply did not stand up under androgynous analysis of the materials. I am also convinced that the standard model for organizing the presentation of the Hindu pantheon, repeated in virtually every textbook or chapter on Hinduism, reflects an androcentric outlook, perhaps on the part of both Hindus and scholars of Hinduism. Feminist biblical scholars can easily and convincingly show us that many standard interpretation of key biblical passages that have prevailed for many generations are the result of an androcentric reading of the text.[11] I have already mentioned Eleanor McLaughlin's challenge to redefine the relevant subject matter of church history. Within the closely allied discipline of anthropology, the shift from androcentrism to androgyny has demolished the "man the hunter" hypothesis[12] and brought significant changes in methods of using primate behavior to hypothesize human evolution and early human behavior.[13] The list could be extended easily.

In sum, every subject that I have studied, whether thoroughly or superficially, *is thoroughly recast,* not just added onto, by androgynous scholarship. Thus, scholarship using the androgynous model of humanity is critical not only for *completeness* but also for *accuracy.* Without the paradigm shift, not only will we not have all the relevant data; we will not have accurate methods for organizing, understanding, and interpreting the data that we do have. So major issues are at stake in the call to study what women have done and thought as seriously as we have always studied what men have done and thought.

Fortunately, most scholars discover, once we concede that androgynous scholarship is necessary, that women are actually much more interesting to study and much more important in the society than was imagined by scholars working under androcentric models. Interestingly, this is the case for even the most male-dominated and patriarchal of societies. Doing androgynous scholarship does not turn out to be some form of academic punishment or exile after all. Or perhaps the judgment that women really are interesting and important is also part of the inevitably value-laden character of all scholarship. After all, at present, most scholars using androgynous methods and models are also feminists and many are women. And most of the androcentric scholars who find studying women uninteresting or unimportant also are men. Can we draw any conclusions about objectivity?

Though my question was, in part, facetious, other considerations regarding objectivity, scholarship, and values must be raised. Can one claim that androgynous scholarship is *better* than androcentric scholarship, or is one left merely stating that one *prefers* androgynous scholarship, perhaps because of one's own values? Recognizing the inevitably political content and implications of scholarship does not, in my view, make it impossible to distinguish better from worse scholarship. Less complete, less accurate scholarship is not as good as more accurate, more complete scholarship. Furthermore, I see no grounds on which one could reasonably argue that the androcentric model of humanity yields more complete and more accurate scholarship than the androgynous model. What one could argue is that some androgynous reconstructions of materials previously analyzed by androcentric scholars are wrong, inappropriate, ill-conceived, illogical, not based on a reasonable reading of the data. But one cannot argue that the *intention* to do androgynous scholarship is wrong or misguided.

In other words, in terms of my own work, some, or conceivably all, of my androgynous reconstruction of aboriginal Australian religion could be wrong, but the fundamental project is nevertheless on target because the androgynous model of humanity is superior to the androcentric model. (I should like to report, in passing, that a major recent field-based discussion of aboriginal women, done by a middle-aged female anthropologist, verifies many of the reconstructions I had suggested and contradicts none.[14] However, its author, who was obviously using androgynous methods, reports that some of her mentors were incredulous about her findings.)

Cross-cultural and historical studies that utilize androgynous methods often involve a much more serious and subtle question concerning the interpenetration of values and scholarship. Once we believe deeply that androgynous scholarship is superior to androcentric scholarship, can we study male dominant cultures and religions without passing judgment on them? Should we be obligated to study them without evaluating them? Does not our very organization and selection of data serve either to highlight or diminish the level of male dominance, thus portraying the religion either more "negatively" or "positivily" than "the facts" may warrent? (This is not to suggest that androcentric scholarship is any less prone to such problems of interpretation and emphasis. But since we are more used to its slant, we are less likely to notice it.)

The general guideline is easy to ascertain. Clearly, when we criticize androcentrism, we are criticizing *methods of scholarship* widely utilized by the scholar's discipline and culture. We are not passing judgment on the historical epoch or the culture being studied; we are not declaring it to be too patriarchal or admirably egalitarian in its values. Furthermore, there can be no easy passage from *studying* a historical epoch or another culture to the *utilizing those materials in one's own world construction*. These are two different enterprises; unless the lines dividing them are clearly delineated, massive misrepresentations will result. Furthermore, we can state that if one wishes to evaluate, it is most appropriate to criticize one's own cultural-religious situation and the scholarly methods derived from it, as is being done in this paper. It is slightly more difficult to evaluate the past of the situation with which one identifies, but also inevitable and appropriate. The most difficult cases are presented by one's studies of "the other," of a culture and religion with which one is not involved but which one studies and finds either exemplary or deplorable. These situations should not be taken as models or antimodels. One should not praise or blame such a context for its values and mores. But can one avoid such evaluations? Following these guidelines can be difficult, and becomes more difficult when one readily admits the normative and prescriptive dimensions found in all scholarship as well as the inevitable subtle self-interest of every scholar.

Perhaps we can more readily construct reasonable guidelines concerning this most difficult interface of descriptive scholarship and normative judgments by contrasting two instances of such scholarship. In *Gyn/Ecology,* Mary Daly includes long chapters on Hindu suttee, Chinese foot binding, African genital operations, and American medical practices, all of which she presents as evidence for "global patriarchy and gynecide."[15] In *Unspoken Worlds,* the chapter on tribal women in Iranian Islam leaves most readers depressed, while the chapter on the Empress Wu reconstructs this usually maligned leader sympathetically.[16] All these writings work with materials from "other" cultures and all of them give the reader a distinct impression as to the *value* or desirability of the phenomena being discussed. Yet I find Mary Daly's treatment of cross-cultural materials problematic, while I obviously find the treatments in *Unspoken Worlds* adequate, even exemplary. What is the difference? For me, a large part of the difference lies with the presence or absence of serious training and credentials to understand otherness empathetically. To use materials from another culture or historical epoch only to strengthen an already formulated hypothesis about gender is not acceptable. To understand and present "the other" empathetically, using androgynous methods and models, with the result that the reader is either repelled or attracted by "the other," is an entirely different enterprise.

My conclusions regarding the study of gender and religion in the cross-cultural and historical wings of the discipline will end with a discussion of the proper subject matters that should be discussed in any complete portrayal of a religion or culture. There are three distinctly separate areas that need to be reseached. Often in androcentric scholarship, the boundaries have been seriously blurred and the most important questions have been overlooked.

Androgynous scholarship stresses and requires, first and foremost, that the actual lives and thoughts of women be studied. Cultural stereotypes and normative laws *about* women cannot, under any circumstances, be substituted for the actual information about what women, in fact, do and think. What they are supposed to do, how they should feel, and the like, are merely cultural projections placed upon women. While interesting and important, they do not tell us about women's religious lives. Unfortunately, the topic of women's actual religious lives and thoughts can be very difficult to research, because it was often overlooked in androcentric scholarship. Nevertheless, this subject is interesting and quite complex, as the table of contents of *Unspoken Worlds* reveals.

If recognized for what it is, the subject of cultural stereotypes and norms about women is also extremely interesting and important. This material is also very easy to research, since men within and androcentric scholarship about the various religions have supplied us liberally with information about how women are supposed to behave and what they should feel and think about those required behaviors. Regarding this information, the critical task for androgynous scholarship is not collecting the data, but reconstructing the interpretations. Quite often, cultural projections about women and androcentric scholarly understandings of women's roles are at odds with androgynous analyses of these same materials. One need only compare the traditional Hindu law code, *The Laws of Manu*,[17] with Susan Wadley's interpretation of Hindu women's domestic rituals in *Unspoken Worlds*[18] to see a fundamental discrepancy between the attitudes women should have and the attitudes they do have. The standard interpretations of cultural attitudes are also often highly androcentric, as my own work on menstruation and childbirth as foci of aboriginal Australian religious concerns can demonstrate.

The record should also include various mythological and theological constructs of "the feminine," popularly known as "the goddess," which, in one form or another, are present in every religious situation. Like cultural stereotypes regarding women, goddesses are often quite easy to research. And, in keeping with androcentric values, they were usually presented to the interested readership as curious aberrations from the norm. A generation of feminist scholars, often without significant training in the study of "the other," has erased the possibility of seeing goddesses as aberrations. But frequently we still have little information, beyond stereotypes, about these goddesses. The most interesting topic of how symbolism of a divine feminine affects both women and men who affirm such images of the divine has not been researched in any significant way, despite the fact that a number of important commentators have expressed themselves strongly on the issue. Despite many books on goddesses,[19] this topic is a gold mine awaiting androgynous scholarship.

ANDROGYNOUS SCHOLARSHIP AND ETHICS: SOME FUNDAMENTAL QUESTIONS

Most scholars in religious studies think of ethics as a normative discipline. Comparativists and historians hardly deal with the topic; somehow, ritual behavior and belief systems dominate most accounts of the religions of other times and places. Ethical norms and ideals are often glossed over quite quickly. Ethicists, on the other hand, seem to pay little attention to what people *do* do, even within their own society; they seem much more interested in determining what they *should* do. To the ethicist, norms from other times and places seem less than central; therefore, cross-cultural and historical studies are usually peripheral to the discipline. Furthermore, if any discipline seems, at least superficially, to aim for abstract universal norms that apply to all humans without exception, despite various differences, it is ethics. At the outset, the need for androgynous ethical studies seems less obvious than the need for androgynous scholarship in cross-cultural and historical studies. And the inevitable blurring of descriptive and normative methods that I both describe and celebrate might seem unlikely.

As with the cross-cultural and historical dimensions of religious studies, other disciplines seem to be more advanced in their thinking regarding gender and ethics than are religious studies. References to important works in philosophy and psychology bear out this observation.[20] Also, as was the case for cross-cultural and historical aspects of religious studies, so in ethical studies, an uneasy, almost nameless feeling that the supposedly neutral and universal norms of ethical discourse simply were not accurate for women first encouraged questioning and questing. The effort "to name our own experience as women" probably was quite developed in the context of consciousness-raising groups well before professional religious ethicists took the question seriously.

For professional ethicists, two interlocking issues, both demanding that women's experience be taken seriously, predominate. First, it is necessary to determine *what women's experience is*. This can only be a *descriptive* task, without presupposition or bias about what women's experience is or should be, whether it is or should be the same as men's experience, and whether or not it conforms with stereotypes about the feminine. Because the first step in feminist ethical discourse must be a thoroughly descriptive exploration of women's experience, the solid line between so-called descriptive and normative disciplines again collapses. Second, it would be pointless to do descriptive analyses of women's experience if professional ethicists were not then willing to modify their conclusions about norms of morality, both public and private, in the light of those discoveries. To take women's experience seriously demands that it be considered *normal* and possibly *normative*, not an aberration from the norm or of no normative consequence.

As a result of this foray on the part of ethicists into descriptive studies and their willingness to take descriptive findings seriously, come other conclusions that would enrich the discipline of ethics immensely. Almost as a side effect of efforts to look into women's experience seriously, we will begin to have some idea of the specificity of men's experience as well, and some idea how it correlates with or deviates from norms of humanity. We need almost to coin and flesh out a new word—"masculinist—" to parallel "feminist." Under this rubric, we could explore experiences specific to men, either biologically or culturally, and determine their positive and negative implications for men, for women, for humanity as a whole. Because in androcentric scholarship, the difference between the masculine and the human has been so thoroughly glossed over and ignored, we discover almost as much about men as about women in androgynous scholarship. Male scholars have, however, been extremely slow to take up the cue, continuing to revel in disembodied attempts at "culture-free" and value-free" discourse. Fortunately, some very sensitive and insightful books on this topic are beginning to appear from religious ethicists.[21]

The feminist push to ground ethical norms in descriptive analysis could lead to a much more far-reaching and transformative result. Feminists often ground ethical discussion not only in discussions of women's experience in present cultural and religious situations, but also in a concern for women's situations in other times and places, as well as the less "mainline" elements of our own situation.[22] In other words, feminist ethicists are more open to cross-cultural studies than many other ethicists. It is very useful to feminist ethics to discuss the ethical norms of prepatriarchal societies and of societies in which patterns of power and equally are different from our own. Alternative views of the body, of sexuality, of the manifold dimensions of sexual ethics, and of work, society, and family can be challenging to ethicists. It is equally useful to feminist ethicists to study patterns of how women cope and find dignity in a variety of patriarchal situations. Unfortunately, however, because so few people are able to work in both ethical theory and cross-cultural studies, such scholarship proceeds at a painfully slow pace.

Nevertheless, this exploration into ethical concerns in cross-cultural perspective begun by feminist ethics has important potential for every ethicist. Ethics is an exercise in "world construction," surely an important concern for scholars in religious studies. Why those who engage in world construction should do so only out of expertise in culturally familiar resources has always puzzled me. Equally, it has puzzled me why those with expertise in culturally foreign materials should be reluctant, or even forbidden, on pain of exile from the company of respectable historians of religion, to engage in world construction. Thus, in another way, from another direction, I hope that androgynous ethical studies will foster a breakdown of the split between descriptive and normative studies in the field of religious studies.

The basic guidelines for androgynous ethical studies—that we must know what is women's experience and that we must take it seriously when suggesting ethical standards—contrasts signifi-

cantly with the two positions that prevailed in prefemininst literature, both popular and scholarly. Most of us were socialized,
academically as well as generally, under two conflicting, largely implicit assumptions regarding women and women's experience.

On the one hand, much in public education gave us the message
that "girls are just as capable as boys," a position known in more
sophisticated terminology as "liberal feminism," or "equal rights"
feminism (as opposed to radical feminism in its many variants).[23]
The older and more conservative position in feminist thought, this
position argues that women have never been given equal opportunity. If given equal opportunity, they will do just as well as men at
all male pursuits, from ship building to writing theology. This version of feminist ethical concern often sees the fundamental problem
as women's exclusion from the valuable tasks usually confined to
men. Thus, though this was not often noted by its proponents, the
liberal feminist position is often subtly androcentric. It does not
advocate major rethinking of basic norms and ideas commonplace
and longstanding in ethics or theology. These concerns and standards, until recently expected only of men, are taken to be adequate
and human. Women can measure up to them and should be judged
by them.

On the other hand, most of us also got another message, which
some of us did not listen to carefully. "Girls are different. There are
some things they just weren't intended to do." Commonly we ran
into some kind of academic "tree house" that had a not-so-subtle
sign across the door: "no girls allowed." We discovered that the liberal values went only so deep; beyond a certain point we were supposed to get the message and contentedly retire into femininity.
Most did, totally unaware that they had been coerced by socialization to drop out. For the very old gender hierarchy and gender du-
alisms were far more powerful than the superficially equal
educations given to boys and girls. The old gender hierarchy proclaimed that men have rights that women do not and the gender dualism gave men the public domain and taught women to value the
private. Sexual stereotypes proclaimed that, after all, women and
men *are* different—that is obvious! Women are intuitive, emotional, caring, nonjudgmental, peaceable. . . . These are also qualities that make women obviously inferior to men, especially in
handling power and important public or communal decisions,
though they do not disqualify women from homemaking. Furthermore, these "feminine" values and experiences have no place in
public policy and values. (Remember Geraldine Ferraro being ques-

tioned during her vice presidential campaign as to whether she was yet through menopause?)

Caught between the rock and the hard place of liberalism and traditional sexual hierarchy and dualism, feminists had no place to go but into another ethical position, at once more androgynous and more radical. Critical of liberalism's subtle androcentrism and rejecting traditional patriarchy, many began to suggest that women's experiences, at present, *are* usually different from men's. Furthermore, though disvalued by patriarchy, these "feminine" traits hold many of the keys to human wholeness and survival. Feminists began to question, not *whether* women could make it in "the system," but whether anyone *should* want to make it in the system, whether the system itself was not incomplete and perhaps very dangerous.

The position that gender differences are in some senses very real and have important ethical implications is, in my view, also potentially quite dangerous. As someone who benefited from and believed in the liberal position and regards any heavily deterministic approach to gender as oppressive, I came reluctantly to appreciate that a fully androgynous view in ethics would go beyond liberalism. Many, both feminists and nonfeminists, slide from recognizing that gender differences matter and are real into justifying limiting men and women to gender-determined attitudes and activities. Therefore, I contend that it is essential to state this position very clearly.

When gender differences are acknowledged and described, it must be emphasized that this is a descriptive, not a normative, exercise. That men and women are found to have certain differences does not mean that *maintaining* those differences is desirable or should be encouraged. However, as in cross-cultural studies, it is difficult to avoid the conclusion that currently women and men often do operate out of subtly different value systems. And it is difficult to avoid the conclusion that women's specific stances have been largely ignored and, when not ignored, dismissed as an aberration from the norm. In patriarchal thinking, to be "abnormal" is to be inferior. Thus, it is easy to understand the early feminist emphasis to minimize gender differences.

But other factors pushed scholars into more direct study of gender *differences*. When differences are focused upon, the major question is whether the discovered and documented differences are biological or cultural. No clear grounding of such differences in biology is sustainable, since variation within one gender of all measurable traits is far greater than the average difference between the genders. Thus, one could not reasonably advocate limiting people to gender-specific tasks and traits on the basis of averages from which individuals may differ significantly. However, both some radical feminists and radical patriarchs strongly ground their pronouncements in biological determinism. Sociobiology is perhaps the most sophisticated scholarly restatement of traditional patriarchy.[24] But some femininsts also use biological determinism to argue that men's innate propensity to aggression, based on their hormonal levels, renders them inevitably dangerous and antisocial.[25] No matter by whom it is used, that conclusion seems dangerous to me. Given current knowledge, it is more appropriate to regard both measurable and more subtle gender differences as due to cultural factors, especially child rearing patterns and gender-role socialization. Such a position both acknowledges the existence of present gender differences and avoids biological determinism.

Regarding present gender differences, the most appropriate conclusion is that gender differences do, in broad outline, follow conventional stereotypes. Women do, on the average, value different things than do men, do react differently. The most influential and scholarly discussion of this thesis has been the work of Carol Gilligan.[26] She demonstrates how, in ethical decision-making situations, girls and women tend to prefer and choose decisions that focus on the well-being of all parties rather than abstract justice. She also demonstrates how these choices were interpreted by other theorists as demonstrations of women's inferior ethical sensibilities, a conclusion she cogently rejects.

Gilligan, and many others, have gone on to draw unconventional conclusions about these "feminine" values and traits. They are not dualistically inferior because they are different. They are valuable *human* traits, essential for life on the planet. Certainly it is very easy to see that the typical women's values of connection and relatedness are at least as vital and valuable as separateness, individuality, and strength. In fact these stereotypical male and public values sound less valuable when they are relabeled devisiveness, alienation, and aggression. However, this new feminist and androgynous ethic goes further. Patriarchy has always valued the feminine traits, *for women and as values regulating private life.* Androgynous ethics insists that the "feminine" values are essential to constructing sane public policy, to constructing ethical theory, theology, art, and all other expressions of human existence. Furthermore, these ethicists tend to expect that in an androgynous society, such valued "feminine" traits will not be limited to women.

If the stereotypical "feminine values" were to become values of public culture, of the society at large, not merely the private realm, what might we expect to change in our common conceptions of morality? At present, I envision three major areas of revalorization. In my own work, they emerge in connection with my femininist analyses of Buddhism, but they are widespread in femininist ethics.

A most saluatory effect of regarding women's values as important values for general physical, psychological, and spiritual well-being would be the recognition that nurturing, relatedness, and caring are necessary for human survival. As such, they would be values, encouraged, and rewarded in our public policy and institutions. Recognizing the centrality of these concerns, it would be impossible to regard spiritual achievement as a lonely, individual quest, or to suggest that spiritual accomplishment is an antisocial task of renouncing human companionship. Such a revalorization would suggest that even in the most radically world denying spiritual traditions, the matrix of human community and caring is, in fact, absolutely essential to the spiritual attainments of its celebrated heroes, though the spiritual tradition may be oblivious, or even hostile, to such considerations. Such a revalorization would emphasize that experiences of companionship and community are central to genuine spiritual experience. Therefore, it will be suggested, skills in being a faithful friend and in reciprocating friendship will be as important in spiritual cultivation as one's meditation, contemplation, or intellectual understanding of the tradition. In short, what is now considered a private concern of little spiritual value, one's life embedded in the matrix of human relatedness, will become an essential aspect of life. It will no longer be regarded as of concern only in one's unimportant private life. Consequently, it will be a central facet in spirituality. In my own work as a Buddhist feminist, I have been advocating just such a revalorization of the third of the three refuges, the refuge of Sangha or community, which, in my estimation, has been seriously and consistently undervalued in Buddhism.[27]

Many feminist ethicists also expect that certain major current public concerns would be significantly revalorized if stereotypical women's values and concerns were taken more seriously. Problems most often cited as linked with the current masculinist values and biases include run-away rampant militarism; wanton, wholesale environmental destruction; and massive global poverty and injustice. In this critique, it is important to note that the critical factor is not putting women instead of men into power, but a transvaluation of values. It is easy to see how alienation, individualism, and aggression result in the current negative and destructive policies of militarism, environmental exploitation, and human oppression. It is also easy to see that values emphasizing relatedness, interdependence, and community among all humans and between humans and the planet would benefit everyone. To call the latter values "feminist" would be agreed upon by most; to call the former set of values "masculinist" would be resisted by many, who might not even recognize them as the current dominant public values. Yet the case has been made convincingly by many, both women and men.

The third major revalorization is linked with the second. Though usually discussed as a theological rather than an ethical issue, some of the most creative and profound feminist thought in religious studies has pointed out that the feminist position argues for a theological and ethical acceptance of finitude.[28] These writers, including Ruether and Christ, have pointed out that the traditional quest in classical Western thought is to escape, usually put as "to transcend," the limits of embodied, mortal, finite human existence by identifying with a transcendent other and its demands. In her many analyses of classical dualism in Western religious thought, Rosemary Ruether has successfully demonstrated that the allegiance to spirit, transcendence, and immorality has had extremely negative repercussions for women, who are linked with the despised finite body. In her book *Laughter of Aphrodite*, Carol Christ then links this despising of finitude with militarism, classism, and environmentally dangerous policies.[29] Because this link seems cogent to me, I feel that it is important to see acceptance of finitude as an *ethical*, as well as a theological, issue.

But why is acceptance of finitude a *feminist* issue? Perhaps because feminist theologians have so consistently brought it up as a major issue. Why? Classical Buddhist though provides perhaps the most succinct definition of finitude—a definition not heretofore used by feminist ethicists, but one which would be useful in their discussions. To be related is be interdependent. To be interdependent is to lack "own-being," to be unable to transcend the matrix—that is to say, to be finite. Buddhism asserts that all things without exception lack own-being and are finite. To accept that finitude is the only possible freedom. In the West, where embracing finitude is still something of a heresy, feminist or androgynous ethicists, who consciously and conspicuously do value embodiedness and relatedness, make the same logical connection between affirming relatedness and affirming finitude. They also then draw the ethical consequences of that affirmation.

After this brief discussion, it becomes clear that taking seriously the stereotypical "feminine" values and experiences as guidelines for important public concerns would lead to a transvaluation of many concerns. But it remains to question how these values could come to be taken seriously, or even articulated. Part of that question has already been dealt with, in the emphasis on studying and describing women's experiences. Part of this enterprise clearly involves women "naming their own reality," which has never been done in androcentric systems. I would emphasize the extent to which it also involves study of prepatriarchal situations, for the reality that patriarchy is a historical discovery, not a biological given is profoundly important in these ethical stances.[30] Finally, to study and name women's experiences must include widespread cross-cultural studies.

But let us leap ahead to the time when we have a good account of women's experiences and values. For those accurate accounts of women's experiences to make much difference, *simultaneously* with expanding knowledge about women's experiences and values, an *increasingly androgynous* life-style will be necessary. That is to say, the more seriously we take women's experiences and values, the less we would restrict and confine them to women. As we see ever more clearly their value and dignity for women and no longer denigrate them as inferior, we see their *human* value. In an androgynous life-style, individuals retain sexual identity, but gender roles cease to be determinative, thus freeing everyone to manifest the human traits for which they have innate talent. This last point is crucially important, for one would not want the effect of recognizing the value of traditional "femininity" to be reinforcement of the prison of gender roles. That too is an ethical matter of ultimate significance for any postpatriarchal but nonseparatist social situation—the only kind of society that offers any hope for the human future.

ANDROGYNY AND THEOLOGY:
THE IMMOVABLE OBJECT MEETS THE IRRESISTIBLE FORCE

The immense topic of feminist theology will not be fully surveyed in this paper. For it is in connection with the queen of the sciences—theology—that the paradigm shift from androcentrism to androgyny has most fully been articulated in religious studies. I am especially interested, as someone with primary training in the history of religions, in how feminist theology could demonstrate or foster dissolving the line between "descriptive" and "normative" disciplines within religious studies. Therefore, I will discuss issues of method in theology and history of religions more directly and will be less directly concerned with the paradigm shift in this section of this paper. I will argue that the most successful androgynous theology would require a blurring of the usual concerns and resources of the theologian and the historian of religions, and will discuss this blurring from the point of view of both disciplines. I will also critique feminist theology for not going far enough into this interdisciplinary task.

To begin, in my view feminist theology has already demonstrated incontrovertibly the extent to which in theology, as in cross-cultural studies and in ethics, one's experience inevitably colors and conditions one's conclusions. In fact, the watchword and rallying cry of early feminist theology was the question of whether conventional theology speaks to women's experience.[31] The answer is a resounding no! A huge body of literature meant to fill the gap.

Though I agree with the conclusion, I would arrive at it by perhaps different methods than would a theologian, due to my stance as a historian of religions. In an approach to religious studies that does not differentiate so sharply between theology and the history of religions, my method of deriving the familiar conclusion of feminist theology may be important. The matter is quite simple. One must first approach theological systems, whether from one's own heritage or the theological symbol systems created by foreign cultures, as *data*, as religious phenomena that one is investigating using the rules of academic scholarship, especially the rules that govern study of cross-cultural or historical phenomena. One simply cannot *begin* to engage in world construction, to evaluate, or to suggest norms for thought or behavior without this kind of empirical study as a basis for one's conclusions. To do otherwise is to engage in an endless circle of apology and unreasonably to privilege one's favorite data from ordinary methods of analysis and evaluation.

Today any good theologian must begin as a historian of religions, must be cognizant of the methods and conclusions of that discipline. Minimally this is the case for the tradition out of which and within which one wishes to theologize. However, I would argue very strongly, as strongly as possible, that there is little excuse, reason, or justification for any contemporary theologian not to be reasonably competent in a tradition that is "other" to the theologian. I would make this argument for two reasons: on the one hand, nothing is so radically relativizing and deabsolutizing as use of "the comparative mirror."[32] On the other hand, any theology would be much richer and more interesting for having input from "other," nontraditional resources. Let us look at these two arguments in turn. In an excellent and highly recommended book, *Religious Worlds: The Comparative Study of Religion*, William Paden has written:

"The comparative study of religion invites self-reflection about the nature of our own cultural systems. Comparative perspective provides a context for the perception of our immediate world. . . . Our own world, instead of being taken for granted, becomes exposed *as* a world, its contents get held up to the comparative mirror, and we become a phenomenon to ourselves."[33]

In this exercise, we cannot help but see the radical historicity of all religious constructs, cannot help but see them reflecting their historical-cultural settings. This experience is especially saluatory for theology precisely because many hope that somehow this discipline can offer some refuge from the all-pervasive "conceptual relativity and cultural pluralism"[34] that characterize our situation. Many hope that, while human institutions, such as the church and the academy may be corrupted by bias and self-interest, religious concepts and symbols of ultimate reality undercut and criticize such bias, rather than participate in it. Such is the expectation and hope of many, especially at the beginning of their journey into consciousness, including feminist consciousness. Nothing is so effective as the comparative mirror in demonstrating that concepts and symbols of ultimate reality are extraordinarily shifty and evanescent, subject to cultural conditioning, dependent on relative worldviews, and liable to promote some interests against others. Theology does not provide some safe haven beyond androcentric distortions. Androgynous consciousness lays bare the entire edifece of familiar theology as a male projection—and as a system whose androcentrism has made it dangerously aggressive, hierarchical, and authoritarian.

Even without much use of the comparative mirror, feminist theologians have demonstrated the androcentrism of familiar theological constructs. With the use of cross-cultural studies, the conclusion would be less painful and more obvious, especially to the theologian not familiar with feminist theology, who may feel threatened by its conclusions. If theological constructs have been deabsolutized by use of the comparative mirror and the theologian is familiar with symbols as projections, at least at some level, then it would not be surprising that the gender is one of the factors that influences the process of theologizing. The theologian would then be prepared to make the same conclusion that the ethicist or the comparative historical scholar must make. The androgynous model of humanity makes for better scholarship and theology than does the androcentric model. In fact, continuing to do theology without thoroughly internalizing the androgynous model of humanity would be recognized as a highly questionable enterprise.

However, the deconstructive, deabsolutizing side of the story is not the only effect of using the comparative mirror. Deabsolutizing one's world provides the matrix of freedom in which to use the comparative mirror further. One is no longer limited by or confined to the culturally familiar set of symbols and myths as one's resources with which to think, to engage in world construction. Given conceptual relativity and cultural pluralism, there is no priviledged set of symbols that anyone should or must use. When one is working on a specific human problem, one need not deprive one's self of any resources that have been used to think about that problem, whatever their cultural source. One might be as instructed by Hindu as by Christian symbols, for example. One need only be thoroughly grounded in scholarly understandings of the symbols one uses. Under such conditions, the reasons for a theologian to be well-trained in cross-cultural studies become overriding. However, the comparative mirror has not been used extensively by feminist theologians, either in deconstruction of andromorphic symbols or in reconstruction of androgynous symbols.

Clearly, the suggestion that one might use the comparative mirror, not only to deabsolutize specific symbols, but also to provide resources with which to think about human existence, has again taken us from descriptive to normative aspects of religious studies. This use of the comparative mirror is somewhat new, both for the scholar originally trained in theology and the scholar based in history of religions. I will conclude this paper with some comments on this use of the comparative mirror, first on the part of the "theologian" and then on the part of the "historian of religions."

Of the many topics important to feminist theology, I have long felt that symbols and constructs of ultimacy are the most interesting and important topic. Understood and used properly, such mythic images are very powerful self-revealing and self-correcting projections. We can learn a great deal about the values and assumptions of cultures, people, and theologians by listening to their God talk. In that sense, God talk is revealing. But used self-consciously and deliberately, God talk can also become a corective for androcentrism, racism, and other unpalatable opinions. In that sense, God talk is a corrective. A theologian familiar with the data of world religions will marvel at the variety of languages about ultimacy available, will be able quite readily to see that, in Tillich's apt phrase, " 'god' is a symbol for god,"[35] and consequently, will be willing to "play" with such images and symbols. And the comparative mirror furnishes many wonderful "playthings."

In the play with symbols and images of ultimacy, a major point seems to me to be worth making. I have often made this point, particularly in the context of Buddhist-Christian dialogue, but theologians less familiar with the history of religions seemto ignore it.[36] The languages of myth, symbol, image, and icon are extremely basic, important, and communicative. They need to be rediscovered and untilized much more in theological discourse, including feminist theological discourse. In mythic God talk, it is impossible, fortunately, to become so abstract that people could ignore the reality that they created an extremely andromorphic God symbol who is said, nevertheless, to be nonsexual and beyond gender, even though he is offended by female references but is comfortable with male pronouns. Such clarity would defuse both popular and sophisticated resistances to androgynous theologizing.

Add to this insight more fuel from the comparative mirror. Often it is overwhelming to people's consciousnesses fully to recognize that God talk about a deity who is personal and andromorphic but not (or barely) gynemorphic *is extremely rare.* Only monotheistic religions have this habit at all, and even in them, there is a recurrent tendency toward covert, sometimes overt, androgynous imagery of deity. As I have often argued, the question is not, "Why do other religions have goddesses?" That is normal and the norm. The question is, "Why did monotheism attempt to get rid of goddesses?" Could it have anything to do with androcentrism and patriarchy? Feminist studies of the Ancient Near East make it overwhelmingly obvious that such is the case.[37] It should be noted, however, that I am not arguing, as might some feminists not sufficiently versed in the data provided by the comparative mirror, that a religion with goddesses *will* be egalitarian. Hinduism is both patriarchal and replete with goddesses. I am only arguing that a religion *without* goddesses will inevitably be androcentric and patriarchal.

A further point needs to be made regarding the use of symbols, metaphors, and myths in androgynous theologizing. While philosophical feminist theology may be quite insightful in an abstract way, by themselves additional or alternative feminist abstractions will not be a sufficient corrective to the conventional abstract, but nevertheless andromorphic God talk. They are quite powerless to undo all the preconceptual and emotional conditioning programed into people by the socialization into a patriarchal religion. Only remythologization in an androgynous fashion, which would include the divine feminine, can solve this problem in any widespread, practical way. Nothing would be so salutary as the simplicity and directness of androgynous mythic images and symbols, which would be empowering for both women and men. One needs to consider well that an abstract ultimate transcending gender, said to be neither male nor female, is only half the story. Such language works well on the absolute level, but by itself has never been sufficient to foster egalitarian practices in the day-to-day relative world.[38] The other half of the story is an everyday familiar image of an ultimate other who is both female and male, as are the humans who symbolize ultimate reality in myriad and diverse ways.

Yet feminist theology, by and large, with some important exceptions, has not taken the route of remythologization but of abstraction.[39] Furthermore, at the more practical level of liturgical reforms, people working within the context of the monotheisms continue that tendency in their reconstructions of images in liturgy. Though the *Inclusive Language Lectionary* does change "God the Father" to "God the Father [*and Mother*],"[40] I have heard many an instance of that phrase turning into "God the Parent." Even many of the options chosen by the *Inclusive Language Lectionary* are more sex neutral than androgynous. But, as I argued many years ago:

> Some who argue for an impersonal God language do so because, while they recognize the limitations of "God-He," they find "God-She" too degrading and unnatural to consider. Deliberately saying "God-She" makes it impossible to mask or hide one's unconscious sexism behind abstract language.[41]

Are there examples of and guidelines for such nonabstract remythologizing? I would point to the work of Carol Christ and Christine Downing, and to some who write of feminist wicca as examples of religious thinkers who have been very daring in their attempts to remythologize divine androgyny.[42] Their work is also challenging and provocative, providing genuinely new ways to look at familiar religious questions. It is important to notice that these two thinkers have also been most willing, among feminist theologians, to make extensive use of the comparative mirror, though their examples are limited to classical Western antiquity. Most probably, there is some connection between their openness to the comparative mirror and their success with androgynous resymbolization. Given the immense lack of such feminine images in familiar religious resources and the richness of feminine imagery available in the comparative mirror, I have always been amazed that feminist theologians use the comparative mirror so sparingly. This tendency must go back to the proclivity of theologians to privilege culturally familiar religious concepts and resources in their world constructions.

My own work with Hindu goddesses and with the feminine principle in Buddhism is the only sustained use of non-Western materials in feminist theology with which I am familiar.[43] The clues and suggestions put forth in those articles have not been widely utilized, however. Nevertheless, I still consider them to be quite relevant to the issues under discussion. Therefore, I will quote, not the specific images I utilized nor the implications for androgynous remythologizing that I see in them, since space does not allow for that, but some of the guidelines for responsible use of a culturally distant comparative mirror:

> I am not suggesting that everyone read a half-dozen books on the Hindu deities and then attempt to utilize the imagery of the Hindu Goddesses in feminist theology. It is much more complex than that, and the Hindu materials are readily susceptible to misinterpretation, both positive and negative. . . . My task is a truly double-edged one. On the one hand, my primary intended audience is feminist theology, not Indology. I intend to *utilize* my conclusions about Hindu materials as a resource for re-imaging the Goddess, not to demonstrate their validity to other scholars of Hinduism. Nor am I attempting a complete description of the Goddesses, either in terms of their historical development or in terms of their contemporary manifestations, since I am looking for useful resources. . . . On the other hand, I am not interested in misrepresenting the Hindu materials for the cause of feminist theology. I am comfortable utilizing only sound conclusions about the symbol-

ism connected with the Hindu Goddesses as suggestions for re-imaging the Goddess. I am suggesting that some real scholarly competence with these materials is a prerequisite, but I am also suggesting that if approached critically and carefully, and if intelligent selection and borrowing are utilized, the Hindu Goddesses are the greatest stimulant to our imagination and to our speculation about the meaning of the Goddess that I have encountered."[44]

Such comments serve as a transition from suggesting that theologians make wider use of the comparative mirror to guidelines for historians of religion engaging in world construction. As I argued in the second section of this paper, in my view, historians of religion always operate out of a value system that affects what they see and how they present their conclusions. The very existence of the cross-cultural comparative approach to religion is a value-laden choice and a rejection of previous approaches to religions.[45] While historians of religion do not usually engage in hierarchic evaluations of religions vis-à-vis each other, it is clear that we reject apologetic justifications of any specific religion as inappropriate. We clearly presuppose that empathetic and accurate presentations of religious points of view are superior to approval or disapproval of religion, depending on similarity to one's own culture. It is time for historians of religion to be much more up-front about these values.

Acknowledging these values basic to history of religions and acknowledging that methodological stances always include values encourages us to take responsibility, in a pluralistic but strife-ridden world, to use the comparative mirror to promote community rather than disunity. After all, the virtue that recommends the history of religions approach is not only that it provides *more accurate* knowledge but that those who have this accurate knowledge about "the other" are more equipped to live in a pluralistic world.[46] There is little other reason for state universities to employ historians of religion to teach undergraduates about Hindu mythology, for example. Furthermore, I would contend that the major reason to spend one's life studying and teaching the history of religions is not merely for the pure accurate knowledge but to promote empathy and respect in a pluralistic world. However, we historians of religion will rarely admit to or talk about such an openly ethical and theological dimension to our work. Some purists are even wont to emphasize that we study other peoples' world construction but do not engage in such work ourselves. However, only a specific world construction allows us pursue our discipline at all. Furthermore, we construct a world every time we construct a course in religion or write an article "about" some phenomenon. So we might as well do it self-consciously and openly.

Once we admit that we do engage in world construction, we can go further. I often feel that historians of religions, who know so much about other cultures and religions, are especially obligated to comment upon, even to evaluate, that about which they know so much. What religious attitudes, phenomena, symbols, or rituals tend to promote a humane world and thus should be encouraged? What attitudes, phenomena, symbols of rituals tend to promote oppression, war, exploitation, or sexism, and therefore should be discouraged? Why are we generally so timid about such questions? In my experience, seeing and naming the androcentric bias in history of religions methodology was only the beginning of a long process of looking into, not only values implicit in the methodological stance of the discipline, but values inherent in the phenomena studied by the discipline. Which of these values serve humane living? Which should we foster? Which ones should we omit from serious consideration? Which ones should we hold up as glaringly deficient in the comparative mirror in which all religious phenomena are ultimately ours and none are ultimately "other"?

I should like to suggest two modes in which the historian of religions might be involved in world construction, and I will present them in terms of work in which I am involved. A historian of religions who engages in world construction need not do so from within a specific religious tradition. My work on Hindu goddesses as resources for Jewish and Christian theology, as well as my work on monotheism and religious diversity, illustrate this possibility. Identifying myself as neither a Hindu nor a monotheist, I nevertheless point out problems, tendencies, needs, and correctives in these perspectives. A historian of religions, deeply familiar with the grammar of symbols, both generally and specifically, can point out that certain symbols go with certain social realities, and that if one wants to promote more humane social realities, specific symbols might be useful. Thus, for example, I suggested six basic images found in connection with Hindu goddesses as useful resources for anyone who wishes to think about the divine feminine as a corrective to patriarchal religion. Correcting patriarchy, I would suggest, is the responsibility of anyone, including historians of religion, who should utilize their vast knowledge to help accomplish this task.

Possibly a historian of religions might also engage in world construction in the context of a religion with which she identifies. For a good historian of religions, this identification would not alter the results of one's scholarship, but it might deepen the passion and the sharpness of one's analysis, as well as explain one's choice of subject matter and emphases. For example, my work on women or feminism and Buddhism[47] grows out of my own involvement with Buddhism, which I have not tried to hide for some time now, as well my own stance as a feminist. In this work, I seek accurate information about women and feminine symbols in Buddhist history. It is important in that account not to gloss over or explain away Buddhist discrimination against or negative stereotypes about women, but it is also important not to blacken the picture out of frustration. In the midst of seeking that balance, I also seek a "usable past," to return to the quotation from Eleanor McClaughlin cited earlier,[48] seeking to do historical scholarship that is at once responsible and usable, in her terms. Beyond such studies of Buddhism as a historical phenomenon, I engage in critical analyses of key Buddhist concepts, asking whether or not they promote sexual hierarchy or egalitarianism. A nonfeminist Buddhalogist or historian of religions might not think to ask that question, but a scholar using androgynous models must, especially in view of Buddhism's repeated lapses into patriarchal practices. Finally, expressing dissatisfaction with Buddhism as currently constituted, I suggest feminist reconstructions of Buddhism, drawing upon my knowledge of Western religion! A non-Buddhist historian of religions would probably not care to become involved in that task. Certainly such work is beyond the conventional repetoire of the historian of religions. But I would contend that such reticence is not an especially responsible use of the knowledge a historian of religions has amassed. Not all historians of religion will want to go so far. But to do so should not be grounds for excommunication from the sacred company of reputable historians of religion.

At this point of analysis and reflection, however, we have definitely accomplished one of the goals set forth at the beginning of this paper. The very thick line dividing descriptive and normative approaches to the study of religion has faded, if not disappeared. Instead, we have a mutual transformation between theology and the history of religions, perhaps parallel to the mutual transformation between religions traditions in dialogue with each other that has been discussed by John Cobb,[49] among others. In neither case does such mutual transformation involve mindless borrowing or deliberate syncretism—a "good parts" artificial synthesis of the disparate traditions. Rather, filtered through dispassionate and passionate minds concerned with understanding at its fullest, these various ways of understanding have mutually transformed each other to the point that neat dotted lines cannot separate them. For this occur, we need theologians who know a lot about several traditions and are not provincial in their use of symbols with which to engage in world construction. And we need historians of religion who not only know a lot about a lot, but are willing to *think with* what they *know about*—to admit that, since world construction is inevitable, we may as well construct the right worlds. For both, taking up this task requires courage and clear-sighted vision.[50]

NOTES

INTRODUCTION

1 "Agreed Statement of the Anglican–Roman Catholic Dialogue of Canada on the Experience of the Ministries of Women in Canada," *Ecumenism*, no. 103, September 1991, 4–5.

2 "Agreed Statement," 7, 9.

3 Bonnie Brennan, "Catholic women: What progress have they made?," *Toronto Star* (Aug. 3, 1991), J10.

4 Ibid.

5 "Agreed Statement," 6–7.

6 Ibid., 15–16.

7 Ibid., 16–17.

8 See Katharina von Kellenbach, *Anti-Judaism in Christian-Rooted Feminist Writings: An Analysis of Major U.S. American and West German Feminist Theologians* (Ann Arbor: UNI, 1987).

9 I would like to thank my colleague Arvind Sharma for suggesting the application of Victor's Turner's theory of liminality and communitas to the analysis at hand.

10 Amrita Chhachhi, "The State, Religious Fundamentalism and Women—Trends in South Asia," *Economic and Political Weekly*, March 18, 1989, 567–78.

11 Ibid., 575.

12 Ibid., 573.

13 Peggy Reeves Sanday, *Female Power and Male Dominance: On the origins of sexual inequality* (Cambridge: Cambridge University Press, 1981), 253–54.

ABORIGINAL WOMEN'S RELIGION

1   This article draws substantially on the Central Australian ethnography
     presented in *Daughters of the Dreaming* (1983) and I gratefully ac-
     knowledge permission of George Allen and Unwin to reprint the ma-
     terial. In writing of women's religious beliefs and practices, one walks
     a fine line, for much is secret. I have consulted (and continue to con-
     sult) with the women who are the "owners" of the knowledge dis-
     cussed here. I am using only material that the women with whom I
     worked have cleared as "open" knowledge. Recently in Australia there
     have been objections raised by certain urban Aboriginal women, re-
     garding the propriety of anyone other than Aboriginal women writing
     about certain matters—this was with reference to rape—but on other
     occasions has included religion and already published material (Bell
     and Nelson 1989, 415 n2). There are problems with descriptions of cer-
     emonies in earlier works and I have avoided direct quotations from
     sources other than those I know to be "open."
2   The Kaytej, Warlpiri, and Warlmanpa land claim was heard before Mr.
     Justice Toohey in 1981. Under the *Aboriginal Land Rights (Northern
     Territory) Act* 1976, title to Aboriginal reserves was transferred to Ab-
     origines and the conditions under which Aborigines could make claim
     to vacant crown land (and land in which all interests were held by, or on
     behalf of Aborigines) were specified. Under the act, Aborigines must
     demonstrate that they satisfy the criteria of traditional ownership and
     this entails presenting evidence of spiritual responsibility and affilia-
     tions to the land and its sites. The claims are heard before a judge who
     sits as the Aboriginal Land Commissioner.
3   See Rohrlich-Leavitt (1975); Bell (1983a, 229–46); Gross (1987) for lit-
     erature reviews from feminist perspectives; and compare Merlan
     (1988). Phyllis Kaberry (1939) provided the first monograph on Aborig-
     inal women in which she presented important data on women's cere-
     monies in the Kimberley region of western Australia, as closed, secret,
     and sustaining, and a refutation of Durkheim's dichotomy as promoted
     by Lloyd Warner (1937). However, Elkin, writing the preface to Kaberry's
     work (xxix-xxx), significantly undercuts her analysis (see Bell 1990, 12–
     15). In various articles Catherine Berndt (1950; 1965), presents material
     on women's closed, secret ceremonies across northern and western
     Australia and also engaged with Durkheim. Jane Goodale (1971) de-
     tailed Tiwi ceremonies and her final chapter explores male and female
     worldviews. Nancy Munn's (1973/86) symbolic analysis of desert ico-
     nography, offers much regarding women's ceremonial life, but privi-
     leges the male experience. Annette Hamilton (1979; 1987), working
     with Pitjantjatjarra in the western desert, has explored the impediment
     to consolidation of male power represented by women's secret ritual
     and indicated the ways in which men seek to infiltrate women's
     worlds. In the last decade or so, a number of women have begun or

completed Ph.D.'s and some have begun to publish: Victoria Burbank (1989), Gillian Cowlishaw (1979), Françoise Dussart (1988), Barbara Glowczewski (1983), André Grau (1983), Jan Lauridsen (1990), Helen Payne (1988), Deborah Bird Rose (1984). Few have engaged with feminist questions or written explicitly situated ethnographies.

4   Kaberry (1939) and Goodale (1971), for instance, presented theirs in the format of a life cycle. In this context one should note that Hart and Pilling's *The Tiwi* (1960) remains *the* ethnography although it is based on work with men. Similarly Mervyn Meggitt's *Desert People* (1962) although about men is *the* desert ethnography.

5   When Rita Gross (1987, 41–42) surveyed the Australian literature, she noted that there were many interpretations, but scanty fieldwork. This is indicative of the slow filtering of Australian material to international markets, but also of the way in which what exists is classified. For instance, in the catalogue of the AIAS, the major research funding body in Australia, there is no category for women (Hill and Barlow, 1985). In other bibliographic sources I find my work classified under "social change," "special problems," "welfare."

6   Unfortunately Annette Hamilton's (1979) Ph.D., which is a most exacting analysis of the shifting ground on which ethnographic observations were made at the time of first contacts in the western desert, remains unpublished. Hamilton (1987) offers a glimpse of this material. See Leacock (1978); Bell (1980; 1983a, 41–106, 246–50; 1988b) for other ethnographic examples.

7   In his review of the literature addressing the study of Aboriginal religion, Stanner (1987) noted that a worldview is hard to dislodge, and even in the face of strong evidence to the contrary, scholars continued to write of Aborigines as primitives with nothing worthy of the name religion. The critical edge of anthropology has dug deeper in ethnocentrism than sexism, and feminist anthropologists are now exploring the intersection of gender and race (Moore, 1988). The theoretical preoccupations, research design, and the nature of the discipline in Australia have all conspired to relegate women to a position of marginality within Aboriginal society and within the discipline (Bell, 1983a; 1984).

8   Hawkeworth's (1989, 535) critique of the divergent arguments concerning the premises of a feminist epistemology, points to the need to move beyond merely declaring interest and bias, to questioning the bases of our knowledge, but is troubled by the tensions this presents for a feminist politic (*ibid:* 556–7). The "postmodernist turn" in anthropology (Marcus and Fischer 1986; Clifford 1988), while claiming self-reflexivity, fails to acknowledge the range of feminist theorizing and ethnographic experimentation, or that critical readings of gendered subjects has long been a central concern of feminist theory (Bell 1983a; Mascia-Lees et al. 1989; Moore 1988; Hondagneu-Sotelo 1988; Stacey 1988; Caplan 1988). Reflexive anthropologists such as Clifford et al. have set gender aside as too difficult, and severely underrepresent the

contribution of feminist anthropologists. Certainly the relationship between feminism and anthropology is not simple (Strathern 1985; Moore 1988; Caplan 1988), but the dialogue belongs in mainstream, and the work of feminists is a fundamental critique. Engaging in this debate is another article, but I am flagging it here for the reader as a shaping force in the debates concerning anthropological practice.

9 One tactic has been to ignore it—Mayne's (1986) bibliography contains no reference to women—or to suggest that womancentric work lacks balance. In reviewing the last twenty-five years of anthropology in Australia, the AIAS commissioned overview papers; Berndt and Tonkinson (1988,6) write of the "earlier feminist anthropological writings" as "overcorrection." Francesca Merlan's (1988) review of gender, which follows their introduction, ignores the intellectual and political importance of feminism as a context for anthropologists, but observes that it is mostly women writing on gender. Her suggestion is a return to the issues of sex, sexuality, and reproduction (ibid, 35ff.). See also Burbank (1989) who quotes Merlan approvingly. Anna Yeatman (1983) is also interested in modeling gender in this way and content to draw on ethnography such as that of Spencer and Allen. She finds nothing in the feminist ethnography to dissuade her.

10 The Aboriginal population at contact is contested and ranges from as low as 150,000 to millions (Bell and Marks 1990, 6–12).

11 The composition of village councils in an excellent example of the intersection of gender politics of Aboriginal society and western notions of representation as gender blind. In many communities, especially in central Australia, it is inappropriate and dangerous for men and women to gather in large meetings. Administrators have looked to men to represent the views of communities (Bell and Ditton 1980/4, 44).

12 For a number of reasons women are less likely to hold a driver's licence than men. They have had fewer opportunities to learn. Men were engaged as drivers during World War II and assisted in stock work, but these work contexts were not routinely available to women.

13 The experiences spoken of as a "dream" do not necessarily occur in sleep, but in a thinking back on an earlier time. Women sometimes have these "dreams" while in especially important country. This use of "dream" in English is not to be confused with "dreaming" or "dream time."

14 The subsections system (also called "skin-system") has eight divisions, into which one is born according to affiliations of one's parents), and is a shorthand form of expressing social relationships (Meggitt 1962, 168; Bell 1983a, 260–64). Siblings will fall within the same subsection but not all members will be siblings. The system is generating by four cross cutting moiety divisions: patri, matri, and generational.

15 In his notes of their trip, Gillen (1968) records the episodes on which the later jointly authored works of Spencer and Gillen are based. Women appear as more vocal and engaged in these accounts but their activities

are classified as squabbles or food-getting, and thus further questions are not asked. There is ample evidence in this source that women's relationship to land mirrored that of men, but this material did not find its way into their ethnography (Bell 1983a, 24–25).

16 The Aboriginal Sacred Sites Protection Authority was a statutory body established under northern territory legislation, the *Sacred Sites Act, 1978*, which is reciprocal legislation to the federal land rights act 1976, but has been significantly amended. Under the *Aboriginal Land Rights (Northern Territory) Act 1976*, land councils, also statutory authorities, were established to handle land claims and represent Aborigines in matters of land.

17 Much debate concerning local and social organization and land tenure systems in Australia focuses on this region, but woman's relationship to land and to ancestors is often explained as derivative of her relationship to someone else, for example, her husband or her father, but not as the mirror image of the male system. In the literature there has also been a stress on patrilineal descent as the basis of group membership. However, evidence forthcoming in land claims where Aboriginal witnesses provide direct statements concerning land, supports the position I have outlined here (Bell 1982; Maddock 1982).

18 Feminist anthropologists (Collier and Rosaldo 1981), arguing the universality of sexual asymmetry, have taken Warner in this way also (Bell, 1990).

19 It is in the shattering of the ritually maintained nexus of land as resource and land as spiritual essence that I have located a shift from female autonomy to male control, from an independent producer to one dependent on social security (Bell 1980, 1983a, 1988b). Thus while Hamilton (1979, 1987) and I are concerned to explore the changing nature of the relations between the sexes from a historical perspective, we have focused from rather differing conceptions of time and place, and upon different institutions and sets of relationships.

WOMEN IN HINDUISM

1 I wish to thank McGill University's humanities research grants committee for funding my research trip to India, from December 1989 to January 1990, which enabled me to collect material and do interviews for this chapter. My particular thanks go to Jyoti Mhapasekara of Bombay who discussed her play, "A Daughter is Born," and her movement called Stri Mukti. I wish to thank Dr. Patel of Ananthacharya Indological Research Institute (Bombay) who paraphrased the aforementioned Marathi play in English, thereby making it accessible to me. I would also like to thank Dr. R. P. Ravindra, S.N.D.T. university (Bombay), an activist with FASDSP (Forum Against Sex Determination and Sex Preselection) who discussed the politics of the movement to ban sex

selection in Maharashtra; Dr. V. Bedekar, president, Institute for Oriental Studies (Thane), who shared his resources and helped me understand the growing Hindu resurgence; the women of the S.N.D.T. Centre for Women's Studies Reference Library where I obtained newspaper articles on suttee and sex selection prior to December 1989; and Vidya Tilak whose daily acts of gracious hospitality nourished body and soul in the best tradition of Hindu womanhood. I would also like to thank Dr. Thomas Coburn, Dr. Paul Nathanson, Leslie Orr, and Zayn Kassam-Hann who offered their comments.

2 Sudesh Vaid, "Ideologies on Women in Nineteenth Century Britain, 1850s–70s," _Economic and Political Weekly_, vol. 20, no. 43, 1985, WS 63-WS 71.

3 Joanna Liddle and Rama Joshi, "Gender and Imperialism in British India," _Economic and Political Weekly_, vol. 20, no. 43, 1985, WS 78.

4 For details of the Brahmin and non-Brahmin reform movements, see Kumari Jayawardena, _Feminism and Nationalism in the Third World_ (London: Zed Books 1986), 73–109: "Women, Social Reform and Nationalism in India."

5 Liddle and Joshi, "Gender," 409.

6 Swami Madhavananda and Ramesh Chandra Majumadar, _Great Women of India_ (Calcutta: Advaita Ashrama, 1953), 404.

7 Shahida Lateef, _Muslim Women in India: Political & Private Realities 1890s–1980s_ (New Delhi: Kali for Women, 1990), 85.

8 Liddle and Joshi, "Gender," WS-74.

9 Madhu Kishwar, "Gandhi on Women," _Economic and Political Weekly_, vol. 20, no. 40, 1985, 1701.

10 Kishwar, "Gandhi on Women," 1692.

11 Jayawardena, _Feminism_, 100.

12 Liddle and Joshi, "Gender," WS-77.

13 Lateef, _Muslim_, 92, quoting _Roshini_, 1946:1.

14 Kishwar, "Gandhi on Women," 1692.

15 Lateef, _Muslim_, 91. See also Katherine K. Young, "From Hindu Strīdharma to Universal Feminism: A Study of the Women in the Nehru Family," in _Traditions in Contact and Change: Selected Proceedings of the XIV Congress of the International Association for the History of Religions_, Peter Slater and Donald Wiebe, eds. (Toronto: Sir Wilfrid Laurier Press, 1983).

16 Lateef, _Muslim_, 93–94.

17 Government of India, _Towards Equality: Report of the Committee on the Status of Women in India_ (New Delhi: Ministry of Education and Social Welfare, Department of Social Welfare, 1974). For a full statistical profile on a state-by-state basis and a critical assessment of various explanations, see Gloria Lalonde, "National Development and the Changing Status of Women in India," M.A. thesis, McGill University, department of anthropology, 1985. Revision of statistics in wake of the 1991 census is awaited.

18 Lateef, *Muslim*, 189–90.
19 January 7–13, 1990.
20 Madhu Kishwar, "Why I do not Call Myself a Feminist," *Manushi* (no. 61, 1990).
21 Ibid., 2.
22 Ibid., 3.
23 Ibid., 7.
24 Ibid.
25 Madhu Kishwar, *Manushi*, "Women Bhakta Poets," *Manushi* (nos. 50, 51, 52, 1989).
26 Madhu Kishwar, "Introduction," *Manushi* (nos. 50, 51, 52, 1989), 5–8.
27 Ibid. (no. 61, 1990), 5.
28 Madhu Kishwar, "In Defence of Our Dharma," *Manushi* (no. 60, 1990), 2.
29 Ibid., 7.
30 Smriti Vohra, "Woman MP No Sanyasini," [sic] *Times of India News Service* (New Delhi, December 21, 1989), 19.
31 Ibid.
32 Ibid.
33 Ibid.
34 Ibid.
35 Ibid.
36 Ibid.
37 Ibid.
38 "BJP's Ramayan," *Manushi* (no. 60, 1990), 4.
39 Sharmila Chandra, "Echoing the Times," *India Today* (January 31, 1990), 54–57.
40 Ibid., 54–55.
41 Ironically, *hindutva* is a polyglot term formed from the Sanskrit neuter suffix *tva* and the foreign loan word *Hindu* used by the Muslims for the people of Sind.
42 Emil D'Cruz, *Indian Secularism: A Fragile Myth* (New Delhi: Indian Social Institute, 1988), 22–23.
43 The term fundamentalism was originally used of Christianity and referred to belief in scripture as a factual record of God's acting in history, belief in a set of doctrines that distill the major events of God's creation and intervention, and belonging to a group defined by such beliefs. In *Fundamentalisms Observed* (Chicago: University of Chicago Press, 1991), Martin E. Marty and R. Scott Appleby, editors, have examined the use of this term and accept a much broader meaning. They argue, for example, that the term "fundamentalism" is here to stay, since it serves to create a distinction over against cognate but not fully appropriate words such as 'traditionalism,' 'conservatism,' or 'orthodoxy' and 'orthopraxis' " (viii). If the term were to be rejected, they suggest, "the public would have to find some other word if it is to make sense of a set of global phenomena which urgently bid to be understood. How-

ever diverse the expressions are, they present themselves as movements which demand comparison even as they deserve fair separate treatment so that their special integrities will appear in bold relief" (viii). They have come to two conclusions. "No other coordinating term was found to be as intelligible or serviceable. And attempts of particular essayists to provide distinctive but in the end confusing accurate alternatives led to the conclusion that they were describing something similar to what are here called fundamentalisms" (viii). The editors then propose to define the term by a "family of resemblances" (what we may also call a polythetic definition). In short, (1) fundamentalisms fight against a threat to their core social and personal identity, (2) they fight for their traditional worldview and their institutions such as the family and its views of gender, sex roles, and child rearing, (3) they fight with selected resources which they regard as fundamental and which will reinforce their identity, often as icons, (4) they fight against others (be they secularists, competing religious groups, or even the moderates of their own tradition, and (5) they fight under a supreme authority (ix-x). One chapter in this large volume is on Hindu "fundamentalists" who are fighting against a perceived threat to Hindu identity by secularists in collusion with members of the minority religions as exemplified by the recent events related to the Hindu desire to build a temple at the supposed birthplace of Lord Rāma.

44 Amrita Chhachhi, "The State, Religious Fundamentalism and Women: Trends in South Asia," *Economic and Political Weekly*, March 18, 1989, 568. According to Chhachhi, communalism is not caused by religious groups that are inherently antagonistic and have their roots in the medieval period. On the contrary, religious groups may be characterized by a lack of unity and caste divisions in some periods but with certain social, economic, and political factors, they unify and take on a new ideological identity to meet certain challenges.

45 *India Today* (Sept. 15, 1990), 34.

46 After the outcry over the proposed increase in reservations and the argument made that they should now be on the basis of economic need rather than birth into a particular group, the government introduced a "reservation" of 10% for the poor.

47 "How India Voted," *India Today* (July 15, 1991), 34.

48 "Poll Stars," *India Today* (May 31, 1991), 77.

49 "The Organisation: The Line of Command," *India Today* (May 15, 1991), 15.

50 Lateef, *Muslim*, 192–93.

51 Lateef notes that although the Indian women's movement up to the time of independence was directed primarily to the emancipation of Hindu women from problems such as suttee, the treatment of widows, and the lack of legal rights to inheritance and divorce, it also took up issues that affected the women of both communities, such as lack of education, child marriage, the seclusion of women, and the practice of

polygamy. Initially, says Lateef, because Muslim women already had rights to inheritance, divorce, and remarriage under traditional law, "Muslims decided that Muslim women's interests would be best served with the restoration of rights under the Shariat or Muslim Personal Law, which had over time been superseded by custom and tradition. . . . Consequently, they supported the passage of the Shariat Act in 1937 and the Dissolution of Muslim Marriages Act in 1939. The enactment of both legislations was endorsed by women's groups as having furthered the cause of women. The basis for these enactments was derived from the eclectic approach adopted in Egypt and Turkey, which amalgamated the different schools of jurisprudence to favour women. . . . However, with Independence and the passage of the Hindu Code Bill, Muslim women's rights and status became an issue both within the community and with other communities, who now regarded it as an indication of Muslim backwardness and intolerable differentiation" (Lateef, *Muslim*, 57). The continuing practice of polygamy and unilateral divorce were the contentious issues. Lateef argues that while Muslim laws on issues that affect women do need to be updated, the position of Muslim women cannot be understood only by looking to religion. On the contrary, the status of Muslim women is often the same as Hindu women in a particular region or class. Lalonde's study corroborates that of Lateef (see "National Development and the Changing Status of Women in India", M.A. thesis, McGill University 1985. Accordingly, Islam has been blamed unduly for the position of women in Indian Muslim communities. Finally, Lateef cannot ignore how Muslim personal law functions as a "symbolic differentiation" for the community (68). All over the Muslim world, "the rise of nationalism with its Islamic symbols in different Muslim societies gave the implementation of the Shariat greater importance, but laws like the family, have been evolving in Muslim societies" (164). At the same time, she notes that "in the case of women's issues, community signals remain mixed, since all communities encourage education and employment, but try to retain control by emphasizing the family and the role of mother and wife. . . . In real terms, therefore, Muslim women share the achievements, goals and expectations for the future with other women in India" (177).

52 Lateef, *Muslim*, 194.
53 For details, see Lateef, *Muslim*, 194.
54 Ibid., 197.
55 Ibid., 198–99.
56 Ibid., 199–200.
57 Ibid., 122.
58 D'Cruz, *Indian*, 77, following Raymond.
59 Ibid., 78–79.
60 See "Christian women urge changes in divorce act," *Indian Express* (Bombay, Jan. 9, 1990), 3; "A Step toward emancipation?," *The Indepen-*

dent (Jan. 15, 1990), 9; "Christian Marriage Act a threat to women," *The Times of India* (Bombay, Jan. 9, 1990), 3.

61 P. C. Chatterji, *Secular Values for Secular India* (New Delhi: P. C. Chatterji, 1984), 223.

62 Amit Rai, "India's New Brahmanism," *Z Magazine* (July/August 1991), 150.

63 Chhachhi, "State," 569.

64 Madhu Kishwar, "Pro Women or Anti Muslim?: The Shahbano Controversy," *Manushi* (no. 32, 1986), 11.

65 Ibid., 4.

66 Ibid.

67 Ibid., 6.

68 Paul R. Brass, *The Politics of India since Independence* (Cambridge: Cambridge University Press, 1990), 191.

69 S. Radhakrishnan, *Recovery of Faith* (Allen and Unwin, 1956), 202.

70 Cited by Chatterji, *Secular*, 15.

71 Kishwar, "Pro Women," (no. 32, 1986), 11.

72 D'Cruz, *Indian*, 22–23.

73 Chhachhi, "State," 571.

74 Sujata Gothoskar, "Pushing Women Out: Declining Employment of Women in the Organised Industrial Sector," *Manushi*, no. 65, 1991, 10–20.

75 Ibid., 10.

76 Chhachhi, "State," 571.

77 Tim Dyson and Mick Moore, "On Kinship Structure, Female Autonomy, and Demographic Behavior in India," *Population and Development Review* (vol. 9, no. 1, 1983), 35–60. Women mostly work in the "unorganized" sector. According to Margot I. Duley in *The Crosscultural Study of Women: A Comprehensive Guide*, Margot I. Duley and M. I. Edwards, eds. (New York: Feminist Press, City University of New York, 1986), 211, there was a 41% decline of women's employment between 1961 and 1971. See also Ursula Sharma, "Segregation and its Consequences in India: Rural Women in Himachal Pradesh" in *Women United, Women Divided: Comparative Studies of Ten Contemporary Cultures*, P. Caplan and J. M. Bujra, eds. (Bloomington: Indiana University Press, 1979).

78 See "Son Preference" in "Report of the Working Group on Traditional Practices Affecting the Health of Women and Children, U.N. Doc. E/CN.4/1986/42 of February 4, 1986, paras. 139–171, pp. 24–30. In this report the origin is attributed to patriarchal structures.

79 S. H. Venkatramani, "Born to Die," *India Today* (June 15, 1986), 31.

80 Barbara D. Miller, *The Endangered Sex* (Ithaca: Cornell University Press, 1981).

81 R. Rao, "Move to Stop Sex-test Abortion," *Nature*, 364, 1986, 202.

82 R. P. Ravindra "The Scarcer Half: A report on amniocentesis and other sex-determination techniques, sex preselection and new reproductive

technologies" *Counterfact*, no. 9, a CED Health Feature, January 1986 (Bombay: Centre for Education and Documentation).

83 Madhu Kishwar, "Towards More Just Norms for Marriage: Continuing the Dowry Debate," *Manushi* (no. 53, 1989), 2–9.

84 T. N. Srivastava, *Women and the Law* (New Delhi: Intellectual Publishing House, 1985), 211–12.

85 Chhachhi, "State," 573.

86 Smt. Girdhar Kanwar (petitioner) [of Jaipur Rajastan] vs. Union of India (respondent): In the Supreme Court of India: Writ Petition of April 1988 (advocate Mr. Shiva Pujan Singh). A copy of this petition was provided by Dr. V. Bedekar of the Institute for Oriental Studies (Thane).

87 "Mrs. Scindia Defends Sati," *Times of India* (Bombay Jan. 22, 1989), reproduced from RCWS/SNDT Holdings.

88 *Indian Express* (Bombay, Jan. 25, 1989).

89 Dr. Baliram Sadashiv Yerkuntawar, "Samvad," *Prajnalok* (in Marathi) no. 119, Dec. 1987; an English translation of this was provided by Dr. V. Bedekar, Institute for Oriental Studies (Thane, Maharashtra).

90 A copy of this letter was provided by Dr. V. Bedekar, Institute for Oriental Studies, Thane, Maharashtra.

91 Lourens P. van den Bosch, "A Burning Question: The Sacred Centre as the Focus of Political Interest," University of Groningen, Netherlands. Delivered to the symposium "The Sacred Centre as the Object of Political Interest," University of Groningen, March 5–8, 1989.

92 Van den Bosh, "Burning Question," 1989.

93 Srivastava, *Woman*, 6.

94 V. V. Prakasa Rao and V. Nandini Rao, *Marriage, the Family and Women in India* (New Delhi: Heritage Publishers, 1982), 3, 148.

95 S. Pothen, *Divorce: Its Causes and Consequences in Hindu Society* (Delhi: Vikas, 1986).

96 Madhu Jain and M. Rahman, "Dating: An Open Embrace," *India Today* (May 15, 1991), 73–75.

97 D'Cruz, *Indian*, 22–23.

98 Klaus Klostermaier, "Truth and Toleration in Contemporary Hinduism," *Papers from the 1990 Symposium on Truth and Tolerance*, E. J. Furcha, ed. (Montreal: Faculty of Religious Studies, McGill University, 1990).

99 Ibid., 140.

100 L. S. Rathore, "Political Culture of India's Ruling Class," *Indian Journal of Political Science*, vol. 51, no. 2, April–June 1990, 277–89.

101 Ursula King, "The Effect of Social Change on Religious Self-Understanding Women Ascetics in Modern Hinduism," *Changing South Asia: Religion and Society*, K. Ballhatchet and D. Taylor, eds. (London: Asian Research, 1984), 80. According to King, Vivekananda also planned a monastic order for women. It was realized only much later, in 1954, with the establishment of Sri Sarada Math and the Ramaskrishna Sarada Mission as an independent women's branch of

the Ramakrishna Order. The latter went on to develop, in turn, a number of branches, some outside Bengal, with members numbering 170 as of 1981.

102 Ibid., 80.

103 Cited in "Ānandamayī Mā and Modern Hinduism" by Katherine K. Young and Lilly Miller in *Boeings and Bullock-carts: Studies in Change and Continuity in Indian Civilization*, vol. 2: *Indian Civilization in its Local, Regional and National Aspects*, Dhirendra Vajpeyi, ed. (Delhi: Chanakya Publications, 1990), 128.

104 Ibid., 134–35.

105 Ibid., 142.

106 Linda Johnsen, "Women Saints of India" *Yoga Journal* (no. 81, July/August 1988), 52. See also Catherine Clementin-Ojha, "The Tradition of Female Gurus," *Manushi* (no. 31, 1985), 2–8; Ursula King, "Effect," 1984; Catherine Ojha, "Feminine Asceticism in Hinduism: Its Tradition and Present Condition," *Man in India*, 61/3 (1981), 254–83.

107 Charles S. White, "Mother Guru. Jñānānanda of Madras, India," in N. A. Falk and R. M. Gross, eds., *Unspoken Worlds: Women's Religious Lives in Non-Western Cultures* (New York: Harper and Row, 1980), 22–37.

108 Vohra, "Woman MP," 19.

109 Chhachhi, "State," 271–73.

110 I thank my colleague Leslie Orr at Concordia University (Montreal) for pointing out how the debate over reservations may be interpreted differently by men and women.

111 Richard John Neuhaus, *The Naked Public Square: Religion and Democracy in America* (Grand Rapids, Michigan: William B. Eerdmans, 1984).

112 Klostermaier, "Truth," 134 and 139.

WOMEN IN BUDDHISM

1 The Sanskrit terms *bhikṣuṇī* and *bhikṣu*, and the Pali terms *bhikkhunī* and *bhikkhu*, mean female and male mendicant, one who begs alms and renounces conventional worldly livelihoods. The translation of these terms as "nun" and "monk" is done for convenience, but it should be kept in mind that Buddhist "monks" and "nuns" did not live like their Christian counterparts.

2 The most widely accepted dates for the Buddha's life are about 560–480 B.C.E. According to tradition the nuns' order was founded about five years after the Buddha's enlightenment and the founding of the monks' order—that is, around 520 B.C.E. Recent research by Kabilsingh (1984, 70–72), however, suggests that the two orders are equally old.

3 On the nuns' order in India: Horner 1975, 95–312; Falk 1980. In ancient Sri Lanka: Lamotte 1958, 291–97; Gombrich 1958, 150ff.; Gunawar-

dana 1979, 37–39. In ancient China: Cissell 1972; Tsai 1981; Schuster 1985b. In ancient Burma: Bechert 1967, 154–55; Gombrich 1988, 168; Gunawardana 1979, 39.

4 Tsai 1981, 8. The Vietnamese ordination ritual, though derived from the Chinese tradition, may be based on texts different from those conventionally used in China itself: Dalai Lama 1987, 7.

5 Jan 1984, 41–42. The total number of monks and nuns in the People's Republic of China in 1982 has been estimated at 25,000 to 28,000, the majority being monks: Jan 1984, 44.

6 The eight precepts are: to abstain from killing, stealing, sexual relations, lying, using intoxicants, eating after midday, dancing or adorning oneself, using comfortable beds and chairs. The ten precepts are these eight, with number seven being split into two parts, and a tenth added: to abstain from touching gold or silver. Lamotte 1958, 59; Bloss 1987, 29, note 4; Allione 1986, xxxv. Most Tibetan renunciant women observe 36 precepts and are regarded as novice nuns: Karma Lekshe Tsomo 1987, 3. Some of the Thai *mae chi* observe only five precepts: Kabilsingh 1982, 73.

7 Theravada, the School of the Elders, is the name of the Buddhist sect to which most south and southeast Asians belong. On female renunciants in modern Thailand, Cambodia, Laos: Kabilsingh 1982; Bunnag 1973; Bechert 1967, 196, 235. In Tibet: Karma Lekshe Tsomo 1987; Dalai Lama 1987. In Sri Lanka: Bloss 1987; Gombrich and Obeyesekere 1988, 274–98.

8 Bechert 1967, 196; P. Van Esterik 1982, 65. In recent decades, however, *mae chi* have been offered opportunities for Buddhist education at Mahamakut University in Bangkok, and by the Institute for Thai Mae Chi: Tambiah 1976, 471; NIBWA 5, 1985, 12–15.

9 NIBWA, 9, 1986, 5–6; NIBWA, 15, 1988, 15–20; Ferguson 1978, 83–84, n. 16.

10 Willis 1984; Aziz 1989. Aziz estimates there are some 600 *ani* now in Tibetan communities in exile, and a few hundred in Tibet itself. Karma Lekshe Tsomo (1987, 5) says there are about 900 *ani* now in India and Nepal.

11 On Mahayana and Theravada Buddhism and some of the differences between them, see Bechert and Gombrich 1984, 41–93; Barnes 1987, 105–15. Mahayana means the "great vehicle" to liberation and enlightenment; it is the name of a broad movement which appeared in India around the beginning of the common era and was carried by missionaries to China and the other lands of the Far East. Theravada is the "school of the elders," the relatively conservative monks and nuns who adhered to the traditions and practices which were well established before the rise of Mahayana Buddhism.

12 The books of rules and explanations for the monastic discipline are called Vinaya. Six Vinaya are extant today, belonging to six of the ancient Buddhist schools. Several more schools than this once existed; ac-

cording to tradition, there were eighteen, and each had its own Vinaya. Only one of the ancient schools survives today, the Theravada. The collection of 200-plus precepts to be observed by monks and nuns is called *Pāṭimokkha* or *Prāṭimoksa,* and is contained in the Vinaya.

13 The Vinaya used for centuries in China and still used in Taiwan and Hong Kong belongs to the Dharmagupta school, which is now extinct as an active branch of Buddhism; only its book of monastic rules continues to be influential (Ch'en 1964, 241; Jan 1984, 41–42). It appears that in the modern People's Republic of China, however, the Vinaya of the Mūlasarvāstivāda school is now being used by monks and nuns (Jan 1984, 41–42). The sections in both these Vinaya listing the rules to be observed by nuns and monks are very similar to those of the Theravada (Kabilsingh 1984). To the Theravada women who advocate the reestablishment of the Theravada *bhikṣuṇī-saṃgha* by way of the Chinese *bhikṣuṇī-saṃgha,* and to the Theravada men who oppose this recourse, it is important to know whether Theravada clergy or texts played a role in the first Chinese *bhikṣuṇī* ordinations. It is known that nuns from Sri Lanka made up the quorum of senior *bhikṣuṇī* at the first full ordination of Chinese nuns, which was held in 433 or 434 C.E. It is quite probable that these nuns belonged to the Theravada which has dominated Sri Lankan Buddhism during most of its history. However, just at the time in question, in the fifth century, other Buddhist schools had become active in Sri Lanka, and had gained a great many adherents. For a time members of other schools outnumbered Theravada clergy (Adikaram 1953, 88–100). Since the Chinese sources which recount the events of the *bhikṣuṇī* ordination say only that the foreign nuns came from Sri Lanka (references in Cissell 1972, 62–70), it is impossible to prove conclusively that they were Theravada. The Vinaya texts used at the ceremony certainly belonged to another Buddhist school or schools, for there is no evidence that Theravada Vinaya texts were ever known in China. Neither was the Indian monk who presided at the Chinese ordination a member of the Theravada. It does seem clear that the monks and nuns who participated in this momentous event, and the Vinaya texts they used, represented various of the ancient Indian Buddhist schools. This was obviously not perceived as a problem by anyone involved. To modern Theravada Buddhists, however, it is a matter of concern.

14 Gombrich and Obeyesekere 1988, 274.

15 Dalai Lama 1987, 6–7; Karma Lekshe Tsomo 1987, 2–3, 9.

16 The Chinese ordination procedure actually has three steps: the "going forth" or novice ordination, the higher ordination of *bhikṣu* and *bhikṣuṇī,* and the *bodhisattva* ordination. Only the latter is a strictly Mahayana ceremony, wherein one vows to bring about the liberation of all beings, not just oneself. A bodhisattva is a heroic being (*sattva*) committed to the attainment of enlightenment (*bodhi*); it is what Mahayana Buddhists call themselves. The bodhisattva ordination has a long

history in China. Theravada Buddhist women who wish to be ordained *bhikṣuṇī* in Chinese monasteries can abstain from this third ordination: NIBWA, 18, 1989, 15.

17 Horner 1975, 149–52.

18 The ten vows are the same as those taken by the quasi nuns in modern Sri Lanka, Thailand, and Burma. The six vows which must be taken by the female probationer according to the Vinaya are the first six of these. As Horner points out (1975, 138) the Vinaya rules allow women fewer rights and also require of them fewer duties than men.

19 For a detailed account of the nuns' *upasaṃpada*, see Horner 1975, 138–58; see also Bechert and Gombrich 1984, 55–56.

20 Horner 1975, 118–61; Bechert and Gombrich 1984, 56; Barnes 1987, 107–8.

21 Falk 1980; Barnes 1987, 106–9, 123–25.

22 Gunawardana 1979, 39; Gombrich 1988, 168. After a long period of genteel decline, followed by a series of ferocious attacks by Muslim invaders, Buddhism finally disappeared from India during the medieval period. Inscriptional evidence suggests that nuns as well as monks survived there to the bitter end, though the nuns' order had nothing like the vigor of the monks' in those latter days. Falk 1980, 222–23; Bechert and Gombrich 1984, 84.

23 Bloss 1987, 22–23, 27–28; Gombrich and Obeyesekere 1988, 291.

24 NIBWA, 12, 1987, 12–13. For the more openminded views of some Theravada clergy in Thailand and Sri Lanka, see NIBWA, 12, 1987, 5–9; 22, 1990, 6–10; 23, 1990, 26–28.

25 Bond 1988, 1–2, 68.

26 Gombrich and Obeyesekere 1988, 276, 285; Bloss 1987.

27 Bloss 1987, 19–21; Gombrich and Obeyesekere 1988, 291.

28 Uchino 1983.

29 The pages of NIBWA, from its founding in 1985 to the latest issue, contain many articles arguing for reinstatement of the *bhikṣuṇī saṃgha*. Four of the most useful are: NIBWA, 4, 1985, 4–10 (Sister Khema, "Is the *Bhikkhunī Saṃgha* Necessary?"); 11, 1987, 13–18 ("Campaign to Start Ordaining Thai Nuns"); 12, 1987, 5–9 ("Rethinking Women's Place in Buddhism"); 12, 1987, 12–15 ("Mindfulness in the International Context"). See also Bloss 1987, 25–26. Jiyu Kennett Roshi, British-born woman Zen master, suggests that women who enter the order should make up their minds why they want to do it: just because men say they cannot, or because they really want to find their own Buddahood: Boucher 1988, 137–38.

30 NIBWA, 12, 1987, 21–25; 10, 1987, 6–11; 9, 1980, 18, 28.

31 NIBWA, 16, 1988, 21–23; 13, 1987, 25.

32 NIBWA, 12, 1987, 12–15. This article was written by Venerable Bhikṣuṇī Karma Lekshe Tsomo, an American woman belonging to a Tibetan nuns' lineage who has been ordained as a *bhikṣuṇī* by Chinese nuns, with the blessing of her Tibetan teacher.

33 For a list of the precepts, see note 6. The Theravada *dasasilmattawa*, *mae chi*, and *thīla shin* who accept these precepts are examples of such pious laywomen. On the ancient Buddhist laity, see Barnes 1987, 109–10; Bechert and Gombrich 1984, 53–54; Horner 1975, 313–79; Willis 1985, 37–58. On the modern Buddhist laity, see Bunnag 1973, 142–79; Bond 1988.

34 Buddhists believe that all sentient beings are caught in the cycle of re-birth. They are reborn again and again until they are able to attain the powerful, liberating insight into the true nature of existence that is nirvana.

35 Lee 1983, 28–37; Koh 1986, 238; Welch 1973, 411–20.

36 Helen Hardacre cites Japanese government statistics compiled in 1981: over 43,000,000 Japanese were then members of the new religions, that is between one-quarter and one-third of the total population of Japan. The influence of the new religions touches even more people and issues than these, moreover. Hardacre 1984, 226; Hardacre 1987, 96.

37 Earhart 1980, 177; Nakamura 1980, 174–75.

38 Lee 1983, 28–37.

39 On Japanese shamanism, see Blacker 1975. On Korean shamanism, see Kendall 1986 and 1988.

40 Lancaster 1986, 145–47; Bechert and Gombrich 1984, 223–24.

41 Nakamura 1980, 186–89; Hardacre 1984, 23–33, 52; Hardacre 1987, 101; Guthrie 1988, 19–22.

42 Hardacre 1984, 55–64, 221–23; Nakamura 1980, 188–89.

43 Hardacre 1984, 57; Hardacre 1979, 458; Hardacre 1986, 121.

44 Hardacre 1979, 458.

45 Hardacre 1984, 5, 188, 208.

46 Hardacre 1984, 208–23.

47 Karma means action. As a principle in Indian religions, karma means the accumulated actions performed by an individual in this life and in all past lives, and the good and bad consequences which inevitably re-sult from them. These consequences color and determine what hap-pens to that person now and in lives to come. As Japanese Buddhists see it, a woman's karmic hindrances will have arisen because of wrong ac-tions in the past.

48 Hardacre 1986, 5, 14, 93; 1984, 203–5.

49 Compare the saga of the Soto Zen nuns recounted above, and also the experiences of the shaman-turned-Zen nun, Satomi Myōdō, recorded in her autobiography: King 1987 and 1988.

50 Hardacre 1984, 206; 1986, 121, 191.

51 Hardacre 1984, 5, 206–8; Guthrie 1988, 20–21; Hardacre 1986, 55–58, 88–98; Nakamura 1980.

52 Hardacre has written at length on the methods used in Reiyūkai to in-duce a woman to subscribe totally to a negative view of women which places all the blame for all family problems squarely on women's shoulders: Hardacre 1979. Risshō Kōsei-kai attains similar results:

Hardacre 1987. Others have commented on women's internalization of notions of female inferiority, in the face of their own obvious accomplishments, in other Buddhist cultures as well: Burma, in NIBWA, 15, 1988, 20; Tibet, in Allione 1986, 9.

53 Men in the new religions do value and praise their partners' accomplishments and superior skills; they acknowledge that women are the center of the sect and that it could never survive without them. Hardacre 1984, 188, and especially 221.

54 Hardacre 1984, 222, 230. Buddhist women meditators in Sri Lanka voiced similar views, that women's lot is very hard, but because of that their spiritual potential is higher than men's: Bond 1988, 184–85.

55 Hardacre 1984, 223.

56 Bond 1988, 177–86, 208–12; J. Van Esterik 1982, 47–52.

57 Gombrich and Obeyesekere 1988, 237; see also Bond 1988, 177.

58 J. Van Esterik 1982.

59 Bechert 1966, 79–80; Bond 1988, 131–33, 189–90; Gombrich and Obeyesekere 1988, 238–39; J. Van Esterik 1982, 47.

60 Bechert and Gombrich 1984, 279–84; Friedman 1987, 135–46, 213–26, 255–68; Boucher 1988, 148–209, 326–82; Fields 1986, 358–90.

61 Bodhisattva means "heroic being committed to the attainment of perfect enlightenment." The term was originally used to refer to the historical Buddha, Gautama, up to the moment he attained enlightenment; at that point he became the Buddha, the Enlightened One. Mahayana Buddhists, who consciously modeled their lives after the Buddha's, called themselves bodhisattvas also.

62 On lay and renunciant bodhisattvas, see Schuster 1985a, 26–56. Recently the Dalai Lama urged nuns of the Tibetan tradition—which is Mahayana—to spend some years practicing and studying in a nunnery and then go out into the world to teach or undertake other worthwhile work: NIBWA, 10, 1987, 6–11.

63 Ch'en 1964, 241–96; Welch 1973, 356–93.

64 Welch 1973, 377–82; Bechert 1967, 333; NIBWA, 16, 1988, 24–25; *Free China Journal*, Nov. 2, 1989, 3, Oct. 8, 1990, 6.

65 Carrithers 1983, 20; Gombrich and Obeyesekere 1988, 254–55.

66 Rahula 1974, 3, quoting the *Mahāvagga*. See also Bond 1988, 250–52, 286.

67 Obeyesekere 1972, 68–73; Gombrich 1988, 188–94, 198–200; Gombrich and Obeyesekere 1988.

68 The ten precepts taken up by the *dasasilmattawa* are the same ones the *anagārika* practices. For the list, see note 6.

69 Bloss 1987, 8–17; Gombrich and Obeyesekere 1988, 286–91.

70 Some groups of *dasasilmattawa* are still directly controlled by laywomen, however, though social service is apparently not required of these renunciant women. Gombrich and Obeyesekere 1988, 286.

71 Gombrich and Obeyesekere 1988, 243–55; Bond 1988, 241–98; Macy 1983. Bond and Macy have written generally sympathetic accounts of

Sarvodaya's ideas. Gombrich and Obeyesekere are highly critical of Ariyaratna's thinking and skeptical about Sarvodaya's effectiveness. The term "sarvodaya" was first coined by Mahatma Gandhi who translated it as "welfare of all." Ariyaratna, who was partly inspired by Gandhi's work, interprets the term to mean "awakening of all"—he gives it, in other words, a distinctive Buddhist coloring.

72 Gombrich and Obeyesekere 1988, 244–45.
73 Bond 1988, 6.
74 Gombrich and Obeyesekere 1988, 249, quoting A. T. Ariyaratna, *In Search of Development* (Moratuwa: Sarvodaya Press, 1981).
75 Tambiah 1976, 434–44.
76 Keyes 1984, 1986.
77 Carrithers 1983, 20. On Western Buddhists engaged in social action at home, see Boucher 1988, 259–325; Oliver 1979, 151–77.
78 See Bechert 1967, 305–72 and especially 334–51 on the Buddhist confrontation with the Diem government and on the Buddhist suicides. Suicide by burning, for a religious goal, was a Chinese Mahayana Buddhist practice imported into Vietnam along with the religion. Inspiration for the practice came principally from the *Lotus Sūtra*, an important Mahayana scripture. The purpose of suicide is not martyrdom—that is, the Buddhist does not choose to *suffer* for the sake of his or her religion. Instead, the act is meant to testify to the suicide's profound understanding of the Buddha's dharma or teachings, and it is performed in a spirit of dedication in order to instruct and inspire others with the force of the Buddha's truth. Only one highly accomplished in meditation—as Thich Quang Duc was—is to carry out a ritual suicide, for the individual must be an adept who has totally mastered mind and feelings. The essence of the Buddha's dharma, which the Mahayana suicide demonstrates by the act, is the teaching that everything exists dependent on other phenomena, and nothing and no one can exist as a unique entity, separated and marked off from the rest. The fate of one is shared by all. Thich Quang Duc was apparently not instigated to his action by the Buddhist hierarchy, but they did approve of it. The other suicides were a different matter, since none of them had had Thich Quang Duc's years of Buddhist discipline and experience in meditation, and some were very young; one was an 18-year-old novice monk. Nevertheless all the suicides were treated with respect by the Buddhist hierarchy after the fact, and all were venerated by the Buddhist faithful. Other suicides occurred during the next few years in protest against the succession of military regimes and their war policies. Nuns and laywomen were among the later group of suicides also.
79 See Bechert 1966, 325–360; Bond 1988, 75–124; Gombrich 1988, 201–3. Sirimavo Bandaranaike was the first of the remarkable modern succession of women prime ministers in traditional South Asian nations. She had originally been one of the new generation of Sinhala Buddhist

politicians, as had her husband. Both found it impossible finally to walk the narrow line of political survival among acrimonious Buddhist interest groups.

80 Bechert and Gombrich 1984, 284–85, quoting a statement issued by the World Buddhist Saṃgha Council.

81 Boucher 1988, 276–84; Bechert and Gombrich 1984, 285.

82 On Tibetan Buddhist women, see Klein 1985b; Willis 1984; Allione 1986; Aziz 1989; Karma Lekshe Tsomo 1987. For the biography of Yeshe Tsogyel and for more information on women and tantric Buddhist practices, see Dowman 1984, and Tarthang Tulku 1983. Tantric Buddhism stresses elaborate rituals and a vast array of esoteric meditative practices, which are imparted directly and secretly by teacher to disciple. Tantric Buddhism, also known as Vajrayana, the diamond vehicle to liberation, belongs doctrinally to the Mahayana. It is only in its esoteric practices that it is unique.

83 The name is transliterated by Tsultrim Allione as A-Yu Khadro. Allione translates the complete biography in 1986, 235–57. Klein offers a summary in 1985b, 115–18.

84 Klein 1985b, 118.

85 Willis 1984, 22–23, quoting Lhalungpa in *Parabola* Magazine, and in the introduction to *Tibet the Sacred Realm: Photographs 1880–1950.* Willis recounts what is known of Ani Lochen's life on pp. 20–22. Ani Lochen died in 1950 at a reputed age of 130 years.

86 Bloss 1987, 14–17; NIBWA, 3, 1985, 11–12.

87 J. Van Esterik 1982, 47–52.

88 NIBWA, 15, 1988, 15–20.

89 *Butsumon,* 1989, 1, 12.

90 NIBWA, 5, 1985, 20–22; NIBWA 11, 1987, 30.

91 Stevens 1987.

92 King 1987 and 1988.

93 On Denison and Stuart, see Friedman 1987, 135–46 and 65–92, and Boucher 1988, 177–84 and 194–205. These two books also present profiles of about twenty other Buddhist women teachers in America.

94 On Jiyu Kennett Roshi, see Friedman 1987, 161–91; Boucher 1988, 133–44; Bechert and Gombrich 1984, 283. Jiyu Kennett has published several books herself, among them *Zen is Eternal Life* (originally published as *Selling Water by the River, A Manual of Zen Training*). Jiyu Kennett attained her high status in the Soto sect because Koho Zenji, one of the sect's most important leaders, forced this change in its policies toward women. This happened in the 1960s, just at the time the Soto nuns' long struggle for their rights was being resolved.

95 Boucher 1988, 141–42, 144, n. 1. See also note 1, above.

96 Friedman 1987, 173–76; Boucher 137, 141.

97 Fields 1986, 169–74.

98 Boucher 1988, 191–94; Fields 1986, 207–8.

99 Fields 1986, 187–92, 197–98, 208–9, 216–17; Boucher 1988, 189.

100 Fields 1986, 277–81; Karma Lekshe Tsomo 1987, 7.

101 On Ayya Khema see: Bloss 1987, 25–26; Bond 1988, 190; Gombrich and Obeyesekere 1988, 290; Friedman 1987, 264–68; Boucher 1988, 108–14; NIBWA, 2, 1985; NIBWA, 4, 1985, 4–10; NIBWA, 6, 1986, 17–18, 22; NIBWA, 20, 1989, 16–20. Ayya Khema has also published a book on *vipassanā* practice, *Being Nobody, Going Nowhere*.

102 NIBWA, 4, 1985, 5–8.

103 Bloss 1987, 26, quoting an article in Colombo's *Daily News*, October 2, 1982.

104 Bloss 1987, 25–26.

105 See NIBWA, 4, 1985, 15–17; NIBWA, 11, 1987, 13–18. Dr. Kabilsingh has published several articles and books, including *A Comparative Study of Bhikkhunī Pātimokkha*.

106 NIBWA, 11, 1987, 13–18, reprint of an interview with Dr. Kabilsingh, which appeared in the *Bangkock Post* in March 1987.

107 Uchino 1983, 185–89.

108 Barnes 1987, 129–133. The arguments of Klein and Gross summarized here appeared in Klein, 1985a, 1987, and Gross, 1986a, 1986b.

109 Klein 1987, 213.

110 Gross, 1986a, 1986b—especially p. 73. It should be observed also that it has often been the imposition of Western values on non-Western societies which have destroyed the security and status of women there— values which accept only men as heads of families and businesses, and as the only rightful owners of property. The diversity in non-Western societies has frequently gone unappreciated by Western colonialists, and by modern Western aid organizations.

111 Klein 1985a, 95.

112 Klein 1985a, 95–98; 1987, 213; Gross 1986b, 72–74.

PEOPLE'S REPUBLIC OF CHINA

1 Merle Goldman suggests convincingly that the Deng leadership is no friendlier to religion than its predecessors. But having realized that fifteen years of strenuous suppression followed by a ten-year attempt to eliminate religion altogether did not destroy it but only drove it underground, the party wants believers to practice their religion in public so that the party could reassert its control. While this seems true, there have been changes. Bishop K. H. Ting observes that "the intellectual milieu has definitely become friendlier to religion and Christianity. . . . The much too easy way of discrediting religion by calling it an opiate has been given up and criticized by more and more writers. Rather, the study of religion as it exists in China today is being advocated. More is being said about the compatibility (within limits) of religious faith and socialism. All of this means that on the national level the policy of religious freedom is gaining a more solid theoretical grounding, and religion is enjoying a more favorable climate" (Ting 1991, 402).

1a   This essay reflects the American middle-class white feminist perspective of its author. I try to raise and answer the question of whether and to what extent women and women's voices are being included today in the revived religious communities and institutions of the People's Republic of China because of three beliefs which to my mind are supported by academic investigation. First, I believe that it is important for the full liberation of women around the world that Chinese women be included, heard, and empowered to lead, at home and abroad. Second, I believe that in most societies and religious traditions it is the case that experiences, perspectives and voices differ according to gender (as well as race, class and place in subtler power and status hierarchies). And third, I believe that religious communities and institutions become more faithful to truth and more helpful to their members by attending fully to all voices.

Chinese political leadership has shared my first belief for most of the twentieth century. Perhaps not all Chinese women would agree with my second belief, while some Chinese women might argue that even if all of my beliefs are worthy ones, attaining full participation for women is properly not the highest priority for China today. However, at this writing what Chinese women and men would say about the relation of women and religion is something we cannot know as much about as we would like; this essay opens a subject not much discussed in print in China. I offer this essay to Chinese women and men in the hope that they will be inspired to contribute to further discussions of the relations between religion and gender in today's China.

2   Kay Ann Johnson (1983) offers a good detailed summary of the "traditional" family system, which, like the "traditional social system," was not as monolithic as our brief summary implies.

3   A good example is the character Xi-feng in the 17th-century novel *Hong Lou Meng (Dream of the Red Chamber)*.

4   There is one fascinating and germane study of the contemporary practice of a folk religious tradition (Berthier 1988). Recent studies of Daoism in the service of folk religion in Fujian province (Dean 1989; 1988) do not tell of any participation by women.

5   I suspect that the issue of gender role equality is not one about which church leaders welcome public discussion, since it would merely divide their followers around an emotional issue in pursuit of a change that would have no great practical benefit. I suspect that church leaders want to discuss only what they perceive to be the real issues facing their church—in this case, survival and relations with the state. Apart from that, they are willing no doubt to discuss such other issues as promote or reflect unity. Another possibility, of course, is that they do not understand at all where the question is coming from, being unfamiliar with the notion that male and female are strong oppositional catego-

ries, with the concept of patriarchy as an institution of domination, and with the feminist critique of Western religion.

6 The church in Fuzhou in Fujian province, for example, supports priests, nuns, and catechists: MacInnis 1989, 288.

7 An interview with Bishop Aloysius Jin Luxian, published in English in *Asia Focus*, Hong Kong, May 24, 1985, quoted in MacInnis 1989, 293. Bishop Jin was ordained a Chinese-appointed auxiliary bishop of Shanghai January 27, 1985, and is the rector of the regional seminary at Sheshan.

8 Prior to 1949 the YWCA, like the YMCA, was a progressive organization that developed native Chinese leaders and took a strong interest in the plight of socially disadvantaged groups. One such effort by the YWCA before 1949 was a campaign to bring literacy and other services to women workers in Shanghai. Mao's wife, Jiang Qing, was involved with the YWCA in this work. In 1951 Zhou En-lai, knowing of this effort, invited progressive women YWCA leaders to the first meeting of Christian leaders with high party officials (conversation with Jean Woo, July 1991; Witke 1977, 82–83; Honig 1986).

9 Nine hundred thousand Protestants and one hundred forty thousand Catholics, out of a population of forty million.

10 This section of this essay is especially indebted to a number of scholars who kindly responded to my plea for information about this as yet little researched subject. My thanks go to Catherine Bell, Steven Bokenkamp, Suzanne Cahill, Ellen Chen, Alvin Chen, Valerie Hansen, Stevan Harrell, Christian Jochim, Terry Kelleher, John Lagerway, Daniel Overmyer, Julian Pas, Jordan Paper, Fabrizio Pregadio, Franciscus Verellen, Tao-chung Yao, and David Yu.

11 *Qian* and *kun* are the names of the pure yang or "heaven" and pure yin or "earth" hexagrams of the *I Ching*.

12 Julian Pas notes that in Taiwan some temples allow women inside the sacred area, while others do not. He sees a trend toward allowing women. Personal communication, August 21, 1991.

13 Pas, personal communication, 1991; Yao, personal communication, 1991. The names taken on ordination by *qiandao* or *kundao* are not gender marked: it is impossible to tell the gender from the name.

14 Figures for the numbers of students are drawn from articles in *Zhongguo Daojiao* on the training programs, which began in 1982 and typically have lasted from nine months to over a year. Curiously, the articles, which give a lot of information about ages and geographical origins of students, do not give information about their gender (Bokenkamp, personal communication, 1991).

15 Catherine Despeux on the basis of her visit in 1984 says of the practice at Tianshidong that the monastics here live by the traditional monastic rules of Quanzhen, recite liturgical texts morning and evening, and practice sitting meditation twice a day. She says further that all the

women at the monastery practice the feminine inner alchemy, including massaging of the breasts and concentration exercise (Despeux 1990, 184–185).

16 The corresponding process in men, which involves avoiding the downward dispersal of the semen, is called "submitting the white tiger" (Pregadio 1991, 90).

17 Welch 1972, 423 reports that Zhaojuesi had 150 monks in the 1940s, 96 in 1951, and 63 in 1953; Jinzusi had 250 in the 1940s (under Neng-hai as abbot?), 151 in 1951, and 80 in 1953.

18 This last does not appear on the list of temples in 1957, but does appear on the list for temples and their addresses in 1964 (32).

19 A small amount of money compared to the 550,000 yuan which the report states has been spent restoring Wenshuyuan, 115,000 of which came from the national government.

20 Makita Tairyo wrote about it in 1958. See Welch 1972, 409.

21 The following discussion is all drawn from Yü 1988.

22 As opposed to bound feet?

23 For a text and translation of six of the pilgrim songs that Yü collected, see Yü 1990, 276–82.

24 In 1987 Antoinette Wire became concerned about whether the Chinese church will gradually revert to male leadership and patriarchal forms to improve its competitive edge in a society in some ways reviving family-based economic structures. She noted that as education improves and more men are attracted into the ministry, women could be left behind. She asked Bishop K. H. Ting whether the church could in fact follow through on its commitment to equal opportunity for women. Ting replied that the more conservative country Christians are used to women leaders and the better educated city people have been raised in a society where women are active leaders in every sector. There are certain advantages, he said, to China's having a very short church history with no deep-seated memory of patriarchal leadership to hold it back (Wire 1989, 197). My own assessment is that Ting's view may prove overoptimistic. The strong tradition of exclusively male leadership in society has been weakened, and some women have been included, but a tendency toward gender hierarchy has certainly not disappeared.

WOMEN AND CHINESE RELIGION IN TAIWAN

1 The Cultural Revolution as an urban mass movement, with Red Guard factions pitted against one another, covered the years 1966 to 1969. But leftists still had great influence until the death of Mao in 1976, so that the Cultural Revolution is held by some to have lasted until 1976.

2   For brief surveys of Chinese religion and society in Taiwan and the People's Republic of China, see Raymond Pong and Carlo Caldarola, "China: Religion in a Revolutionary Society" and Michael Saso, "Taiwan: Old Gods and Modern Society" in *Religions and Societies: Asia and the Middle East*, Carlo Caldarola, ed. (New York: Mouton, 1982).

3   The general fertility rate for all women in Taiwan dropped from 184/10,000 in 1958 to 60/10,000 in 1987.

4   Except where indicated, all translations from Chinese texts are my own. I have used the Wade-Giles system for romanizing Chinese names and terms because it is more widely used in Taiwan than *pinyin*.

5   For discussions of the roles of women in Buddhism, Confucianism, and Taoism, see the relevant chapters by Nancy Shuster Barnes, Theresa Kelleher, and Barbara Reed in *Women in World Religions*, Arvind Sharma, ed. (Albany: SUNY Press, 1987).

6   The Monkey King is one of the main characters of the popular Chinese novel *Hsi yu-chi* [Journey to the West].

7   According to people's own religious identification, 44 percent are Buddhist and 34 percent belong to the popular (folk) religion. But if people are classified according to their beliefs and religious activities, anthropologist Ch'ü Hai-yuan would consider at least 66 percent of Taiwan's population as belonging to Chinese popular religion. The discrepancy is due to the historical preference of the Chinese to identify themselves as Buddhist (Ch'ü 1985, 69).

8   Hsing-t'ien Temple has been supported by officials in the Nationalist government because its deities and rituals are pan-Chinese and thus reduce regional (and specifically Taiwanese) allegiances commonly promoted by community-based temples. The temple also prohibits elaborate offerings. Therefore the government welcomes the temple as a force against what they view as the waste and superstition found in traditional Taiwanese community temples. (See Feuchtwang, 293–301.)

9   The only religious activity surveyed by Ch'ü Hai-yuan in which men were more active than women was in *feng-shui*, the Chinese form of geomancy based on the configuration of yin and yang forces. Since *feng-shui* is used primarily to determine the most auspicious location for homes, temples, and graves, it is not surprising that men would be more likely to participate in this public role.

10   An excellent example of a poor working-class woman's views of ancestor reverence and filial piety is found in the life of a Mrs. Ning as reported by Ida Pruitt. *A Daughter of Han: The Autobiography of a Chinese Working Woman* (Stanford: Stanford University Press, 1967).

11   Marriage property laws were reformed in 1985 to remove some of the worst biases against women, but laws still give married men great control over their wives' property. Divorced women still have great difficulties gaining property or custody of their children. See Chiang and Ku 1985, 13–21.

TODAY'S JEWISH WOMEN

1 See Debra Kaufman, "Coming Home to Jewish Orthodoxy: Reactionary or Radical Women?," *Tikkun*, vol. 2, no. 3 (1987), 60–63. See also Lis Harris, *Holy Days: The World of a Hasidic Family* (New York: Summit Books, 1985). *Tikkun* and *Journal of Feminist Studies in Religion* have been especially helpful general sources. Two useful anthologies are Elizabeth Koltun, ed., *The Jewish Woman: New Perspectives* (New York: Schocken, 1976) and Susannah Heschel, ed., *On Being a Jewish Feminist* (New York: Schocken, 1983). I owe special thanks to Judith Plaskow, Susannah Heschel, and Cynthia Ozick for kind help. None is responsible for the defects in this study.

2 *New York Times*, March 21, 1989, p. 3.

3 Ibid.

4 Galia Golan, "Movement toward Equality for Women in Israel," *Tikkun*, vol. 2, no. 1 (1987), 19–20.

5 Ibid., 20.

6 Shulamith Koenig, "A Jewish Perspective from Israel," in *Speaking of Faith*, Diana L. Eck and Devaki Jain, eds. (Philadelphia: New Society Publishers, 1987), 67–69.

7 See Merle Feld, "Sinai," and Chava Weissler, "Standing at Sinai," *Journal of Feminist Studies in Religion*, vol. 1, no. 2 (fall 1985), 89–92.

8 Cynthia Ozick, "Ruth," in *Congregation: Contemporary Writers Read the Jewish Bible*, David Rosenberg, ed. (New York: Harcourt, Brace, Jovanovich, 1987), 362.

9 Ibid., 373.

10 See Paula Hyman, "Gender and Jewish History," *Tikkun*, vol. 3, no. 1 (1988), 35–38.

11 Rachel Adler, "The Virgin in the Brothel and Other Anomalies: Character and Context in the Legend of Beruriah," *Tikkun*, vol. 3, no. 6 (1988), 28.

12 Ibid., 104.

13 Martha Ackelsberg, "Spirituality, Community, and Politics: B'not Esh and the Feminist Reconstruction of Judaism," *Journal of Feminist Studies in Religion*, vol. 2, no. 2 (fall 1986), 112–13.

14 Ibid., 119.

15 Marian Henriquez Neudel, "Innovation and Tradition in a Contemporary Midwestern Jewish Congregation," in *Unspoken Worlds; Women's Religious Lives*, 2d ed., Nancy Auer Falk and Rita M. Gross, eds. (Belmont, Calif.: Wadsworth, 1989), 180.

16 Ibid., 186.

17 "Jewish Roots: An Interview with Betty Friedan," *Tikkun*, vol. 3, no. 1 (1988), 27.

18 Marcia Falk, "Notes on Composing New Blessings: Toward a Feminist-Jewish Reconstruction of Prayer," in *Weaving the Visions: New Pat-*

terns in Feminist Spirituality, Judith Plaskow and Carol P. Christ, eds. (San Francisco: Harper & Row, 1989), 128.

19 Ibid., 135.

20 Ellen M. Umansky, "Creating a Jewish Feminist Theology: Possibilities and Problems, ibid., 188.

21 Ibid., 198. See also "Roundtable Feminist Reflections on Separation and Unity in Jewish Theology," *Journal of Feminist Studies in Religion*, vol. 2, no. 1 (spring 1986), 113–30. See Plaskow's *Standing Again at Sinai: Judaism from a Feminist Perspective* (San Francisco: Harper & Row, 1990), pp. 121–169.

CHRISTIANITY AND WOMEN

1 Figures derived from *The World Almanac and Book of Facts* (New York: World Almanac, 1988), 591.

2 See below, (Women in Christianity).

3 For example, the works of Mary Daly, Elizabeth S. Fiorenza and other North American feminists are regularly translated into German. Rosemary Ruether's *The Radical Kingdom* (Harper & Row, 1970) is available in Spanish (1971). Her *Liberation Theology* (Paulist, 1971) is available in Japanese. Her *Faith and Fratricide* (Seabury, 1974) is in German. Her *New Woman, New Earth* (Seabury, 1975) is in Spanish, Korean, and German. Her *Mary: The Feminine Face of the Church* (Westminster, 1977) is in German and Dutch. Her *To Change the World* (Crossroads, 1981) is in Dutch. Her *Sexism and God-Talk* (Beacon, 1983), is in Korean and German. Her *Womanguides* (Beacon, 1985) and *Woman-church* (Beacon, 1986) are in German.

4 See *Women in American Law: From Colonial Times to the New Deal*. Marlene Stein Wortman, ed. (New York: Holmes and Meier, 1983), 13–15.

5 Ibid., 17–19. Also Linda Koehler, *A Search for Power: The Weaker Sex in17th Century New England* (Urbana: University of Illinois Press, 1981).

6 See Eleanor Flexner, *Century of Struggle: The Woman's Movement in the United States* (New York: Atheneum, 1972), 29–30.

7 Thomas Woody, *History of Women's Education in the United States* (New York: 1929).

8 Flexner, *Century*, 113–30.

9 See Jean Donnison, *Midwives and Medical Men: A History of Inter-Professional Rivalries and Women's Rights* (New York: Schocken, 1977) for the history of the elimination of women from gynecology and obstetrics.

10 See *Feminism: Essential Historical Writings*, Miriam Schneir, ed. (New York: Random House, 1972), 35–48 for a selection of Grimke's "Letters on the Equality of the Sexes and the Condition of Women" (1837).

11 See Carolyn Gifford, "Women in Social Reform Movements," in *Women and Religion in America: The Nineteenth Century*, Rosemary

Ruether and Rosemary Keller, eds. (San Francisco: Harper and Row, 1981), vol. 1, 294–340.

12 See Schneir, *Feminism*, 76–82.

13 Elizabeth Cozden, *Antoinette Brown Blackwell: A Biography*. (Old Westbury, N.Y.: Feminist Press, 1982).

14 See Barbara Brown Zikmund, "The Struggle for the Right to Preach," in Ruether and Keller, *Women and Religion*, vol. 1, 193–241.

15 See Gerda Lerner, *The Creation of Patriarchy* (New York: Oxford University Press, 1986).

16 Cardinal James Gibbons, spokesman for the American bishops, delivered several speeches and addresses against women's suffrage between 1911 and 1916. See documents on Gibbons in the Sophia Smith Collection, Smith College.

17 See Lorine Getz, "Women's Struggle for an American Catholic Identity," in *Women and Religion in America: 1900–1968*, Rosemary Ruether and Rosemary Keller, eds. (San Francisco: Harper and Row, 1986), vol. 3, 175–222.

18 See Letha D. Scanzoni and Susan Setta, "Women in Evangelical, Holiness and Pentacostal Traditions," in Ruether and Keller, *Woman and Religion*, vol. 3, 223–65.

19 See Letha D. Scanzoni, "The Great Chain of Being and the Chain of Command," in *Women's Spirit Bonding*, Janet Kalven, ed. (New York: Pilgrim Press, 1984), 41–55.

20 Ruether and Keller, *Women and Religion*, vol. 3, 232.

21 For a history of American women in the depression era, see Lois Scharf, *To Work and to Wed: Female Employment, Feminism and the Great Depression* (New York: Greenwood, 1982).

22 This pattern of government sponsored propaganda for women to enter the labor force during World War II and to depart after the war has been graphically documented in the documentary film "Rosie the Riveter" (NY: Ivy Films).

23 This propaganda by psychological "experts" declaring that children will be developmentally impaired without "full-time" mothering and its coincidence with the loss of cheap servants and nannies has been documented in British society by Ann Dally, *Inventing Motherhood: The Consequences of an Ideal* (New York: Schocken, 1983).

24 Flexner, *Century*, 143.

25 For expressions of this anger of movement women at radical men, white and black, see Marlene Dixon, "The Rise of Women's Liberation," and Gayle Rubin, "Women as Nigger" in *Masculine/Feminine*, Betty and Theodore Roszak, eds. (New York: Harper, 1969), 192, 239.

26 See Jane J. Mansbridge, *Why We Lost the ERA* (Chicago: University of Chicago Press, 1986).

27 See Barbara Brown Zikmund, in Ruether and Keller, *Women and Religion*, vol. 3, 339–84.

28 *Yearbook of American and Canadian Churches*, Constant H. Jacquet, ed. (Nashville: Abingdon Press, 1988, p. 278.

29 Figures for the number of women in twenty U.S. denominations are derived from a report of the National Council of Churches of Christ in the USA. The percentages were derived by comparing these NCC figures with the total number of clergy in each of these denominations as reported in the *Yearbook*. The figures for the Unitarian Universalists were not included in this list and were supplied by the national headquarters of the Unitarian-Universalists in Boston.

30 Ann Naylor of the national office of the United Church of Canada supplied these figures from statistics kept in her files. Information on women and feminist studies in theological education in the United Church of Canada was supplied by Shelley Finson, Atlantic School of Theology, Halifax.

31 Karen Evans of the national office of the Anglican Church of Canada supplied these figures from statistics kept by the national church.

32 For an account of black women in the Sanctified Church, where women have often held the title of bishop, see Jualyne Dodson and Cheryl Townsend Gilkes, "Something Within: Social Change and Collective Endurance in the Sacred World of Black Christian Women," in Ruether and Keller, *Woman and Religion*, vol. 3, 80–130.

33 See picture and report on Matthews, *Women and Religion*, 349.

34 Marjorie Matthews is deceased and Leontyne Kelly, a black woman, is retired. The six women serving in 1992 are Judith Craig (Ohio), Sharon Brown-Christopher (Minnesota), Susan Morrison (Philadelphia), Ann Sherer (Kansas), Mary Ann Swenson (Denver), and Sharon Rader (Wisconsin).

35 See the "Barbara Harris: Bishop," articles by Li Tim-Oi, Marjorie Farmer, Pamela Darling, Susan Pierce, J. Antonio Ramos, Rosemary Ruether, Robert L. DeWitt, Monica Furlong, and Carter Heyward in *The Witness*, vol. 72, no. 4, April 1989, 4–27.

36 Kathy Nickerson, "Clergywomen Statistics and Charts" in *Wellsprings: A Journal of United Methodist Clergywomen*, vol. 2, no. 1, Summer 1989, 27–29.

37 Figures from Kathy Nickerson, Division of Ordained Ministry, General Board of Higher Education and Ministry of the United Methodist Church, Nashville.

38 Ruether and Keller have edited the three-volume *Women and Religion in America* (San Francisco: Harper and Row, 1981, 1983, and 1986). Rosemary Keller has also edited the two-volume *Women in New Worlds: Historical Perspectives on the Wesleyan Tradition*. (Nashville: Abingdon, 1981, 1982).

39 Phyllis Bird wrote the chapter "Images of Women in the Old Testament" in Religion and Sexism: Images of Women in the Jewish and Christian Traditions, Rosemary Ruether, ed. (New York: Simon and Schuster, 1974), 41–88. She is presently completing two major monographs, one showing that the whole concept of "sacred prostitution" in

ancient Near Eastern religion is questionable historically and the other on the roles of women in ancient Israelite religion.

40 This program, offered in the summers in Chicago since 1983, is called "Women in Ministry in the City." For the acceptance of women in ministry in mainline American Protestant denominations, see *Women of the Cloth*, compiled by Jackson Carroll, Barbara Hargrove, and Adair Mummis (San Francisco: Harper and Row, 1981).

41 See *An Inclusive Language Lectionary, Readings for Year A* (New York: National Council of Churches of Christ in the U.S.A., 1983), and *An Inclusive Language Lectionary: Readings for the Year B.* (New York: National Council of Churches of Christ in the U.S.A., 1984).

42 For a study of the power dynamics of God-language and how this must be reconceived in relations of mutuality, see Sallie McFague, *Models of God: Theology for an Ecological, Nuclear Age* (Philadelphia: Fortress Press, 1987).

43 Rebecca Chopp, *Proclamation, Women and the Word* (New York: Crossroads Press, 1989).

44 See Rosemary Ruether, *Women-church: Theology and Practice* (San Francisco: Harper and Row, 1986).

45 In response to the survey on women in world Christianity, I received information from the following countries and persons: (1) Germany: Eva Renate Schmidt and Anita Losch, Frankfurt and Gelnhausen, and Hildburg Wegner, Evangelische Frauenarbeit in Deutschland E.V., Frankfurt; (2) Norway: Gunvor Lande, Mellomkirkelig Rad for den Norske Kirke, Oslo; (3) Scotland: Fiona Hulbert, Church of Scotland, Edinburgh; (4) Ireland: Delma Sheridan, Catholic Church, Dublin; (5) Netherlands: Nel Bennema de Rijcke, secretary, Feminisme en Christendom, University of Nijmegen, who gathered information of women in theological education as students and faculty, and women's studies courses for the University in Heerlen, the Free University and the Catholic University in Amsterdam, the University of Groningen, the University of Kampen, the University of Tilburg, Nijmegen University, the University of Utrecht, and the University of Leiden; (6) France: Pasteur France Beydon, Eglise Reforme, Chartres; (7) Japan: Aiko Carter, NCC Women's Desk, Tokyo; (8) Korea: Rene Pak, Korean-American Campus Ministry, Chicago, and Sun Ai Park, *In God's Image*, c/o McCormick Seminary, Chicago; (9)Argentina: Mabel de Filippini, Centro de Estudios Cristianos, Buenos Aires; (10) Philippines: Virginia Fabella and Margaret Lacson, EATWOT, Asian Office, Manila; (11) India: Jessie Tellis Nayak, WINA, Mangalore, and Rita Monteiro, Satyashodak, Bombay.

46 *World Christian Encyclopedia*, David B. Barrett, ed. (Oxford: Oxford University Press, 1982) lists both the percentage of Christians in each country and the percentage of those practicing. For France 73% are listed as Christian, mainly Roman Catholic, 35% of which are non practicing, p. 295.

47 Kenya, with 82% Christians has 74% practicing (ibid., 432).

48 The *World Christian Encyclopedia* lists deaconess organizations worldwide under the heading of "women in ordained ministry." The fact that women are ordained to the presbyterate is ignored, and there are no statistics on women in the church in any category (ibid., 848).

49 Between 1966 and 1985 the number of U.S. American nuns declined from the peak of 180,000 to 130,000; see Mary Joe Weaver, *New Catholic Women: A Contemporary Challenge to Traditional Religious Authority* (San Francisco: Harper and Row, 1985), 86.

50 The need for a female ministry in early Christianity had much to do with this social pattern of female segregation; see Stevan L. Davies, *The Revolt of the Widows: The Social World of the Apocryphal Acts* (Carbondale: Southern Illinois University Press, 1980). In 19th-century missionary work, male missionaries could not visit women in their homes in most African and Asian cultures, so the female missionary became essential to evangelize women; see Rosemary Keller, "Lay Women in the Protestant Tradition" in Ruether and Keller, *Women and Religion*, vol. 1, 246–53.

51 In most Protestant churches full ordination to the presbyterate was not granted all at once, but rather there were a series of stages that led to it. For example, in Germany, women were admitted to theological study in 1919. Those with theological training were allowed to teach religious education in high schools in the 1920s. By the 1930s some churches also allowed such women to do catechetics in local churches and pastoral work in hospital and prison chaplancies. Their office was inaugurated by a ceremony of blessing, but not recognized as full ordination. In World War II these theologically trained women were asked to take over parishes and granted "limited ordination," but they were all taken out of these offices after the war. At the end of the 1950s women again became incorporated into parish ministry, but could exercise sacramental ministry only in specialized work with youth, hospitals, etc. Women lost ordination when they married. Only at the end of the 1960s was full ordination on equal terms for men and women begun in some German churches: account compiled by Eva Renate Schmidt, Church of Hessen and Nassau, Frankfurt.

52 There are presently 2,000 female graduates of theological courses in Korea, according to Rene Pak, Korean-American Campus Ministry, Chicago.

53 Copies available from Aiko Carter, Women's desk, National Christian Council, 2-3-18 Nishiwaseda, Shinjuku-ku, Tokyo. See also Matsui Yayori, "Japan's Emergence as a Super Economic Power—Are Japanese Women Happy?," in *In God's Image*, September 1987, 31–35.

54 The papers from this conference were published as *Doing Theology in a Divided World*, Virginia Fabella and Sergio Torres, eds. (Maryknoll, N.Y.: Orbis Books, 1985).

55 These papers were published in Spanish in 1986 under the title *El Rostro Femenino de la Teología*. Most of these papers appear in English translation in *Through Her Eyes: Women's Theology from Latin American*, Elsa Tamez, ed. (Maryknoll, N.Y.: Orbis, 1989).

56 Maryknoll, N.Y.: Orbis Books, 1988.

57 Copies available from the Asian Women's Resource Center for Culture and Theology, 134-5 Nokbun-Dong, Eunpyong-Ku, Seoul, 122-020 Korea.

58 In addition to Orbis Books, Meyer-Stone Books has published third-world feminist theology, such as the reprint of the WCC volume, *New Eyes for Reading: Biblical and Theological Reflections by Women from the Third World*, 1987.

59 See Antonio Gonzalez-Dorado, *Mariología popular Latinoamericano: de la María conquistadora a la María liberatadora* (Asuncion, 1985). Indian Catholic women also participated in a consultation on mariology, discussion this topic from a feminist perspective. See Leelamma Athyal, "Mariology: A Feminist Perspective" in *Towards a Theology of Humanhood: Women's Perspective*, Aruna Gnanadason, ed. (Delhi: ISPCK, 1986), 49–61; also the papers on mariology from the 1985 Asian women's theology conference in Manila and the 1987 Singapore conference, in *In God's Image*, December 1988, 6–12.

60 The writings of Asian feminists in *In God's Image* reflect this more pastoral perspective, with its optimistic belief that scripture can be readily correlated with women's liberation.

61 See note 3, above.

62 The document of the French groupe Orsay, "Droits et Cultures: Françaises, immigrées, estrangères, Quel avenir pour les femmes à l'Horizon 93? Quid de la Théologie féministe?" is more like the liberation theology hermeneutic of Latin American feminist and liberation theologians than like the Dutch and German Protestant academic feminist theology that they are concerned to translate: 47 rue de Clichy, 75009 Paris.

63 For the hermeneutic of popular Bible reading in the Base Christian Communities, see Carlos Mesters, "The Use of the Bible in Christian Communities of the Common People" in *The Challenge of Basic Christian Communities*, Sergio Torres and John Eagleson, eds. (Maryknoll, N.Y.: Orbis Books, 1982).

64 The major ideas of this Korean feminist theology of national unification can be found in *In God's Image*, June 1988.

65 For the roots of the Nazi ideology of German nature religion in German romanticism, see George L. Mosse, *The Crisis of German Ideology: Intellectual Origins of the Third Reich* (New York: Grosset and Dunlap, 1964).

66 For example, matriarchal feminist Elizabeth Gould Davis, *The First Sex* (Baltimore: Penguin, 1971), declares that the great matriarchal cultures

of the ancient Near East, Babylonian and Egyptian, were Indo-European, not Semitic. The Semites, notably Jews, never had any true culture, but have been the major source of patriarchal militarist monotheism; see 140–42. See also Rosemary Ruether, "Radical Victorians: The Quest for an Alternative Culture" in *Women and Religion*, vol. 3, 6–7, 30–32.

67 Susanna Heschel, in her lectures in Germany in 1988, challenged German feminism on their anti-Semitism. Louise Schottroff particularly took up this challenge to examine German feminist anti-Semitism. The critique of anti-Judaism has become a major concern of German Christian feminism.

68 See the writings of Peruvian feminist theologian, Aurora Lapiedra, "religiosidad popular y mujer Andina" in *El Rostro Femenino de la Teologia*, 49–73; also *Christianismo y Sociedad*, nr. 88, 24 (1986), vol. 2, 75–89.

69 For example, Sun Ai Park, "Theology of Han from a Woman's Perspective" (unpublished).

70 The primary exponent of this African theology is John S. Mbiti, *African Religions and Philosophy* (Garden City, N.Y.: Doubleday, 1971).

71 Mercy Amba Oduyoye, *Hearing and Knowing: Theological Reflections on Christianity in Africa* (Maryknoll, N.Y.: Orbis Books, 1986), 120–37.

72 See Lee Oo Jung, "Korean Culture and Feminist Theology" in *In God's Image*, September 1987, 36–38.

73 See Rita Monteiro, "The Indian Socio-Cultural Reality: A Feminist Perspective," in *Socio-Cultural Analysis in Theologizing*, Kunchina Patil, ed. (Bangalore: Indian Theological Association, 1987), 81–109.

74 Trees Dahm and Hedwig Meyer-Wilmes, "Metaphorphosis of 'Feminisme en Christendom': Development of the Discipline of Feminist Theology," working paper, to be published in the *Journal of Feminist Studies in Religion*.

75 See reports by Rommie Nauta and Berma Klein Goldewijk, "Feminist Perspective on Latin American Liberation Theology" and "Latin American Women Theology," in *Exchange: Bulletin of Third World Christian Literature and Ecumenical Research*, IIMO, Netherlands, vol. 16, no. 48, December 1987, 1–31.

76 The groupe Orsay publishes translations of feminist theology in *Femme Théologie à Minuit*, 47 rue de Clichy, 75009 Paris.

77 Mercy Amba Oduyoye, "Reflections from a Third World Woman's Perspective: Women's Experience and Liberation Theology" in *Irruption of the Third World: Challenge to Theology* (Maryknoll, N.Y.: Orbis Books, 1983), 246–55.

78 *Against Machismo: Ruben Alves, Leonardo Boff, Gustavo Gutiérrez, José Míquez Bonino, Juan Luis Segundo and Others Talk about the Struggle of Women*, interviews by Elza Tamez (Oak Park, Ill.: Meyer-Stone Books, 1987).

79 See Sook Ja Chung, "The Relation of Korean Feminist Theology and Minjung Theology" in her *An Attempt of Feminist Theology,* (np,n.d.), 34–66.

80 Rommie Nauta, "Latin American Women Theology" in *Exchange,* 15–17.

WOMEN IN ISLAM

1 The Western reader is cautioned that such labels do not necessarily connote in Middle East cultures what they generally mean in the West.

2 A number of articles have appeared recently attempting to describe and explain the phenomenon of Islamic dress. Two helpful pieces are those of Valerie J. Hoffman-Ladd, "Polemics on the Modesty and Segregation of Women in Contemporary Egypt" in *International Journal of Middle East Studies,* 19 (1987), 23–50, and Fadwa el Guindi, "Veiled Activism: Egyptian Women in the Contemporary Islamic Movement," in *Femmes de la Méditerranée, Peuples Méditerranéens,* 22–23 (Janv.-Juin 1983), 79–89.

3 Articles in recent Cairo newspapers, for example, contain warnings from sheikhs of al-Azhar such as this from Dr. Salim 'Abd al-Ra'uf: "The styles which are worn by some of our women and girls following the latest fashion are not within the confines of Islam. This is not Islamic dress and it is not *higab.* . . . The woman today is creative. She makes her dress tight, shortens it, wears it tight and decorates her head. All this is contrary to Islamic dress."

4 Interview in *Middle East Times* (February 21–27, 1989), 19. Ms. Saadawi has expressed such convictions to the author a number of times over the last seven years.

5 As Nesta Ramazani observed in "Arab Women in the Gulf" (*Middle East Journal,* 39 [1985], 259): "[The Saudi woman] is entrusted with the surgeon's scalpel or the obstetrician's forceps, but not with her own morality."

6 For a brief history of the development of educational opportunities for women in Saudi Arabia, see Ibtissam al-Bassam, "Institutions of Higher Education for Women in Saudi Arabia" in *International Journal of Educational Development,* 4 (1984), 255–58.

7 See Louay Bahry, "The New Saudi Woman: Modernizing in an Islamic Framework" in *Middle East Journal,* 34, 4 (1982), 502–15. Bahry notes on p. 508 that "some modernists have even proposed the establishment of women's courts, with female judges."

8 Soraya Altorki, *Women in Saudi Arabia* (New York: Columbia University Press, 1986), explores some of the changing circumstances among the upper classes of Saudi society.

9 Among a number of analyses of these events, see Nahid Yeganeh, "Women's Struggles in the Islamic Republic of Iran" in Azar Tabari and Na-

hid Yeganeh, eds., *In the Shadow of Islam: The Women's Movement in Iran* (London: Zed Press, 1982), 26–74.

10 Eliz Sanasarian details many of these reversals in *The Women's Rights Movement in Iran* (New York: Praeger, 1981), especially pp. 124–49.

11 See Freda Hussein and Kamelia Radwan, "The Islamic Revolution and Women: Quest for the Quranic Model," in Freda Hussein, ed., *Muslim Women* (New York: St. Martin's Press, 1984), 12.

12 Abdolrahamane Mahdjoube, "La révolution intérieure d'une militante Khomeinyste," in *Femmes de la Méditerranée, Peuples Méditerranéens*, 22–23 (Janv.-Juin 1983), 102, translated from the French.

13 For a good exposition of the influence of the system of seclusion (*purdah*) in the country, see Hanna Papanek, "Purdah in Pakistan: Seclusion and Modern Occupations for Women," in Hanna Papanek and Gail Minault, eds., *Separate Worlds* (Columbia, Mo.: South Asia Books, 1982), 190–215.

14 Freda Hussein in "The Struggle of Women in the National Development of Pakistan," in *Muslim Women*, 202–3, quotes some of Mawdudi's declarations that apart from child bearing, women are not fit for any job and that women are not only incapable but are demonstrably inferior to men.

15 For a full report of this event and its aftermath, see H. Mintjes, "The Doctor and the Ladies: A New Debate on 'Women and Islam' in Pakistan," in *al-Mushir* 25 (1983), 5–73.

16 "Not much imagination is required to realize that the vision of an Islamic social order entertained by the Ulema differs radically from that envisaged by educated and articulate women. But even Sunni politicians of the religious-oriented parties are by no means unanimous in their conception of an Islamic state." (Lucy Carroll, "Nizan-I-Islam: Processes an Conflicts in Pakistan's Programme of Islamisation, with Special Reference to the Position of Women," in *Journal of Commonwealth and Comparative Politics*, 20 [1982], 85).

17 There has been a dramatic change in the demographics of the Middle East, for example. More than half of the population now lives in urban areas with implications for mobility, family relationships, child care, and the like.

18 Jordanian women, unlike many others, do take positions as nurses and secretaries.

19 In the mid-1980s, for example, 20% of the work force and 41% of university-degree holders were women.

20 "As long as women are perceived, consciously or unconsciously, as symbols and repositories of cultural purity and authority, their full liberation will continue to pose a dilemma." (Amal Rassam, "Revolution Within the Revolution? Women and the State in Iraq" in *Iraq: The Contemporary State* [New York: St. Martin's Press, 1982], 99).

21 Recent headlines in the *Middle East Times* suggest the nature of this challenge: "Furor over Islamic Dress Heats up Turkey's Religious-

Secular Debate" (January 11–17, 1987, 5); "Turkish-Iranian Ties Take Nose Dive over Headscarf Ban" (March 28–April 3, 1989, 4), followed by a notation that "Subsequent Iranian agitation on the issue included a demonstration by chador-clad Iranian women in Tehran urging Turkish women to revolt against the country's secular ideology."

22 See, for example, Nancy and Richard Tapper, "The Birth of the Prophet: Ritual and Gender in Turkish Islam." (Man 22, 1 [March 1987], 72): "Not only do women too practice the central, day-to-day rites of Islam, but in their performance they may carry a religious load often of greater transcendental importance to the community than that borne by men."

23 Negiba Megademeni, as cited in "Muslim Women Developing a Theory of Islamic Feminism" in *Unitarian Universalist World*, 16, 8 (August 15, 1985), 10.

CONCLUSIONS TWENTY-FIVE YEARS LATER

1 See Rita M. Gross, "Tribal Religions: Aboriginal Australia," *Women in World Religions*, Arvind Sharma, ed. (Albany: State University of New York Press, 1987), 41–42, for a summary of that literature and its refutation.

2 Rita M. Gross, "Menstruation and Childbirth as Ritual and Religious Experience among Native Australians," *Unspoken Worlds: Women's Religious Lives*, Nancy Auer Falk and Rita M. Gross, eds. (Belmont, Calif.: Wadsworth, 1989), 257–66, and Rita M. Gross, "Tribal Religions: Aboriginal Australia," *Women In World Religions*, Arvind Sharma, ed. (Albany: State University of New York Press, 1987), 37–58.

3 Nancy Auer Falk and Rita M. Gross, *Unspoken Worlds: Women's Religious Lives* (Belmont, Calif.: Wadsworth, 1989.)

4 Rita M. Gross, *Exclusion and Participation: The Role of Women in Australian Aboriginal Religion* doctoral dissertation, U. of Chicago, 1975.

5 Some examples include Margrit Eichler, *Nonsexist Research Methods: A Practical Guide* (Boston: Allen and Unwin, 1988); Sandra Harding, ed., *Feminism and Methodology* (Bloomington: Indiana University Press, 1987); Sandra Harding, *The Science question in Feminism* (Ithaca: Cornell University Press, 1986); Elizabeth Langland and Walter Grove, *A Feminist Perspective in the Academy: The Difference It Makes* (Chicago: University of Chicago Press, 1981); Joyce McCarl Nielsen, *Feminist Research Methods: Exemplary Readings in the Social Sciences* (Boulder, Colo.: Westview Press, 1990); and Dale Spender, ed., *Men's Studies Modified: The Impact of Feminism on the Academic Disciplines* (Oxford: Pergamon Press, 1981).

6 Simone De Beauvoir, *The Second Sex* (New York: Bantom Books, 1961), xv.

7   This phrase, which so well captures the silencing of women by patri-
    archy and androcentrism, was first used by Mary Daly in *Beyond God
    the Father: Toward a Philosophy of Women's Liberation* (Boston: Bea-
    con Press, 1973), 8. The theme is also echoed in the title of the book
    edited by myself and Nancy Falk, *Unspoken Worlds: Women's Reli-
    gious Lives*, which was the first major exploration of women's religious
    lives, as opposed to cultural stereotypes *about* women, in cross-
    cultural perspective.

8   Henrietta L. Moore, *Feminism and Anthropology* (Minneapolis: Uni-
    versity of Minnesota Press, 1988), and Margot I. Duley and Mary I Ed-
    wards, *The Cross-Cultural Study of Women: A Comprehensive Guide*
    (New York: Feminist Press, 1986).

9   Eleanor McLaughlin, "The Christian Past: Does It Hold a Future for
    Women?," *Womanspirit Rising* (San Francisco: Harper and Row,
    1979), 96.

10 *Unspoken Words: Women's Religious Lives*, p. xv.

11 An important early article was Phyllis Trible, "Eve and Adam: Genesis
    2–3 Reread," *Womanspirit Rising*, 74–83. See also Phyllis Trible, *God
    and The Rhetoric of Sexuality* (Philadelphia: Fortress Press, 1978) and
    Elizabeth Schüssler Fiorenza, *Bread not Stone: The Challenge of Fem-
    inist Biblical Interpretation* (Boston: Beacon Press, 1984).

12 Frances Dahlberg, *Woman the Gatherer* (New Haven: Yale University
    Press, 1981) and Sally Slocum, "Woman the Hunter: Male Bias in An-
    thropology," *Toward an Anthropology of Women*, Ranya Reiter, ed.
    (New York and London: Monthly Review Press, 1975) 36–50.

13 Shirley Strum, *Almost Human: A Journey into the World of Baboons*
    (New York: Random House, 1987).

14 Diane Bell, *Daughters of the Dreaming* (North Sydney, N.S.W., Austra-
    lia: McPhee Grible/George Allen and Unwin, 1983).

15 Mary Daly, *Gyn/Ecology: The Metaethics of Radical Feminism* (Bos-
    ton: Beacon Press, 1978), 109–292.

16 Gross and Falk, *Unspoken Worlds: Women's Religious Lives*, 125–33,
    145–54.

17 George Buhler, tr. *The Laws of Manu* (New York: Dover Publications,
    1969), esp. pp. 195–98.

18 Falk and Gross, *Unspoken Worlds*, 72–81.

19 Many semipopular books on goddesses, often of questionable scholarly
    accuracy, have appeared. Among the most popular and influential of
    such books is Merlin Stone, *When God Was a Woman* (New York: Har-
    court Brace Javonovich, 1978). Two reliable cross-cultural surveys of
    goddesses in major religions, both ancient and modern, are David Kin-
    sley, *The Goddesses' Mirror: Visions of the Divine from East and West*
    (Albany: State University of New York, 1989) and Carl Olsen, *The Book
    of the Goddess* (New York: Crossroad, 1983).

20 Important and influential works include Carol Gilligan, *In a Different
    Voice: Psychological Theory and Women's Development* (Cambridge:

Harvard University Press, 1982), Nancy Chodorow, *The Reproduction of Mothering: Psychoanalysis and the Psychology of Gender* (Berkeley: University of California Press, 1978), Dorothy Dinnerstein, *The Mermaid and the Minotaur: Sexual Arrangements and Human Malaise* (New York: Harper and Row, 1977), Joyce Treblicot, ed., *Mothering: Essays in Feminist Theory* (Towana, N.J.: Rowman and Allenhold, 1983), and Belenky, Clinchy, Goldberger, and Tarule, *Women's Ways of Knowing: The Development of Self, Voice, and Mind* (New York: Basic Books, 1986).

21 For example, see James B. Nelson, *The Intimate Connection: Male Sexuality, Male Spirituality* (Philadelphia: Westminster Press, 1988).

22 For an example, see Katie G. Cannon, *Black Womanist Ethics* (Atlanta: Scholars' Press, 1988).

23 For an excellent presentation of this distinction, see Rosemarie Tong, *Feminist Thought: A Comprehensive Introduction* (Boulder: Westview Press, 1989).

24 The book that originated the debate is E. O. Wilson, *Sociobiology: The New Synthesis* (Cambridge: Harvard University Press, 1975). A feminist discussion is found in Marion Lowe, "Sociobiology and Sex Differences," *Signs: Journal of Women and Culture*, vol. 4, 1 (autumn 1978), 118–25.

25 Charlene Spretnek, ed., *The Politics of Women's Spirituality: Essays on the Rise of Spiritual Power Within the Feminist Movement* (Garden City, N.Y.: Anchor Books, 1982), esp. pages xv-xxi and 565–73.

26 Carol Gilligan, *In a Different Voice* (Cambridge: Harvard University Press, 1982).

27 Rita M. Gross, "I Go For Refuge to the Sangha," *Buddhist-Christian Studies*, vol. 11 (forthcoming).

28 Carol P. Christ, "Finitude, Death and Reverence for Life," *Laughter of Aphrodite: Reflections on a Journey to the Goddess* (San Francisco: Harper and Row, 1987), 213–27. Rosemary Ruether, "Motherearth and Megamachine," *WomanSpirit Rising: A Feminist Reader in Religion*, Judith Plaskow and Carol Christ, eds. (San Francisco: Harper and Row, 1979), 43–52.

29 Christ, "Finitude," 213–227.

30 Three sources are especially useful in demonstrating this position. Ann Barstow, "The Prehistoric Goddess," *The Book of the Goddess*, 7–15; Gerda Lerner, *The Creation of Patriarchy* (New York: Oxford University Press, 1986); and Marija Gimbutas, "Women and Culture in Goddess Oriented Old Europe," *The Politics of Women's Spirituality*, 22–32.

31 Christ and Plaskow, *Womanspirit Rising*, 1–62.

32 Paden, *Religious Worlds: The Comparative Study of Religion* (Boston: Beacon Press, 1988), 164.

33 Ibid,. 164–65.

34 Ibid., 12.

35 Quoted by Carol Christ, *Laughter of Aphrodite*, 135.

36 For example, I brought up this point in response to Gordon Kaufman's paper, "God and Emptiness: An Experimental Essay," at the 1986 meetings of the Cobb-Abe Buddhist-Christian theological encounter, but this was not a comment to which he chose to respond in any way, while I thought it was the most important point I had made. For published accounts, see *Buddhist-Christian Studies*, vol. 9 (1989), 175–212.

37 Judith Ochshorn, *Female Experience and the Nature of the Divine* (Bloomington: Indiana University Press, 1981) and Gerda Lerner, *The Creation of Pariarchy*.

38 Buddhism and Christianity share a similar abstract believe and a similar failure to institutionalize genuine equality on an ordinary day-to-day basis. Christians cite the Pauline phrase that in Christ there is neither male nor female when pressed on beliefs about gender equality, and Buddhists, similarly say "the dharma is neither male nor female" when asked about women's spiritual capabilities. But because neither religion has examined sexist attitudes and practices, there is a great gulf between abstract ideal and everyday realities in both.

39 Certainly this is true of the work of Mary Daly, and to a lesser extent of Rosemary Ruether, especially in her earlier work. Though both make a philosophical case for the use of female pronouns and images of ultimacy, they do not actually give many models of such language in their own work. See also Sally TeSelle, for an example of a theologian who works with metaphor, but is more comfortable with sex neutral images, such as friend, than with full-blown feminine-androgynous images.

40 *An Inclusive Language Lectionary: Readings for Year A, Revised Edition* (National Council of the Churches of Christ in the U.S.A., 1986), 13.

41 Rita M. Gross, "Female God Language in a Jewish Context," *Woman-Spirit Rising*, 172.

42 Christine Downing, *The Goddess: Mythological Images of the Feminine* (New York: Crossroad, 1981), Carol P. Christ, *Laughter of Aphrodite*, and Starhawk, *The Spiral Dance: A Rebirth of the Ancient Religion of the Great Goddess* (San Francisco: Harper and Row, 1979) are my favorites.

43 Rita M. Gross, "Hindu Female Deities as a Resource for the Contemporary Rediscovery of the Goddess," *Journal of the American Academy of Religion*, 46, 3 (Sept. 1978), 269–91; "Steps Toward Feminine Imagery of Deity in Jewish Theology, *On Being A Jewish Feminist: A Reader*, Susannah Heschel, ed. (New York: Schocken Books, 1983); "The Feminine Principle in Tibetan Vajrayana Buddhism: Reflections of a Buddhist Feminist," *Journal of Transpersonal Psychology*, 16:2 (1984), 179–92; "I Will Never Forget to Visualize that Vajrayogini is My Body and Mind," *Journal of Feminist Studies in Religion*, 3:1 (spring 1987), 77–89.

44 Gross, "Hindu Female Deities as a Resource in the Contemporary Rediscovery of the Goddess," *Journal of the American Academy of Religion,* 46:3 (September 1978), 277–78.

45 William E. Paden, *Religious Worlds,* 15–49.

46 Rita M. Gross, "Religious Diversity: Some Implications for Monotheism," *Wisconsin Dialogue,* vol. 11 (1991). Another version of these comments, aimed specifically at Jewish monotheism, is "Religious Pluralism: Some Issues for Judaism," *Journal of Ecumenical Studies,* vol. 26:1 (winter 1989).

47 Rita M. Gross, "Buddhism and Feminism: Toward the Mutual Transformation," *Eastern Buddhist,* vol. 19:1 and 2 (spring and fall 1986); "The Dharma is Neither Male nor Female: Buddhism on Gender and Liberation," *Mens's and Women's Liberation: Testimonies of Spirit,* Grob, Gordon, and Hassan, eds., (Greenwood Press); "Buddhism after Patriarchy," *After Patriarchy: Feminist Reconstructions of the World's Religions,* Cooey, Eakin, and McDaniel (Orbis Books, 1992) and *Buddhism After Patriarchy: A Feminist History, Analysis, and Reconstruction of Buddhism* (Albany: State University of New York Press, 1993.

48 See n. 9.

49 John Cobb, *Beyond Dialogue: Toward a Mutual Transformation of Buddhism and Christianity* (Philadelphia: Fortress Press, 1982).

50 Some material in this essay has been incorporated from my book: *Buddhism After Patriarchy: A Feminist History, Analysis and Reconstruction of Buddhism.*

BIBLIOGRAPHY

INTRODUCTION

"Agreed Statement of the Anglican-Roman Catholic Dialogue of Canada on the Experience of the Ministries of Women in Canada." In *Ecumenism*, no. 103. Sept., 1991: 4–5.

Brennan, Bonnie. "Catholic women: What progress have they made?" In *The Toronto Star*. Aug. 3, 1991: J10.

Chhachhi, Amrita. "The State, Religious Fundamentalism and Women—Trends in South Asia." In *Economic and Political Weekly*. March 18, 1989: 567–78.

Sanday, Peggy Reeves. 1981. *Female Power and Male Dominance: On the origins of sexual inequality.* Cambridge: Cambridge University Press.

von Kellenbach, Katharina. 1987. *Anti-Judaism in Christian-Rooted Feminist Writings: An Analysis of Major U.S. American and West German Feminist Theologians.* Ann Arbor: UNI.

ABORIGINAL WOMEN'S RELIGION

Bell, Diane. 1992. "Considering gender: are human rights for women too?" In *Human Rights in Cross Cultural Perspectives.* Abdullahi An-Na'im, ed. University of Pennsylvania Press, Philadelphia. 339–362.

———. 1989. "The sacred and the profane revisited: religion and gender in Aboriginal Australia." Roundtable presentation, A.A.R. Annual Conference. Anaheim, Calif., November.

———. 1988a. "The politics of separation." In *Dealing with Inequality*. Marilyn Strathern, ed. C.U.P. Cambridge. 112–29.

———. 1988b. "Choose your mission wisely: Christian colonials and Aboriginal marital arrangements on the northern frontier." In *Aboriginal Australians and Christianity*. Deborah Bird Rose and Tony Swain, eds. A.A.S.R., Adelaide. 338–52.

———. 1988c. "We are hungry for our land." In *A Most Valuable Acquisition*. Verity Burgman and Jenny Less, eds. McPhee Gribble/Penguin, Melbourne. 29–41.

———. 1987a. "Aboriginal women and customary law." In *Indigenous Law and the State*. Bradford W. Morse and Gordon R. Woodman, eds. Foris, Holland. 297–314.

———. 1987b. "Exercising discretion: sentencing Aborigines for murder in the Northern Territory." In *Indigenous Law and the State*. Bradford W. Morse and Gordon R. Woodman, eds. Foris, Holland. 367–96.

———. 1987c. "Aboriginal women and the religious experience." In *Traditional Aboriginal Society: A Reader*. W. H. Edwards, ed. MacMillan, South Melbourne. 237–56 (first published 1982).

———. 1984–5. "Aboriginal women and land: learning from the Northern Territory experience." *Anthropological Forum*, vol. 5, no. 3. 353–63.

———. 1984. "Women and Aboriginal religion." In *Religion in Aboriginal Australia*. Max Charlesworth, Ken Maddock, Diane Bell and Howard Morphy, eds. Q.U.P., St. Lucia. 295–303.

———. 1983a. *Daughters of the Dreaming*. Allen and Unwin, Sydney.

———. 1983b. "Sacred sites: the politics of protection." In *Aborigines and Land Rights*. Nicolas Peterson and Marcia Langton, eds. A.I.A.S., Canberra. 278–93.

———. 1981. "Daly River (Malak Malak) Land Claim: women's interests." Submission to the Daly River (Malak Malak) Land Claim prepared on behalf of the Northern Land Council. Darwin, Exhibit no. 8 (34 pp.); Exhibit no. 65 (12 pp.) (restricted).

———. 1982. "In the Tracks of the Munga-Munga." Submission to Cox River Land Claim, prepared on behalf of the Northern Land Council. Darwin, Exhibit no. 27 (35 pp.).

———. 1980. "Desert politics: choices in the 'marriage market'." In *Women and Colonization: Anthropological Perspectives*. Mona Etienne and Eleanor Leacock, eds. Praeger, New York. 239–69.

Bell, Diane, and Pam Ditton. 1980/4. *Law: The Old and the New*. Aboriginal History, Canberra.

Bell, Diane, and Genée Marks. 1990. *Aborigines and Australian Society*. UNESCO, Paris.

Bell, Diane, and Topsy Napurrula Nelson. 1989a. "Speaking about rape is everyone's business." *Women's Studies International Forum*, vol. 12, no. 4. 404–16.

Bern, John. 1979a. "Politics in the conduct of a secret male ceremony." *Journal of Anthropological Research*, vol. 35, no. 1. 47–60.

———. 1979b. "Ideology and domination." *Oceania*, vol. 50, no. 2. 118–32.

Berndt, Catherine. 1970. "Digging sticks and spears, or, the two-sex model." In *Women's Role in Aboriginal Society*. Fay Gale, ed. AIAS, Canberra. 39–48.

———. 1950. "Women's changing ceremonies in Northern Australia." *L'Homme*, vol. 1, 1–87.

———. 1965. "Women and the 'secret life.'" In *Aboriginal Man in Australia*. R. M. and C. H. Berndt, eds. Angus and Robertson, Sydney. 236–82.

Berndt, R. M. 1951. *Kunapipi*. Cheshire, Melbourne.

Berndt, R. M., and R. Tonkinson. 1988. "Foreword: a contemporary overview." In *Social Anthropology and Australian Aboriginal Studies*. R. M. Berndt and R. Tonkinson, eds. Aboriginal Studies Press, Canberra. 1–13.

Burbank, Victoria. 1989. "Gender and the anthropological curriculum: Aboriginal Australia." In *Gender and Anthropology: Critical Reviews for Research and Teaching*. Sandra Morgen, ed. AAA, Washington. 116–31.

Caplan, Pat. 1988. "Engendered knowledge." *Anthropology Today*, vol. 14, no. 5, 8–12; no. 6, 14–17.

Clifford, James. 1988. *The Predicament of Culture*. Harvard University Press, Cambridge.

Collier, Jane, and Michelle Rosaldo. 1981. "Politics and gender in simple societies." In *Sexual Meanings: The Cultural Construction of Gender and Sexuality*. Sherry B. Ortner and Harriet Whitehead, eds. Cambridge University Press, London. 275–329.

Cowlishaw, Gillian. 1979. "Woman's Realm: A study of socialisation, sexuality and reproduction." Ph.D Thesis, University of Sydney.

Dussart, Françoise. 1988. "Warlpiri Women's Yawulyu Ceremonies: A forum for socialization and innovation." Ph.D. Thesis, ANU, Canberra.

Elkin, A. P. 1961. "The Yabuduruwa." *Oceania*, vol. 31. 166–209.

Gillen, Francis James. 1968. *Gillen's Diary: The Camp Jottings of F. J. Gillen on the Spencer and Gillen Expedition across Australia, 1910–2*. Libraries Board of South Australia, Adelaide.

Glowczewski, Barbara. 1983. "Death, women and 'value production': the circulation of hairstrings among the Walpiri of the Central Australian Desert." *Ethnology*, vol. 22, no. 3. 225–39.

Goodale, Jane. 1971. *Tiwi Wives*. University of Washington Press, Seattle.

Grau, Andrée. 1983. "Dreaming, Dancing, Kinship: The Melville and Bathurst Islands, North Australia." Ph.D. Thesis, Queen's University of Belfast, Northern Ireland.

Gross, Rita. 1987. "Tribal religions: Aboriginal Australia." In *Women and World Religions*. Arvind Sharma, ed. SUNY Press, Albany. 37–58.

Hamilton, Annette. 1987. "Dual social systems: technology, labour and women's secret rites in the eastern Western Desert of Australia." In *Traditional Aboriginal Society: A Reader*. W. H. Edwards, ed. Mac-Millan, South Melbourne. 34–52 (first published 1980).

————. 1979. "Timeless Transformations: Women, men and history in the Australia Western Desert." Ph.D. thesis, University of Sydney.

Hart, C. W. M., and A. R. Pilling. 1960. *The Tiwi of North Australia.* Holt Rinehart and Winston, New York.

Hawkesworth, Mary E. 1989. "Knowers, knowing and known: feminist theory and claims of truth." *Signs*, vol. 14, no. 3. 533–37 (see also commentaries and reply, *Signs*, 1990, vol. 15, no. 2, 417–28).

Hiatt, L. R. 1987. "Aboriginal political life." In *Traditional Aboriginal Society: A Reader.* W. H. Edwards, ed. MacMillan, South Melbourne. 174–88 (first published 1984).

Hill, Marji, and Alex Barlow. 1985. *Black Australia 2: An Annotated Bibliography and Teachers' Guide to Resources on Aborigines and Torres Strait Islanders.* AIAS, Canberra.

Hondagneu-Sotelo, Pierrette. 1988. "Gender and fieldwork: review essay." *Women's Studies International Forum*, vol. 11, no. 6. 611–18.

Kaberry, Phyllis M. 1939. *Aboriginal Women: Sacred and Profane.* George Routledge and Sons, London.

Kendon, Adam. 1988. *Sign Language of Aboriginal Australia: Cultural Semiotic and Communicative Perspectives.* C.U.P., Cambridge.

Kuhn, T. S. 1970. *The Structure of Scientific Revolutions.* University of Chicago Press, Chicago.

Lauridsen, Jan. 1990. "Women's jarata of North Central Australia." Manuscript.

Leacock, Eleanor. 1978. "Women's status in egalitarian society." *Current Anthropology*, vol. 19, no. 2. 247–75.

Maddock, Kenneth. 1982. *The Australian Aborigines: A Portrait of their Society* (second edition). Penguin, Ringwood (first edition 1972).

Marcus, George E., and Michael M. J. Fischer. 1986. *Anthropology as Cultural Critique.* University of Chicago Press, Chicago.

Mascia-Lees, Frances E., Patricia Sharpe, and Colleen Ballerino Cohen. 1989. "The postmodern turn in Anthropology: cautions from a feminist perspective." *Signs*, vol. 15, no. 1. 7–35.

Mayne, Tom. 1986. *Aborigines and the Issues.* Australian Council of Churches, Sydney.

Meggitt, M. J. 1962. *Desert People: A Study of the Walbiri Aborigines of Central Australia.* Angus and Robertson, Sydney.

Merlan, Francesca. 1988. "Gender in Aboriginal social life: a review." In *Social Anthropology and Australian Aboriginal Studies.* R. M. Berndt and R. Tonkinson, eds. Aboriginal Studies Press, Canberra. 15–76.

————. 1989. "The objectification of 'culture': an aspect of current political process in Aboriginal affairs." *Anthropological Forum*, vol. 6, no. 1. 105–16.

Moore, Henrietta. 1988. *Feminism and Anthropology.* University of Minnesota Press, Minneapolis.

Munn, Nancy D. 1973/1986. *Walbiri Inconography: Graphic Representations and Cultural Symbolism in a Central Australian Society* (with a new afterword). University of Chicago Press, Chicago.

Payne, Helen. "Singing a Sister's Sites: Women's Land Rights in the Australian Musgrave Ranges." Ph.D. Thesis, University of Queensland.
Róheim, Geza. 1933. "Women and their life in Central Australia." *RAIJ*, no. 63. 207–65.
Rohrlich-Leavitt, Ruby, Barbara Sykes, and Elizabeth Weatherford. 1975. "Aboriginal woman: male and female anthropological perspectives." In *Towards and Anthropology of Woman*. Rayna Reiter, ed. Monthly Review Press, New York.
Rose, Deborah Bird. 1984. "Dingo makes us Human: Being and purpose in Australian Aboriginal culture." Ph.D. Thesis, Bryn Mawr College.
Spencer, Baldwin, and F. J. Gillen. 1899. *The Native Tribes of Central Australia*. Macmillan, London.
Stacey, Judith. 1988. "Can there be a feminist ethnography?" *Women's Studies International Forum*, vol. 11, no. 1. 21–27.
Stanner, W. E. H. 1979. "Religion, totemism and symbolism." In *White Man Got No Dreaming*. A.N.U. Press, Canberra. 106–43 (first published 1962).
Strathern, Marilyn. 1985. "Dislodging a world view: challenge and counter challenge in the relationship between feminism and anthropology." *Australian Feminist Studies*, no. 1. 1–25.
Strehlow, T. G. H. 1971. *Songs of Central Australia*. Angus and Robertson, Sydney.
Warner, Lloyd W. 1969. *A Black Civilization: A Social Study of an Australian Tribe*. Peter Smith, Glouchester, Mass. (first published 1937, Harper and Row).
White, I. M. 1975. "Sexual conquest and submission in Aboriginal myths." In *Australian Aboriginal Mythology*. L. R. Hiatt, ed. AIAS, Canberra.
Yeatman, Anna. 1983. "The procreative model: the social ontological bases of the gender-kinship system." *Social Analysis*, no. 14. 3–30 (see also comments and rejoinder, *Social Analysis*, 1984, no. 16, 3–43.)

HINDUISM

"A step toward emancipation?" In *The Independent*. Jan. 15, 1990; 9.
"BJP's Ramayan." In *Manushi*. no. 60. 1990.
Brass, Paul R. 1990. *The Politics of India since Independence*. Cambridge: Cambridge University Press.
Chandra, Sharmila. "Echoing the Times." In *India Today*. Jan. 31, 1990.
Chatterji, P. C. 1984. *Secular Values for Secular India*. New Delhi: P. C. Chatterji.
Chhachhi, Amrita. "The State, Religious Fundamentalism and Women: Trends in South Asia." In *Economic and Political Weekly*. March 18, 1989.
"Christian Marriage Act a threat to women." In *The Times of India*. Bombay. Jan. 9, 1990: 3.

"Christian women urge changes in divorce act." In *Indian Express*. Bombay. Jan. 9, 1990: 3.

Clementin-Ojha, Catherine [see also Ojha]. "The Tradition of Female Gurus." In *Manushi*. no. 31. 1985.

D'Cruz, Emil. 1988. *Indian Secularism: A Fragile Myth*. New Delhi: Indian Social Institute.

Duley, Margot I. 1986. *The Cross-cultrual Study of Women: A Comprehensive Guide*. Eds. Margot I. Duley and M. I. Edwards. New York: Feminist Press, City University of New York.

Dyson, Tim and Mick Moore. "On Kinship Structure, Female Autonomy, and Demographic Behavior in India." In *Population and Development Review*. vol. 9. no. 1. 1993.

Gothoskar, Sujata. "Pushing Women Out: Declining Employment of Women in the Organised Industrial Sector." In *Manushi*. no. 65. 1991.

Government of India. 1974. *Towards Equality: Report of the Committee on the Status of Women in India*. New Delhi: Ministry of Education and Social Welfare, Department of Social Welfare.

"How India Voted." In *India Today*. July 15, 1991: 34.

India Today. Sept. 15, 1990: 34.

Indian Express. Bombay. Jan. 25, 1989.

Jain, Madhu and M. Rahman. "Dating: An Open Embrace." In *India Today*. May 15, 1991: 73–75.

Jayawardena, Kumari. 1986. "Women, Social Reform and Nationalism in India." *Feminism and Nationalism in the Third World*. London: Zed Books.

Johnsen, Linda. "Women Saints of India." In *Yoga Journal*. no. 81. 1988.

King, Ursula. 1984. "The Effect of Social Change on Religious Self-Understanding: Women Ascetics in Modern Hinduism." In *Changing South Asia: Religion and Society*. Eds. K. Ballhatchet and D. Taylor. London: Asian Research.

Kishwar, Madhu. "In Defence of Our Dharma." In *Manushi*. no. 60. 1990.

———. "Why I do not Call Myself a Feminist." In *Manushi*. no. 61. 1990.

———. "Towards More Just Norms for Marriage: Continuing the Dowry Debate." In *Manushi*. no. 53. 1989.

———. "Introduction." In *Manushi*. no. 50–52. 1989.

———. "Women Bhakta Poets." In *Manushi*. no. 50–52. 1989.

———. "Pro Women or Anti Muslin?: The Shahbano Controversy." In *Manushi*. no. 32. 1986.

———. "Gandhi on Women." In *Economic and Political Weekly*. vol. 20. no. 40. 1985.

Klostermaier, Klaus. 1990. "Truth and Toleration in Contemporary Hinduism." In *Papers from the 1990 Symposium on Truth and Tolerance*. Ed. E. J. Furcha. Montreal: Faculty of Religious Studies, McGill University.

Lalonde, Gloria. 1985. "National Development and the Changing Status of Women in India." M.A. Thesis. Montreal: McGill University, Department of Anthropology.

Lateef, Shahida. 1990. Muslim Women in India: Political & Private Realities 1890s–1980s. New Delhi: Kali for Women.

Liddle, Joanna and Rama Joshi. "Gender and Imperialism in British India." In Economic and Political Weekly. vol. 20. no. 43. 1985.

Madhavananda, Swami and Ramesh Chandra Majumadar. 1953. Great Women of India. Calcutta: Advaita Ashrama.

Marty, E. Martin and R. Scott Appleby. 1991. Fundamentalisms Observed. Chicago: University of Chicago Press.

Miller, Barbara D. 1981. The Endangered Sex. Ithaca: Cornell University Press.

"Mrs. Scindia Defends Sati." In Times of India. Bombay. Jan. 22, 1989.

Neuhaus, Richard John. 1984. The Naked Public Square: Religion and Democracy in America. Grand Rapids, Michigan: William B. Eerdmans.

Ojha, Catherine. 1981. "Feminine Asceticism in Hinduism: Its Tradition and Present Condition." In Man in India. 61/3.

"Poll Stars." In India Today. May 31, 1991: 77.

Pothen, S. 1986. Divorce: Its Causes and Consequences in Hindu Society. Delhi: Vikas.

Radhakrishnan, S. 1956. Recovery of Faith. London: Allen and Unwin.

Rai, Amit. "India's New Brahmanism." In Z Magazine. July/Aug. 1991.

Rao, R. "Move to Stop Sex-test Abortion." In Nature. 364. 1986.

Rao, V. V. Prakasa and V. Nandini Rao. 1982. Marriage, the Family and Women in India. New Delhi: Heritage Publishers.

Rathore, L. S. "Political Culture of India's Ruling Class." In Indian Journal of Political Studies. vol. 51. no. 2. 1990.

Ravindra, R. P. "The Scarcer Half: A report on amniocentesis and other sex-determination techniques, sex preselection and new reproductive technologies." Counterfact no. 9. CED Health Feature. Bombay: Centre for Education and Documentation. Jan. 1986.

Sharma, Ursula. 1979. "Segregation and its Consequences in India: Rural Women in Himachal Pradesh." In Women United, Women Divided: Comparative Studies of Ten Contemporary Cultures. Eds. P. Caplan and J. M. Bujra. Bloomington: Indiana University Press.

"Son Preference." In Report of the Working Group on Traditional Practices Affecting the Health of Women and Children. U.N. Doc. E/CN.4/1986/42 of Feb. 4, 1986: paras. 139–171, 24–30.

Srivastava, T. N. 1985. Woman and The Law. New Delhi: Intellectual Publishing House.

"The Organisation: The Line of Command." In India Today. May 15, 1991.

Vaid, Sudesh. "Ideologies on Women in Nineteenth Century Britain, 1850s–70s." In Economic and Political Weekly. vol. 20. no. 43. 1985.

van den Bosch, Lourens P. "A Burning Question: The Sacred Centre as the Focus of Political Interest." Paper delivered to the symposium "The Sacred Centre as the Object of Political Interest." Groningen, Netherlands: University of Groningen. March 1989.

Venkatramani, S. H. "Born to Die." In *India Today*. June 15, 1986.

Vohra, Smriti. "Woman MP No Sanyasini." In *Times of India News Service*. New Delhi. Dec. 21, 1989: 19.

White, Charles S. 1980. "Mother Guru: Jñānānanda of Madras, India." In *Unspoken Worlds: Women's Religious Lives in Non-Western Cultures*. Eds. N. A. Falk & R. M. Gross. New York: Harper and Row.

Yerkuntawar, Baliram Sadashiv. "Samvad." In *Prajnalok* (Marathi). no. 119, Dec. 1987.

Young, Katherine K. and Lilly Miller. 1990. "Ānandamāyī Mā and Modern Hinduism." In *Boeings and Bullock-carts: Studies in Change and Continuity in Indian Civilization*. vol. 2: *Indian Civilization in its Local, Regional and National Aspects*. Ed. Dhirendra Vajpeyi. Delhi: Chanakya Publications.

Young, Katherine K. 1983. "From Hindu Stridharma to Universal Feminism: A Study of the Women in the Nehru Family." In *Traditions in Contact and Change: Selected Proceedings of the XIV Congress of the International Association for the History of Religions*. Eds. Peter Slater and Donald Wiebe. Toronto: Sir Wilfred Laurier Press.

WOMEN IN BUDDHISM

Adikaram, E. W. 1953. *Early History of Buddhism in Ceylon*. Colombo: M. D. Gunasena and Company.

Allione, Tsultrim. 1986. *Women of Wisdom*. London: Arkana Paperbacks.

Aziz, Barbara Nimri. 1989. "Buddhist Nuns." *Natural History*. March. 40–49.

Barnes, Nancy J. 1987. "Buddhism." In *Women in World Religions*, Arvind Sharma, ed. Albany: State University of New York Press.

Bechert, Heinz. 1966. *Buddhismus, Staat und Gesellschaft in den Ländern des Theravāda Buddhismus*. Band XVII, 1. Hamburg: Schriften des Instituts für Asienkunde.

────. 1967. *Buddhismus, Staat und Gesellschaft in den Ländern des Theravāda Buddhismus*. Band XVII, 2. Hamburg: Schriften des Instituts für Asienkunde.

Bechert, Heinz, and Richard Gombrich, eds. 1984. *The World of Buddhism, Buddhist Monks and Nuns in Society and Culture*. New York: Facts on File Publications.

Blacker, Carmen. 1975. *The Catalpa Bow: A Study of Shamanistic Practices in Japan*. London: George Allen & Unwin.

Bloss, Lowell W. 1987. "The Female Renunciants of Sri Lanka: The *Dasasil-mattawa.*" *Journal of the International Association of Buddhist Studies.* 10, no. 1. 7–32.

Bond, George D. 1988. *The Buddhist Revival in Sri Lanka: Religious Tradition, Reinterpretation and Response.* Columbia: University of South Carolina Press.

Boucher, Sandy. 1988. *Turning the Wheel: American Women Creating the New Buddhism.* New York: Harper and Row.

Bunnag, Jane. 1973. *Buddhist Monk, Buddhist Layman. A Study of Urban Monastic Organization in Central Thailand.* Cambridge: Cambridge University Press.

Butsumon. 1989. Volume 4, Fall Ohigan. Publication of the Buddhist Bookstore, Buddhist Churches of America of Jodo Shinshu Hongwanji-ha, San Francisco.

Carrithers, Michael. 1983. *The Forest Monks of Sri Lanka.* Delhi: Oxford University Press.

Carroll, Theodora Foster. 1983. *Women, Religion and Development in the Third World.* New York: Praeger.

Ch'en, Kenneth. 1964. *Buddhism in China, A Historical Survey.* Princeton: Princeton University Press.

Cissell, Kathryn Ann A. [Kathryn A. Tsai]. 1972. *The Pi-ch'iu-ni chuan: Biographies of Famous Chinese Nuns from 317–516 C.E.* Ann Arbor, Mich. University Microfilms.

Dalai Lama [His Holiness Tenzin Gyatso the 14th Dalai Lama]. 1987. "Advice to the Nuns of Geden Choeling." *Newsletter on International Buddhist Women's Activities,* 10. 6–11.

Dowman, Keith. 1984. *Sky Dancer, The Secret Life and Songs of the Lady Yeshe Tsogyel.* London: Routledge & Kegan Paul.

Earhart, H. Byron. 1980. "Toward a Theory of the Formation of the Japanese New Religions: a Case Study of Gedatsu-kai." *History of Religions,* 20, 1–2. 175–97.

———. 1989. *Gedatsu-kai and Religion in Contemporary Japan.* Indiana University Press.

Falk, Nancy A. 1980. "The Case of the Vanishing Nuns: The Fruits of Ambivalence in Ancient Indian Buddhism." In *Unspoken Worlds, Women's Religious Lives in Non-Western Cultures.* Nancy A. Falk and Rita M. Gross, eds. San Francisco: Harper & Row.

Ferguson, John P. 1978. "The Quest for Legitimation by Burmese Monks and Kings: The Case of the Shwegyin Sect (19th–20th Centuries)." In *Religion and Legitimation of Power in Thailand, Laos and Burma.* Bardwell Smith, ed. Chambersburg, Pa.: Anima Books.

Fields, Rick. 1986. *How the Swans Came to the Lake: A Narrative History of Buddhism in America.* Boston: Shambhala Publications.

Free China Journal. Taipei, ROC. U.S. Edition: Los Angeles. Nov. 2, 1989; Oct. 18, 1990.

Friedman, Lenore. 1987. *Meetings with Remarkable Women: Buddhist Teachers in America.* Boston: Shambhala Publications.

Gombrich, Richard. 1988. *Theravāda Buddhism, A Social History from Ancient Benares to Modern Colombo.* London: Routledge & Kegan Paul.

Gombrich, Richard, and Gananath Obeyesekere. 1988. *Buddhism Transformed. Religious Change in Sri Lanka.* Princeton: Princeton University Press.

Gross, Rita. 1986a. "Buddhism and Feminism: Toward their Mutual Transformation, 1." *Eastern Buddhist,* 19, 1. 44–58.

————. 1986b. "Buddhism and Feminism: Toward their Mutual Transformation, 2." *Eastern Buddhist,* 19, 2. 62–74.

Gunawardana, R. A. L. H. 1979. *Robe and Plough, Monasticism and Economic Interest in Early Medieval Sri Lanka.* Tucson: University of Arizona Press.

Guthrie, Stewart. 1988. *A Japanese New Religion: Risshō Kōsei-kai in a Mountain Hamlet.* Ann Arbor. University of Michigan Press.

Hamilton-Merritt, Jane. 1986. *A Meditator's Diary, A Western Woman's Unique Experiences in Thailand Monasteries.* London: Unwin Paperbacks.

Hardacre, Helen. 1979. "Sex-Role Norms and Values in Reiyūkai." *Japanese Journal of Religious Studies.* 6, no. 3. 445–59.

————. 1984. *Lay Buddhism in Contemporary Japan: Reiyūkai Kyōdan.* Princeton University Press.

————. 1986. *Kurozumikyō and the New Religions of Japan.* Princeton: Princeton University Press.

————. 1987. "Hōza: the Dharma Seat." In *Japanese Buddhism: Its Tradition, New Religions and Interaction with Christianity.* Minoru Kiyota, ed. Tokyo: Buddhist Books International.

Hopkinson, Deborah, et al. 1986. *Not Mixing Up Buddhism.* New York: White Pine Press.

Horner, I. B. 1975. *Women Under Primitive Buddhism, Laywomen and Almswomen.* Delhi: Motilal Banarsidass (originally published, London: Routledge & Kegan Paul, 1930).

Jan, Yun-hua. 1984. "The Religious Situation and the Studies of Buddhism and Taoism in China: An Incomplete and Imbalanced Picture." *Journal of Chinese Religions,* 12. 37–64.

Kabilsingh, Chatsumarn. 1982. "Buddhism and the Status of Women." *Southeast Asian Review,* 7, nos. 1–2. 63–74.

————. 1984. *A Comparative Study of Bhikkunī Pātimokkha.* Varanasi: Chaukhambha Orientalia.

Kajiyama, Yuichi. 1982. "Women in Buddhism." *Eastern Buddhist,* 15, 2. 53–70.

Kendall, Laurel. 1986. *Shamans, Housewives and Other Restless Spirits.* Honolulu: University of Hawaii Press.

————. 1988. *The Life and Hard Times of a Korean Shaman.* Honolulu: University of Hawaii Press.

Kennett, Jiyu. 1972. *Selling Water by the River, A Manual of Zen Training.* New York: Vintage Books (reissued as *Zen is Eternal Life*).

Keyes, Charles F. 1984. "Mother or Mistress but Never a Monk: Buddhist Notions of Female Gender in Rural Thailand." *American Ethnologist,* 11, no. 2. 223–41.

———. "Ambiguous Gender: Male Initiation in a Northern Thai Buddhist Society." In *Gender and Religion: On the Complexity of Symbols.* Caroline Walker Bynum, Stevan Harrell, and Paula Richman, eds. Boston: Beacon Press.

Khema, Ayya. 1987. *Being Nobody, Going Nowhere, Meditations on the Buddhist Path.* London: Wisdom Publications.

King, Sallie B. 1987. *Passionate Journey: The Spiritual Autobiography of Satomi Myōdō.* Boston: Shambhala Publications.

———. 1988. "Egalitarian Philosophies in Sexist Institutions: The Life of Satomi-san, Shinto Miko and Zen Buddhist Nun. *Journal of Feminist Studies in Religion,* 4. 7–26.

Kirsch, Thomas. 1982. "Buddhism, Sex-roles and the Thai Economy." In *Women of Southeast Asia,* Penny Van Esterick, ed. DeKalb, Illinois: Northern Illinois University, Center for Southeast Asian Studies.

Klein, Anne C. 1985a. "Nondualism and the Great Bliss Queen, A Study in Tibetan Buddhist Ontology and Symbolism." *Journal of Feminist Studies in Religion,* 1. 73–98.

———. 1985b. "Primordial Purity and Everyday Life: Exalted Female Symbols and the Women of Tibet." In *Immaculate and Powerful, The Female in Sacred Image and Social Reality.* Clarrissa W. Atkinson, Constance H. Buchanan, and Margaret R. Miles, eds. Boston: Beacon Press.

———. 1987. "Finding a Self: Buddhist and Feminist Perspectives." In *Shaping New Vision: Gender and Values in American Culture.* Clarissa W. Atkinson, Constance H. Buchanan, and Margaret R. Miles, eds. Ann Arbor: UMI Research Press.

Koh, Hesung Chun. 1986. "Religion and Socialization of Women in Korea." In *Religion and the Family in East Asia.* George A. DeVos and Takao Sofue, eds. Berkeley: University of California Press.

Lamotte, Etienne. 1958. *Histoire du Bouddhisme Indien, des Origines à l'ère Saka.* Louvain: Publications Universitaires, Institut Orientaliste.

Lancaster, Lewis. 1986. "Buddhism and Family in East Asia." In *Religion and the Family in East Asia.* George A. DeVos and Takao Sofue, eds. Berkeley: University of California Press.

Lebra, Takie Sugiyama. 1984. *Japanese Women: Constraint and Fulfillment.* Honolulu: University of Hawaii Press.

Lee, Young-jo. 1983. "Current State of Buddhism among Women in Korea." *Korea Journal,* 23, no. 9. 28–37.

Levering, Miriam L. 1982. "The Dragon Girl and the Abbess of Mo-Shan: Gender and Status in the Ch'an Buddhist Tradition." *Journal of the International Association of Buddhist Studies,* 5, no. 1. 19–36.

Macy, Joanna. 1983. *Dharma and Development: Religion as Resource in the Sarvodaya Self-Help Movement.* West Hartford, Conn.: Kumarion Press.

Nakamura, Kyoko Motomochi. 1980. "No Women's Liberation: The Heritage of a Woman Prophet in Modern Japan." In *Unspoken Worlds: Women's Religious Lives in Non-Western Cultures.* Nancy A. Falk and Rita M. Gross, eds. San Francisco: Harper & Row Publishers.

NIBWA. 1985--. *Newsletter on International Buddhist Women's Activities.* Dr. Chatsumarn Kabilsingh, ed. (Bangkok, Thailand). No. 1--.

Obeyesekere, Gananath. 1972. "Religious Symbolism and Political Change in Ceylon." In *The Two Wheels of Dhamma, Essays on the Theravāda Tradition in India and Ceylon.* Bardwell L. Smith, ed. Chambersburg, Pa.: American Academy of Religion.

Oliver, Ian P. 1979. *Buddhism in Britain.* London: Rider and Company.

Rahula, Walpola. 1974. *The Heritage of the Bhikkhu, A Short History of the Bhikkhu in Educational, Cultural, Social, and Political Life.* Trans. K. P. G. Wijayasurendra and revised by the author. New York: Grove Press (originally published as *Bhiksuvagē Uramaya,* 1946).

Sakyadhita. 1990--. International Association of Buddhist Women. Honolulu, vol. 1, no. 1--.

Sankar, Andrea. 1984. "Spinster Sisterhoods: Jing Yih Sifu: Spinster-Domestic-Nun." In *Lives: Chinese Working Women.* Mary Sheridan and Janet W. Salaff, eds. Bloomington: Indiana University Press.

Schuster, Nancy J. [Nancy Barnes]. 1985a. "The Bodhisattva Figure in the *Ugraparipṛcchā.*" In *New Paths in Buddhist Research.* A. K. Warder, ed. Durham, North Carolina: Acorn Press.

———. 1985b. "Striking a Balance: Women and Images of Women in Early Chinese Buddhism." In *Women, Religion and Social Change.* Yvonne Y. Haddad and Ellison B. Findly, eds. Albany: State University of New York Press.

Sidor, Ellen S. 1987. *A Gathering of Spirit: Women Teaching in American Buddhism.* Cumberland, R.I.: Primary Point Press.

Stevens, John. 1987. "Lotus Moon: the Art of the Buddhist Nun Rengetsu." *Arts of Asia,* September-October. 89–96.

Tabrah, Ruth M. 1983. "Reflections on Being Ordained." *Eastern Buddhist,* 16, 2. 124–33.

Tambiah, S. J. 1976. *World Conqueror and World Renouncer, A Study of Buddhism and Polity in Thailand Against a Historical Background.* Cambridge: Cambridge University Press.

Taring, Rinchen D. 1970. *Daughter of Tibet.* Delhi: Allied Publishers.

Tarthang Tulku, tr. 1983. *Mother of Knowledge: The Enlightenment of Ye-shes mTsho-rgyal.* Oakland: Dharma Press.

Topley, Marjorie. 1978. "Marriage Resistance in Rural Kwangtung." In *Studies in Chinese Society.* Arthur P. Wolf, ed. Stanford: Stanford University Press.

Tsai, Kathryn A. [Kathryn A. Cissell]. 1981. "The Chinese Buddhist Monastic Order for Women: The First Two Centuries." In *Women in China, Current Directions in Historical Scholarship.* Richard W. Guisso and Stanley Johannesen, eds. Youngstown, N.Y.: Philo Press.

Tsomo, Karma Lekshe. 1987. "Tibetan Nuns and Nunneries." *The Tibet Journal,* 12, no. 4. 1–14. Reprinted in *Feminine Ground, Essays on Women and Tibet,* Janice D. Willis, ed. Ithaca, N.Y.: Snow Lion Publications, 1989.

———. 1989. *Sakyadhita: Daughters of the Buddha.* Ithaca, N.Y.: Snow Lion Publications.

Uchino, Kumiko. 1983. "The Status Elevation Process of Sōtō Sect Nuns in Modern Japan." *Japanese Journal of Religious Studies,* 10, nos. 2–3. 177–94.

Van Esterik, John. 1982. "Women Meditation Teachers in Thailand." In *Women of Southeast Asia,* Penny Van Esterik, ed. DeKalb, Ill.: Northern Illinois University, Center for Southeast Asian Studies.

Van Esterik, Penny. 1982. "Laywomen in Theravāda Buddhism." In *Women of Southeast Asia,* Penny Van Esterik, ed. DeKalb, Ill.: Northern Illinois University, Center for Southeast Asian Studies.

Welch, Holmes. 1973. *The Practice of Chinese Buddhism, 1900–1950.* Cambridge, Mass.: Harvard University Press (originally published 1967).

Willis, Janice D. 1984. "Tibetan Ani-s, the Nun's Life in Tibet." *The Tibet Journal,* 9, no. 4. 14–32. Reprinted in *Feminine Ground, Essays on Women and Tibet,* Janice D. Willis, ed. Ithaca, N.Y.: Snow Lion Publications, 1989.

———. 1989. *Feminine Ground, Essays on Women and Tibet.* Ithaca, N.Y.: Snow Lion Publications.

PEOPLE'S REPUBLIC OF CHINA

Anagnost, Ann. 1989. "Transformations of Gender in Modern China." In *Gender and Anthropology; Critical Reviews for Research and Teaching.* Sandra Morgen, ed. Washington, D.C.: American Anthropological Association.

Andors, Phyllis. 1983. *The Unfinished Liberation of Chinese Women, 1949–1980.* Bloomington: Indiana Univesity Press.

Barlow, Tani, and Donald M. Lowe. 1987. *Teaching China's Lost Generation.* San Francisco: China Books and Periodicals, Inc. (first published as *Chinese Reflections* by Praeger Publishers in 1985).

Barlow, Tani. 1989. "Introduction." In Barlow with Gary Bjorge, *I Myself am a Woman: Selected Writings of Ding Ling.* Boston: Beacon Press.

Beijing Review. 1990. "Beijing's first group of new nuns." Sept. 17–23. 27 (translated from New Century, *Xin Shiji,* issue no. 2, 1990).

Belden, Jack. 1949. "Goldflower's Story." In *China Shakes the World.* New York: Harper and Brothers.

Berry, Chris. 1985. "Sexual Difference and the Viewing Subject in *Li Shuang-shuang* and *The In-Laws.*" In Chris Berry, ed., *Perspectives on Chinese Cinema.* Ithaca: China-Japan Program, Cornell University.

Berthier, Brigitte. 1988. *La Dame-du-Bord-de-l'Eau.* Nanterre: Société d'Ethnologie.

Brown, G. Thompson. 1983. *Christianity in the People's Republic of China.* Philadelphia: John Knox Press.

Brown, Lowell H. 1991. "The Amity Consultation in Nanjing." *China Notes,* vol. 29, no. 1 (Winter 1990–91). 617.

Cao Shengjie. 1986. "What Womanhood Means to Us in New China." In *Ecumenical Sharing: A New Agenda.* New York: Publications Committee for the Nanjing Conference, c/o Dr. Franklin J. Woo, 475 Riverside Drive, New York, N.Y. 10115–0050.

Chan, Anita, et al. 1984. *Chen Village: The Recent History of a Peasant Community in Mao's China.* Berkeley: University of California Press.

Chan, Kim-Kwong. 1987. *Toward a Contextual Ecclesiology: The Catholic Church in the People's Republic of China. 1979–1983.* Hong Kong: Phototech System.

Chan Shih-ch'uang. 1990. *Tao-chiao yü nu-hsing.* Shanghai: Ku-chi ch'u-pan-she.

Chao, Jonathan, and Richard Van Houten. 1988. *Wise as Serpents, Harmless as Doves.* Pasadena, Calif.: William Carey Library.

Chen Tingting. 1991. "The 'Bitter-Sweet' of a Woman Evangelist." *China News Update,* July. 3–4.

China Daily. 1991. "Village Catholics rebuild church." Jan. 28.

Cone, James H. 1986. "EATWOT visits China: Some theological implications." *China Notes,* vol. 24, no. 4, Autumn. 407–11.

Croll, Elizabeth. 1978. *Feminism and Socialism in China.* London: Routledge and Kegan Paul.

Dean, Kenneth. 1988. "Taoism and Popular Religion in Southeast China: History and Revival." Ph.D. dissertation, Stanford University.

———. 1989. "Revival of Religious Practices in Fujian: A Case Study." In *The Turning of the Tide: Religion in China Today.* Julian F. Pas, ed. Oxford: Oxford University Press. 51–78.

Despeux, Catherine. 1990. *Immortelles de la Chine ancienne: Taoisme et alchimie féminine.* Puiseaux: Pardes.

Diamond, Norma. 1975. "Collectivization, Kinship and the Status of Women in Rural China." *Bulletin of Concerned Asian Scholars,* 7, no. 1.

Far Eastern Economic Review. 1990. "Fighting the good fight: Underground church reaps the fruits of religious boom" and "Trouble under heaven: Religious fervour grows despite suppression." July 5. 39–41.

Fung, Raymond. 1983. *Households of God on Chinese Soil* (first published in 1982). Maryknoll, N.Y.: Orbis Books.

Farley, Margaret A. 1991. "A New Form of Communion: Feminism and the Chinese Church." *America*, vol. 164, no. 7. 199–204.

Garrett, Shirley S. 1985. "Images of Chinese Women." In John C. B. and Ellen Low Webster, eds., *The Church and Women in the Third World*. Philadelphia: Westminster Press.

Ge Baojuan. 1991. "Lessons for a Teacher." *China News Update*, July. 2–3.

Goldman, Merle. 1986. "Religion in Post-Mao China." *Annals of the American Academy of Political and Social Science*, 483. 146–56.

Goonatilake, Dr. Hema. 1988. "Nuns of China: Part I: The Mainland." In Karma Lekshe Tsomo, ed., *Sakyadhita: Daughters of the Buddha*. Ithaca, N.Y.: Snow Lion Publications.

Gu Hua. 1983. *A Small Town Called Hibiscus*. Beijing: Panda Books.

Hachiya Kunio. 1990. *Chūgoku Dōkyō no Genjo* (2 volumes). Tokyo: Tokyo University Tōyōbunka Kenkyūjo.

Hahn, Thomas H. 1989. "New Developments Concerning Buddhist and Taoist Monasteries." In Julian F. Pas, ed., *The Turning of the Tide: Religion in China Today*. Oxford: Oxford University Press.

Hareven, Tamara K. 1987. "Divorce, Chinese Style." *Atlantic Monthly*, 259, no. 4. 70–76.

Honig, Emily. 1986. *Sisters and Strangers: Women in the Shanghai Cotton Mills, 1919–1949*. Stanford: Stanford University Press.

Honig, Emily, and Gail Hershatter. 1988. *Personal Voices: Chinese Women in the 1980's*. Stanford: Stanford University Press.

Hunter, Alan, and Don Rimmington. 1990. "Survey Article: Christianity in the People's Republic of China." *Religion*, vol. 20. 177–83.

Johnson, Chalmers A. 1962. *Peasant Nationalism and Communist Power*. Stanford: Stanford University Press.

Johnson, Kay Ann. 1983. *Women, the Family and Peasant Revolution in China*. Chicago: University of Chicago Press.

Lai Shu-fen. 1987. "Qingchengshan Daozong nuli wei zuguo sihua zuo gongxian" [Taoists work hard to make contributions to our country's four modernizations]. *Zhongguo Daojiao*, no. 3.

————. 1985. "Waiguo youren fang Qingcheng." *Lu-you Tian-fu* [Traveling in Szechwan], no. 2 (March 27), 15–16.

Levering, Miriam. 1985. Field notes, August.

————. 1988a. Field notes, July and August.

————. 1988b. "Buddhist Convents in Taiwan: Communities of Liberation?" Unpublished paper delivered at Duke University, Sept.

————. 1989. Field notes, March and April.

MacInnis, Donald E. 1989. *Religion in China Today: Policy and Practice*. Maryknoll, N.Y.: Orbis Books.

Madsen, Richard. 1989. "The Catholic Church in China: Cultural Contradictions, Institutional Survival, and Religious Renewal." In *Unofficial China: Popular Culture and Thought in the People's Republic of China*, Perry Link, Richard Madsen, and Paul G. Pickowicz, eds. 103–20. Boulder, Colo.: Westview Press.

Overmyer, Daniel L. 1980. "Dualism and Conflict in Chinese Popular Religions." In *Transitions and Transformations in the History of Religions*, Frank E. Reynolds and Theodore M. Ludwig, eds. Leiden: E. J. Brill.

Parish, William L., and Martin King Whyte. 1978. *Village and Family in Contemporary China*. Chicago: University of Chicago Press.

Pregadio, Fabrizio. 1991. Review of *Immortelles de la Chine ancienne. Taoisme et alchimie féminine*, by Catherine Despeux. *Taoist Resources*, vol. 3, no. 1 (July). 85–93.

Stacey, Judith. 1983. *Patriarchy and Socialist Revolution in China*. Berkeley: University of California Press.

Ting, K. H. 1991a. "The Chinese Church as I See It." *Christian Century*, April 10.

Towery, Britt. 1987. *The Churches of China, Taking Root Downward, Bearing Fruit Upward*. Waco, Texas: Long Dragon Publishers.

Ting, K. H. 1991b. "Dui *Tian Feng* zhu yuan [My Hopes for *Tian Feng*]," *Tian Feng*, April 1991, 10–11. Translated and excerpted by Jean Woo in *China News Update*, July 1991, 12.

Ting, Yen Ren. 1991. "The Amity Foundation and Social Development in China." *China Notes*, vol. 29, no. 1. 611–16.

Wang, Erh-feng, and Hsiao Chou, eds. 1989. *Chin-tan*. Beijing: Chung-kuo fu-nu ch'u-pan-she.

Wei, Zhangling. 1989. *Status of Women: China*. Bangkok: Unesco Principal Regional Office for Asia and the Pacific.

Welch, Holmes. 1967. *The Practice of Chinese Buddhism: 1900–1950*. Cambridge: Harvard University Press.

———. 1968. *The Buddhist Revival in China*. Cambridge: Harvard University Press.

———. 1972. *Buddhism Under Mao*. Cambridge: Harvard University Press.

Whyte, Bob. 1988. *Unfinished Encounter: China and Christianity*. Harrison, Pa.: Morehouse Publishing.

Wickeri, Philip L. 1990. "Christianity in Zhejiang: A Report from a Recent Visit to Protestant Churches in China." *China Notes*, Spring and Summer. 575–82.

Wire, Antoinette Clark. 1989. "The Chinese Christian Three-Self Movement: A Model of Solidarity for Women." *Union SQR*, vol. 43/no. 1–4. 181–200.

Witke, Roxane. 1977. *Comrade Chiang Ch'ing*. Boston: Little, Brown and Company.

Wolf, Margery. 1972. *Women and the Family in Rural Taiwan*. Stanford: Stanford University Press.

———. 1985. *Revolution Postponed: Women in Contemporary China*. Stanford: Stanford University Press.

Woo, Jean. 1988. "The Movement of the Spirit in China." *China Notes*, Autumn. 493–98.

Young, Marilyn. 1989. "Chicken Little in China: Some Reflections on Women." In Arif Dirlik and Maurice Meisner, eds., *Marxism and the Chinese Experience: Issues in Contemporary Socialism.* Armonk, N.Y., and London: M.E. Sharp.

Yü, Chün-fang. 1989. "Miracles, Pilgrimage Sites and the Cult of Kuan-yin," unpublished paper presented at the Conference on Pilgrimage in China, 1989. A different version of this paper, entitled "Pu-to and the Creation of the Chinese Potalaka," is found in Susan Naquin and Chün-fang Yü, eds., *Pilgrims and Sacred Sites in China.* Berkeley: University of California Press, 1992, 190–245.

————. 1990. "Images of Kuan-yin in Chinese Folk Literature." *Chinese Studies,* vol. 8, no. 1 (June). 221–85.

WOMEN AND CHINESE RELIGION IN TAIWAN

Chan, Wing-tsit. Trans. 1967. *Reflections on Things at Hand: the Neo-Confucian Anthology.* New York: Columbia University Press.

Chiang, Lan-hung Nora, and Yenlin Ku. 1985. *Past and Current Status of Women in Taiwan.* Taipei: Women's Research Program, Population Studies Center, National Taiwan University.

Ch'ü Hai-yuan. 1986. "Hsien-tai jen te tsung-chiao hsing-wei yü t'ai-tu" [Religious actions and attitudes of contemporary people]. *Chung-hua wen-hua fu-hsing yueh-k'an* [Chinese cultural renaissance monthly], 19/1. 68–82.

———— (Chiu, Hei-yuan). 1988. "Faiths in Transition." *Free China Review,* 38/1. 4–8.

Feuchtwang, Stephan. 1974. "City Temples in Taipei Under Three Regimes." In *The Chinese City Between Two Worlds,* Mark Elvin and G. William Skinner, eds. Stanford: Stanford University Press.

Huang Chien-hou. 1989. "Hsien-tai sheng-huo chung hsiao te shih-chien" [The realization of filial piety in contemporary life]. In *Chung-kuo jen te hsin-li* [The Chinese mind], Yang Kuo-shu, ed. Taipei: Kui kuan Publishing.

Jordan, David K., and Daniel L. Overmyer. 1986. *The Flying Phoenix: Aspects of Chinese Sectarianism in Taiwan.* Princeton: Princeton University Press.

Legge, James. Trans. 1966 reprint of 1923 edition. *The Four Books: Confucian Analects, the Great Learning, the Doctrine of the Mean, and the Works of Mencius.* New York: Paragon.

Lin Mei-jung. 1989. *Jen-lei hsueh yü t'ai-wan* [Anthropology and Taiwan]. Pan-ch'ao, Taiwan: Tao-hsiang Publishing.

Lü Hsiu-lien. 1974. *Hsin nü-hsing chu-yi* [New feminism]. Taipei: Yu-shih Publishing.

————. 1985 "Chen-chieh p'ai-fang" [Chaste widow memorial arch], in *Che san-ke nü-jen* [These three women]. Taipei: Tzu-li wan-pao [Independence evening post].

Pong, Raymond, and Carlo Caldarola. 1982. "China: Religion in a Revolutionary Society." In *Religions and Societies: Asia and the Middle East*, Carlo Caldarola, ed. New York: Mouton.

Pruitt, Ida. 1967. *A Daughter of Han: The Autobiography of a Chinese Working Woman*. Stanford: Stanford University Press.

Sangren, P. Steven. 1987. *History and Magical Power in a Chinese Community*. Stanford: Stanford University Press.

Saso, Michael. 1982. "Taiwan: Old Gods and Modern Society." In *Religions and Societies: Asia and the Middle East*, Carlo Caldarola, ed. New York: Mouton.

Sharma, Arvind, ed. 1987. *Women in World Religions*. Albany: State University of New York Press.

Social Welfare Indicators, Republic of China. 1989. Taipei: Manpower Planning Department, Council for Economic Planning and Development, Executive Yuan.

Statistical Yearbook of the Republic of China. 1988. Taipei: Directorate-general of Budget, Accounting and Statistics, Executive Yuan.

Tsui, Elaine Yi-lan. 1987. *Are Married Daughters "Spilled Water"? A Study of Working Women in Urban Taiwan*. Taipei: Women's Research Program, Population Studies Center, National Taiwan University.

Wolf, Margery. 1972. *Women and the Family in Rural Taiwan*. Stanford: Stanford University Press.

Yü Te-hui. 1985. *T'ai-wan min-su hsin-li pu-tao* [The psychological guidance of Taiwanese folk psychology]. Taipei: Chang lao-shih Publishing.

————. 1987. *Chung-kuo jen te hsing-fu kuan* [The Chinese view of happiness]. Taipei: Chang lao-shih Publishing.

JUDAISM

Penina Adelman, *Miriam's Well: Rituals for Jewish Women Around the Year* (Fresh Meadows, NY: Biblio Press, 1986).

Rachel Biale, *Women and Jewish Law* (New York: Schocken Books, 1984).

Menachem M. Brayer, *The Jewish Woman in Rabbinic Literature* (Hoboken, NJ: KYAV Publishing House, 1986).

Steven M. Cohen and Paula Hyman, eds., *The Jewish Family: Myths and Reality* (New York: Holmes & Meyer, 1986).

Lis Harris, *Holy Days: The World of a Hasidic Family* (New York: Summit Books, 1985).

Lesley Hazleton, *Israeli Women: The Reality Behind the Myth* (New York: Simon & Schuster, 1977).

Susannah Heschel, ed., *On Being a Jewish Feminist: A Reader* (New York: Schocken Books, 1983).

Melanie Kaye Kantrowitz and Irena Klepfisz, eds., *The Tribe of Dina: A Jewish Women's Anthology* (Boston: Beacon Press, 1989).

Elizabeth Koltun, ed., *The Jewish Woman: New Perspectives* (New York: Schocken Books, 1976).

Judith Plaskow, *Standing Again at Sinai: Judaism from a Feminist Perspective* (San Francisco: Harper & Row, 1990).

Savina Teubal, *Sarah the Priestess: The First Matriarch of Genesis* (Athens, OH: Swallow Press, 1984).

Chava Weissler, *Making Judaism Meaningful: Ambivalence and Tradition in a Havurah Community* (New York: AMS Press, 1988).

CHRISTIANITY AND WOMEN IN THE MODERN WORLD

An Inclusive Language Dictionary, Readings for Year A. 1983. New York: National Council of Churches of Christ in the U.S.A.

An Inclusive Language Dictionary, Readings for Year B. 1984. New York: National Council of Churches of Christ in the U.S.A.

Barrett, David B., ed. 1982. *World Christian Encyclopedia.* Oxford: Oxford University Press.

Bird, Phyllis. 1974. "Images of Women in the Old Testament". In Rosemary Ruether, ed. *Religion and Sexism: Images of Women in Jewish and Christian Traditions.* New York: Simon and Schuster.

Chopp, Rebecca. 1989. *Proclamation, Women and the Word.* New York: Crossroads Press.

Cozden, Elizabeth. 1982. *Antoinette Brown Blackwell: A Biography.* Old Westbury, N.Y.: The Feminist Press.

Dahm, Trees and Hedwig Meyer-Wilmes. "Metamorphosis of 'Feminisme en Christendom': Development of The Discipline of Feminist Theology". *Journal of Feminist Studies in Religion* (forthcoming).

Daily, Ann. 1983. *Inventing Motherhood: The Consequences of an Ideal.* New York: Schocken.

Davies, Stevan L. 1980. *The Revolt of the Widows: The Social World of the Apocryphal Acts.* Carbondale: Southern Illinois University Press.

Davis, Elizabeth Gould. 1971. *The First Sex.* Baltimore: Penguin.

Dixon, Marlene. 1969. "The Rise of Women's Liberation". In Betty and Theodore Roszak, eds. *Masculine/Feminine.* New York: Harper.

Dodson, Jualyne and Cheryl Townsend Gilkes. 1986. "Something Within: Social Change and Collective Endurance in the Sacred World of Black Christian Women". In Rosemary Ruether and Rosemary Keller, eds. *Women and Religion in America: 1900–1968.* San Francisco: Harper & Row. Vol. III.

Donnison, Jean. 1977. *Midwives and Medical Men: A History of Inter-Professional Rivalries and Women's Rights.* New York: Schocken.

Fabella, Virginia and Sergio Torres, eds. 1985. *Doing Theology In a Divided World.* Maryknoll, N.Y.: Orbis Books.

Flexner, Eleanor. 1972. *Century of Struggle: The Woman's Movement in the United States.* New York: Atheneum.

Getz, Lorine. 1986. "Women's Struggle for an American Catholic Identity". In Rosemary Ruether and Rosemary Keller, eds. *Women and Religion in America: 1900–1968.* San Francisco: Harper & Row, Vol. III.

Gifford, Carolyn. 1981. "Women in Social Reform Movements". In Rosemary Ruether and Rosemary Keller, eds., *Women and Religion in America.* San Francisco: Harper & Row. Vol. I.

Gnanadason, Aruna. ed. *Towards a Theology of Humanhood: Women's Perspective.* Delhi: ISPCK.

In God's Image. June 1988.

Jackson, Carroll, Barbara Hardgrove and Adair Mummis, compilers. 1981. *Women of the Cloth.* San Francisco: Harper & Row.

Jacquet, Constant H., ed. 1988. *Yearbook of American and Canadian Churches.* Nashville: Abingdon Press.

Jung, Lee Oo. 1987. "Korean Culture and Feminist Theology." *In God's Image.* Sept. 1987.

Keller, Rosemary, ed. 1981–1982. *Women in New Worlds: Historical Perspectives on Wesleyan Traditions.* Nashville: Abingdon.

————. 1981. "Lay Women in The Protestant Tradition". In Rosemary Ruether and Rosemary Kelleher, eds. *Women and Religion in America: The Nineteenth Century.* San Francisco: Harper & Row. Vol. I.

Koehler, Linda. 1981. *A Search for Power: The Weaker Sex in 17th Century New England.* Urbana: University of Illinois Press.

Lerner, Gerrda. 1986. *The Creation of Patriarchy.* New York: Oxford University Press.

Mansbridge, Jane J. 1986. *Why We Lost the E.R.A.* Chicago: Chicago University Press.

Mbiti, John S. 1971. *African Religions and Philosophy.* Garden City, N.Y.: Doubleday.

McFague, Sallie. 1987. *Models of God: Theology for an Ecological, Nuclear Age.* Philadelphia: Fortress Press.

Mesters, Carlos. 1982. "The Use of the Bible in Christian Communities of the Common People". In Sergio Torres and John Eagleson, eds. *The Challenge of Basic Christian Communities.* Maryknoll, N.Y.: Orbis Book.

Monteiro, Rita. 1987. "The Indian Socio-Cultural Reality: A Feminist Perspective". In Kunchina Patil, ed. *Socio-Cultural Analysis in Theolizing.* Bangalore: Indian Theological Association.

Mosse, George L. 1964. *The Crisis of German Ideology: Intellectual Origins of the Third Reich.* New York: Grosset and Dunlap.

Nauta, Rommie and Berma Klein Goldewijk. 1987. "Feminist Perspective on Latin American Liberation Theology" and "Latin American Women Theology". *Exchange: Bulletin of Third World Christian Literature and Ecumenical Research* 16:48:1–31.

Nickerson, Kathy. 1989. "Clergywomen Statistics and Charts". *Wellsprings: A Journal of United Methodist Clergywomen*. 2:1:27–29.

Oduyoye, Mercy Amba. 1986. *Hearing and Knowing: Theological Reflections on Christianity in Africa*. Maryknoll, N.Y.: Orbis Books.

Rubin, Gayle. 1969. "Women as Nigger". In Betty and Theodore Roszak, eds. *Masculine/Feminine*. New York: Harper.

Ruether, Rosemary R. 1970. *The Radical Kingdom*. New York: Paulist Press.

────. 1971. *Liberation Theology*. New York: Paulist Press.

────. 1974. *Faith and Fratricide*. New York: Seabury Press.

────. 1975. *New Woman, New Earth*. New York: Seabury Press.

────. 1977. *Mary: The Feminine Face of the Church*. Philadelphia: Westminster Press.

────. 1981. *To Change the World*. New York: Crossroads Press.

────. 1983. *Sexism and God Talk*. Boston: Beacon Press.

────. 1985. *Womanguides*. Boston: Beacon Press.

────. 1986. *Woman-Church*. Boston: Beacon Press.

────. 1986. *Woman-Church.: Theology and Practice*. San Francisco: Harper & Row.

────. 1992. *Gaia and God: An Ecofeminist Theology of Earth Healing*. San Francisco: Harper.

────. 1986. "Radical Victorians: The Quest for an Alternative Culture". In Rosemary Ruether and Rosemary Keller, eds. *Woman and Religion in America 1900–1968*. San Francisco: Harper & Row. Vol. III.

Scanzoni, Letha D. and Susan Setta. 1984. "The Great Chain of Being and the Chain of Command". In Janet Kalven, ed., *Women's Spirit Rising*. New York: Pilgrim Press.

────. 1986. "Women in Evangelical, Holiness and Pentacostal Traditions". In Rosemary Ruether and Rosemary Keller, eds. *Women and Religion in America: 1900–1968*. San Francisco: Harper & Row. Vol. III.

Scharf, Lois. 1982. *To Work and to Wed: Female Employment, Feminism and the Great Depression*. New York: Greenwood.

Schneir, Miriam, ed. 1972. *Feminism: Essential Historical Writings*. New York: Random House.

Tamez, Elsa, ed. 1989. *Through Her Eyes: Women's Theology in Latin America*. Maryknoll, N.Y.: Orbis Books.

────. Interviews by. 1987. *Against Machismo: Ruben Alves, Leonardo Boff, Gustavo Gutierrez, José Míquez Bonio, Juan Luis Segundo and Others Talk About the Struggle for Women*. Oak Park, Illinois: Meyer-Stone Books.

Weaver, Mary Jo. 1985. *New Catholic Women: A Contemporary Challenge to Traditional Religious Authority*. San Francisco: Harper & Row.

Woody, Thomas. 1966. *History of Women's Education in the United States*. New York: Octagon Books.

Wortman, Marlene Stein, ed. 1983. *Women in American Law: From Colonial Times to the New Deal*. New York: Holmes and Meier.

Yayori, Matsu. 1987. "Japan's Emergence as a Super Economic Power—Are Japanese Women Happy?" In *God's Image*. September 1987.

Zikmund, Barbara Brown. 1981. "The Struggle for Right to Preach." In Rosemary Ruether and Rosemary Keller, eds. *Women and Religion in America: The Nineteenth Century*. San Francisco: Harper & Row. Vol. I.

ISLAM

Afshar, Haleh. 1987. *Women, State and Ideology: Studies from Africa and Asia*. Albany: State University of New York Press.

Ahmed, Leila. 1992. *Women and Gender in Islam. Historical Roots of a Modern Debate*. New Haven: Yale University Press.

Altorki, Soraya. 1986. *Women in Saudi Arabia. Ideology and Behavior Among the Elite*. New York: Columbia University Press.

Azari, Farah. 1983. *Women of Iran, The Conflict with Fundamentalist Islam*. London: Ithaca Press.

Bahry, Louay. 1982. "The New Saudi Woman: Modernizing in an Islamic Framework." In *Middle East Journal* 34(4):502–15.

El Guindi, Fadwa. 1983. "Veiled Activism: Egyptian Women in the Contemporary Islamic Movement." In *Femmes de la Mediterranee, Peuples Mediterraneens* 22–23:79–89.

Fathi, Asghar, ed. 1985. *Women and the Family in Iran*. Leiden: E. J. Brill.

Haddad, Yvonne Y. 1984. "Islam, Women and Revolution in Twentieth-Century Arab Thought." In *Muslim World* 74:137–60.

Haeri, Shahla. 1989. *Law of Desire. Temporary Marriage in Shi'i Iran*. Syracuse, NY: Syracuse University Press.

Al-Hibri, Azizah, ed. 1982. *Women and Islam*. Elmsford, NY: Pergamon Press.

Hijab, Nadia. 1988. *Womanpower. The Arab Debate on Women at Work*. Cambridge: Cambridge University Press.

Hoffman-Ladd, Valerie J. 1987. "Polemics on the Modesty and Segregation of Women in Contemporary Egypt." In *International Journal of Middle East Studies* 19:23–50.

Hussein, Freda, ed. 1984. *Muslim Women. The Ideal and Contextual Realities*. New York: St. Martin's Press.

Keddi, N. R., ed. 1991. *Women in Middle East History: Shifting Boundaries in Sex and Gender*. New Haven: Yale University Press.

Mernissi, Fatima. 1991. *The Veil and the Male Elite*. Reading, MA: Addison-Wesley Publishing Comapny.

Milani, Farzaneh. 1991. *Veils and Words. The Emerging Voices of Iranian Women Writers*. Syracuse, NY: Syracuse University Press.

Minai, Naila. 1981. *Women in Islam. Tradition and Transition in the Middle East*. New York: Seaview Books.

Moghadam, Val. 1988. "Women, Work and Ideology in the Islamic Republic." In *International Journal of Middle East Studies* 20:221–43.

Mumtaz, Khawar and Farida Shaheed, eds. 1988. *Women of Pakistan. Two Steps Forward, One Step Back?* London: Zed Press.

Nashat, Guity, ed. 1983. *Women and Revolution in Iran*. Boulder, CO: Westview Press.

Olson, E. 1985. "Muslim Identity and Secularism in Contemporary Turkey. The Headscarf Debate." In *Anthropology Quarterly* 58:161–70.

Papanek, Hanna and Gail Minault, eds. 1982. *Separate Worlds*. Columbia, MO: South Asia Books.

Ramazani, Nesta. 1985. "Arab Women in the Gulf." In *Middle East Journal* 39:258–76.

Rugh, Andrea B. 1984. *Family in Contemporary Egypt*. Syracuse, NY: Syracuse University Press.

———. 1986. *Reveal and Conceal. Dress in Contemporary Egypt*. Syracuse, NY: Syracuse Univeristy Press.

Sanasarian, Eliz. 1981. *The Women's Rights Movement in Iran*. New York: Praeger.

Shaaban, Bouthaina. 1988. *Both Right and Left Handed. Arab Women Talk About Their Lives*. Bloomington: Indiana University Press.

Sullivan, Soraya Paknazar, tr. 1991. *Stories by Iranian Women Since the Revolution*. Austin: Center for Middle East Studies.

Tabari, Azar and Nahid Yeganeh, eds. 1984. *In the Shadow of Islam. The Women's Rights Movement in Iran*. New York: St. Martin's Press.

TWENTY-FIVE YEARS

Barstow, Ann. "The Prehistoric Goddess." In *The Book of the Goddess*. Ed. by Carl Olson. New York: Crossroad, 1983.

Belenky, Mary Field, et al. *Women's Ways of Knowing: The Development of Self, Voice, and Mind*. New York: Basic Books, 1986.

Bell, Diane. *Daughters of the Dreaming*. North Sydney, N.S.W., Australia: McPhee Grible/ George Allen and Unwin, 1983.

Cannon,Katie G. *Black Womanist Ethics*. Atlanta: Scholars Press, 1988.

Christ, Carol P. *Laughter of Aphrodite: Reflections on a Journey to the Goddess*. San Francisco: Harper and Row, 1987.

Dahlber, Frances. *Woman the Gatherer*. New Haven: Yale University Press, 1981.

Daly, Mary. *Beyond God the Father: Toward a Philosophy of Women's Liberation*. Boston: Beacon Press, 1973.

Daly, Mary. *Gyn/Ecology: The Metaethics of Radical Feminism*. Boston: Beacon Press, 1978.

deBeauvoir, Simone. *The Second Sex*. New York: Bantam Books, 1961.

Dinnerstein, Dorothy. *The Mermaid and the Minotaur: Sexual Arrangements and Human Malaise*. New York: Harper and Row, 1977.

Downing, Christine. *The Goddess: Mythological Images of the Feminine.* New York: Crossroad, 1981.

Duley, Margot I. and Edwards, Mary I. *The Cross-Cultural Study of Women: A Comprehensvie Guide.* New York: Feminist Press, 1986.

Falk, Nancy Auer and Gross, Rita M., eds. *Unspoken Worlds: Women's Religious Lives.* Belmont, CA: Wadsworth, 1989.

Fiorenza, Elizabeth Schussler. *Bread Not Stone: The Challenge of Feminist Biblical Interpretation.* Boston: Beacon Press, 1984.

Gilligan, Carol. *In a Different Voice: Psychological Theory and Women's Development.* Cambridge: Harvard University Press, 1982.

Gimbutas, Marija. "Women and Culture in Goddess Oriented Old Europe." In *The Politics of Women's Spirituality.* Ed. by Charlene Spretnek. Garden City, NY: Anchor Books, 1982.

Gross, Rita M. *Buddhism after Patriarchy: A Feminist History, Analysis, and Reconstruction of Buddhism.* Albany, NY: State University of New York Press, 1993.

————. "Female God Language in a Jewish Context." In *Womanspirit Rising: A Feminist Reader in Religion.* Ed. By Carol P. Christ and Judith Plaskow. San Francisco: Harper and Row, 1979.

————. "Hindu Female Deities as a Resource in the Contemporary Rediscovery of the Goddess." *Journal of the American Academy of Religion* XLVII:3 (1978), pp. 269–91.

————. "I Will Never Forget to Visualize That Vajrayogini is my Body and Mind." *Journal of Feminist Studies in Religion* III:1 (1987), pp. 269–91.

————. "Menstruation and Childbirth as Ritual and Religious Experience among Native Australians." In *Unspoken Worlds: Women's Religious Lives.* Ed. by Nancy Auer Falk and Rita M. Gross. CA: Wadsworth, 1989.

————. "Steps Toward Feminine Imagery of Deity in Jewish Theology." *On Being a Jewish Feminist.* Ed. by Susannah Heschel. New York: Schocken Books: 1983.

————. "Tribal Religions: Aboriginal Australia." In *Women in World Religions.* Ed. by Arvind Sharma. Albany, NY: State University of New York Press, 1987.

Harding, Sandra M. ed. *Feminism and Methodology.* Bloomington: Indiana University Press, 1987.

Kinsley, David. *The Goddesses' Mirror: Visions of the Divine from East and West.* Albany, NY: State University of New York Press, 1989.

Lerner, Gerda. *The Creation of Patriarchy.* New York: Oxford University Press, 1986.

Lowe, Marion. "Sociobiology and Sex Differences." *Signs: Journal of Women and Culture* IV:1 (Autumn 1978), pp. 118–25.

McLaughlin, Eleanor. "The Christian Past: Does it Hold a Future for Women?" In *Womanspirit Rising: A Feminist Reader in Religion.* Ed. by Carol P. Christ and Judith Plaskow. San Francisco: Harper and Row, 1979.

Moore, Henrietta L. *Feminism and Anthropology*. Minneapolis: University of Minnesota Press, 1988.

Nelson, James B. *The Intimate Connection: Male Sexuality, Male Spirituality*. Philadelphia: Westminster Press, 1988.

Ochshorn, Judith. *The Female Experience and the Nature of the Divine*. Bloomington: Indiana University Press, 1981.

Olson, Carl, ed. *The Book of the Goddess*. New York: Crossroads, 1983.

Paden, William E. *Religious Worlds: The Comparative Study of Religion*. Boston: Beacon Press, 1988.

Ruether, Rosemary. "Motherearth and the Megamachine." In *Womanspirit Rising: A Feminist Reader in Religion*. Ed. by Carol P. Christ and Judith Plaskow. San Francisco: Harper and Row, 1979.

Slocum, Sally. "Woman the Hunter: Male Bias in Anthropology." In *Toward an Anthropology of Women*. Ed. by Ranya Reiter. New York and London: Monthly Review Press, 1975.

Spretnek, Charlene, Ed. *The Politics of Women's Spirituality: Essays on the Rise of Spiritual Power Within the Feminist Movement*. Garden City, NY: Anchor Books, 1982.

Starhawk. *The Spiral Dance: A Rebirth of the Ancient Religion of the Great Goddess*. San Francisco: Harper and Row, 1979.

Tong, Rosemarie. *Feminist Thought: A Comprehensive Introduction*. Boulder, CO: Westview Press, 1989.

Trible, Phyllis. "Eve and Adam: Genesis 2–3 Reread." In *Womanspirit Rising: A Feminist Reader in Religion*. Ed. by Carol P. Christ and Judith Plaskow. San Francisco: Harper and Row, 1979.

CONTRIBUTORS

ARVIND SHARMA (B.A. Allahabad 1958; M.A. Syracuse 1970; M.T.S. Harvard Divinity School 1974; Ph.D. Harvard University 1978) lectured at the University of Sydney, Australia before moving to Montreal, Canada where he is a Professor of Comparative Religion at McGill University. He has published several papers and monographs dealing with the position of women in Indian Religions, some of which are incorporated in *Sati: Historical and Phenomenological Essays* (1988). He is the editor of a trilogy on women and religion of which this book is one; the other two are *Women in World Religions* (1987) and *Religion and Women* (1993).

KATHERINE K. YOUNG is Associate Professor, History of Religions, McGill University. She publishes in the areas of South Indian religions, gender and religion, and comparative ethics. She has coauthored with H. C. Coward and Julius J. Lipner *Hindu Ethics: Purity, Abortion, and Euthanasia* (State University of New York Press) and has edited *Hermeneutical Paths to the Sacred Worlds of India* (Scholar's Press). She has a forthcoming book entitled *New Perspectives on Women in Hinduism*. Along with being the general editor of a series with State University of New York Press called McGill Studies in the History of Religions: A Series Devoted to International Scholarship, she is one of the editors of *The Annual Review of Women in World Religions* (State University of New York Press) and *Gender in World Religions* (McGill).

DIANE BELL is professor of Religion, Economic Development and Social Justice, College of the Holy Cross, Worcester, Massachusetts. Prior to taking up this position, she was professor of Australian studies and director, Center for Australian Studies, Deakin University, Victoria, Australia. She received her B.A. in anthropology from Monash University, and a Ph.D. in anthropology from Australia National University. Professor Bell is author of *Daughters of the Dreaming* (1983), *Generations: Grandmothers, Mothers & Daughters* (1987), and co-author of *Law: The Old and the New* (1980/4). She has also coedited several books and published numerous articles and chapters on women's issues, religion, and Aboriginal rights and problems. She has written many papers and reports and participated in commissions and committees in Australia.

NANCY J. BARNES received her Ph.D. from the University of Toronto in Sanskrit and Indian Studies, with specialization in Buddhism in India and China. She has taught at Wesleyan University, the Hartford Seminary Foundation, and the Hartford College for Women, and at present she is teaching in the Religion Department of Trinity College and the Art History Department of the University of Hartford. She has published in the fields of women in Buddhism, and Mahayana Buddhist thought and practice. Currently, she is studying ritual practices in Indian and Chinese Buddhism, and the early history of the Mahayana movement. She is also at work on a monograph on the Great Stupa at Sanchi, in India.

MIRIAM LEVERING received her Ph.D. from Harvard University in the Comparative History of Religion. She is Associate Professor of Religious Studies at the University of Tennessee, Knoxville, where she teaches about Buddhism, Chinese religion and women and religion. She is the editor of *Rethinking Scripture* (SUNY Press, 1989) and the author of three historical essays on gender and women in Ch'an and Zen Buddhism, as well as other articles.

BARBARA REED is Associate Professor of Religion and the Director of Asian Studies at St. Olaf College, Northfield, Minnesota. She received a Ph.D in religion from the University of Iowa in 1982 and also did graduate work in Chinese philosophy at National Taiwan Normal University (Taipei, Taiwan). Her research and publications have focused on women in Chinese religion. She is currently studying contemporary legends and rituals concerning Kuan-yin Bodhisattva.

DENISE L. CARMODY received her Ph.D. from Boston College in 1970 in the philosophy of religion. She has taught at Boston College, Notre Dame of Maryland, Pennsylvania State University, and Wichita State University. Since 1985 she has been the head of the Department of Religion in the University of Tulsa, Tulsa, Oklahoma. Her publications include *Women and World Religions* (Nashville: Abingon, 1979), *Seizing the Apple: a feminist spirituality of personal growth* (New York: Crossroad, 1984), *Religious Women: contemporary reflections on Eastern texts* (New York: Crossroad, 1991), *The Good Alliance: Feminism, Religion and Education* (Lanham, Md.: University Press of America, 1991) and *Virtuous Woman: theological reflections on Christian feminist ethics* (Maryknoll, N.Y.: Orbis Books, 1992).

ROSEMARY RADFORD RUETHER is the Georgia Harkness professor of applied theology at the Garrett-Evangelical Theological Seminary and a member of the graduate faculty of the joint program in theological and religious studies of Northwestern University in Evanston, Illinois. She is the author or editor of twenty books and numerous articles on the subject of Christian theological history and social justice. She has written on such topics as sexism and racism, economic exploitation, and war and peace. Among her recent books is *Sexism and Godtalk: Toward a Feminist Theology* (Beacon Press), a three volume documentary history entitled *Women and Religion in America* (Harper and Row) and *Gaia and God: An Ecofeminist Theology of Earth Healing* (Harper San Francisco). Dr. Ruether holds the Ph.D. degree in classics and patristics from the Claremont Graduate School in Claremont, California. She is a frequent lecturer on university campuses and church conventions, and has been actively involved in movements for social justice for over twenty years. She is married and is the mother of three children.

JANE I. SMITH is vice-president for academic affairs and professor of Islamic Studies at Iliff School of Theology in Denver. She is the author of several books on Islam, including *The Islamic Understanding of Death and Resurrection* and *Mission to America: Five Islamic Sectarian Movements in the United States* (with Yvonne Haddad). She is the editor of *Women in Contemporary Muslim Society*, editor of the Islamic section of the *Encyclopedia of Women in World Religions*, and has written numerous articles on the historical and present circumstances of Islamic women. As associate director of the Center for the Study of World Religions at Harvard, she was editor of the Center's "Studies in World Religions" publications series. She has traveled widely throughout the Middle East and other parts of the Islamic world, and is a regular participant in Muslim-Christian dialogue sessions abroad and in the United States.

RITA M. GROSS received her Ph.D. in the History of Religions from the University of Chicago for the first dissertation on women studies in religion, *Exclusion and Participation: The Role of Women in Aboriginal Australian Religion*. In 1990, she received the annual Award for Excellence in Scholarship from the University of Wisconsin-Eau Claire. She has been a leader in feminist studies in religion for twenty years. A founder of the Women and Religion section of the American Academy of Religion, she served as its program chair for five years. She has written many articles and essays on a wide variety of topics pertaining to women and religion. Her book *Unspoken Worlds: Women's Religious Lives* (edited with Nancy Auer Falk) is widely used in courses on women and world religions. *Buddhism After Patriarchy: A Feminist History, Analysis, and Reconstruction of Buddhism*, was published by SUNY Press in 1993. Currently, she is writing a textbook on religious studies for basic women studies courses, *Feminism and Religious Studies: Transformations of a Discipline*. In addition to her work in feminist scholarship in religious studies, Rita Gross has played a leading role in Buddhist-Christian dialogue in North America. A member of the Buddhist-Christian Theological Encounter (the Cobb-Abe group), she is a past president of the Society for Buddhist-Christian Studies and served as program chair for its 1992 International Conference. Her articles and essays have been translated into Dutch, German, French, Spanish, and Japanese.

INDEX OF NAMES

INDEX OF TERMS

SUBJECT INDEX